Communications in Computer and Information Science 1789

Rationale

The CCIS series is devoted to the publication of proceedings of computer science conferences. Its aim is to efficiently disseminate original research results in informatics in printed and electronic form. While the focus is on publication of peer-reviewed full papers presenting mature work, inclusion of reviewed short papers reporting on work in progress is welcome, too. Besides globally relevant meetings with internationally representative program committees guaranteeing a strict peer-reviewing and paper selection process, conferences run by societies or of high regional or national relevance are also considered for publication.

Topics

The topical scope of CCIS spans the entire spectrum of informatics ranging from foundational topics in the theory of computing to information and communications science and technology and a broad variety of interdisciplinary application fields.

Information for Volume Editors and Authors

Publication in CCIS is free of charge. No royalties are paid, however, we offer registered conference participants temporary free access to the online version of the conference proceedings on SpringerLink (http://link.springer.com) by means of an http referrer from the conference website and/or a number of complimentary printed copies, as specified in the official acceptance email of the event.

CCIS proceedings can be published in time for distribution at conferences or as post-proceedings, and delivered in the form of printed books and/or electronically as USBs and/or e-content licenses for accessing proceedings at SpringerLink. Furthermore, CCIS proceedings are included in the CCIS electronic book series hosted in the SpringerLink digital library at http://link.springer.com/bookseries/7899. Conferences publishing in CCIS are allowed to use Online Conference Service (OCS) for managing the whole proceedings lifecycle (from submission and reviewing to preparing for publication) free of charge.

Publication process

The language of publication is exclusively English. Authors publishing in CCIS have to sign the Springer CCIS copyright transfer form, however, they are free to use their material published in CCIS for substantially changed, more elaborate subsequent publications elsewhere. For the preparation of the camera-ready papers/files, authors have to strictly adhere to the Springer CCIS Authors' Instructions and are strongly encouraged to use the CCIS LaTeX style files or templates.

Abstracting/Indexing

CCIS is abstracted/indexed in DBLP, Google Scholar, EI-Compendex, Mathematical Reviews, SCImago, Scopus. CCIS volumes are also submitted for the inclusion in ISI Proceedings.

How to start

To start the evaluation of your proposal for inclusion in the CCIS series, please send an e-mail to ccis@springer.com.

Emmanouel Garoufallou · Andreas Vlachidis
Editors

Metadata and Semantic Research

16th Research Conference, MTSR 2022
London, UK, November 7–11, 2022
Revised Selected Papers

Editors
Emmanouel Garoufallou
International Hellenic University
Thessaloniki, Greece

Andreas Vlachidis
University College London
London, UK

ISSN 1865-0929 ISSN 1865-0937 (electronic)
Communications in Computer and Information Science
ISBN 978-3-031-39140-8 ISBN 978-3-031-39141-5 (eBook)
https://doi.org/10.1007/978-3-031-39141-5

This Springer imprint is published by the registered company Springer Nature Switzerland AG
The registered company address is: Gewerbestrasse 11, 6330 Cham, Switzerland

Preface

Metadata and semantics are integral to any information system and important to the sphere of Web of Data, Semantic Web, and Linked Data. Research and development addressing metadata and semantics is crucial to advancing how we effectively discover, use, archive, and repurpose information. In response to this need, researchers are actively examining methods for generating, reusing, and interchanging metadata. Integrated with these developments is research on the application of computational methods, linked data, and data analytics. A growing body of literature also targets conceptual and theoretical designs providing foundational frameworks for metadata, knowledge organization, and semantic applications. There is no doubt that metadata weaves its way through nearly every aspect of our information ecosystem, and there is great motivation for advancing the current state of understanding in the fields of metadata and semantics. To this end, it is vital that scholars and practitioners convene and share their work and research findings.

Since 2005, the International Metadata and Semantics Research Conference (MTSR) has served as a significant venue for the dissemination and sharing of metadata and semantic-driven research and practices. This year marked the 16th edition of MTSR, drawing scholars, researchers, and practitioners who are investigating and advancing our knowledge on a wide range of metadata and semantic-driven topics. The 16th International Conference on Metadata and Semantics Research (MTSR 2022) was organized by the Department of Information, University College London (UCL), UK, taking place between November 7th and 11th, 2022, in central London (Bloomsbury Campus). The 16th edition marked the return to in-person events following the COVID-19 pandemic. The MTSR 2022 Organizing Committee decided to organize the conference as a hybrid event to accommodate the diverse requirements of delegates.

The MTSR conference series has grown in terms of the number of participants and paper submission rates over the past decade, marking it as a leading international research conference. Continuing the successful legacy of previous MTSR conferences, MTSR 2022 brought together scholars and practitioners who share a common interest in the interdisciplinary field of metadata, Linked Data, ontologies, and the Semantic Web. In total, 54 in-person and 303 online delegates from 29 countries registered for the MTSR 2022 conference. The program and the proceedings show a rich diversity of research and practices from metadata and semantically focused tools and technologies to linked data, cross-language semantics, ontologies, metadata models, semantic systems, and meta-data standards. The sessions of the conference included 27 papers covering a broad spectrum of topics, proving the interdisciplinary view of metadata. The benefits and challenges of making data findable, accessible, interoperable, and reusable (FAIR) across domains and disciplines have been recognized and the opportunities for reuse, repurposing, and redeployment of data using semantic technologies have been verified. Recent advances in neural networks, natural language processing, and knowledge graphs have been presented, promoting innovations and methods for topic modelling, semantic annotation, and automatic metadata generation.

Metadata as a research topic is maturing, and the conference supported the following eight tracks: Digital Libraries, Information Retrieval, Big, Linked, Social, and Open Data; Agriculture, Food, and Environment; Open Repositories, Research Information Systems, and Data Infrastructures; Digital Humanities and Digital Curation; Cultural Collections and Applications; European and National Projects; Knowledge IT Artifacts in Professional Communities and Aggregations; and Metadata, Identifiers, and Semantics in Decentralized Applications, Blockchains, and P2P Systems. Each of these tracks had a rich selection of short and full research papers, giving broader diversity to MTSR that spans across health records, cultural heritage collections, environmental data, and manufacturing, enabling deeper exploration of significant topics. MTSR 2022 also brought together researchers, scholars, practitioners, educators, and information professionals coming from libraries, archives, museums, cultural heritage institutions, and organizations from the educational sector and industry.

All the papers underwent a thorough and rigorous peer-review process, with two to five reviewers assigned to each paper. The review and selection for this year was highly competitive, and only papers containing significant research results, innovative methods, or novel and best practices were accepted for publication. From the general session, only 10 submissions were accepted as full research papers, representing 12.6% of the total number of submissions, and one submission was accepted as a short paper. An additional 11 contributions from tracks covering noteworthy and important results were accepted as full research papers, and three were accepted as short papers, bringing the total of MTSR 2022 accepted contributions to 25. The acceptance rate of full research papers for both the general session and tracks was 27.8% of the total number of submissions.

University College London (UCL) was founded in 1826 in the heart of London and is amongst the best universities in the world, 8th in the world (QS World University Rankings 2022) and 2nd in UK for research power (REF 2021). UCL is London's leading multidisciplinary university, with more than 16,000 staff and 50,000 students from over 150 different countries. The UCL Department of Information Studies is an international centre for knowledge creation and transfer in the fields of librarianship, archives and records management, publishing, information science, and digital humanities. It is the only department in the UK which brings together in one place programmes in library and information studies, information science, archives and records management, publishing, and digital humanities. Starting as the first British School of Librarianship in 1919, the department paved the way for other Higher Education institutions in Britain, leading training programmes for information professionals in an expanding job market. The success helped to establish its worldwide reputation, promoting professional standards that influenced information management practices worldwide through an international cohort of students.

MTSR 2022 was pleased to host a remarkable keynote presentation by Jenny Bunn, Head of Archives Research, The National Archives, UK. In her presentation "Modelling Metadata for Archives and Records Management", Jenny addressed the field of archival metadata and computerised development of the material through the lenses of an archivist, delivering an important historical account whilst setting the scene of current challenges of datafication and opportunities of semantic systems. Dr. Bunn argues that "Metadata modelling can be seen to have become a subject of interest to the archives and records management (ARM) domain from the late 1970s onwards. From that point, modelling activity has increased, culminating in the recent development of the Records in Contexts conceptual model and ontology". In her presentation she placed the Records in Contexts-Conceptual Model (RiC-CM) in its own contexts, highlighting past metadata modelling activity within the ARM community, the models that arose because of it, and the perspectives thereby surfaced. She concluded with reflections on recent modelling activity at The National Archives, in connection with the Towards a National Collection funded research project (UKRI-AH/W00321X/1) 'Our Heritage, Our Stories', and Project Omega, which aims to create a pan-archival catalogue from an ecosystem of more than 10 separate databases."

We conclude this preface by thanking the many people who contributed their time and efforts to MTSR 2022 and made this year's conference possible despite the unforeseen obstacles caused once more by COVID-19. We also thank all the organizations that supported this conference. We thank all the institutions and universities that co-organized MTSR 2022. We extend our sincere gratitude to the members of the Program Committees (both main and special tracks), the Steering Committee, and the Organizing Committees (both general and local), to all the special track chairs, and to the conference reviewers who invested their time generously to ensure the timely review of the submitted manuscripts. A special thanks to keynote speaker Jenny Bunn. Also, a special thank you goes to Anxhela Dani, Esmeralda Dudushi, Vasiliki Georgiadi, and Chrysanthi Chatzopoulou, for supporting us on social media platforms, in the organization and communication tasks, as well as in the technical support of the website throughout the year for this event. To Anxhela Dani, Esmeralda Dudushi, Chrysanthi Chatzopoulou and Vasiliki Georgiadi who assisted us with the preparation of these proceedings and the Book of Abstracts, and to Nikoleta, Vasiliki, and Stavroula for their endless support and patience. Our thanks go to our best paper and best student paper awards sponsor euroCRIS, and to this year's Premier sponsor EBSCO. Finally, our deepest thanks go to the MTSR community, all the authors and participants of MTSR 2022 for making the event a great success.

December 2022

Emmanouel Garoufallou
Andreas Vlachidis

Organization

General Chair

Emmanouel Garoufallou	International Hellenic University, Greece

Chair for MTSR 2022

Andreas Vlachidis	University College London, UK

Special Track Chairs

Miguel-Ángel Sicilia	University of Alcalá, Spain
Francesca Fallucchi	Guglielmo Marconi University, Italy
Riem Spielhaus	Georg Eckert Institute for International Textbook Research, Germany
Ernesto William De Luca	Georg Eckert Institute for International Textbook Research, Germany
Armando Stellato	University of Rome Tor Vergata, Italy
Nikos Houssos	Sentio Solutions, Greece
Michalis Sfakakis	Ionian University, Greece
Lina Bountouri	Publications Office of the European Union, Luxembourg
Emmanouel Garoufallou	International Hellenic University, Greece
Jane Greenberg	Drexel University, USA
Richard J. Hartley	Manchester Metropolitan University, UK
Stavroula Antonopoulou	Perrotis College, American Farm School, Greece
Rob Davies	Cyprus University of Technology, Cyprus
Fabio Sartori	University of Milano-Bicocca, Italy
Angela Locoro	Università Carlo Cattaneo, Italy
Arlindo Flavio da Conceição	Federal University of São Paulo (UNIFESP), Brazil
Rania Siatri	International Hellenic University, Greece

Steering Committee

Juan Manuel Dodero	University of Cádiz, Spain
Emmanouel Garoufallou	International Hellenic University, Greece
Nikos Manouselis	AgroKnow, Greece
Fabio Santori	Università degli Studi di Milano-Bicocca, Italy
Miguel-Ángel Sicilia	University of Alcalá, Spain

Local Organizing Committee

Michela Montesi	Complutense University of Madrid, Spain
Isabel Villaseñor-Rodríguez	Complutense University of Madrid, Spain
Patricia-Gema Acevedo-Zarco	Complutense University of Madrid, Spain

Organizing Committee

Chrysanthi Chatzopoulou	Frontiers Media, Switzerland
Anxhela Dani	LIBER Europe, The Netherlands
Vasiliki Georgiadi	International Hellenic University, Greece
Esmeralda Dudushi	CERN, Switzerland
Chrysanthi Theodoridou	International Hellenic University, Greece

Technical Support Staff

Ilias Nitsos	International Hellenic University, Greece

Program Committee Members

Trond Aalberg	Norwegian University of Science and Technology, Norway
Rajendra Akerkar	Western Norway Research Institute, Norway
Getaneh Alemu	Solent University, UK
Arif Altun	Hacettepe University, Turkey
Stavroula Antonopoulou	Perrotis College, American Farm School, Greece
Ioannis N. Athanasiadis	Wageningen University, the Netherlands
Panos Balatsoukas	King's College London, UK
Wolf-Tilo Balke	TU Braunschweig, Germany
Tomaz Bartol	University of Ljubljana, Slovenia
José Alberto Benítez	University of León, Spain
Ina Bluemel	German National Library of Science and Technology TIBm, Germany

Mehmet C. Okur	Yaşar University, Turkey
Gabriela Ossenbach	UNED, Spain
Laura Papaleo	Metropolitan City of Genova, Italy and Rensselaer Polytechnic Institute, USA
Juan Antonio Pastor	University of Murcia, Spain
Christos Papatheodorou	National and Kapodistrian University of Athens and Digital Curation Unit, IMIS, Athena RC, Greece
María Poveda-Villalón	Universidad Politécnica de Madrid, Spain
Marios Poulos	Ionian University, Greece
T. V. Prabhakar	Indian Institute of Technology Kanpur, India
Aurelio Ravarini	Università Carlo Cattaneo, Italy
Maria Cláudia Reis Cavalcanti	Military Institute of Engineering, Brazil
Cristina Ribeiro	INESC TEC, University of Porto, Portugal
Eva Méndez Rodríguez	Universidad Carlos III of Madrid, Spain
Dimitris Rousidis	International Hellenic University, Greece
Athena Salaba	Kent State University, USA
Salvador Sánchez-Alonso	University of Alcalá, Spain
Ricardo Santos-Muñoz	Spanish National Library, Spain
Fabio Sartori	University of Milano-Bicocca, Italy
Noemi Scarpato	San Raffaele University of Rome, Italy
Christian Scheel	Georg Eckert Institute for International Textbook Research, Germany
Jochen Schirrwagen	University of Bielefeld, Germany
Birgit Schmidt	University of Göttingen, Germany
Joachim Schöpfel	University of Lille, France
Michalis Sfakakis	Ionian University, Greece
Cleo Sgouropoulou	University of West Attica, Greece
Kathleen Shearer	Confederation of Open Access Repositories, Germany
Rania Siatri	International Hellenic University, Greece
Miguel-Ángel Sicilia	University of Alcalá, Spain
Flávio Soares Corrêa da Silva	University of São Paulo, Brazil
Ahmet Soylu	Norwegian University of Science and Technology, Norway
Riem Spielhaus	Georg Eckert Institute for International Textbook Research, Germany
Lena-Luise Stahn	Freie Universität Berlin, Germany
Armando Stellato	University of Rome Tor Vergata, Italy
Imma Subirats	Food and Agriculture Organization of the United Nations, Italy
Shigeo Sugimoto	University of Tsukuba, Japan
Maguelonne Teisseire	INRAE, France

Jan Top	Wageningen Food & Biobased Research, The Netherlands
Robert Trypuz	John Paul II Catholic University of Lublin, Poland
Giannis Tsakonas	University of Patras, Greece
Chrisa Tsinaraki	Technical University of Crete, Greece
Andrea Turbati	University of Rome Tor Vergata, Italy
Yannis Tzitzikas	University of Crete and ICS-FORTH, Greece
Christine Urquhart	Aberystwyth University, UK
Evgenia Vassilakaki	EIOPA, Germany
Sirje Virkus	Tallinn University, Estonia
Andreas Vlachidis	University College London, UK
Zhong Wang	Sun Yat-sen University, China
Katherine Wisser	Simmons College, USA
Georgia Zafeiriou	University of Macedonia, Greece
Cecilia Zanni-Merk	INSA Rouen Normandie, France
Fabio Massimo Zanzotto	University of Rome Tor Vergata, Italy
Marcia Zeng	Kent State University, USA
Marios Zervas	Cyprus University of Technology, Cyprus
Thomas Zschocke	World Agroforestry Centre (ICRAF), Kenya
Maja Žumer	University of Ljubljana, Slovenia

Special Track on Metadata & Semantics for Agriculture, Food & Environment (AgroSEM'22)

Track Chairs

Miguel-Ángel Sicilia	University of Alcalá, Spain

Program Committee

Ioannis Athanasiadis	Wageningen University, The Netherlands
Patrice Buche	Institut National de la Recherche Agronomique (INRAE), France
Caterina Caracciolo	Food and Agriculture Organization of the United Nations, Italy
Stasinos Konstantopoulos	NCSR Demokritos, Greece
Claire Nédellec	INRAE, France
Ivo Pierozzi	Embrapa Agricultural Informatics, Brazil
Armando Stellato	University of Rome Tor Vergata, Italy
Maguelonne Teisseire	INRAE, France

Jan Top	Wageningen Food & Biobased Research, The Netherlands
Robert Trypuz	John Paul II Catholic University of Lublin, Poland

Track on Metadata and Semantics for Cultural Collections and Applications

Special Track Chairs

Michalis Sfakakis	Ionian University, Greece
Lina Bountouri	Publications Office of the European Union, Luxembourg

Program Committee

Trond Aalberg	Oslo Metropolitan University, Norway
Karin Bredenberg	National Archives of Sweden, Sweden
Enrico Francesconi	EU Publications Office, Luxembourg and Consiglio Nazionale delle Recerche, Firenze, Italy
Manolis Gergatsoulis	Ionian University, Greece
Sarantos Kapidakis	University of West Attica, Greece
Christos Papatheodorou	National and Kapodistrian University of Athens and Digital Curation Unit, IMIS, Athena RC, Greece
Chrisa Tsinaraki	Joint Research Centre, European Commission, Italy
Andreas Vlachidis	University College London, UK
Maja Žumer	University of Ljubljana, Slovenia

Track on Metadata & Semantics for Digital Libraries, Information Retrieval, Big, Linked, Social & Open Data

Special Track Chairs

Emmanouel Garoufallou	International Hellenic University, Greece
Jane Greenberg	Drexel University, USA
Rania Siatri	International Hellenic University, Greece

Program Committee

Panos Balatsoukas	King's College London, UK
Özgü Can	Ege University, Turkey
Sissi Closs	Karlsruhe University of Applied Sciences, Germany
Mike Conway	University of North Carolina at Chapel Hill, USA
Phil Couch	University of Manchester, UK
Milena Dobreva	Sofia University St Kliment Ohridski, Bulgaria
Ali Emrouznejad	Aston University, UK
Panorea Gaitanou	Hellenic National Defence College, Greece
Jane Greenberg	Drexel University, USA
Richard J. Hartley	Manchester Metropolitan University, UK
Nikos Korfiatis	University of East Anglia, UK
Rebecca Koskela	Research Data Alliance, USA
Dimitris Rousidis	International Hellenic University, Greece
Athena Salaba	Kent State University, USA
Miguel-Ángel Sicilia	University of Alcalá, Spain
Christine Urquhart	Aberystwyth University, UK
Evgenia Vassilakaki	EIOPA, Germany
Sirje Virkus	Tallinn University, Estonia
Georgia Zafeiriou	University of Macedonia, Greece
Marios Zervas	Cyprus University of Technology, Cyprus

Track on Metadata and Semantics for European and National Projects

Track Chairs

Richard J. Hartley	Manchester Metropolitan University, UK
Stavroula Antonopoulou	Perrotis College, American Farm School, Greece
Robert Davies	Cyprus University of Technology, Cyprus

Program Committee

Panos Balatsoukas	King's College London, UK
Mike Conway	University of North Carolina at Chapel Hill, USA
Emmanouel Garoufallou	International Hellenic University, Greece
Jane Greenberg	Drexel University, USA
Nikos Houssos	Sentio Solutions, Greece
Nikos Korfiatis	University of East Anglia, UK
Damiana Koutsomiha	American Farm School, Greece

Paolo Manghi	Institute of Information Science and Technologies, National Research Council, Italy
Dimitris Rousidis	International Hellenic University, Greece
Rania Siatri	International Hellenic University, Greece
Miguel-Ángel Sicilia	University of Alcalá, Spain
Armando Stellato	University of Rome Tor Vergata, Italy
Sirje Virkus	Tallinn University, Estonia

Track on Metadata & Semantics for Open Repositories, Research Information Systems & Data Infrastructures

Track Chairs

Nikos Houssos	Sentio Solutions, Greece
Armando Stellato	University of Rome Tor Vergata, Italy

Honorary Track Chairs

Imma Subirats	Food and Agriculture Organization of the United Nations, Italy

Program Committee

Gordon Dunshire	University of Strathclyde, UK
Jan Dvorak	Charles University of Prague, Czech Republic
Jane Greenberg	Drexel University, USA
Siddeswara Guru	University of Queensland, Australia
Keith Jeffery	Keith G. Jeffery Consultants, UK
Nikolaos Konstantinou	University of Manchester, UK
Rebecca Koskela	University of New Mexico, USA
Jessica Lindholm	Malmö University, Sweden
Paolo Manghi	Institute of Information Science and Technologies-Italian National Research Council (ISTI-CNR), Italy
Brian Matthews	Science and Technology Facilities Council, UK
Eva Mendez Rodriguez	University Carlos III of Madrid, Spain
Joachim Schöpfel	University of Lille, France
Kathleen Shearer	Confederation of Open Access Repositories, Germany
Jochen Schirrwagen	University of Bielefeld, Germany

Birgit Schmidt	University of Göttingen, Germany
Chrisa Tsinaraki	European Commission Joint Research Centre, Italy
Yannis Tzitzikas	University of Crete and ICS-FORTH, Greece
Zhong Wang	Sun Yat-sen University, China
Marcia Zeng	Kent State University, USA
Manuel Fiorelli	University of Rome Tor Vergata, Italy

Track on Metadata & Semantics for Digital Humanities and Digital Curation (DHC2022)

Track Chairs

Ernesto William De Luca	Georg Eckert Institute for International Textbook Research, Germany
Francesca Fallucchi	Guglielmo Marconi University, Italy
Riem Spielhaus	Georg Eckert Institute for International Textbook Research, Germany

Program Committee

Maret Nieländer	Georg Eckert Institute for International Textbook Research, Germany
Elena González-Blanco	Universidad Nacional de Educación a Distancia, Spain
Steffen Hennicke	Georg Eckert Institute for International Textbook Research, Germany
Ana Garcia-Serrano	Universidad Nacional de Educación a Distancia, Spain
Philipp Mayr	GESIS, Germany
Noemi Scarpato	San Raffaele University of Rome, Italy
Andrea Turbati	University of Rome Tor Vergata, Italy
Christian Scheel	Georg Eckert Institute for International Textbook Research, Germany
Armando Stellato	University of Rome Tor Vergata, Italy
Wolf-Tilo Balke	TU Braunschweig, Germany
Andreas Lommatzsch	TU Berlin, Germany
Ivo Keller	TH Brandenburg, Germany
Gabriela Ossenbach	Universidad Nacional de Educación a Distancia, Spain
Francesca Fallucchi	Guglielmo Marconi University, Italy

Track on Knowledge IT Artifacts (KITA) in Professional Communities and Aggregations (KITA 2022)

Track Chairs

Fabio Sartori	University of Milano-Bicocca, Italy
Angela Locoro	Università Carlo Cattaneo, Italy
Arlindo Flavio da Conceição	Federal University of São Paulo, Brazil

Program Committee

Federico Cabitza	University of Milano-Bicocca, Italy
Riccardo Melen	University of Milano-Bicocca, Italy
Aurelio Ravarini	Università Carlo Cattaneo, Italy
Carla Simone	University of Siegen, Germany
Flávio Soares Corrêa da Silva	University of São Paulo, Brazil
Cecilia Zanni-Merk	INSA Rouen Normandie, France

Special Track on Metadata, Identifiers and Semantics in Decentralized Applications, Blockchains and P2P systems

Track Chair

Miguel-Ángel Sicilia	University of Alcalá, Spain

Program Committee

Sissi Closs	Karlsruhe University of Applied Sciences, Germany
Ernesto William De Luca	Georg Eckert Institute for International Textbook Research, Germany
Juan Manuel Dodero	University of Cádiz, Spain
Francesca Fallucchi	Guglielmo Marconi University, Italy
Jane Greenberg	Drexel University, USA
Nikos Houssos	Sentio Solutions, Greece
Nikos Korfiatis	University of East Anglia, UK
Dimitris Rousidis	International Hellenic University, Greece
Salvador Sánchez-Alonso	University of Alcalá, Spain
Michalis Sfakakis	Ionian University, Greece

Rania Siatri	International Hellenic University, Greece
Armando Stellato	University of Rome Tor Vergata, Italy
Robert Trypuz	John Paul II Catholic University of Lublin, Poland
Sirje Virkus	Tallinn University, Estonia

Contents

Track on Open Repositories, Research Information Systems & Data Infrastructures, and Metadata, Linked Data, Semantics and Ontologies - General Session

Metadata, Linked Data, Semantics and Ontologies - General Session, and Track on European and National Projects

Metadata, Linked Data, Semantics and Ontologies - General Session, and Track on Knowledge IT Artifacts (KITA)

Knowledge Artifacts to Support Dietary: The Diet Module of the PERCIVAL Project

Fabio Sartori(✉), Klaus Shala, Andrea Moglia, Jacopo Talpini, and Marco Savi

REDS Lab - Department of Computer Science, Systems and Communication, University of Milan - Bicocca, viale Sarca, 336, 20126 Milan, Italy
{fabio.sartori,marco.savi}@unimib.it,
{k.shala,a.moglia1,j.talpini}@campus.unimib.it

Abstract. This paper describes the Diet module of the PERCIVAL project, that aims at improving the quality of life (QoL) of patients affected by chronic diseases through the promotion, sharing, deliberation and monitoring of decisions about their different aspects among all the actors involved. The module is composed of two Android apps developed according to the principles of behavior change theories, in order to maximize the acceptability level by the user and the overall benefits for him/her. The paper focuses on the architectural, design and implementation aspects, presenting how the two apps are correlated to provide an adequate support to the user.

Keywords: Behavior Change · Knowledge Artifacts · mHealth · Quality of Life

1 Introduction

In this paper, a recent development of the PERCIVAL [11] project is presented, namely the *Diet Module*. Quality of life (QoL) of patients affected by chronic diseases and caregivers is a very important and interdisciplinary research topic, as shown in [4,9] the need for new methodologies capable to reduce the impact of neuro-degenerative disorders on everyday life of affected people and their relatives.

Chronic diseases are often characterized by the emerging of multiple disorders. Thus, chronic patients are subject to different, contemporary and heterogeneous therapies. The main problem from the medical point of view is to find a correct trade-off among them: drugs must be taken at different or the same time according to possible side-effects, possible psychological support could be necessary as well as adequate physical training and diet programs.

The main aim of the PERCIVAL project is increasing the QoL of patients and caregivers through the development of an integrated framework that supports them at different levels of granularity.

E. Garoufallou and A. Vlachidis (Eds.): MTSR 2022, CCIS 1789, pp. 3–13, 2023.
https://doi.org/10.1007/978-3-031-39141-5_1

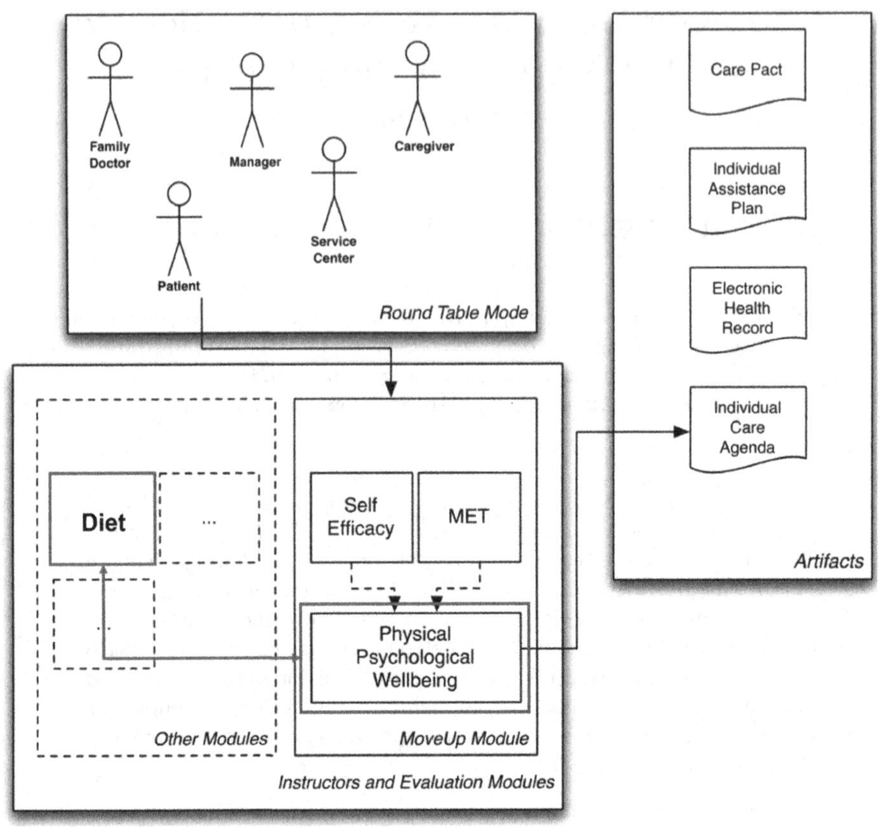

Fig. 1. The main elements of PERCIVAL.

Figure 1 shows a sketch of the main elements of the PERCIVAL project. From the conceptual point of view, PERCIVAL is composed by three main parts: the *Round Table Mode*, the *Artifacts* and the *Instructors and Evaluation Modules*. The first one is devoted to the design of the community of users involved in the system. Each of them has a specific interface to register in the system, specifying its role and permissions, as well as the values for the main attributes. The role defines the set of operations a specific user can perform on artifacts, that are passive entities representing the documents necessary to register all the information about the chronic disorder of the patient. Operations are accomplished by means of opportune modules. In the figure, the flow from *Patient* role to *Individual Care Agenda* by means of the *MoveUp* module is shown. MoveUp has inspired the development of the overall architecture of PERCIVAL system, being directly involved in collecting, representing and using physiological data from wearable devices: the adoption of wearable expert systems paradigm [10] has allowed to extend the MoveUp approach to develop new prototypes in order

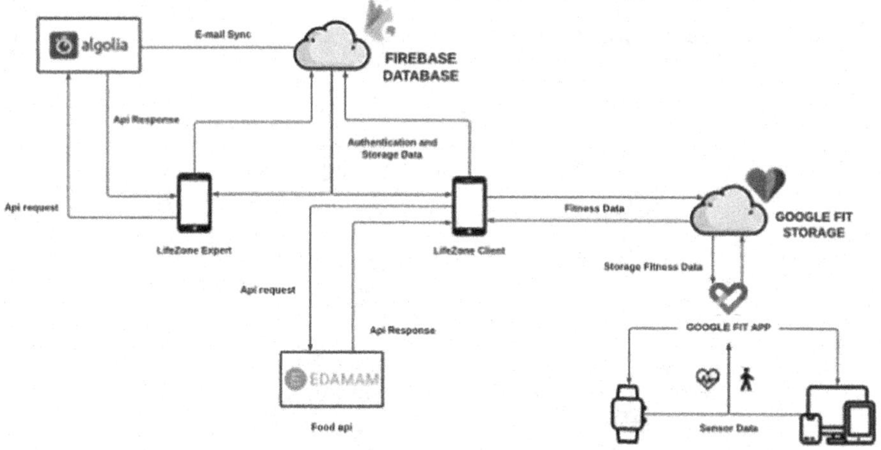

Fig. 2. The draft architecture of PERCIVAL Diet Module.

to improve the support level for community roles; in this paper, the Diet module will be considered.

Diet is composed of two Android app, namely LifeZone Client and LifeZone Expert; the former is devoted to support the user, i.e. the patient, in his/her decision making process about the dietary management, from the suggestion about the meal characteristics to interconnection with the physical activity module; the latter concerns the communication between the patient the healthcare professional involved in round table by the him/her to obtain help to maintain that process under control, i.e. the dietitian. The rest of the paper is organized as follows: Sect. 2 will briefly review the state of the art; Sect. 3 will describe the architecture, design and implementation of both apps composing the Diet module of PERCIVAL; finally, Sect. 4 will briefly conclude the paper addressing some possible future work.

2 Motivation and Background

As pointed out in [8], *malnutrition is an independent risk factor that negatively influences patients' clinical outcomes, quality of life, body function, and autonomy.* It is crucial being able to identify early and precisely patients at risk of malnutrition in order to start a timely and opportune nutritional support.

Indeed, the world-wide diffusion of mHealth apps available in the app stores today can be useful to this aim: data collected can support users in the implementation of effective behavior change strategies as well as make more efficient the communication with health care professionals [2]. Among them, great interest in nutrition and diet monitoring apps has been witnessed by their significantly high number of downloads, making them one of the most mHealth exploited services to promote behavior in people lifestyle [3].

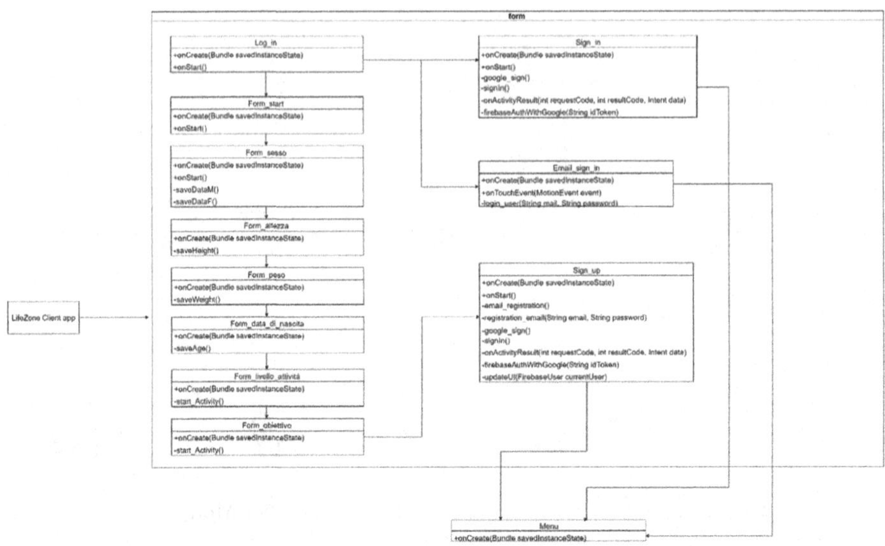

Fig. 3. The classes of the LifeZone Client app.

The gratifications obtained from the use of diet and fitness apps is another key factor motivating users continuing to use them, as demonstrated in [6]. Results showed that the five gratifications of recordability, networkability, credibility, comprehensibility, and trendiness significantly were significant to predict user intention to persist in using diet/fitness apps, while accuracy and entertainment were not.

In [12], iPhone apps to promote healthier diets are analyzed from the health behavior theory adoption point of view. The study consisted of 58 diet apps from iTunes' Health & Fitness category, showing that most apps were theory deficient and provided just general information/assistance. The authors concluded that opportunities exist for health behavior change experts to collaborate with app developers to incorporate health behavior theories into the development of personalized apps.

3 Case Study: The Diet Module of Percival

As emerging from the previous section, one of the most important successful factors in the development of diet and nutrition apps is the inclusion of behavior change strategies in their design and implementation. The Diet module of the Percival system has been integrated with the MoveUp one to this aim: the evaluation of physical and psychological wellbeing of a person is a key aspect for tailored support of person in the Percival framework.

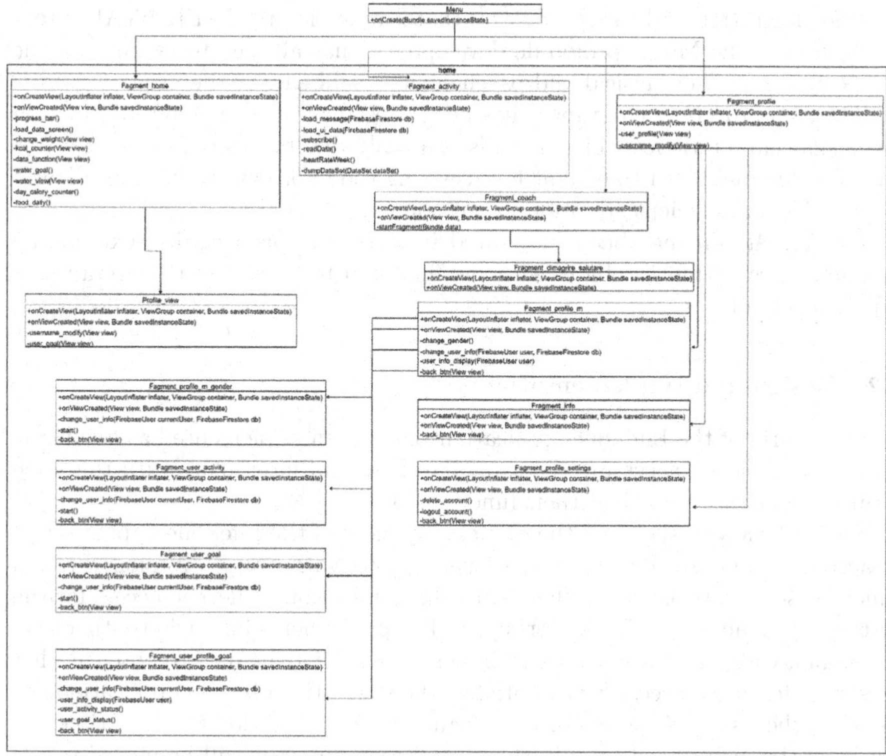

Fig. 4. The classes of the Menu activity in the LifeZone client app.

3.1 The System Architecture

Figure 2 shows the draft architecture of the diet module. The heart of the system is *LifeZone* application, an Android-based application split into two main parts, according to the principles of the round table abstraction:

- *LifeZone Client*, that allows a patient to take care of the amount of calories and nutrients to be consumed day-by-day by him/her in a simple a user-friendly way to reach personalized goals, on the basis of his/her own lifestyle (thanks to the connection with the MoveUp module);
- *LifeZone Expert*, that enables professionals invited to the user round table to access useful information about the patient, monitoring him/her at distance giving useful suggestions to him/her as well as exchanging opinions about on how to operate for reaching the final objectives.

Storage of data and user authentications are managed by means of Firebase platform, a standard de-facto provided by *Google*^{TM} that allows to manage NoSql databases in a transparent way by means of opportune APIs for synchronizing and accessing data elaborated by the LifeZone application.

The integration with $GoogleFit^{TM}$, that is crucial part of PERCIVAL extensively used in the MoveUp module development, has allowed to retrieve all the data concerning the physical and psychological wellbeing of the user.

The *Edamam* online database has been chosen as the source on information for meals characteristics: this choice is primarily due to the existence of a free and very complete API to exploit for accessing the information that has allowed its effective and efficient adoption in our context.

Finally. *Algolia* has been integrated in order to optimize the text mining functionalities within Firebase, with the final aim to maximize the overall user experience level.

3.2 Design and Implementation

The two parts of the LifeZone applications have been implemented as two interconnected projects, accessing the same database and interfacing with the same supporting classes to deliver their functionalities.

Figure 3 shows a sketch of the client component of the LifeZone app, in terms of activities organization. LifeZone Client starts with a *login* session through which a user can register him/herself to the application, if he/she access for the first time) or accessing it recovering his/her personnel information, otherwise. In the first case, the login activity will continue asking the user to enter his/her personnel features, necessary to initialize the suggestions by the application. At the end, the user will be enabled to login in the system for the first time, by means of the *sign up* activity; in the second case, the user will be moved to the *sign up* activity to select the access mode to the app (i.e. Google profile or email and password). Then, the user will have the possibility to start the *evaluation* strategy of the LifeZone app, that is implemented in the *Menu* activity, depicted in Fig. 4.

The Menu activity is divided into four main parts, namely *food diary*, *monitoring of physical activity*, *personal coach* and *user profile*. The first one is devoted to take care calories and nutrients consumed during the day, add/remove meals to/from the diary, take a look at the characteristics of what has been eaten or drunk, annotate the amount of water drunk during a given period of time and understand how many goals have been reached or failed. To do this, three opportune activities are exploited:

- *Api_result*, through which the connection to the $Edamam^{TM}$ platform is made possible;
- *Item_implementation*, that allows to visualize in user-friendly manner the consumed amount of macronutrients and calories per 100 g of meal, possibly modifying this value;
- *Food_daily_list*, through which the user can list the meals taken during the day, possibly modifying the collection.

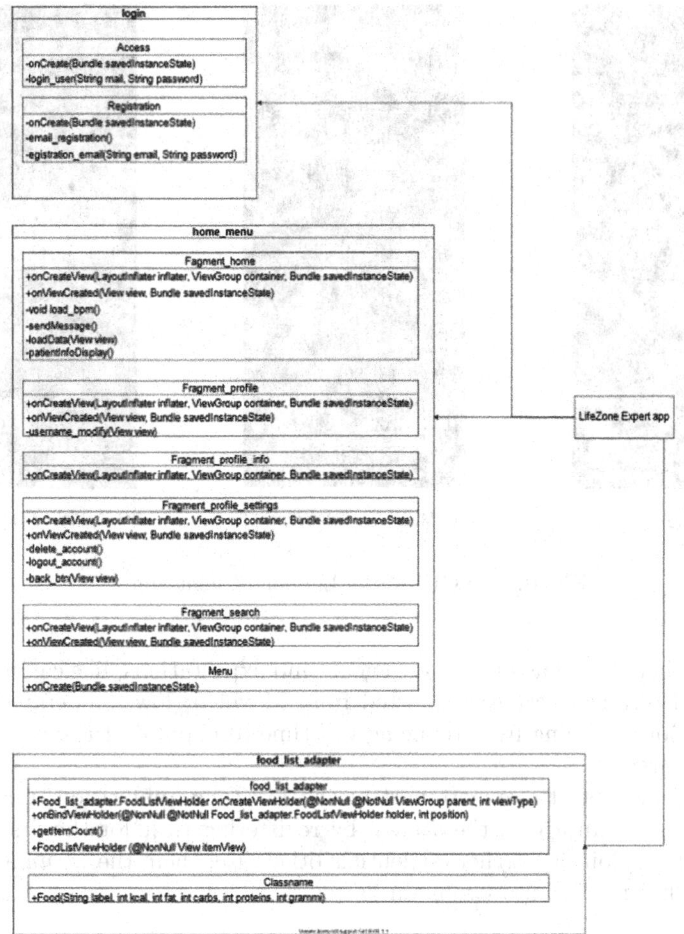

Fig. 5. The classes of the LifeZone Expert app.

The second one connects to the MoveUp module to extract some data about the physical wellbeing of the subject, like the heartbeat rate monitoring, the amount of MET or steps of physical activity made during the day (if available). Such information can be exploited to vary the food diary initially proposed to the user: for example, in case of intense physical activity made during the day, it will be possible to increase the amount of calories to assume or to add a meal rich in potassium. This suggestions could be made automatically by the system as well as by the expert connected with the user by means of the LifeZone expert app.

Third, the *coach fragment* gives the user suggestions about good practices to follow in order to organize his/her food diary. Finally the profile of the user can be managed by means of the last part of the Menu activity, to modify information

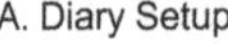
A. Diary Setup

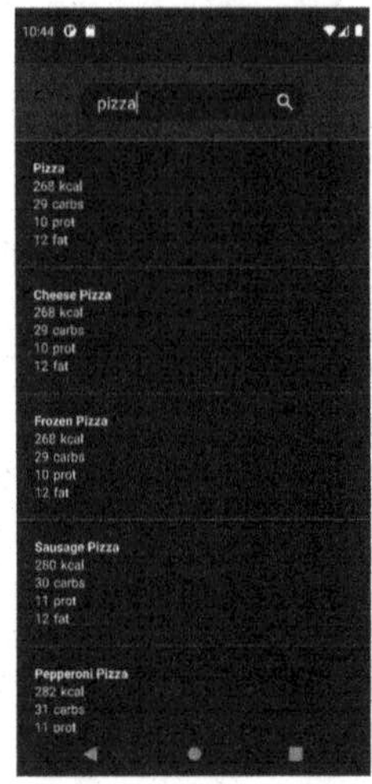

B. Meal Characteristics

C. Achieved Goals

Fig. 6. The GUI of the LifeZone Client app.

about him/her as well as his/her own goals and expectations, like e.g. modifying the level of physical activity imported from MoveUp (low, moderated, active, very active)or switching from reducing waistline to maintain the current weight as desired target.

Figure 5 presents the expert part of the LifeZone application. First of all, the expert user can access the system by registering to it for the first time or signing in it exploiting his/her credentials otherwise; then, the *Menu* activity is launched, that is split into two main parts:

- *Patients visualization*, that allows a professional to select a patient through text mining functionalities, monitoring all his/her data and parameters, food diary with calories and macronutrients and communicate with him/her to suggest modifications according to his/her overall status;
- *Profile*, that enables an expert to modify personal data and settings.

3.3 A Complete Case Study

The *Diary* functionality is shown in Fig. 6. The user can setup the agenda of meals to consume according to the calories balance reported on the top of Part A. in the figure; the daily goal of calories to get by means of meals is presented together with the effective amount of calories obtained from meals consumed (dynamically updated according to diary changes) and the amount of calories burnt during the day (thanks to physical activity). A user can have an idea of a given meal impact on the calories summary thanks to the interface with the *Edamam*^{TM} platform implemented in Part B. of the figure; doing so, he/she can decide if that aliment should be added to the diary or not to reach the daily

Fig. 7. The GUI of the LifeZone Client app: Coach functionalities and link with LifeZone Expert and MoveUp.

goal. Finally, Part C. of the figure shows the virtual prize obtained by a user for the goal achievement, in order to increase his/her motivation to continue using the app.

According to what stated above, behavior change strategies are crucial to encourage people to download and use these kind of applications. In our approach, the behavior change interventions are mediated by physical activity monitoring and continuous collaboration with healthcare professionals, who are active members of the patient round table. Figure 7 depicts sketches of the *Coach* functionalities and links to *LifeZone Expert* and *MoveUp* modules of Percival. Parts A. and B. gives explanations about the different goals a user should try to achieve according to his/her capabilities, presenting in clear manner the benefits/drawback of each of them. From the link to MoveUp, the LifeZone app can import some useful data about the physical conditions of the person, like e.g. the heart-beat rate during the day, the number of steps walked or the MET amount of physical activity performed (if available). Looking at this data, the professional can give the patient useful suggestion, communicating directly with him/her via email messages. In this way, the Diet module of Percival can provide the user with a more comfortable set of functionalities than other apps he/she can download from app stores, being sure that his/her actions will be evaluated by competent people if and only if he/she agree with this possibility: according to the Percival framework principles, in fact, all the people sitting at the round table of a patient have been explicitly invited by him/herself.

Deliberations of the expert are taken on the basis of the LifeZone Expert app functionalities, as shown in Fig. 8. An healthcare professional can select a specific patient from the different round tables he/she participates to (Part A. of the figure), then he/she can access all the information concerning him/her, about the food diary followed that day, the physiological data, and so on. Finally, the expert can send notifications to the person about the evaluation of such data, if

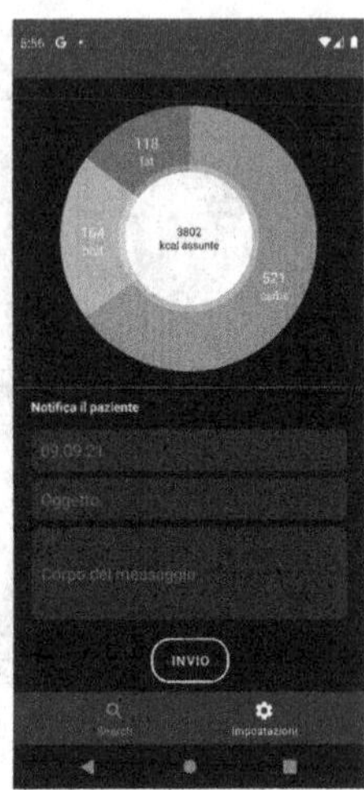

A. Patient research B. Patient data summary C. Patient notification

Fig. 8. The GUI of the LifeZone Expert app.

necessary, for example giving suggestion on how correcting a problematic diary. In this way, the connection between the LifeZone Expert and the LifeZone Client apps is established.

4 Conclusions and Future Work

This paper has presented the Diet Module of PERCIVAL project, that aims to develop a framework to share information, knowledge and documents among all the subjects involved in the recent reform of Lombardy Healthcare System. In particular, the project is oriented to improve the QoL of patients affected by chronic diseases and their caregivers, through the monitoring of physiological and psychological parameters, exploiting them to help users following prescriptions, therapies and suggestions for optimal life-styles. In this sense, Diet module is crucial in the management of patients affected by diseases like e.g. diabetes and, generally speaking, to promote a behavior change interventions devoted to improve the physical and psychological wellbeing thanks to the interconnection with the MoveUp module of the project [1].

As reported in Sect. 2, the domain of apps diet support is continuously expanding. The challenge of the Percival project is making them usable by people characterized by low levels of self-efficacy, i.e. the typical users of the Percival system, in order to maximize the impact of behavior change strategies implemented. Indeed, diet apps have been mainly used in the past by very motivated people, like sport dietitians [5]. One of the most recent approaches is the inclusion of artificial intelligence methods for dietary assessment, like in $goFOOD^{TM}$ [7]. This app is capable to estimate the content of a meal in terms of calories and macronutrient amount starting from an image captured by a phone. Although substituting human expert by means of artificial intelligence is not considered in the context of Percival at the moment, the goFOOD approach is indeed more interesting than the one currently adopted by the LifeZone Client app to recognize the characteristics of meals to be added to the food diary, based on simpler textual research. The user motivation could be significantly increased if the app would be able to recognize if an aliment could be added to the diary or not simply taking a picture of it.

Future work will consider other aspects of the chronic disease treatment cycle: in particular, the PERCIVAL project will focus on the interconnection among dietary, physical activity and pharmacological therapies to build up a complete, integrated framework to improve the QoL of patients. To this aim, new figures and roles will be added to the round table abstraction, in order to deliver a configurable environment for the sharing of knowledge and information among all the roles involved. Finally, an intense testing campaign will be organized, considering that it was not possible till now due to COVID restrictions.

References

1. Baretta, D., et al.: Wearable devices and AI techniques integration to promote physical activity. In: Proceedings of the 18th International Conference on Human-Computer Interaction with Mobile Devices and Services Adjunct, pp. 1105–1108. ACM (2016)
2. Buis, L., et al.: Implementation: the next giant hurdle to clinical transformation with digital health. J. Med. Internet Res. **21**(11), e16259 (2019)
3. Franco, R.Z., Fallaize, R., Lovegrove, J.A., Hwang, F.: Popular nutrition-related mobile apps: a feature assessment. JMIR Mhealth Uhealth **4**(3), e5846 (2016)
4. Gauthier, A., et al.: A longitudinal study on quality of life and depression in ALS patient-caregiver couples. Neurology **68**(12), 923–926 (2007)
5. Jospe, M.R., Fairbairn, K.A., Green, P., Perry, T.L.: Diet app use by sports dietitians: a survey in five countries. JMIR Mhealth Uhealth **3**(1), e3345 (2015)
6. Lee, H.E., Cho, J.: What motivates users to continue using diet and fitness apps? application of the uses and gratifications approach. Health Commun. **32**(12), 1445–1453 (2017)
7. Lu, Y., et al.: $goFOOD^{TM}$: an artificial intelligence system for dietary assessment. Sensors **20**(15), 4283 (2020)
8. Reber, E., Gomes, F., Vasiloglou, M.F., Schuetz, P., Stanga, Z.: Nutritional risk screening and assessment. J. Clin. Med. **8**(7), 1065 (2019)
9. Riedijk, S., et al.: Caregiver burden, health-related quality of life and coping in dementia caregivers: a comparison of frontotemporal dementia and Alzheimer's disease. Dement. Geriatr. Cogn. Disord. **22**(5–6), 405–412 (2006)
10. Sartori, F., Melen, R.: Wearable expert system development: definitions, models and challenges for the future. Program **51**(3), 235–258 (2017)
11. Sartori, F., Melen, R., Lombardi, M., Maggiotto, D.: Knowledge artifacts for the health: the PERCIVAL project. In: Garoufallou, E., Sartori, F., Siatri, R., Zervas, M. (eds.) MTSR 2018. CCIS, vol. 846, pp. 257–267. Springer, Cham (2019). https://doi.org/10.1007/978-3-030-14401-2_24
12. West, J.H., Hall, P.C., Arredondo, V., Berrett, B., Guerra, B., Farrell, J.: Health behavior theories in diet apps. J. Consum. Health Internet **17**(1), 10–24 (2013)

Ontology Based Skill Matchmaking Between Contributors and Projects in Open Source Hardware

Erik Paul Konietzko(✉) and Sonika Gogineni(✉)

Fraunhofer Institute for Production Systems and Design Technology IPK, Pascalstraße 8-9, 10587 Berlin, Germany

{Erik.Paul.Konietzko,Sonika.Gogineni}@ipk.fraunhofer.de

Abstract. Open source hardware (OSH) projects are dynamic with respect to those actively participating in them. In addition, often-stated challenges in OSH projects are the difficulty to find suitable collaborators and to motivate them to stay for the longer run. This paper addresses these challenges to balance the workload between the project core team and the community. For this purpose, an ontology-based demonstrator for skill-based matching in OSH communities was developed and evaluated. A sample project and user data from a collaborative online OSH development platform was enriched with skills and connected with a semantic network consisting of two ontologies. On one hand, the demonstrator enables finding users with particular capabilities to match certain project requirements. On the other hand, users of the development platform can be matched to projects based on their skill interests. A use case scenario was evaluated using the demonstrator. The results show that an integration of a semantic network with a collaborative OSH development platform is realisable and presents potentials for further utilization.

Keywords: Open source hardware · open source product development · skill-based matchmaking · community management · OWL · Protégé · data mapping · ontology

1 Introduction

The main challenges of collaboration in the OSH community result from unpredictable processes and varying structure of the projects, as well as a high turnover [9]. The turnover results from the non-completion of tasks by contributors leaving a project. A high turnover often leads to knowledge loss and unstructured information. This leads to lack of continuity of the development process and reduces project efficiency. Although counter-strategies have been developed (e.g. documentation guides, templates or trainings), there is a lack of standardized procedures, methods and tools [5, 9].

Accordingly, OSH community collaboration requires increased management efforts in contrast to closed innovation [28]. Building a community requires an understanding of how to initiate a collaborative process and to apply structuring and collaboration methods. The complexity and management effort to ensure project progression increases

E. Garoufallou and A. Vlachidis (Eds.): MTSR 2022, CCIS 1789, pp. 14–25, 2023.
https://doi.org/10.1007/978-3-031-39141-5_2

with the size of the community and the level of decentralisation. Boisseau et al. describe a shift from vertical hierarchies to horizontal forms of organisation in OSH projects [4]. In this context, the motivation of contributors vary from an interest in developing technically sophisticated solutions, to personal or social development, to having fun [5, 7, 25]. Heyer and Seliger categorize the motivation accordingly as pragmatic, social or hedonistic [19]. In particular, encouraging so-called hobby contributors is a major challenge, as their participation fluctuates more than the participation of contributors that are interested in the progress of the product [5]. Nevertheless, maintaining a diverse range of users and contributors is an important point for successful collaboration [4].

Further challenges arise from the vague definition of roles in OSH communities [4]. Although roles are identifiable (cf. e.g. [3, 25, 28]), they are not clearly separated or subject to recognizable formalisms [3]. Stakeholders can take on different roles at the same time, e.g. users of a product can be developers of the same. This increases the interdependencies within the community and the coordination effort [4, 28].

Additional challenges in task and skill management result from the variety of specialisations required in the development of complex products [34]. Established practices in task coordination show to build a modular product structure and define the requirements and demands for tasks, e.g. requisite knowledge or skills [2, 26, 34].

To address these challenges a systematic research approach was followed as detailed in Sect. 3. Based on the research approach, a solution based on skill-based matchmaking was derived and developed. The solution can help both community members and the core project team to find each other and facilitate motivated collaboration within OSH projects. It is based on the deployment of ontologies in the background to connect the various elements of OSH projects. The reason for the selection of an ontology-based approach is detailed in Sect. 2. This paper documents the methodical procedure from the requirements analysis of the working procedure within open source product development via the extraction of a use case to the implementation and evaluation of a demonstrator. The implementation is outlined in Sect. 4 and the evaluation of the demonstrator is described in Sect. 5. The demonstrator is documented in a repository[1] for deeper insights into this work [23]. It includes work from the OPEN_NEXT[2] project, which explores the dynamics within OSH collaborations and seeks to establish co-design and co-manufacturing processes between producers and clients.

2 State of the Art

The section briefly outlines the benefits that ontologies provide for the use case and describes a development approach for ontologies. As mentioned, the use case is based on OSH projects and skill-based matchmaking on online platforms. In this regard, Sect. 3 breaks down the process of identifying this focus.

Skill-based matchmaking is found in dynamic environments of discrepant skill demand and supply. This extends across many domains, such as multiplayer online games [21] or HR hiring processes [33], but also the manufacturing domain [20], which

[1] https://github.com/OPEN-NEXT/WP3_Skillmatching.

[2] https://www.opennext.eu.

is the focus here. There are a number of approaches to skill-based matchmaking, but they all share a common goal: A simple and optimized work process, i.e. workload handling or effort reduction. [20] Matchmaking approaches can be implemented using different technologies and formalisms [22]. However, they often assume defined product, resource or process structures on which they build.

In order to implement such approaches in OSH projects and to benefit from the advantages, ontologies respond to the unsteady and undefined ways of working in OSH projects. The definition of an ontology used in this research is that of Studer et al. [36], which combines the definitions of Gruber [17] and Borst [6]: *"An ontology is a formal, explicit specification of a shared conceptualisation."* [36, p. 185] Further details of this definition can be found in e.g. Studer et al. [36] or Guarino et al. [18].

Ontologies offer some advantages that make them suitable for skill-based matchmaking [33] as well as the OSH development environment. Ontologies offer the possibility to analyze a domain, so that domain knowledge can be explicitly modelled in a general understanding [30]. Munir and Sheraz Anjum also mention the advantage of keeping queries comprehensible and close to the user even with growing knowledge, in contrast to e.g. databases, which in such cases can show a higher complexity [29]. Ontologies facilitate the distribution of a common and reusable understanding and offer the possibility of reasoning above it [12, 30]. An additional factor is the Open World Assumption (OWA), which allows incomplete data sets [1]. This is particularly important to consider due to the voluntary nature of participation and documentation in OSH projects. Durán-Muñoz and Bautista-Zambrana list aspects that are also advantageous for OSH projects, such as the handling of dynamic changes in terminologies and information or the possibility to represent multilingual terms [11].

Many ontology development methods and methodologies have been introduced. For a comprehensive overview, Corcho et al. [8] and Pan et al. [31] can be referenced, among others.

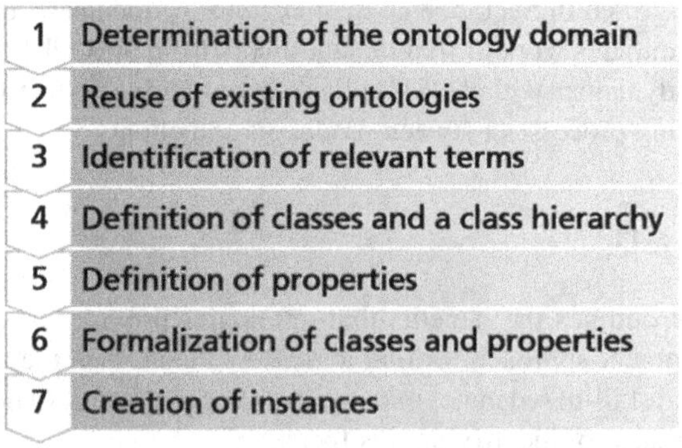

1 Determination of the ontology domain
2 Reuse of existing ontologies
3 Identification of relevant terms
4 Definition of classes and a class hierarchy
5 Definition of properties
6 Formalization of classes and properties
7 Creation of instances

Fig. 1. Ontology development approach

The development approach used in this work is shown in Fig. 1. It is a combination of the approaches from Stuckenschmidt [35] and Noy and McGuinnes [30], which provides a detailed overview and describes general steps of ontology development [37]. In the first step, the domain of ontology is determined and its concrete use is defined. Competency questions (CQ) can provide support in the development of an ontology. CQ are formulated directly to the ontology to check whether it contains enough information to answer the question or corresponds to a required level of detail [35]. In the second step, research is conducted to find existing ontologies or standards in the relevant domain. Followed by an assessment if they can be reused or adapted for the domain purpose. Relevant terms used in the domain context are identified in the third step. Such vocabularies and terms enable in identifying relevant schemata for the ontology. This is further utilized in steps 4 and 5 to define classes and their properties. The sixth step involves – if necessary – an optional formalization of these classes and properties. This includes axioms or explicit rules on the classes and properties. This is advantageous when, e.g. transformations are necessary or automatic inferring is required. Finally, the ontology is instantiated in the last step. The layout of the individual steps in the context of the study is described in more detail in Sect. 4.

3 Research Approach

The research approach is illustrated in Fig. 2. It is based on the methodological collaboration approach followed by Gogineni et al. [14].

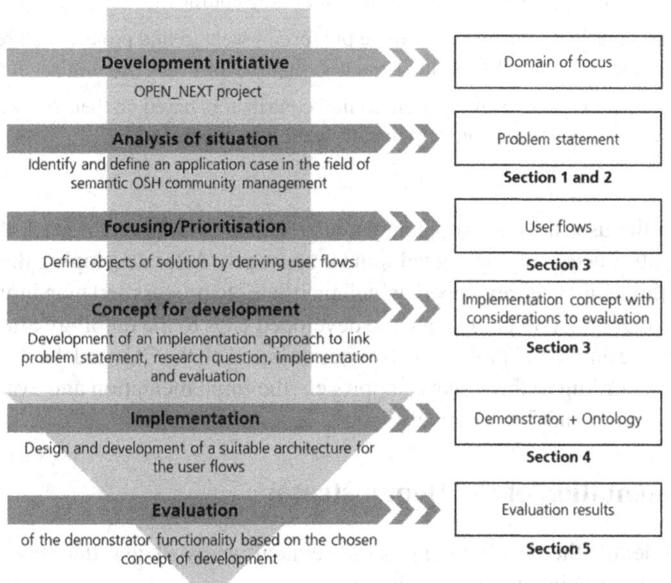

Fig. 2. Research approach

The architecture, developed for a semantic assistance system, is based on the design science research methodology (DSRM) from Peffers et al. [32]. They emphasize the positive influence of an iterative collaboration with domain experts on the development outcome [16]. The results documented in this paper represent one iteration of this approach.

The left-hand side of Fig. 2 shows individual steps of the development approach, while the right-hand side shows respective outcomes of each step and in which section of the paper they are detailed in. The initiative for the research and development of the demonstrator was the project OPEN_NEXT, which set the focus on improving OSH collaboration. Within this project, an analysis of the initial situation through interviews provided insights into challenges and possible solutions (cf. [15]), as mentioned in the introduction. The challenges were narrowed down in the next step by the development of user flows, which serve to identify necessary functionalities for the implementation of the demonstrator. This ensures a user-centered development. The user flows were then prioritized in workshops with project members.

Based on the workshop results the user flows shown in Table 1 were recognized as among the highest priority user flows and were grouped for concept development.

Table 1. User flows

Number	User flow (UF)
UF 1	As a contributor on an OSH online platform, I want to add my skills and interests to my profile, so that others know more about my abilities
UF 2	As a contributor on an OSH online platform, I want to find projects that require my specific skills in tasks, so that I can use, improve or evolve my skills
UF 3	As a project core team, we want to find contributors based on their skills and interests so that they can help in carrying out a specific task

Based on the user flows, competency questions were formed that mark the starting point of the introduced ontology development approach. After developing the ontology, a suitable architecture was developed, which facilitates to process and map input data and to instantiate it at first, and to evaluate the developed CQs to the ontology afterwards. In the third step, the ontology is validated via queries based on the CQs and the demonstrator is assessed. According to the research approach, the implementation and evaluation are described in Sect. 4 and 5 respectively.

4 Implementation of the Demonstrator

This section details the development of the semantic network and the development of the demonstrator architecture around it.

4.1 Development of the Semantic Network

The semantic network consists of two integrated ontologies. The first ontology (*OSH project ontology)* illustrates the project landscape of OSH projects. The second ontology ("skill ontology") consists two main classes namely user and skill entity.

Figure 3 depicts the connections between projects, issues/tasks, users and skills within the OSH work process. The semantic network was built from two ontologies to enable an independent development or an exchange of an individual ontology.

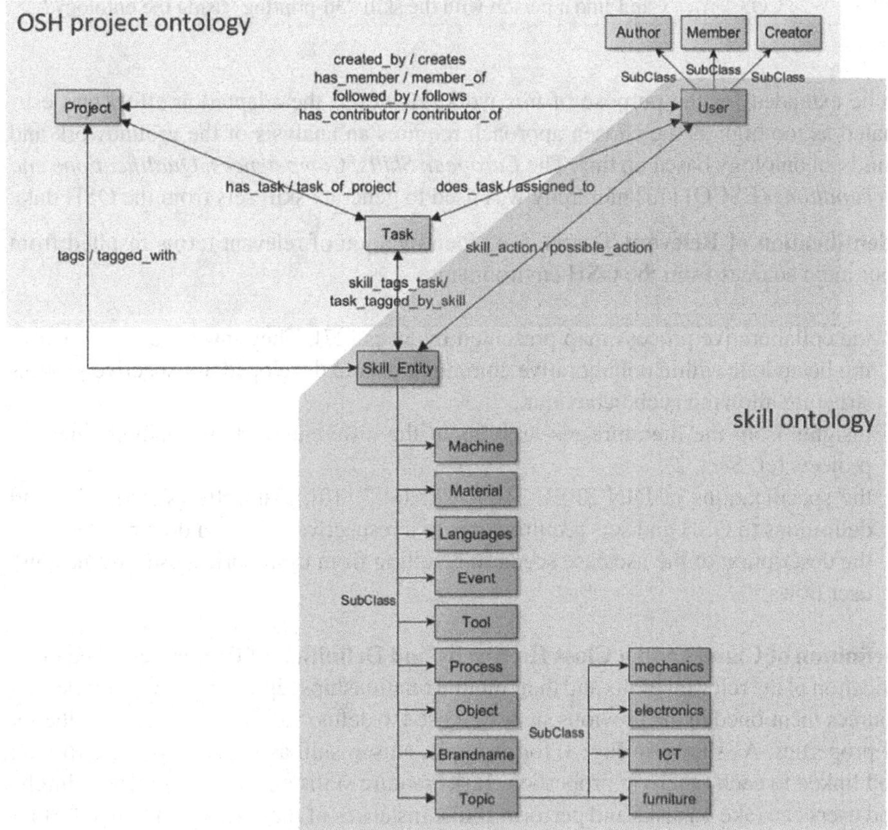

Fig. 3. Representation of semantic network consisting of two ontologies

The development of the semantic network is briefly explained according to Fig. 1.

Determination of the Ontology Domain. The delimitation of the domain for the ontology was achieved by developing the user flows, which were explained in more detail in Sect. 3. To illustrate the further development and evaluation process, Table 2 shows an example of two CQ and the UF they relate to. CQ2.1 is constructed from the perspective of matching, which suggests possible interesting projects to users. From the other perspective, CQ3.1 helps to find users with specific skills, for example for engaging with projects that need them.

Reuse of Existing Ontologies. A thorough research revealed that there are no relevant and general ontologies relating to the landscape of OSH project work. Being domain specific, existing open ontologies tend to focus on a specific use case and would need

Table 2. Competency question relating to UF2

UF No.	CQ No.	Competency question
UF2	CQ2.1	Can I find a project with a need for skills that a user can provide?
UF3	CQ3.1	Can I find a person with the skill "3d-printing" using the ontology?

to be extended for the purpose of this work. However, the adaptation effort was estimated as too high as the chosen approach requires an analysis of the groundwork and builds an ontology based on this. The *European Skills, Competences, Qualifications and Occupations* (ESCO) [13] hierarchy was used to generate skill sets from the OSH data.

Identification of Relevant Terms. The identification of relevant terms resulted from four main sources from the OSH environment:

- the collaborative process map presented by Mies [27]. They investigated the working behaviour within collaborative communities and developed a respective process structure allowing such behaviour.,
- insights from the literature research about the different working methods in OSH projects (cf. Sect. 2),
- the specifications of DIN SPEC:3105-1:2020-07 [10], that delivers principles and definitions to OSH and sets requirements to a respective technical documentation
- the description of the use case scenario resulting from user stories, user journey and user flows.

Definition of Classes and a Class Hierarchy and Definition of Properties. The identification of the relevant terms and their mutual relationships represented in the individual sources mentioned in the previous step were used to define the class structure and the set of properties. As shown in Fig. 3, for example, a user, skill and task class were formed and linked to each other via properties. Tasks require skills and are tagged accordingly, and users can take on tasks and perform skills. Instances of these classes are then further refined with additional attributes such as "name", "ID" or "description".

Formalization of Classes and Properties. In the first iteration step, formalization was performed fundamentally. A deeper formalization of axioms requires a sufficient outstanding data analysis. Nevertheless, formalisation has been carried out in order to link user skills to the needs of projects or tasks. Figure 4 exemplarily shows an object property chain that states a user who follows a project on an online platform is also interested in the topics with which the followed project is tagged. This makes it possible to identify and attract interested users for further project work and issues.

$$\textit{User follows\_project Project} \land \textit{Project tagged\_with Tag} \triangleq \textit{User interested\_in Tag}$$

Fig. 4. Object property chain

Creation of Instances. For the instantiation, a data mapping based on Méndez et al. [24] was used. A data input set was generated from a GraphQL API and was formatted in JSON. Within the ontology, the individual classes and properties are annotated with the respective JSON pointer referring to the location of information in the JSON file. At first, the pointers are read from the annotations in the ontology and formulated as a query to the input data. Afterwards, the query results are instantiated as the corresponding classes and properties.

4.2 Development of Demonstrator Architecture

An architecture was developed around the ontologies which enables instantiation, implementation and querying of the ontology and instances. The architecture is inspired by the works of Gogineni et al. [14, 16], which also followed a user-centered approach to develop a semantic assistance system in the aerospace domain. The architecture of the first validation step is shown in Fig. 5.

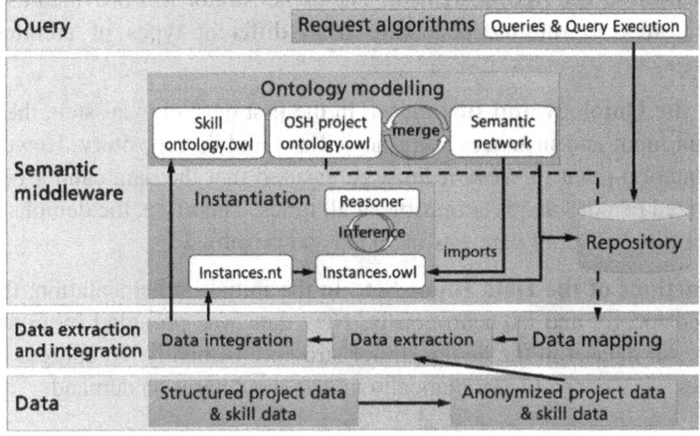

Fig. 5. Demonstrator architecture in first evaluation step

It includes a data layer in which anonymized project, skill and user data is stored. In an extraction and integration layer, the information is instantiated based on the mappings defined in the ontology. The semantic middleware layer handles the instances including the semantic network. The query layer enables the final query of the ontologies including instances.

5 Evaluation

In the following, the evaluation of the semantic network and the demonstrator architecture is discussed. To evaluate the ontology, SPARQL queries were developed with consideration to every CQ and the initially defined user flows. Based on the results returned, it was possible to assess whether a CQ could be answered correctly. Figure 6 shows sections of exemplary result sets from the queries relating to CQ 2.1 and CQ3.1.

?User	?Skill_Entity	?Project
:uid113	:laser-cutting	:UHJvamVjdDo0MTAz
:uid62	:robotics	:UHJvamVjdDoxMDAw

?User	?Skill_Entity
:uid41	:3dprinting
:uid105	:3dprinting

Fig. 6. Section of query results for (a) CQ2.1 and (b) CQ3.1

For CQ2.1, the results show a connection between seven users that are connected to 25 projects over eleven different skills. This shows that the ontology is able to match project requirements with user capabilities. In case of CQ3.1, the results show that all three users with the skill "3d-printing" from the test set were found using the ontology. Following this procedure, all the CQs were positively evaluated.

After the function of the demonstrator and the ontology was established, a first evaluation step regarding implementation and use of the demonstrator on an existing online development platform took place. The demonstrator was evaluated and first measures were implemented:

Containerization of the Demonstrator. The demonstrator was provided as a Docker container in order to run independently from different types of architectures or infrastructures.

Privatizing the Ontology and Instances. In the first development step, the semantic network, data input and instances were hosted in a public repository. However, from an implementation point of view, it must be ensured that the data cannot be changed by unauthorized persons and is accessible at all times. Therefore, the demonstrator was adapted accordingly and all data was included and privatized.

Update Functions of the Data Input Set. In the initial implementation, the dataset was deployed locally and asynchronously. New data was provided by querying and saving the result dataset in the demonstrator structure manually. To address this issue, microservices were added to automatically update the dataset on demand.

6 Conclusion and Outlook

Based on the research approach (cf. Fig. 2.) an application case of skill-based matchmaking in OSH community collaboration was developed. By means of the semantic network, it was possible to connect skills with users, issues and projects and to make them accessible in queries. The concept is based on a user-centric approach, in which formulated user flows were converted into competency questions. This enabled the evaluation on a functional level with simultaneous consideration of the user perspective. Further analyses of need and feasibility were not conducted, but should be considered when pursuing individual measures of implementation.

Measures to extract skill matching possibilities in existing project data can be evaluated in the future (e.g. automated skill assignment mechanisms with AI or ML approaches). In addition, measures to the expand the skill set and/or enriching it with possible axioms or prioritization and weighting mechanisms between the demands and supplies of different skill sets can enhance the usability.

Measures relating to testing the application with more use cases and further investigation of instantiated data would help in examining regularities, axioms or rules. Another future possibility would be the integration of task sequences to display (co-) dependencies of the tasks and their respective skill requirements.

Measures relating to demonstrator interfaces refer to the functional implementation of the demonstrator and aim at the development for data continuous integration and synchronous use within a user interface. This includes the expansion of the demonstrator with other mapping approaches for different data sources as well as the real time synchronisation between the data sources and the instantiated data from the ontology.

It is also possible to adapt the skill-based matchmaking approach to other domains. The semantic network is divided between the skills ontology and OSH project ontology in the domain of OSH product development, so that the ontologies can be adapted separately or transferred to other domains by exchanging or integrating other ontologies.

Acknowledgements. This project has received funding from the European Union's Horizon 2020 research and innovation programme under grant agreement no. 869984.

References

1. Antoniou, G., Harmelen, F.V.: Web ontology language: OWL. In: Staab, S., Studer, R. (eds.) Handbook on Ontologies. IHIS, pp. 91–110. Springer, Heidelberg (2009). https://doi.org/10.1007/978-3-540-92673-3_4
2. Antoniou, R., Pinquié, R., Boujut, J.-F., Ezoji, A., Dekoninck, E.: Identifying the factors affecting the replicability of open source hardware designs. Proc. Des. Soc. **1**, 1817–1826 (2021)
3. Balka, K., Raasch, C., Herstatt, C.: Open source enters the world of atoms: a statistical analysis of open design. First Monday **14**(11) (2009). https://doi.org/10.5210/fm.v14i11.2670
4. Boisseau, É., Omhover, J.-F., Bouchard, C.: Open-design: a state of the art review. Des. Sci. **4**, e3 (2018)
5. Bonvoisin, J., Thomas, L., Mies, R., Gros, C., Boujut, J.-F.: Current state of practices in open source product development. In: Proceedings of the 21st International Conference on Engineering Design (ICED17). 21st International Conference on Engineering Design (ICED17), Vancouver, Canada, 21–25 August 2017 (2017)
6. Borst, W.N.: Construction of engineering ontologies for knowledge sharing and reuse. CTIT Ph.D.-thesis series, no. 97-14. Centre for Telematics and Information Technology, Enschede, NL (1997)
7. Boujut, J.-F., Pourroy, F., Marin, P., Dai, J., Richardot, G.: Open source hardware communities: investigating participation in design activities. Proc. Int. Conf. Eng. Des. **1**, 2307–2316 (2019)
8. Corcho, O., Fernández-López, M., Gómez-Pérez, A.: Ontological engineering: what are ontologies and how can we build them? In: Cardoso, J. (ed.) Semantic Web Services, pp. 44–70. IGI Global (2007)
9. Dai, J.X., Boujut, J.-F., Pourroy, F., Marin, P.: Issues and challenges of knowledge management in online open source hardware communities. Des. Sci. **6**, e24 (2020)
10. DIN SPEC 3105-1:2020-07: DIN SPEC 3105-1:2020-07, Open Source Hardware_- Teil_1: Anforderungen an die technische Dokumentation; Text Englisch. Beuth Verlag GmbH, Berlin
11. Durán-Muñoz, I., Bautista-Zambrana, M.R.: Applying ontologies to terminology: advantages and disadvantages. HERMES - J. Lang. Commun. Bus. **26**(51), 65–77 (2013). https://doi.org/10.7146/hjlcb.v26i51.97438

12. Di Sciascio, E., Donini, F.M., Mottola, M., Mongiello, M., Colucci, S., Di Noia, T.: A formal approach to ontology-based semantic match of skills descriptions (2003)
13. Europäische Kommission: ESCO handbook. European skills, competences, qualifications and occupations. Publication Office of the European Union, Luxembourg (2017)
14. Gogineni, S., Exner, K., Stark, R., Nickel, J., Oeler, M., Witte, H.: Semantic assistance system for providing smart services and reasoning in aero-engine manufacturing. In: Garoufallou, E., Fallucchi, F., William De Luca, E. (eds.) MTSR 2019. CCIS, vol. 1057, pp. 90–102. Springer, Cham (2019). https://doi.org/10.1007/978-3-030-36599-8_8
15. Gogineni, S.: Deliverable 3.1 - user stories of collaborative engineering needs (2020)
16. Gogineni, S., et al.: Systematic design and implementation of a semantic assistance system for aero-engine design and manufacturing. IJMSO **15**, 87 (2021)
17. Gruber, T.R.: A translation approach to portable ontology specifications. Knowl. Acquis. **5**, 199–220 (1993)
18. Guarino, N., Oberle, D., Staab, S.: What is an ontology? In: Staab, S., Studer, R. (eds.) Handbook on Ontologies. IHIS, pp. 1–17. Springer, Heidelberg (2009). https://doi.org/10.1007/978-3-540-92673-3_0
19. Heyer, S., Seliger, G.: Open manufacturing for value creation cycles. In: Matsumoto, M., Umeda, Y., Masui, K., Fukushige, S. (eds.) Design for Innovative Value Towards a Sustainable Society, pp. 110–115. Springer, Dordrecht (2012). https://doi.org/10.1007/978-94-007-3010-6_23
20. Järvenpää, E., Siltala, N., Hylli, O., Lanz, M.: Product model ontology and its use in capability-based matchmaking. Procedia CIRP **72**, 1094–1099 (2018)
21. Jiménez-Rodrıguez, J., Jiménez-Dıaz, G., Dıaz-Agudo, B.: Matchmaking and case-based recommendations. In: 19th International Conference on Case Based Reasoning (2011)
22. Joshi, M., Bhavsar, V.C., Boley, H.: Knowledge representation in matchmaking applications. Adv. Knowl. Based Syst.: Model. Appl. Res. 29–49 (2010)
23. Konietzko, E.P.: WP3_Skillmatching. Zenodo (2021). https://doi.org/10.5281/ZENODO.5512214
24. Méndez, S.J.R., Haller, A., Omran, P.G., Wright, J., Taylor, K.: J2RM: an ontology-based JSON-to-RDF mapping tool. In: Taylor, K., Goncalves, R., Lecue, F., Yan, J. (eds.) Proceedings of the ISWC 2020 Demos and Industry Tracks: From Novel Ideas to Industrial Practice co-located with 19th International Semantic Web Conference (ISWC 2020). ISWC (Demos/Industry), Globally Online, 1–6 November 2020, pp. 368–373 (2020)
25. Mies, R., Bonvoisin, J., Jochem, R.: Harnessing the synergy potential of open source hardware communities. In: Redlich, T., Moritz, M., Wulfsberg, J.P. (eds.) Co-Creation. MP, pp. 129–145. Springer, Cham (2019). https://doi.org/10.1007/978-3-319-97788-1_11
26. Mies, R., Bonvoisin, J., Jochem, R.: Cross-sectional study on the collaborative capacity of open source hardware communities. In: First International workshop on Open Design and Open Source Hardware Product Development, Grenoble (France) (2020)
27. Mies, R.: OPEN!_D2.1_Open source product development process models (2021). https://zenodo.org/record/5341253#.YS3hSOdCTRY
28. Moritz, M., Redlich, T., Wulfsberg, J.: Best practices and pitfalls in open source hardware. In: Rocha, Á., Guarda, T. (eds.) ICITS 2018. AISC, vol. 721, pp. 200–210. Springer, Cham (2018). https://doi.org/10.1007/978-3-319-73450-7_20
29. Munir, K., Sheraz Anjum, M.: The use of ontologies for effective knowledge modelling and information retrieval. Appl. Comput. Inform. **14**, 116–126 (2018)
30. Noy, N., McGuinnes, D.: Ontology development 101: a guide to creating your first ontology. Knowledge Systems Laboratory (2001)
31. Pan, J.Z., Vetere, G., Gomez-Perez, J.M., Wu, H.: Exploiting Linked Data and Knowledge Graphs in Large Organisations. Springer, Cham (2017). https://doi.org/10.1007/978-3-319-45654-6

32. Peffers, K., Tuunanen, T., Rothenberger, M.A., Chatterjee, S.: A design science research methodology for information systems research. J. Manag. Inf. Syst. **24**, 45–77 (2007)
33. Petrican, T., Stan, C., Antal, M., Salomie, I., Cioara, T., Anghel, I.: Ontology-based skill matching algorithms. In: 2017 13th IEEE International Conference on Intelligent Computer Communication and Processing (ICCP). 2017 13th IEEE International Conference on Intelligent Computer Communication and Processing (ICCP), Cluj-Napoca, 07–09 September 2017, pp. 205–211. IEEE (2017). https://doi.org/10.1109/ICCP.2017.8117005
34. Raasch, C.: Product development in open design communities: a process perspective. Int. J. Innov. Technol. Manage. **08**, 557–575 (2011)
35. Stuckenschmidt, H.: Ontologien. Springer, Heidelberg (2011)
36. Studer, R., Benjamins, V., Fensel, D.: Knowledge engineering: principles and methods. Data Knowl. Eng. **25**, 161–197 (1998)
37. Synak, M., Dabrowski, M., Kruk, S.R.: Semantic web and ontologies. In: Kruk, S.R., McDaniel, B. (eds.) Semantic Digital Libraries, pp. 41–54. Springer, Heidelberg (2009). https://doi.org/10.1007/978-3-540-85434-0_3

GOLDCASE: A Generic Ontology Layer for Data Catalog Semantics

Johannes Schrott[2(✉)], Sabine Weidinger[1], Martin Tiefengrabner[3], Christian Lettner[1], Wolfram Wöß[2], and Lisa Ehrlinger[1,2(✉)]

[1] Software Competence Center Hagenberg GmbH, Hagenberg, Austria
{sabine.weidinger,christian.lettner,lisa.ehrlinger}@scch.at

[2] Johannes Kepler University Linz, Linz, Austria
{johannes.schrott,wolfram.woess,lisa.ehrlinger}@jku.at

[3] PIERER Innovation GmbH, Wels, Austria
martin.tiefengrabner@pierer-innovation.com

Abstract. Data catalogs automatically collect metadata from distributed data sources and provide a unified and easily accessible view on the data. Many existing data catalog tools focus on the automatic collection of technical metadata (e.g., from a data dictionary) into a central repository. The functionality of annotating data with semantics (i.e., its meaning) in these tools is often not expressive enough to model complex real-world scenarios. In this paper, we propose a generic ontology layer (GOLDCASE), which maps the semantics of data in form of a high-expressive data model to the technical metadata provided by a data catalog. Hence, we achieve the following advantages: 1) users have access to an understandable description of the data objects, their relationships, and their semantics in the domain-specific data model. 2) GOLDCASE maps this knowledge directly to the metadata provided by data catalog tools and thus enables their reuse. 3) The ontology layer is machine-readable, which greatly improves automatic evaluation and data exchange. This is accompanied by improved FAIRness of the overall system. We implemented the approach at PIERER Innovation GmbH on top of an Informatica Enterprise Data Catalog to show and evaluate its applicability.

Keywords: Data catalogs · Ontologies · Business data model · FAIR principles

1 Introduction

Robust metadata (i.e., "data that defines or describes other data" [11]) is a key success factor for any data governance strategy along with its components, such as, data quality measurement, data modeling, access security, and the fulfillment of the FAIR principles [18]. The acronym FAIR stands for findability, accessibility, interopability, and re-use of data [21]. Data catalogs promise to solve the challenge of metadata management by providing an automated solution to "collect, create, and maintain metadata" [15]. While the focus of the first

E. Garoufallou and A. Vlachidis (Eds.): MTSR 2022, CCIS 1789, pp. 26–38, 2023.
https://doi.org/10.1007/978-3-031-39141-5_3

data catalogs was on the *cataloging* functionality, i.e., the collection of technical metadata [6], a broader view has been established meanwhile [2,12]. Recent research states that data catalogs should ideally cover all aspects of metadata management, that is, from automated gathering of technical metadata, over data modeling for IT professionals, to a high-level business data model for domain experts [2,12,14]. A business (also: enterprise) data model "is a data model independent of any implementation" [20], which describes the domain knowledge of an organization.

However, many state-of-the-art data catalog tools do not fully implement this wide range of functionalities, especially with respect to the expressiveness of the data semantics. An example is our use case at PIERER Innovation GmbH (PInno), formerly known as KTM Innovation GmbH. The product Informatica Enterprise Data Catalog (EDC) is used to automatically collect technical metadata from a large amount of heterogeneous data sources (e.g., relational databases, proprietary files from the R&D manufacturing site, and NoSQL stores like MongoDB). While EDC is excellent for this task and the provision of data lineage, it lacks a high-expressive business data model providing an abstract view on the underlying technical data sources. For example, it is not possible to model relationships between semantic annotations. Thus, we declare the EDC data model as "too less expressive" to model the domain knowledge for PInno. For our implementation, we selected ontologies as suitable technology since they provide the required level of semantic expressiveness [4,20].

In this paper, we introduce GOLDCASE (Sect. 3), a Generic Ontology Layer for Data Catalog Semantics, which allows organizations to (1) build a high-expressive business data model in form of a Web Ontology Language (OWL) ontology, and to (2) connect this ontology to the technical metadata collected by their already used data catalog. GOLDCASE is evaluated in a proof-of-concept implementation deployed at PInno to highlight its positive effect on the FAIRness compared to the usage of EDC only (Sect. 4). We evaluate FAIRness by verifying the fulfillment of the FAIR principles[1] published by [21].

2 Background on Data Catalogs and Related Work

In literature [2,6,12,16,22], the term data catalog and consequently the scope of data catalog tools is not clearly defined (as also reported by Labadie et al. [14]). When data catalogs were first mentioned in the early 2000s (as part of the "dataspaces" concept – see [6]), the focus was on the *cataloging* functionality only. In the meantime, a broader view has been established. Korte et al. [12] present a reference model of data catalogs, which consists of three components that depend on each other. The *role model* defines user groups and use cases, the *functional model* defines functional groups and functions, e.g., data inventory, governance, or discovery, and the *information model* defines data objects, attributes, and their relations. The information model is considered future work [12].

[1] https://www.go-fair.org/fair-principles (Oct. 2022).

In a systematic literature review, Ehrlinger et al. [2] identified the four components of a data catalog: (i) *metadata management*, (ii) *business context*, (iii) *data responsibility roles*, and the (iv) *FAIR principles.* (i) Metadata management describes the collection, creation, and maintenance of metadata [15]. We refer to metadata that is already available in a company and can be collected automatically as *technical metadata.* The counterpart of technical metadata is the (ii) business context, which describes the high-level view of business users on the data. Many data catalog tools allow users to manually define business context in the form of simple annotations or as a separate business glossary [2,14]. While glossaries are a good basis to enrich technical metadata, they are less expressive than ontologies when it comes to the modeling of domain knowledge (cf. [4]). In summary, technical metadata reflects the current state of data sources and business context enriches technical metadata with domain knowledge [2]. The (iv) FAIR guiding principles proposed by Wilkinson et al. [21] provide guidelines for the publishing of (meta)data. They received increasing popularity in the enterprise context [14] as a standardized way to measure the expressiveness and quality of metadata. Thus, we also make use of the FAIR principles to evaluate GOLDCASE in Table 1.

The establishment of (iii) data responsibility roles (e.g., data steward, data owner) and the assignment of these roles to people and data assets is an essential part of the broader topic data governance [2,14], and considered future work. Also, Sequeda and Lassila [16] as well as Gartner Inc. [22] see data catalogs as a part of data governance solutions. The main application areas of data catalogs are the management of data assets in an inventory and the provision of business context, which increases the findability and understanding of these data assets [22].

However, most traditional data catalogs do not make use of ontologies [8] and therefore lack expressiveness in their business context. While this might be sufficient for smaller companies or simple use cases (see [4] for an analysis of when to use ontologies), large enterprises like PIERER Innovation GmbH, which is part of the PIERER Mobility AG Group, need maximal expressiveness to model their domain knowledge.

There exist some commercial products that use ontologies or knowledge graphs internally. Examples that follow the World Wide Web Consortium (W3C) recommendations Resource Description Framework (RDF) and OWL and support SPARQL are Semantic Web Company's PoolParty[2], Collibra's Data Catalog[3], Cambridge Semantic's Anzo Platform[4], and data.world[5]. Although not using ontologies, dataspot[6] is worth to be mentioned as it features extensive modeling capabilities, including conceptual relationships. Vancauwenbergh et

[2] https://www.poolparty.biz (Oct. 2022).
[3] https://www.collibra.com/us/en/platform/data-catalog (Oct. 2022).
[4] https://cambridgesemantics.com/anzo-platform (Oct. 2022).
[5] https://data.world (Oct. 2022).
[6] https://www.dataspot.at (Oct. 2022).

al. [19] demonstrate on how to use Collibra as a semantic layer to enhance the expressiveness of an existing research information system.

An approach, which is conceptually different from GOLDCASE due to a different application domain, but follows similar objectives, are the high-expressive metadata annotations for open government data by Křemen and Nečaský [13].

Considering existing research on data catalogs, we summarize that an expressive high-level view is a key requirement for application in practice [2,12,14,22]. Since not all data catalog tools offer this high-level view on semantics and there is, to the best of our knowledge, no directly comparable solution for a vendor-agnostic generic business layer based on ontologies, we propose GOLDCASE to fulfill this requirement.

3 A Generic Ontology Layer for Data Catalog Semantics

In this section, we first describe the structure of GOLDCASE, a generic ontology layer for data catalog semantics, and subsequently a guideline for its use. GOLDCASE is built on ontologies (following the W3C recommendations RDF and OWL), since ontologies allow to connect heterogeneous information sources and can abstract individual sources to a global view [17]. Feilmayr and Wöß [4] extend the original definition by Gruber [7] and describe ontologies as "a formal, explicit specification of a shared conceptualization that is characterized by high semantic expressiveness required for increased complexity." This definition emphasizes the high semantic expressiveness as key factor for modeling very complex domains.

3.1 Structure of GOLDCASE

GOLDCASE covers three of the four components a data catalog should consist of (cf. [2]): (i) metadata management, (ii) business context, and (iv) the FAIR principles. (iii) Data responsibility roles are not considered in the current state of GOLDCASE and are planned for future work. Figure 1 shows the structure of GOLDCASE, which is divided into the following two parts:

1. **Representation of technical metadata.** For representing the data sources, we combine the W3C recommendation Data Catalog Vocabulary (DCAT)[7], which is a vocabulary for publishing data catalogs on the web, and the Data Source Description (DSD)[8] vocabulary, which provides classes to represent data within a data source [3]. From DCAT, the following classes are used: *Catalog* for modeling an instance of the data catalog, *DataService* for a resource within a data catalog, and *Dataset* for a specific data source. Since existing data catalog tools also analyze the structure within a data source and *Dataset* is the most fine-grained class in DCAT, the DSD vocabulary is used to model concepts of the data dictionary within a data source (e.g., schemas, tables, attributes).

[7] https://www.w3.org/TR/vocab-dcat-2 (Oct. 2022).

[8] http://dqm.faw.jku.at/ontologies/dsd (Oct. 2022).

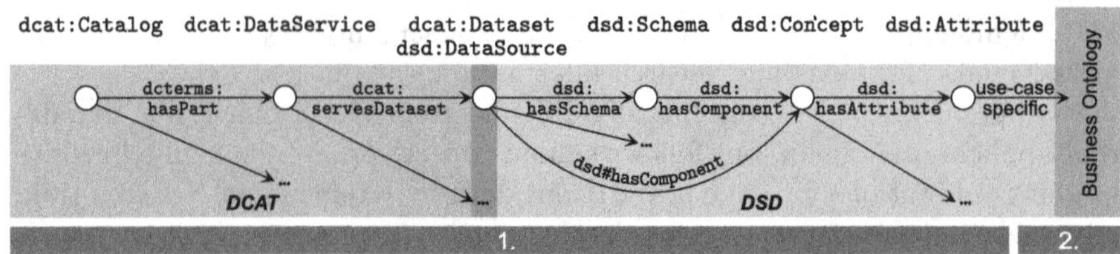

Fig. 1. GOLDCASE: ontology structure

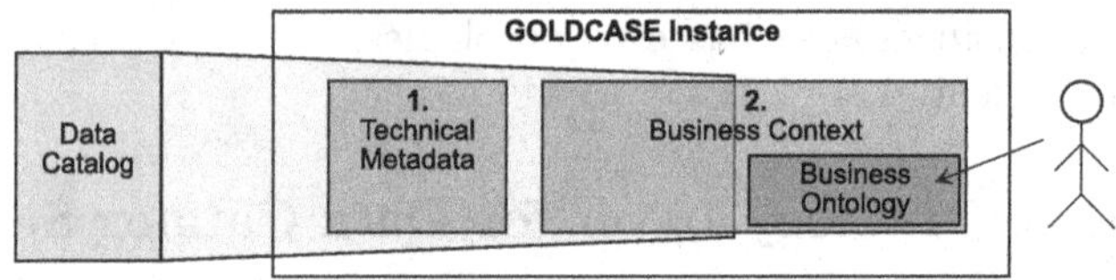

Fig. 2. GOLDCASE: architecture and interface to an existing data catalog tool

2. **Business context.** The modeling of an ontology as business context depends on the use case and company. Therefore, no generic structure is provided in the right outer part of Fig. 1. It is recommended to use one of the many methodologies (see [5] for an overview) for the creation of the business ontology. Some data catalog tools already provide business context to some extent (e.g., the *data domains* in EDC as described in Sect. 4.2). However, these structures are often not expressive enough to model real-world scenarios. To reuse the business context of a data catalog tool like EDC, it is necessary to customize GOLDCASE with use-case-specific ontology classes and properties. For an example, see the proof-of-concept implementation in Sect. 4.3.

3.2 Role in Organization and Implementation Guideline

GOLDCASE does not provide all data catalog functionalities, but focuses on the provision of semantics for metadata already collected by an existing data catalog tool. Consequently, a data catalog tool needs to be in use by the organization to apply GOLDCASE. Figure 2 illustrates the two structural parts (i.e., technical metadata and business context) of GOLDCASE and how they are connected with an existing data catalog within an organization. To implement GOLDCASE in such a setting, the following five steps need to be taken:

S1 **Download:** GOLDCASE is publicly available[9].
S2 **Customization:** After investigating the structure of the existing data catalog tool, GOLDCASE can be customized with vendor-specific classes and properties.

[9] http://dqm.faw.jku.at/ontologies/GOLDCASE (Oct. 2022).

S3 **Business Ontology Creation:** An business ontology, which serves as business context, has to be created.
S4 **Program Logic:** A program that instantiates the customized GOLDCASE and populates it with data from the data catalog needs to be created.
S5 **Interface:** To allow users the interaction and querying of GOLDCASE, an interface is required. This can either be an application programming interface (API) or an User interface (UI).

4 Implementation and Discussion of Benefits

Based on a specific use case at PIERER Innovation GmbH, we demonstrate the applicability of GOLDCASE through a Python-based proof of concept (POC) in Sect. 4.3. We evaluate the POC and summarize its benefits in Sect. 4.4.

4.1 Use Case at PIERER Innovation GmbH

PIERER Innovation GmbH (PInno) aims at developing new products, services, and business models around the digital ecosystem of vehicles, especially for KTM AG. The vision of PInno is to enable internal and external partners to work collaboratively on data-driven use cases, without requiring them to have detailed knowledge about the internal data landscape and processes.

For our proof of concept, we considered the following use case: A defect in a motorcycle's component leads to a warranty claim. To analyze the cause of such defects, profound knowledge of the data structure (in terms of databases and business processes) is currently necessary. In a first step, the motorcycle models equipped with the affected components must be retrieved from the bills of material. Using this list of motorcycle models, the relevant warranty claims can then be extracted from KTM dealer management system. To allow the analysis of the respective defect in detail, diagnostic data recorded at the workshops (as part of warranty processing) must be extracted from the motorcycle diagnostic system and made available to the data scientists and analysts.

4.2 Informatica Enterprise Data Catalog (EDC)

PInno uses EDC to manage their data sources. Informatica is classified as a leader in the "Magic Quadrant for Metadata Management Solutions" by Gartner Inc. [1] and offers two products that can be classified as data catalogs: EDC[10], with a focus on metadata management, and Axon[11], with a focus on data collaboration and data governance [12]. At the time of the project, PInno uses EDC only.

In the terminology of EDC, the most general concept is a so-called *resource*, which can be scanned to retrieve technical metadata from data sources [9]. As

[10] https://www.informatica.com/products/data-catalog/enterprise-data-catalog.html (Oct. 2022).

[11] https://www.informatica.com/products/data-quality/axon-data-governance.html (Oct. 2022).

an example, the scanned metadata of a relational database is structured in the following hierarchy, with *Attribute* having the highest granularity:

$$Resource \rightarrow DataSet \rightarrow Schema \rightarrow Table \rightarrow Attribute$$

Instances of these classes are known as *assets*. So-called *business terms*, which can originate from EDC-wide business glossaries, can be assigned to assets to introduce a common naming. *Data domains* are common terms to define the meaning of a *column* and can be grouped to *data domain groups* for categorization [9,10]. However, it is not possible to model relationships (e.g., same-as, sub-data-domain) between data domains nor business terms. As an example at PInno, the *vehicle identification number (VIN)* should be modeled as sub-data-domain of the *serial number*, since every VIN is a serial number for vehicles, but not every serial number is a VIN (e.g., for vehicle parts).

4.3 Proof-of-Concept Implementation

The aim of our POC implementation is to simplify the complex process described in Sect. 4.1 by providing a single and clear interface for non-technical users (e.g., domain users, customers) that want to query (meta)data based on domain knowledge. To achieve this, we build an abstraction layer on top of EDC using GOLDCASE.

From a technical perspective, the POC offers a client application, which requests the data domains and structure of the data sources from the EDC using its REST API. The gathered information is integrated into a customized GOLDCASE instance, which is newly created for each query. We followed the implementation guideline from Sect. 3.2 for the creation of our POC. Since the first step (Download) is trivial, only the actions taken during the steps S2–S5 are described in the following. We assume basic knowledge about ontologies.

S2 – Customization: EDC provides business context to some extent through *data domains* (cf. Sect. 4.2). To reuse this information, we customize the GOLDCASE template with an additional concept "data domain" and connect this concept to the PInno business ontology with an annotation property. Figure 3 depicts the structure of the customized GOLDCASE, which matches the structure of EDC. For simplicity, inverse object properties are not displayed.

S3 – Business Ontology Creation: We implemented a business data model in form of an OWL ontology for PInno. Figure 4 shows an excerpt of this ontology, which is subsequently used to demonstrate the functionality of our POC[12]. Please note that the example ontology is only an excerpt of the full business ontology, which cannot be published due to confidentiality.

[12] Ontology excerpt published on our website: http://dqm.faw.jku.at/ontologies/goldcase-application-example-1/goldcase-application-example.ttl.

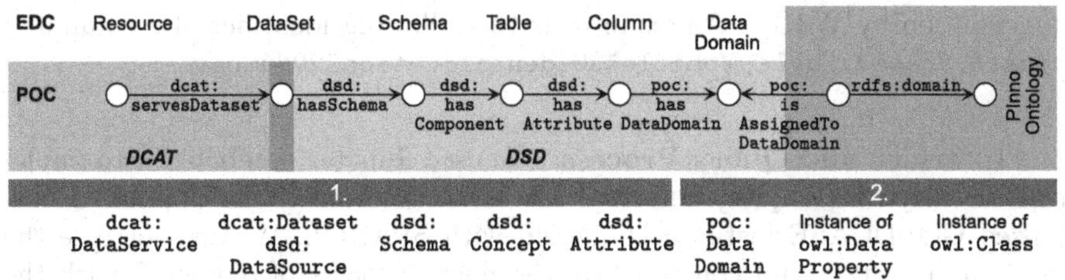

Fig. 3. Structure of the customized GOLDCASE and the corresponding EDC classes

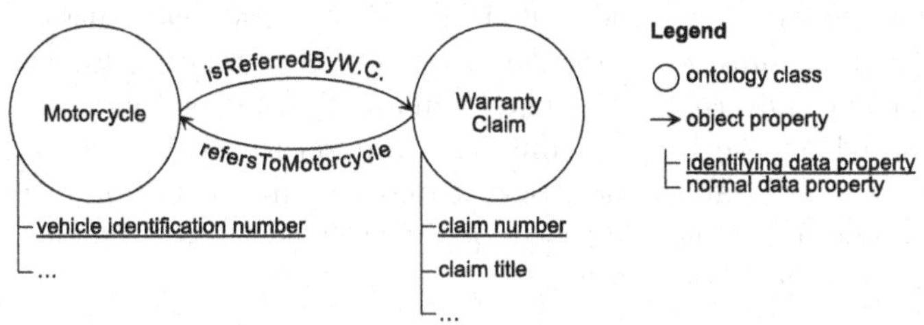

Fig. 4. Excerpt of the PInno business ontology

In addition to the technical metadata, semantics from EDC are retrieved in form of the data domains (cf. S2). To enable their reuse, we introduce a mapping between data domains and the data properties of our business ontology. The mapping is realized as a key-value store, where for each data domain a corresponding data property of the business ontology is assigned. Consequently, the business context of EDC (data domains organized in a list) is connected with the more expressive business context of GOLDCASE realized as an ontology.

S4 – Program Logic: We implemented a Python-based program, which instantiates the customized GOLDCASE and queries the EDC using REST requests. For every new query that is passed to the POC, a new copy of the customized GOLDCASE, including the mapping and the PInno business ontology from Fig. 4, is instantiated. We refer to these instantiated ontologies as the *customized GOLDCASE instance.* After instantiation, all information required to answer the query (i.e., data sources and data domains) are retrieved from EDC and the customized GOLDCASE instance is populated on-the-fly without any persistence. We decided for a virtual integration scenario since it reduces the size of the graph inside the POC and redundant storage of the information from EDC is not feasible.

Subsequently, the customized GOLDCASE instance is populated with asset representations from EDC using the classes described in Sect. 3.1. The identifiers of the asset representations are based on the "path of an asset" (obtained from EDC) and are encoded according to the "IRI-safe version of a string" recommendation by W3C[13]. An example is the following identifier of a column[14]: `Dataset.Schema.Table.Vehicle%20Identification%20Number`.

S5 – Interface and Query Process: We used Jupyter notebooks[15] to implement an easy-to-use query interface for users. Internally, the populated customized GOLDCASE instance is queried with SPARQL. We demonstrate the use of the interface and consequently the query process of our POC with the central question from our use case in Sect. 4.1: "Which motorcycle has which warranty claims?".

On a more general level, the POC in its current state can answer queries of the type "Which *business ontology class (subject)* has a relationship with *another business ontology class (object)*?". The UI allows to select subject and object for the query based on the business ontology and returns information about the data structures (i.e., tables) necessary to create the query for retrieving the actual data. The following exemplary query process is based on the excerpt of the business ontology shown in Fig. 4.

1. A user enters a query to the business ontology through the Jupyter UI. *Example:* "Which *motorcycle* has which *warranty claims*?"
2. The customized GOLDCASE instance is initialized as described in S4.
3. Using all data properties from the subject and the identifying data property(s) from the object, the data domains that are relevant for the respective query are determined using the *mapping*. *Example:* Through the mapping (cf. S3), `VIN` is determined as the corresponding data domain in EDC for the data property `Vehicle_Identification_Number`.
4. For each data domain, technical metadata about the tables the data domain is assigned to, are retrieved from EDC and the GOLDCASE instance is populated with representations of the tables.
5. The POC determines the representations of the data sources that hold the requested information via SPARQL. *Example:* The POC returns (1) the representation of all tables that define a motorcycle and (2) the representations of the tables, where warranty claims are in a relationship with a motorcycle.

4.4 Evaluation and Summary of the Benefits

To highlight the added value of GOLDCASE, we assess both, the EDC and our POC by means of the components a data catalog should consist of (cf. [2]). Table 1 shows a direct comparison of these requirements, where ✓ denotes complete fulfillment, ∼ partial fulfillment (justification in the description column), and × no fulfillment. For a description of the single FAIR principles, we refer to [21] and the GO FAIR website[1]. The arrows in column GOLDCASE indicate the influence GOLDCASE has on the fulfillment of the POC compared to EDC

[13] https://www.w3.org/TR/2012/REC-r2rml-20120927/#dfn-iri-safe (Oct. 2022).

[14] Parts of the example have been redacted due to confidentiality.

[15] https://jupyter.org (Oct. 2022).

Table 1. Evaluation of our POC by means of the data catalog components by [2]

	EDC	POC	GOLDCASE	Description
Metadata Management	✓	✓	→	
Business Context	~	✓	↑	EDC supports *data domains*, which however cannot be contextualized with semantic relationships.
Data Responsibility Roles	~	×	↓	Data roles can be assigned to data assets in EDC, but comprehensive role management is part of Axon. Roles were not in the focus of the current version of POC, but are subject to future work.
FAIR Principles				
Findable				
F1	✓	✓	↑	EDC uses proprietary identifiers. GOLDCASE uses IRIs.
F2	~	✓	↑	OWL features a higher expressiveness than the data structure of EDC.
F3	✓	✓	→	
F4	✓	✓	→	
Accessible				
A1	✓	✓	→	EDC offers a REST API. The POC can be queried with SPARQL.
A1.1	✓	✓	→	
A1.2	✓	✓	→	The POC depends on data from EDC, the fulfillment is therefore inherited.
A2	~	~	→	In EDC, data assets can be deleted, but the resulting behavior regarding the metadata is unclear. The POC inherits this information from EDC.
Interoperable				
I1	~	✓	↑	The Informatica-specific data structures of EDC may be formal and are accessible via REST, but not broadly applicable outside the Informatica universe. OWL and SPARQL are W3C recommendations.
I2	~	✓	↑	While EDC is tied to the Informatica universe, OWL is a linked open data standard.
I3	~	✓	↑	Qualified relationships are supported for technical metadata, but not for business context.
Reusable				
R1	~	✓	↑	OWL features a higher expressiveness than the data structure of EDC.
R1.1	~	~	→	The availability of license information depends on the maintenance of EDC by its users. The POC inherits this information from EDC.
R1.2	✓	✓	→	EDC supports data lineage, which is inherited by the POC.
R1.3	×	✓	↑	Since EDC does not meet domain-relevant community standards, we developed GOLDCASE and our POC.

alone. Aspects that are improved by the use of GOLDCASE are denoted with $\uparrow$, $\rightarrow$ means no influence, whereas $\downarrow$ shows a negative influence. The only $\downarrow$ is attributed to the data responsibility roles, since they are considered future work.

We see components as well as the FAIR principles fulfilled if a function serving the needed functionality is present in the software. While the management of (technical) metadata is already supported by EDC alone, business context is only fulfilled partially by EDC through the concept of data domains. Since data domains cannot be structured in a hierarchy nor put into context with semantic relationships, full support of the business context is only enabled when using GOLDCASE and therefore supported in our POC. For completeness, we also included data responsibility roles in Table 1, which are supported by EDC, but not by the POC due to our different research focus (planned for future work). With respect to the fulfillment of the FAIR principles, a clear improvement of FAIRness can be seen when comparing the POC to EDC. While the POC fully supports the *findability* and *interoperability* sections, the functionalities at the *accessibility* section are mainly inherited from EDC. In addition to that, the *reusability* section depends on the input of users. One of the most important aspects for PInno was *reusability* to prevent locking into one vendor's ecosystem. Since GOLDCASE is based on open standards, it can be applied to any data catalog tool, and therefore allows the creation of an independent global business data model.

In summary, on a scale from 1 (best) to 5 (worst), the domain experts at PInno ranked the overall usability of the POC with 2, whereas EDC was ranked with 4. The main reason for this is the high-level business data model, which has been put upon EDC using GOLDCASE. Considering the use case from Sect. 4.1, the sum of all queries required to retrieve the information about which motorcycle(s) correspond to a warranty claim, is handled through the program logic of our POC and only one query in the language of the user is necessary.

5 Conclusion and Research Outlook

In this paper, we propose GOLDCASE, a generic ontology layer, which can be applied on top of existing data catalog tools and extends them with a high-level view on the semantics of data. To demonstrate the applicability in real-world scenarios and to evaluate the benefits of GOLDCASE, we implemented a proof of concept at PInno. The customized GOLDCASE instance at PInno seamlessly connects the automatically collected technical metadata from an existing Informatica EDC with a high-expressive business data model for domain experts and external partners.

We show that the use of GOLDCASE improves the FAIRness of the overall system and enables clear semantics, which leads to better metadata. Metadata management, in turn, is the basis for all data governance tasks, such as, data quality assurance and access security [18].

For future work, we plan to extend our POC at PInno with additional use cases and to implement more complex query types in the UI. With respect to

GOLDCASE, we plan to add versioning of the ontology by using RDF-star and SPARQL-star[16], since they allow RDF predicates to have properties.

Considering the components of a data catalog (cf. [2]), our focus so far was technical metadata, business context, and the fulfillment of the FAIR principles. We argue that data responsibility roles are essentially to enable data FAIRness. Thus, this will be the next step in our research. While software enables FAIRness to a certain degree (by providing the technical basis for storing and managing the data), people are eventually responsible for using the provided software and for maintaining the metadata.

Acknowledgements. The research reported in this paper has been funded by BMK, BMDW, and the State of Upper Austria in the frame of the COMET Programme managed by FFG.

References

1. De Simoni, G., et al.: Magic Quadrant for Metadata Management Solutions (2020). www.gartner.com/en/documents/3993025
2. Ehrlinger, L., Schrott, J., Melichar, M., Kirchmayr, N., Wöß, W.: Data catalogs: a systematic literature review and guidelines to implementation. In: Kotsis, G., et al. (eds.) DEXA 2021. CCIS, vol. 1479, pp. 148–158. Springer, Cham (2021). https://doi.org/10.1007/978-3-030-87101-7_15
3. Ehrlinger, L., Wöß, W.: Semi-automatically generated hybrid ontologies for information integration. In: Joint Proceedings of the Posters and Demos Track of 11th International Conference on Semantic Systems, SEMANTiCS2015 and 1st Workshop on Data Science: Methods, Technology and Applications (DSci15), vol. 1481, pp. 100–104. CEUR Workshop Proceedings, Aachen (2015)
4. Feilmayr, C., Wöß, W.: An analysis of ontologies and their success factors for application to business. Data Knowl. Eng. **101**, 1–23 (2016)
5. Fernández-López, M., Gómez-Pérez, A.: Overview and analysis of methodologies for building ontologies. Knowl. Eng. Rev. **17**(2), 129–156 (2002)
6. Franklin, M., et al.: From databases to dataspaces: a new abstraction for information management. SIGMOD Rec. **34**(4), 27–33 (2005)
7. Gruber, T.R.: A translation approach to portable ontology specifications. Knowl. Acquis. **5**(2), 199–220 (1993)
8. Hilger, J., Wahl, Z.: Data catalogs and governance tools. In: Hilger, J., Wahl, Z. (eds.) Making Knowledge Management Clickable, pp. 187–192. Springer, Cham (2022). https://doi.org/10.1007/978-3-030-92385-3_11
9. Informatica LLC: Informatica Catalog Administrator Guide (2021)
10. Informatica LLC: Informatica Enterprise Data Catalog User Guide (2021)
11. ISO/IEC 25012:2008 Systems and Software Engineering - Systems and Software Quality Requirements and Evaluation (SQuaRE) - Measurement of Data Quality. Standard, International Organization for Standardization, Geneva (2008). www.iso.org/standard/35736.html
12. Korte, T., et al.: Data Catalogs - Integrated Platforms for Matching Data Supply and Demand. Reference Model and Market Analysis (Version 1.0). Fraunhofer Verlag, Stuttgart (2019)

[16] https://w3c.github.io/rdf-star/cg-spec/editors_draft.html (Oct. 2022).

13. Křemen, P., Nečaský, M.: Improving discoverability of open government data with rich metadata descriptions using semantic government vocabulary. J. Web Semant. **55**, 1–20 (2019)
14. Labadie, C., et al.: FAIR enough? Enhancing the usage of enterprise data with data catalogs. In: 2020 IEEE 22nd Conference on Business Informatics (CBI), Antwerp, pp. 201–210. IEEE (2020)
15. Quimbert, E., Jeffery, K., Martens, C., Martin, P., Zhao, Z.: Data cataloguing. In: Zhao, Z., Hellström, M. (eds.) Towards Interoperable Research Infrastructures for Environmental and Earth Sciences. LNCS, vol. 12003, pp. 140–161. Springer, Cham (2020). https://doi.org/10.1007/978-3-030-52829-4_8
16. Sequeda, J., Lassila, O.: Designing and Building Enterprise Knowledge Graphs. Synthesis Lectures on Data, Semantics, and Knowledge, no. 20. Morgan & Claypool (2021)
17. Studer, R., et al.: Knowledge engineering: principles and methods. Data Knowl. Eng. **25**(1–2), 161–197 (1998)
18. Talburt, J.: Data Speaks for Itself: Data Littering (2022). https://tdan.com/data-speaks-for-itself-data-littering/29122
19. Vancauwenbergh, S., et al.: On research information and classification governance in an inter-organizational context: the flanders research information space. Scientometrics **108**(1), 425–439 (2016)
20. West, M.: Developing High Quality Data Models. Elsevier (2011)
21. Wilkinson, M.D., et al.: The FAIR guiding principles for scientific data management and stewardship. Sci. Data **3**(1), 160018 (2016)
22. Zaidi, E., et al.: Data Catalogs Are the New Black in Data Management and Analytics (2017). https://www.gartner.com/en/documents/3837968

Evaluation of Search Methods on Community Documents

Kushagra Singh Bisen[1,5], Sara Assefa Alemayehu[1], Pierre Maret[1,4](✉), Alexandra Creighton[2], Rachel Gorman[2], Bushra Kundi[2], Thumeka Mgwgwi[3], Fabrice Muhlenbach[1], Serban Dinca-Panaitescu[2], and Christo El Morr[2]

[1] Université Jean Monnet, Saint Étienne, France
pierre.maret@univ-st-etienne.fr
[2] School of Health Policy and Management, York University, Toronto, Canada
[3] School of Gender, Sexuality and Women's Studies, York University, Toronto, Canada
[4] The QA Company, Saint Étienne, France
[5] IDLab, Ghent University - imec, Ghent, Belgium

Abstract. Searching for domain-specific information on the web is tough. Community documents are therefore made searchable with a dedicated search platform. Search Methods employed on a document corpora are often evaluated over the aspect of efficiency and not focusing on the often-overlooked user experience. In the paper, we present an evaluation of search methods over domain-specific document corpora over search methods. The document corpora are represented in RDF as well as free-text. We describe the search methods as well as present the evaluation environment prepared. Moreover, we present the result of the user study to understand the experience of a user with the search methods.

Keywords: Meta-Data · Domain-Specific Documents · Question Answering · Information Retrieval · UEQ · Human-Computer Interaction

1 Introduction

Search for domain-specific information is tough on the web. Search engine usually returns a response from pages which are popular and indexed above. Communities with an interest in a particular domain often find results which are not relevant to their query searching on the web. For instance, this is the case for activists in disability and human rights advocacy groups. This community, as well as many other distributed communities, need domain-specific repositories where they will have more chances to find the information they are searching for. These data and document repositories may implement a different mechanism for accessing the information. Moreover, the questions asked by stakeholders in a project can utilise the meta-data, the document's content or both. Therefore,

E. Garoufallou and A. Vlachidis (Eds.): MTSR 2022, CCIS 1789, pp. 39–49, 2023.
https://doi.org/10.1007/978-3-031-39141-5_4

there is a need for an evaluation of methods that can be employed for searching over community data and documents. In this paper, we present an evaluation of search techniques available over domain-specific document corpus. The paper is organised as follows, In Sect. 2, we describe the existing work done in this direction. In Sect. 3, we explain the experiment we conducted and the evaluation methods. We further show the results in Sect. 4.2. We conclude and point to future work in the Sect. 5

2 Related Work

The evaluation of search methods generally concentrates on the performance of the search mechanism: calculation of precision, recall, and F-Measure. Benchmarks have been proposed for this kind of task. Apart from the quality of the search method, it is also important to provide the user with an efficient search experience to retrieve the information in the corpus. Therefore, there is a need for evaluating the quality of the user search experience when searching for information. And this is especially necessary because of the emergence and popularity of new search techniques such as Elastic search [17,27], Question Answering over free text [2,4,5,7], and Question Answering over knowledge graphs [9,10,28,30]. The search techniques are *one-field one-shot search* i.e. users retrieve information by building a question/query through only a text field and receive the answer in response. There have been end user evaluations on semantic web to improve the human-semantic web interaction [11,22]. There are various methods for evaluating a method such as Concept Testing [23], Heuristic Evaluation [24] and User Experience Evaluation [29]. We need to adapt the evaluation of user experience to the search methods. To the best of our knowledge, there has been no user experience evaluation on search methods over community documents.

3 Description of an Evaluation Environment for Search Methods

In this section, we describe the environment prepared to experiment with and evaluate the search methods on community documents. In the Subsect. 3.1 we describe the search methods we compare and in the Subsect. 3.2 we describe the experiment.

3.1 Search Methods

QAnswer over Knowledge Graphs. QAnswer KG [9] is a search engine over RDF datasets with which users can search information with both questions as well as keywords. The data stored in a knowledge graph can be exported as a triple pattern for QAnswer KG. The input query is expanded and n-grams from the query are mapped with the properties and resources. The properties and resources are used to generate possible SPARQL queries by combining the triples which share a variable. The queries are ranked with a machine-learning model and the query with the highest confidence is chosen as the response to the user's input.

Elastic Search over Documents. Elastic Search over Documents (ESDoc) Elastic Search [13] is a JSON based full-text search engine capable to search over big data in a real-time fashion. Elastic Search can be used out of the box, although some users prefer to tweak parameters. Elastic Search is built over Apache Lucene, a java library. The elastic search uses algorithms such as okapi bm25 and NMSLIB to return a relevant document in response to the query.

An elastic search system's architecture is composed of [18]

- *Document* for storing an entity, it has an identifier and is part of an index where it is stored. They can be separated over multiple nodes.
- *Node* is an instance of elastic search active for a query. Connected active nodes are referred to as a *cluster*.
- *Shards* are used to improve efficiency through processing in parallel by further dividing the index into shards. Shards are often stored as *Replicas* to provide throughput of the data for efficiency in search.

QAnswer Search over Documents. QAnswer Search over Documents (QADoc) employs RoBERTa [20] for question answering over the document corpus. The documents are uploaded, split into paragraphs and pre-processed. The questions to the documents are answered with the content of the document.

3.2 Experiment

Search Instruction Questionnaire. An experiment was conducted where the candidates were requested to search for domain-specific information as illustrated in the Table 2. The instructions provided are *search-method agnostic*. We did not propose questions but rather proposed search instructions to which a user can formulate the question by himself in a search technique. The reason was to prevent biases that could arise by providing questions to search the method, as the methods are different in their implementation. For example, telling the users to search for "*keyword1, keyword2, keyword3*" will work in keyword-based elastic search but could not be good in other search methods. The candidates used each search method listed in the Sect. 3.1 to search for the domain-specific information. The candidates have presented a questionnaire with the search instructions with a 7-point Likert Scale [14] from −3 to 3 (the higher the better) to record the relevancy of the information retrieved, as per the user. We present 6 search instructions to the candidate of which 5 are True i.e. there is any information related to the instruction in the community document corpus and 1 is False i.e. there is no information related to the instruction in the community document corpus (see Table 1). The candidates use a stopwatch to record the time they spent searching for the information. The candidates are instructed to stop searching if more than 2 min are spent and further record that they didn't find an answer. The candidates are also instructed to record if they found an answer with three scales which are yes, no and maybe. We chose two minutes as a threshold for search as the search method should be able to provide an answer in that time, if not the search method is not considered efficient.

User Experience Questionnaire. The second questionnaire presented to the candidate after each search method was a user experience questionnaire (UEQ) [19]. We choose UEQ as it provides a benchmark to classify the values obtained from the result. The objective of UEQ is to allow a quick assessment done by end users covering a preferably comprehensive impression of user experience. It should allow users to express feelings, impressions and attitudes that arise when experiencing the search method under investigation simply and immediately [25]. We employ the standard version of UEQ which contains 26 items. The items are divided into 6 scales. The 6 scales focus on different experience aspects of the search method:

- Attractiveness: Signifying the overall impression of the search method.
- Perspicuity: Describing if it is easy to get familiar with the search method and if it is easy to understand.
- Efficiency: Describing if the search method is fast to provide them with information.
- Dependability: Describing if the user feels confident while using the search method.
- Stimulation: Describing if the user finds the search method exciting and motivating.
- Novelty: Describing if the user finds the search method innovative and creative.

We use the UEQ scales to find how the candidates feel about the attractiveness of the search method (with the scale *Attractiveness*), the usefulness of the search method i.e. Pragmatic Value (employing the scales *Perspicuity, Efficiency and Dependability*), the ease of use of the search method i.e. Hedonic Value (employing the scales *Stimulation and Novelty*).

4 Experimental Results

4.1 Domain of Experiment

The communities working for disability rights advocacy require better information access [1,21]. In the domain of healthcare, the stakeholders perform a variety of search tasks like literature reviews, scoping reviews, rapid evidence reviews and systematic reviews [6]. The domain of the documents employed in the experiment is disability studies. The motivation to choose disability studies documents was to provide a better search experience for the disability documents in the WikiDisability Project [12]. We search over the disability documents which are annotated with the Disability Wiki Website[1] in the Disability Knowledge

[1] https://disabilityrightsweb.univ-st-etienne.fr/.

Graph[2] as well as in free-text in PDF to be searchable by Elastic Search 3.1 and QAnswer Search over Documents 3.1. The Table 2 describes the disability domain-specific search instructions given to the user. The search instructions, as well as the UEQ, were provided to the user in form of a response form[3] to be filled.

Table 1. The table shows the details related to the search instruction questionnaire experiment

Documents	**Candidates**	Search Methods	True Questions	False Questions
24	**17**	3	5	1

Table 2. The table shows the search instructions given to the user for search with each method

Instruction to the User	Is answer available?
Find text about the racism faced by black feminists	Yes
Find text about elitism in american womens movement	Yes
Find text about human rights of minors	No
Find text about racism in United States	Yes
Find text about ableism in prison	Yes
Find text about police violence for disabled people	Yes

4.2 Results of the Experiment

The value for UEQ scales are described in the Table 4. We further compare the search methods with an ANOVA test [8] on each 6 sub-scale of UEQ for the 17 candidates. However, there was a statistically significant difference between the groups as determined by One-Way ANOVA of the scales Perspicuity, Efficiency and Novelty. An ANOVA test signifies if there is an overall difference between the groups. We, therefore, perform a Tukey-Kramer Test [15] to find out the differences between the groups. The results from the experiment are summarised as,

- ESDoc provided the most relevant answers as per the candidates of the experiment, although it provided them with a false sense of information as the users found information for the instruction with no information available in the community corpus (see Fig. 1).

[2] https://disabilitywiki.univ-st-etienne.fr/wiki/The_Disability_Wikibase.
[3] https://forms.gle/bjKqpdRGCuFSQFFG9.

- For search instruction with information available in the document corpus, users found most information with ESDoc followed by QAnswer KG and QADoc. However, for the instruction with no information available, users *found* most information with ESDoc as well (see Fig. 2).
- The values obtained from UEQ (see Table 4) falls in the category of *bad* according to the UEQ benchmark [26]
- There were no statistically significant differences between the group means as determined by One-Way ANOVA of the scales Attractive, Dependability and Stimulation (see Table 5)
- There was a statistically significant difference between the groups as determined by One-Way ANOVA of the scales Perspicuity, Efficiency and Novelty (see Table 5).
- From Tukey-Kramer Test, we find that there is a significant difference between ESDoc vs QAnswer KG and ESDoc vs QADoc in the Perspicuity Scale.
- There is a significant difference between ESDoc vs QADoc for both Novelty and Efficiency scale (see Table 6)
- QADoc had the highest Hedonic Value i.e. users found QADoc to be the most pleasant while interacting with it. It is followed by ESDoc and QAnswer KG (see Fig. 3).

Table 3. Benchmark scores for classifying the experiences of users to the scales of UEQ [26]. The scores obtained in the experiment belong to the scale **bad**.

	Att.	Eff.	Per.	Dep.	Sti.	Nov.
Excellent	≥1.75	≥1.78	≥1.9	≥1.65	≥1.55	≥1.4
Good	≥1.52	≥1.47	≥1.56	≥1.48	≥1.31	≥1.05
	<1.75	<1.78	<1.9	<1.65	<1.55	<1.4
Above Avg	≥1.17	≥0.98	≥1.08	≥1.14	≥0.99	≥0.71
	<1.52	<1.47	<1.56	<1.48	<1.31	<1.05
Below Avg	≥0.7	≥0.54	≥0.64	≥0.78	≥0.5	≥0.3
	<1.17	<0.98	<1.08	<1.14	<0.99	<0.71
Bad	**<0.7**	**<0.54**	**<0.64**	**<0.78**	**<0.5**	**<0.3**

Table 4. The scores obtained from UEQ on different scales

Scales	QAnswer KG	ESDoc	QADoc
Attractive	−0.272	**−0.114**	−0.433
Perspicuity	**−0.014**	−1.205	−0.05
Efficiency	−0.22	**0.014**	−0.583
Dependability	−0.132	**−0.014**	−0.266
Stimulation	−0.161	**0.0588**	−0.1
Novelty	−0.088	−0.191	**0.266**

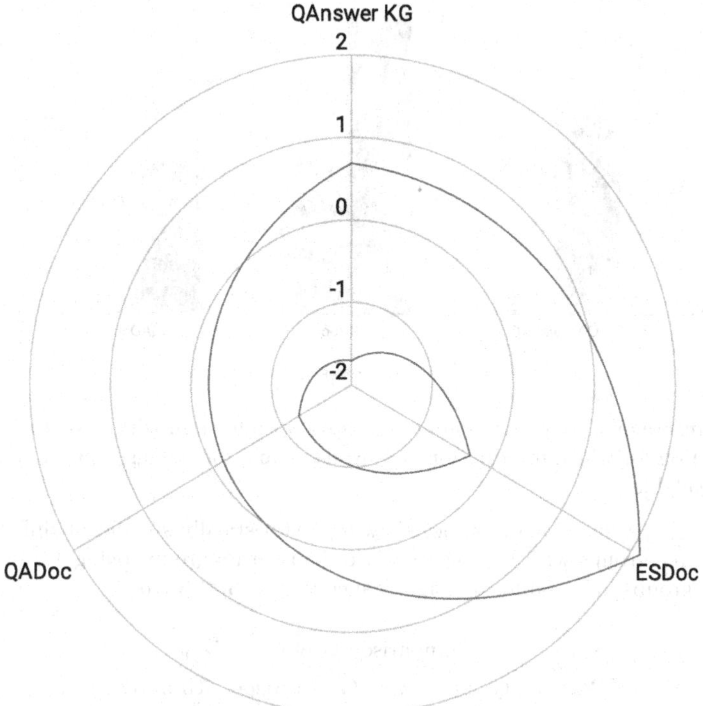

Fig. 1. Likert scale scores for the search methods in the relevancy of the information found from the search methods on instructions with information was available and for the instruction, information was not available

Table 5. Values of F-Ratio and P-Value for One-Way Anova with $df_{between} = 2$ and $df_{within} = 46$ on the UEQ data for Search Methods

Scale	F-Ratio	P-Value
Attractive	1.269	0.29
Perspicuity	36.20	<0.001
Efficiency	5.284	0.008
Dependability	0.861	0.429
Stimulation	1.78	0.179
Novelty	3.2	0.049

- QAnswer KG had the highest Pragmatic Value i.e. users found QAnswer KG to be the most efficient and useful. It is followed by QADoc and ESDoc (see Fig. 3) (Table 3).

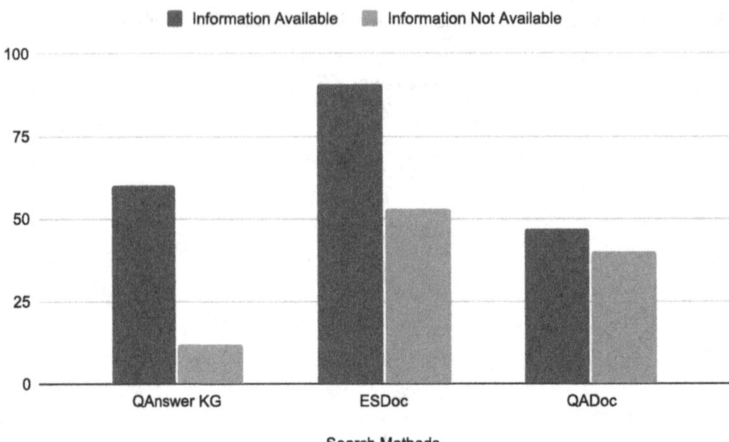

Fig. 2. Percentage of users who found an answer within 2 min with search methods on the instruction for which information was available and for the instruction information was not available

Table 6. q_{tukey} values for the scales showing a statistically significant difference. As there are three groups with the degree of freedom within groups being 46, the critical value for 3 groups, df = 46 for 5% significance level is **3.425** [16]

Scale	Comparison Groups	q_{tukey}
Perspicuity	QAnswerKG vs ESDoc	**10.6742**
	ESDoc vs QADoc	**10.029**
	QAnswerKG vs QADoc	0.306
Efficiency	QAnswerKG vs ESDoc	1.86
	ESDoc vs QADoc	**4.579**
	QAnswerKG vs QADoc	2.777
Novelty	QAnswerKG vs ESDoc	0.798
	ESDoc vs QADoc	**3.439**
	QAnswerKG vs QADoc	2.665

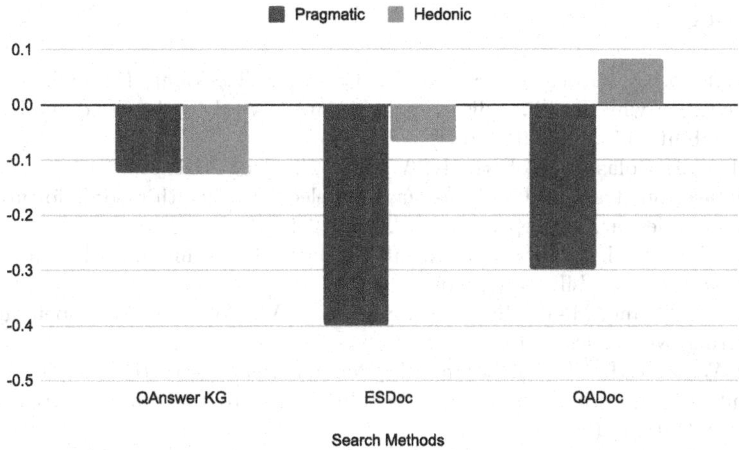

Fig. 3. Pragmatic (i.e. perceived use-fullness, efficiency) and Hedonic (i.e. perceived innovation) values for the search methods

5 Conclusion and Future Work

In the paper, we have presented the evaluation of search methods on domain-specific community document corpus based on the user experience. We found out that using Elastic search over the documents can provide relevant answers. Although, it also provided a false sense of relevancy of the information to the user for the search instruction with no information available in the document corpora. Thus, for non-exploratory question answering with an exact answer, we need more than the Elastic search technique. We find out that QADoc was the search method with perceived innovation by the users, but it did not perform as well as ESDoc or QAnswer KG for information retrieval. QAnswer KG was perceived as the most useful search method by the users. We conclude that we need to combine various search methods over community documents to provide a better search experience to the user. After conclusion, we developed a demo[4] on the same document corpus where we combine the three search methods [3]. We used wikibase as a knowledge graph to store data around the document (the meta-data) and QADoc for data inside the document (the actual content). We introduced a fallback to other search methods in case the confidence of the response to the query is below a predefined threshold. In future, we have planned for a heuristic evaluation of the user interface for each search method to improve the search experience. We have also planned to introduce a new set of documents from the same domain to the corpus and evaluate the search with the application where the search methods are combined.

[4] http://demo-disabilityrightsweb.univ-st-etienne.fr/.

References

1. Abualghaib, O., Groce, N., Simeu, N., Carew, M.T., Mont, D.: Making visible the invisible: why disability-disaggregated data is vital to "leave no-one behind". Sustainability **11**(11), 3091 (2019)
2. Bardhan, J., Colas, A., Roberts, K., Wang, D.Z.: DrugEHRQA: a question answering dataset on structured and unstructured electronic health records for medicine related queries. arXiv preprint arXiv:2205.01290 (2022)
3. Bisen, K.S., et al.: Wikibase as an infrastructure for community documents: the example of the disability wiki platform (2022)
4. Chen, W., Chang, M.-W., Schlinger, E., Wang, W., Cohen, W.W.: Open question answering over tables and text (2020)
5. Chen, W., Zha, H., Chen, Z., Xiong, W., Wang, H., Wang, W.: HybridQA: a dataset of multi-hop question answering over tabular and textual data. arXiv preprint arXiv:2004.07347 (2020)
6. Collins, A., Coughlin, D., Miller, J., Kirk, S.: The production of quick scoping reviews and rapid evidence assessments: a how to guide. Technical report, December 2015. Freely available via Official URL link
7. Cucerzan, S., Agichtein, E.: Factoid question answering over unstructured and structured web content. In: TREC, vol. 72, p. 90 (2005)
8. Cuevas, A., Febrero, M., Fraiman, R.: An anova test for functional data. Comput. Stat. Data Anal. **47**(1), 111–122 (2004)
9. Diefenbach, D., Giménez-García, J., Both, A., Singh, K., Maret, P.: QAnswer KG: designing a portable question answering system over RDF data. In: Harth, A., et al. (eds.) ESWC 2020. LNCS, vol. 12123, pp. 429–445. Springer, Cham (2020). https://doi.org/10.1007/978-3-030-49461-2_25
10. Diomedi, D., Hogan, A.: Question answering over knowledge graphs with neural machine translation and entity linking (2021)
11. García, R., Gil, R.: Improving human-semantic web interaction: the Rhizomer experience. In: SWAP (2006)
12. Gorman, R., et al.: The potential of an artificial intelligence for disability advocacy: the WikiDisability project. In: Public Health and Informatics, pp. 1025–1026. IOS Press (2021)
13. Gormley, C., Tong, Z.: Elasticsearch: The Definitive Guide: A Distributed Real-Time Search and Analytics Engine. O'Reilly Media, Inc. (2015)
14. Joshi, A., Kale, S., Chandel, S., Pal, D.K.: Likert scale: explored and explained. Br. J. Appl. Sci. Technol. **7**(4), 396 (2015)
15. Keselman, H.J., Rogan, J.C.: The Tukey multiple comparison test: 1953–1976. Psychol. Bull. **84**(5), 1050 (1977)
16. Kokoska, S., Nevison, C.: Critical values for the studentized range distribution. In: Kokoska, S., Nevison, C. (eds.) Statistical Tables and Formulae, pp. 64–66. Springer, New York (1989). https://doi.org/10.1007/978-1-4613-9629-1_12
17. Kononenko, O., Baysal, O., Holmes, R., Godfrey, M.W.: Mining modern repositories with elasticsearch. In: Proceedings of the 11th Working Conference on Mining Software Repositories, MSR 2014, pp. 328–331. Association for Computing Machinery, New York (2014)
18. Kuc, R., Rogozinski, M.: Elasticsearch Server. Packt Publishing Ltd. (2013)
19. Laugwitz, B., Held, T., Schrepp, M.: Construction and evaluation of a user experience questionnaire. In: Holzinger, A. (ed.) USAB 2008. LNCS, vol. 5298, pp. 63–76. Springer, Heidelberg (2008). https://doi.org/10.1007/978-3-540-89350-9_6

20. Liu, Y., et al.: RoBERTa: a robustly optimized BERT pretraining approach (2019)
21. Loeb, M.: Disability statistics: an integral but missing (and misunderstood) component of development work. Nord. J. Hum. Rights **31**(3), 306–324 (2013)
22. McCool, R., Cowell, A.J., Thurman, D.A.: End-user evaluations of semantic web technologies. Technical report, Pacific Northwest National Lab. (PNNL), Richland, WA, United States (2005)
23. Moore, W.L.: Concept testing. J. Bus. Res. **10**(3), 279–294 (1982)
24. Nielsen, J.: How to conduct a heuristic evaluation, vol. 1, no. 1, p. 8. Nielsen Norman Group (1995)
25. Schrepp, M., Hinderks, A., Thomaschewski, J.: Design and evaluation of a short version of the user experience questionnaire (UEQ-S). Int. J. Interact. Multimedia Artif. Intell. **4**(6), 103–108 (2017)
26. Schrepp, M., Thomaschewski, J., Hinderks, A.: Construction of a benchmark for the user experience questionnaire (UEQ) (2017)
27. Shahi, D.: Apache Solr. Springer, Heidelberg (2016). https://doi.org/10.1007/978-1-4842-1070-3
28. Shin, S., Jin, X., Jung, J., Lee, K.-H.: Predicate constraints based question answering over knowledge graph. Inf. Process. Manag. **56**(3), 445–462 (2019)
29. Vermeeren, A.P.O.S., Law, E.L.-C., Roto, V., Obrist, M., Hoonhout, J., Väänänen-Vainio-Mattila, K.: User experience evaluation methods: current state and development needs. In: Proceedings of the 6th Nordic Conference on Human-Computer Interaction: Extending Boundaries, pp. 521–530 (2010)
30. Zheng, W., Yu, J.X., Zou, L., Cheng, H.: Question answering over knowledge graphs: question understanding via template decomposition. Proc. VLDB Endow. **11**(11), 1373–1386 (2018)

Track on Digital Humanities and Digital Curation, and Track on Cultural Collections and Applications

Semantic Annotation of Ancient Greek Mathematical Texts

Vasileios Siochos[(✉)], Michalis Sialaros, Jean Christianidis, and Christos Papatheodorou

Department of History and Philosophy of Science, National and Kapodistrian University of Athens, Athens, Greece
{vsiochos,msialaros,ichrist,papatheodor}@phs.uoa.gr

Abstract. In his *Commentary on Book I of Euclid's Elements*, Proclus Lycius, a famous Neoplatonic philosopher of the fifth century CE, proposed a scheme for analyzing complete mathematical propositions into six parts: proposition, enunciation, setting out, determination, construction, proof and conclusion. Leaving content aside, most of these parts can be identified based on specific formulaic expressions. Still, neither all parts are always identifiable by such expressions, nor do they always appear in a strictly sequential order with no intermingling with each other. This paper focuses on developing a tool which will allow scholars to semantically annotate ancient Greek mathematical texts according to Proclus' scheme. To this end, we apply machine learning algorithms to the first seven books of Euclid's *Elements*.

Keywords: digital humanities · semantic annotation · classification algorithms · Euclid · *Elements* · Greek mathematics · Proclus

1 Introduction

In the mid-5th century CE, Proclus compiled a commentary on Book I of Euclid's *Elements* in which he proposed that every complete mathematical proposition could be analyzed into six internal parts: enunciation (πρότασις - *protasis*), setting out (ἔκθεσις - *ekthesis*), determination (διορισμός - *diorismos*), construction (κατασκευή - *kataskeue*), proof (ἀπόδειξις - *apodeixis*), and conclusion (συμπέρασμα - *symperasma*) [12, 18].

For centuries, Proclus' scheme was thought to adequately describe not only Euclid's practice in the *Elements*, but also the majority of Greek mathematical texts. This idea was challenged by Netz, who argued that the scheme must have been a much later formularization, perhaps by Proclus himself [19]. Following Cretney, [3] who points out that there is still a lot of research to be done using other forms of output, and Masià, who claims that using computational tools for an automated analysis of ancient Greek mathematical texts (henceforth AGMT) could be productive [16], we started encoding the results of recent historical research on the logical syntax and stylistic structure of Greek mathematics [1, 7–9, 20].

E. Garoufallou and A. Vlachidis (Eds.): MTSR 2022, CCIS 1789, pp. 53–64, 2023.
https://doi.org/10.1007/978-3-031-39141-5_5

Encoding provides a formal way to store structured and reusable information. Apart from structure, mathematical objects and letter denotations, for which the preprocessing led quickly to a specific encoding methodology, a challenging part that did not lead to a clear solution was the semantic annotation of the text, and in particular according to the Proclus' scheme. In general, a first level of research questions for such corpora, given their structure as well as their scientific orientation and vocabulary, is the (semi)automated generation of metadata and the knowledge discovery from them by processing their semantics. The extracted knowledge is necessary for historians who investigate, among others, the logical and syntactical structure of the propositions in AGMT.

In this paper, we explore the possible use of machine learning techniques to achieve the semantic annotation of AGMT corpora; we also present an experiment to discover the Proclus' scheme of the six parts of mathematical propositions on a sample corpus of Euclid's *Elements*. It is worth noting that, as a rule, AGMT consists of propositions. Moreover, some of the aforementioned internal parts might appear more than once in a proposition, while it is not necessary that all parts exist in a proposition. For example, there are no instances of the category 'construction' in propositions with arithmetic content. Therefore, given the number of their editions, as well as the heterogeneity of these texts due to their stylistic differences, there is a need for a process to classify automatically AGMT to the parts (categories) defined by the Proclus' scheme. Thus, the research problem is defined as follows: To semantically annotate the text of a given set of mathematical propositions, according to the categories of the Proclus' scheme.

In Sect. 2, a brief review of related literature is presented. In Sect. 3, the implemented experiment methodology is described. In Sect. 4, the most important experiment results are presented. In Sect. 5, a discussion about the experiment results is conducted and, finally, in Sect. 6, conclusions are drawn and directions for future work steps are set.

2 Related Work

The employment of information processing methods and tools gave scholars a new research domain that gradually shaped the field of Digital Humanities. In this context, Büchler demonstrates an approach using text mining algorithms for identifying 'terminology or textual reuse' in ancient Greek texts [2]. His goal was to compute 'semantic co-occurrences' by observing the words in the sentences and therefore utilizes visual analytics on text mining results. Developing models based on technology can unlock the cooperative potential between artificial intelligence and historians. Moreover, technology may assist historians in answering research questions concerning the practices followed, the connections between texts of different authors or between different propositions in the same text, as well as about the kind of methodologies and tools that could be used to classify and achieve deeper understanding of a text, or, more generally, about the kind of information that could be extracted from it.

Although several works exist regarding text analysis of ancient Greek literature, the corresponding works which study AGMT is comparatively poor. Indeed, AGMT have not yet received much scholarly attention, despite that there are scholars who have argued recently in favor of this research direction; for example, Masià [16] claims that AGMT are 'appropriate texts to be analyzed automatically' and utilizes computational tools. He constructs tables of the distribution of verbal occurrences and the number of particle occurrences related to each corresponding part of proposition. Moreover, he examines whether the lemmatized terms follow Zipf's Law. In his view, automated computational tools would be productive provided that their design should be adapted to the specific characteristics of AGMT and to the relevant textual aspects. Schiefsky suggests that 'information technology can open up new perspectives for the study of source materials in the history of mathematics and science' and he continues by mentioning that technology may contribute to 'both by making it possible to pursue old questions in new ways and by raising new questions that cannot easily be addressed using traditional means of investigation' [23]. Moreover, he considers that further study is needed to explore the concrete ways in which different structures of argument are expressed in AGMT language. Netz in his PhD thesis [21] provides lengthy catalog of formulaic expressions used in AGMT. Still, as Schiefsky points out, 'the study of the linguistic expression of mathematical argumentation is still very much in its early stages, and stands to benefit greatly from a more thorough and systematic approach' [23]. Roughan agrees with the fact that when information is meaningfully encoded in digital formats it 'can be well-suited for quantitative analyses' [22], and Hyman states that 'semantic networks provide a powerful tool for studying conceptual development in the history of science' [13].

The availability of large corpora in collections such as the Perseus Digital Library [21], provides the opportunity to semantically annotate [10, 11, 26] and classify them under particular criteria [4, 17]. Based on these directions, our research focuses on developing a tool exploiting supervised machine learning methods capable of semantically annotating the ancient Greek mathematical texts according to Proclus' scheme.

3 Methodology

In this section, the employed methodology is documented, by describing the datasets used for the experiments, the used algorithms and their configuration, and the evaluation metrics utilized to assess the derived results.

3.1 Dataset

Euclid's *Elements* is not only the most famous ancient mathematical treatise, but also the most formally structured Greek mathematical text. For this reason, our datasets were drawn from this Work. The *Elements* consists of thirteen books, and each book consists of a number of propositions that are either theorems or problems. In particular, in our study, we have chosen to deal with the first seven books [6, 21], the first six of which deal with geometry while the seventh contains propositions in arithmetic. Hence, the dataset includes all propositions from the first seven books, reaching a total number of 212 propositions containing 1838 instances from the eight annotation categories, based on Proclus' scheme. These categories, as mentioned, are Enunciation (*protasis*), Setting out (*ekthesis*), Determination (*diorismos*), Construction (*kataskeue*), Proof (*apodeixis*) and Conclusion. The category Conclusion was further divided to the sub-categories Particular Conclusion (*symperasma_part*), General Conlusion (*symperasma_gen*) and Quod erat (*oper_edei*). The last sub-category includes just two phrases existing in every proposition of each book; the first, 'ὅπερ ἔδει δεῖξαι' (quod erat demonstrandum, Q.E.D.), appears when the proposition is a theorem, while the second, 'ὅπερ ἔδει ποιῆσαι' (quod erat faciendum, Q.E.F.), appears when the proposition is a problem.

3.2 Preprocessing

The annotation of the experimental corpus has been realized by two mathematicians-historians of mathematics, supervised by a senior one who resolved any discrepancies. Actually, the experts studied one by one the propositions of each of the seven books of the *Elements* and annotated the text of each proposition.

Table 1. Number of propositions and instances by using 8 annotating categories.

Euclid's Book from *Elements*	I	II	III	IV	V	VI	VII	Total
Number of propositions	48	14	37	16	25	33	39	212
Number of instances	382	115	332	143	230	306	330	1838
Attributes	687	423	720	555	334	826	450	-
Enunciation	48	14	37	16	25	33	39	212
Setting out	48	14	34	15	25	34	46	216
Determination	57	16	47	19	32	43	51	265
Construction	43	14	54	24	26	45	37	243
Proof	52	16	53	26	44	51	73	315
Particular Conclusion	51	15	37	14	27	41	42	227
General Conclusion	35	12	33	12	25	26	3	146
Quod erat	48	14	37	17	26	33	39	214

There is no standard methodology on annotating AGMT, thus the annotation was conducted based on the following observations/heuristic rules [1, 19, 20]: Enunciation includes the first sentences until just before the word "ἔστω" ('Let there be'). Setting out starts with "ἔστω" ('Let there be') until just before "λέγω ὅτι" ('I claim that') or "δεῖ δή" ('Thus it is required to'), which indicate Determination. Construction includes verbs in the imperative clause. Proof starts with "καὶ ἐπεί" ('And since') or "ἐπεί" ('Since'). Particular Conclusion is a repentance of the previous Determination containing the word "ἄρα" (Therefore). General Conclusion is a repentance of the previous Enunciation containing the word "ἄρα" (Therefore). Finally Quod erat includes the exact phrases "ὅπερ ἔδει ποιῆσαι" (Q.E.D.) or "ὅπερ ἔδει δεῖξαι" (Q.E.F). Table 1 provides analytical information about the number of propositions of each book, the instances of the categories and their attributes (words/tokens) and the number of instances for each category.

3.3 Experimental Setup

The Waikato Environment for Knowledge Analysis (Weka) [5] was used as the machine learning workbench for preprocessing our datasets and for applying machine learning algorithms to them. The preprocessing of the dataset resulted to Attribute-Relation File Format (ARFF) files. The upper box of the Fig. 1 shows a fragment of a proposition. The raw unstructured text was annotated and transformed into an attribute-relation file with two attributes. The first attribute is a text string and the second is the category attribute (middle box of the Fig. 1). The text string was treated as a bag of words and was filtered with an TF-IDF transformation forming a vector {0 c_i, t_1 w_1, t_2 w_2,...}, where c_i (i = 1, 2, ..., 8) is one of the eight categories, t_i is the id number of the attribute and w_i the TF-IDF weight of the attribute (lower box of the Fig. 1). Note that the tuple (0, c_i) which indicates the annotated category, is missing when the text is annotated in the first Category, Enunciation (*protasis*).

ἐπὶ τῆς δοθείσης εὐθείας πεπερασμένης τρίγωνον ἰσόπλευρον συστήσασθαι. ἔστω ἡ δοθεῖσα εὐθεῖα πεπερασμένη ἡ ΑΒ. δεῖ δὴ ἐπὶ τῆς ΑΒ εὐθείας τρίγωνον ἰσόπλευρον συστήσασθαι. κέντρῳ μὲν τῷ Α διαστήματι δὲ τῷ ΑΒ κύκλος γεγράφθω ὁ ΒΓΔ, καὶ πάλιν κέντρῳ μὲν τῷ Β διαστήματι δὲ τῷ ΒΑ κύκλος γεγράφθω ὁ ΑΓΕ, καὶ ἀπὸ τοῦ Γ σημείου, καθ' ὃ τέμνουσιν ἀλλήλους οἱ κύκλοι, ἐπὶ τὰ Α, Β σημεῖα ἐπεζεύχθωσαν εὐθεῖαι αἱ ΓΑ, ΓΒ.

Raw unstrustured text

'ἐπὶ τῆς δοθείσης εὐθείας πεπερασμένης τρίγωνον ἰσόπλευρον συστήσασθαι',protasis
'ἔστω ἡ δοθεῖσα εὐθεῖα πεπερασμένη ἡ ΑΒ.',ekthesis
'δεῖ δὴ ἐπὶ τῆς ΑΒ εὐθείας τρίγωνον ἰσόπλευρον συστήσασθαι.',diorismos
'κέντρῳ μὲν τῷ Α διαστήματι δὲ τῷ ΑΒ κύκλος γεγράφθω ὁ ΒΓΔ, καὶ πάλιν κέντρῳ μὲν τῷ Β διαστήματι δὲ τῷ ΒΑ κύκλος γεγράφθω ὁ ΑΓΕ, καὶ ἀπὸ τοῦ Γ σημείου, καθ' ὃ τέμνουσιν ἀλλήλους οἱ κύκλοι, ἐπὶ τὰ Α, Β σημεῖα ἐπεζεύχθωσαν εὐθεῖαι αἱ ΓΑ, ΓΒ.',kataskeui

Annotated text

{30 3.160146,45 1.564115,97 3.359552,125 2.525021,141 1.382258,153 1.049843,183 1.176219,204 2.525021}
{0 ekthesis,48 1.482474,200 0.506334,231 0.957286,282 2.291796,292 3.160146,309 1.513986}
{0 diorismos,22 2.243974,45 1.564115,125 2.525021,141 1.382258,153 1.049843,183 1.176219,204 2.525021,231 0.957286,285 1.530296}
{0 kataskeui,1 0.994362,37 0.97188,49 1.740793,56 0.495123,78 1.318622,122 2.010749,139 1.271611,149 1.26034,156 1.217004,165 1.637145,183 1.176219,219 2.879099,230 1.676765,231 0.957286,243 1.978504,244 2.157218,253 1.656672,290 2.044568,326 2.525021,328 2.525021,357 3.640599,362 2.679692,405 3.005474,407 3.005474,412 3.005474,413 4.121052,415 4.121052,416 3.005474,417 4.121052,422 3.359552,426 4.121052,431 4.121052,441 2.772249,455 3.005474}

TF-IDF representation

Fig. 1. The annotation and the preprocessing of the annotated text

A variety of algorithms were trained using this dataset and several configurations were tested to explore their efficiency. The algorithms applied on the datasets are the following: Naive Bayes, Random Forest, Random Tree, Support Vector Machines (SVM), which Weka calls it Sequential minimal optimization (SMO) and a functionality of Weka named AutoWeka [15, 25] that combines several classification algorithms. For the applied algorithms we used the default settings of WEKA.

To validate the efficiency of the classifiers, the following partition methods were applied on the datasets to create the training and test subsets: (i) the default testing method of WEKA that specifies a 10 fold cross-validation and (ii) a randomized 2/3 training-1/3 test split of the dataset.

3.4 Evaluation Measures

While applying machine learning algorithms, the most common evaluation measures used are: (i) the true positive classified rate (the rate of instances that are correctly classified in a category), (ii) the false positive classified rate (the rate of instances that are false classified in a category), (iii) precision (the fraction of the true positive instances related to all the positive classified instances in a specific category) and (iv) recall (the fraction of the true positive instances related to all the correctly classified instances in a specific category), (v) F-measure, which is calculated as the harmonic mean of precision and recall, and (vi) the weighted average of each measure. Additionally to these quantitative measures, a quality measure, the confusion matrix was used to evaluate and analyze the results (Fig. 2). The confusion matrix provides information regarding the false positive classifications of the instances of a dataset and, thus, the researcher has an assistive tool to identify and justify the mismatches of the used algorithm or the configuration of the experiment.

```
 a  b  c  d  e  f <-- classified as
11  0  0  0  0  4 |   a = protasis
 0 14  0  2  0  0 |   b = ekthesis
 1  0 20  1  0  0 |   c = diorismos
 0  0  0 15  0  0 |   d = kataskeue
 0  0  1  0 16  0 |   e = apodeixis
 1  0  0  0  0 15 |   f = symperasma
```

Fig. 2. A confusion matrix example showing how many instances were classified to each category.

4 Results

4.1 Initial Experiment

Before the experiments, an initial investigation took place in order to familiarize ourselves with the data. Thus, we run Naive Bayes deploying two alternative configurations. In the first the algorithm run only on the propositions of the First Book of the *Elements*. Its performance exhibited an average F-measure equal to 90%. Using the same configuration SVM exhibited an average F-measure equal to 93.2%.

The second configuration applied a part of speech filtering to the same data, only to the propositions of the First Book. This configuration was based on Netz [20] and Acerbi [1], who remarked that ancient Greek mathematicians employed specific formulaic expressions for different parts in the propositions. These expressions include verbs, articles, adverbs, prepositions, conjunctions and particles. Hence, the expert annotators filtered the data by keeping only the terms of the expressions that are considered as the most semantically significant. Additionally, regarding the denotative letters used to refer objects in the propositions [1], it was decided all the letter-labels to be excluded from the data. Naive Bayes exhibited improved results on this configuration, both for the weighted average F-measure (92.3%) as well as for the F-measure of each category. However, when SVM applied to the first data configuration, the non-filtered data, outperformed (as mentioned weighted average F-measure = 93.2%) the results of Naive

Bayes on both configurations. Hence, we could claim that this filtering does not improve significantly the derived results. Therefore, the filtering of the second configuration was not further used in the experiments.

Thus, the experiments started using only the propositions of the first three books of the *Elements;* furthermore, Naive Bayes algorithm was the first applied and its results are used as the baseline to compare the results of the exploited semantic annotation methods. Table 2 reveals that SVM exhibits an encouraging performance (weighted average F-measure 93.9%). The results of Random Forest and Naive Bayes are not satisfying especially for the classes 'Enunciation and 'General Conclusion'. Observing F-measure for each category (Table 2) we notice that the low average weight derives from the 'Enunciation' and 'General Conclusion' with just a 48.6% and 30.8% F-measure respectively. The same observation applies to the Naive Bayes which results a F-measure 51.9% and 66.7% for the categories 'Enunciation' and 'General Conclusion' respectively.

Table 2. Initial experiment: F-measure per classification algorithm.

Classifier	Naive Bayes	SVM		Random Forest
Testing method	Split 2/3–1/3	Split 2/3–1/3	Crossvalidation 10 Folds	Split 2/3–1/3
Enunciation	0.519	0.923	0.932	0.486
Setting out	0.882	0.909	0.907	0.938
Determination	0.811	1.000	0.983	0.865
Construction	0.897	0.933	0.914	0.968
Proof	0.933	0.963	0.941	0.966
Particular Conclusion	0.813	0.882	0.874	0.848
General Conclusion	0.667	0.903	0.879	0.308
Quod erat	0.971	1.000	1.000	0.971
Weighted Average	**0.808**	**0.939**	**0.932**	**0.793**

This behavior could be explained by observing two facts. Firstly, as Acerbi points out [1] 'Enunciation and conclusion of a mathematical proposition go together: they are nearly identical'. None of them include denotative letters and the General Conclusion contains additionally the word "ἄρα" (therefore). Secondly the 'Particular Conclusion' is very similar, share almost the same words, expressions and label letters, to the instances of the 'Determination' class. These two classes actually differ to the tenses of the verbs; Determination phrases are in Present tense (e.g. prove that …), while Particular Conclusion phrases are in Past tense (e.g. we proved that …). In the next experiments the F-measure results of Random Forest and Naive Bayes algorithms are improving due to the dataset's enrichment with more Books of Euclid's *Elements*.

4.2 Expanding the Dataset

In the next phase, the dataset was expanded by including the propositions of all the first seven books of the *Elements*. This setup resulted to more than 1800 instances of the predefined categories. Table 3 presents that the baseline classifier, Naive Bayes, performed in general better than in the initial experiment. SVM was applied using two different testing methods (the random split of the dataset into 2/3 training and 1/3 testing data and the 10 folds cross validation) and performed slightly worse than the initial experiment, though stable close to 93%. It is remarkable that SVM improves significantly the performance of the categories exhibiting low performance, 'Enunciation', 'General Conclusion' and 'Particular Conclusion', as compared with the results of the experiments on the expanded dataset. For instance, the F-measure of the 'Enunciation' category increased from 92.3% to 100%, for the 'Particular Conclusion' from 88.2% to 90.9% and for the 'General Conclusion' from 90.3% to 92%. After several dozens of experiments, using different machine learning algorithms, configurations and testing methods, it seems that the SVM algorithm has a stable performance with an F-measure close to 93%.

Table 3. Expanded dataset: F-measure results.

Classifier	Naive Bayes	SVM		Random Forest
Testing method	Split 2/3–1/3	Split 2/3–1/3	Crossvalidation 10 Folds	Split 2/3–1/3
Enunciation	0.806	1.000	0.981	0.539
Setting out	0.863	0.898	0.923	0.925
Determination	0.913	0.953	0.957	0.938
Construction	0.780	0.846	0.848	0.852
Proof	0.865	0.915	0.908	0.919
Particular Conclusion	0.821	0.909	0.912	0.867
General Conclusion	0.698	0.920	0.938	0.225
Quod erat	1.000	1.000	1.000	1.000
Weighted Average	**0.851**	**0.927**	**0.931**	**0.821**

5 Discussion

Based on the experimental results, utilizing five different classification algorithms and performing hundreds of classification experiments, we observe that the overall results (Fig. 3) are promising, given the average performance of this classification process. Regarding the question of which algorithm fits better to the data, it is observed that

SVM provides a relatively stable attitude exhibiting an average F-measure over 92%. An interesting remark is that the F-measure for SVM remains greater than 92%, even when the data scale.

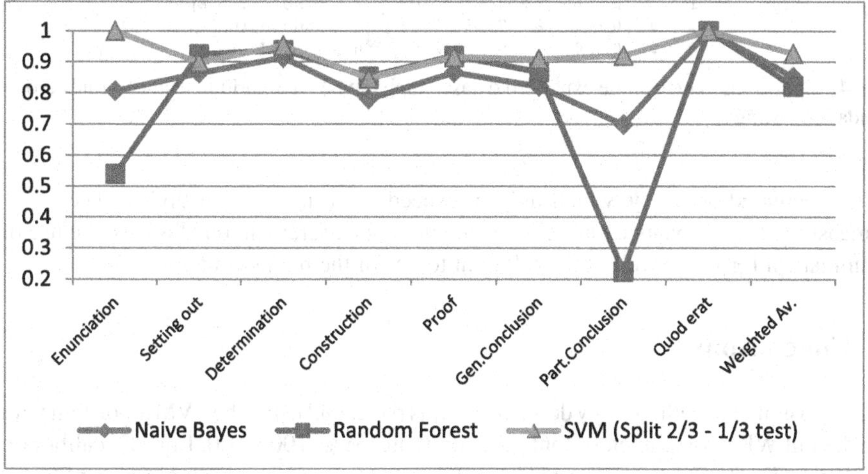

Fig. 3. F-measure per class and classification algorithm

Focusing on each part of a mathematical proposition it should be noted that the category 'Enunciation' and 'Particular Conclusion' can be hardly estimated by Random Forest and Naïve Bayes. Regarding SVM, the 'Construction' class has steadily the lowest F-measure, but still over 80% in average. Observing the style (morphology) of the instances (text) of the 'Construction' category, the verbs are in the imperative clause [1]. A limitation of our experimental setup is that we did not take into account the grammatical forms of the words. Probably, if these parameters were included in the training process, then the performance would be improved. This observation is confirmed by the Confusion matrices; the category 'Construction' demonstrates (Fig. 4, line 'd = *kataskeue*') several wrong classifications and signifies that the grammatical forms might play significant role to correctly annotate this category.

Another observation from the Confusion matrices is that a percentage of the instances of the category 'Proof' were wrongly classified. In particular, the majority of these instances were classified to the category 'Construction' (12 of the total 33 wrongly classified, Fig. 4, line 'e = *apodeixis*'). This is probably due to the content of the Book VII which is the unique arithmetic Book, whereas the content of the propositions of the other books is geometric.

As mentioned, the AutoWeka functionality of Weka software was utilized in all the experiments. In general, this mixed-method that integrates the results of a set of classification algorithms, combining feature selection techniques and classification approaches (ensemble methods, meta-methods, base classifiers and hyperparameter setting) [25]. AutoWeka achieved a weighted F-measure of 96.3% in the initial experiment and 86.6% in the expanded dataset, all after a 120 min run. Following the bibliography recommendation [15], we conducted longer runs, up to 360 min, but there was no improvement

```
  a   b   c   d   e   f   g   h   <-- classified as
210   0   0   2   0   0   0   0 |   a = protasis
  0 203   0  12   1   0   0   0 |   b = ekthesis
  0   2 254   5   3   1   0   0 |   c = diorismos
  0  13   7 207  13   4   0   0 |   d = kataskeue
  4   5   3  12 281   7   2   0 |   e = apodeixis
  1   1   2   6   5 206   6   0 |   f = conclusion_spe
  1   0   0   0   2   7 136   0 |   g = conclusion_gen
  0   0   0   0   0   0   0 214 |   h = operedei
```

Fig. 4. Confusion matrix of the expanded dataset applying SVM algorithm using 10 folds cross-validation testing

of the weighted accuracy, which did not exceed the F-measure of 96.3%. The lower F-measure of the expanded dataset may be due to the aforementioned issues, the use of grammatical forms, as well as the different topics of the books contents.

6 Conclusions

In conclusion, the methodology described in this paper and using the SVM algorithm with the default WEKA parameters configuration (batchSize: 100, c:1.0, Logistic calibrator, epsilon:1.0E-12, filtertype: Normalize training data, PolyKernel, numDecimanPlaces: 2, tolerance parameter: 0.001, random seed: 1), appears to be capable of classifying the AGMT voluminous collections according to Proclus' scheme in a satisfying degree. Still, our work is just a starting point for further research. Moreover, the use of grammatical analysis or a stemmer for ancient Greek might lead to more precise results. This could improve the performance of the annotation process of AGMT, not only for Proclus' scheme but also for other semantic categories.

Obviously, the expansion of datasets by adding more arithmetic books from the *Elements,* or apply the methodology to other ancient Greek mathematicians' books, might improve the up to now obtained good results and will reveal some extra needs and peculiarities of the data. Additionally, for the further improvement of the derived results some add-on functionalities of the used learning algorithms, such as the utilization of feature selection algorithms will be tested and assessed in detail.

In general, classification, such as the presented methodology, could contribute to the following research directions mentioned by Schiefsky [23]:

(1) The identification of formulaic language in AGMT: the proposed methodology classifies the mathematical propositions to particular parts and therefore facilitates the discovery of the desired formulaic expressions.
(2) The analysis of the translations of AGMT to other languages (Latin, Arabic) would transfer useful patterns that could be exploited to AGMT analysis: the described approach could be exploited to other AGMT translations.
(3) The study of deductive structures, which is defined as the characterization of the structure of argumentation within specific propositions as well as the identification of deductive relationships between different propositions: the discovery of deductive relationships could be modeled as a semantic annotation process that discovers phrases and symbols that signify such deductions.

The primary orientation for planning the future work, will be to address the need for the shift of the focus of Digital Humanities on 'providing intergraded tools for solving research problems' [14]. In this direction, feature selection methods, e.g. the information gain algorithm, will be tested to leverage the existing results.

References

1. Acerbi, F.: The Logical Syntax of Greek Mathematics. Springer, Cham (2021). https://doi.org/10.1007/978-3-030-76959-8
2. Büchler, M., Geßner, A., Eckart, T., Heyer, G.: Unsupervised detection and visualization of textual reuse on ancient Greek texts. J. Chicago Colloq. Digit. Humanit. Comput. Sci. **1**, 1–17 (2010)
3. Cretney, R.: Editing and reading early modern mathematical texts in the digital age. Hist. Math. **43**, 87–97 (2016). https://doi.org/10.1016/j.hm.2015.05.002
4. Dhar, A., Mukherjee, H., Dash, N.S., Roy, K.: Text categorization: past and present. Artif. Intell. Rev. **54**(4), 3007–3054 (2020). https://doi.org/10.1007/s10462-020-09919-1
5. Eibe F., Hall, M.A., Witten, I.H.: The WEKA workbench. In: Online Appendix for "Data Mining: Practical Machine Learning Tools and Techniques, Fourth Edn.. Morgan Kaufmann (2016)
6. Heiberg, J.L.: Euclid. Euclidis Elementa. Leipzig. Teubner (1883–1888)
7. Federspiel, M.: Sur l'élocution de l'ecthèse dans la géométrie grecque classique. L'Antiquité Classique **79**, 95–116 (2010)
8. Federspiel, M.: Sur l'opposition défini/indéfini dans la langue des mathématiques grecques. Les études Classiques **63**, 249–293 (1995)
9. Federspiel, M.: Sur la locution ἐφ' οὗ/ἐφ' ᾧ servant a désigner des êtres géométriques par des lettres. In: Guillaumin, J.-Y., (ed.), Mathématiques dans l'Antiquité, pp. 9–25. Publications de l'Université de Saint-Etienne (1992)
10. Foka, A., et al.: Heritage metadata: a digital Periegesis. In: Information and Knowledge Organisation in Digital Humanities, pp. 227–242. Routledge (2021). https://doi.org/10.4324/9781003131816
11. Frank, A., Bögel, T., Hellwig, O., Reiter, N.: Semantic annotation for the digital humanities – using Markov logic networks for annotation consistency control. In: Linguistic Issues in Language Technology, vol. 7 (2012). https://doi.org/10.33011/lilt.v7i.1275
12. Friedlein, G.: Proclus: Commentarii in Primum Euclidis Elementorum Librum. Teubner (1873)
13. Hyman, M.D.: Semantic networks: a tool for investigating conceptual change and knowledge transfer in the history of science. In: Übersetzung und Transformation, pp. 355–368. De Gruyter (2011). https://doi.org/10.1515/9783110896657.355
14. Hyvönen, E.: Using the Semantic Web in digital humanities: shift from data publishing to data-analysis and serendipitous knowledge discovery. Semant. Web. **11**, 187–193 (2020). https://doi.org/10.3233/SW-190386
15. Kotthoff, L., Thornton, C., Hoos, H.H., Hutter, F., Leyton-Brown, K.: Auto-WEKA: automatic model selection and hyperparameter optimization in WEKA. In: Hutter, F., Kotthoff, L., Vanschoren, J. (eds.) Automated Machine Learning. TSSCML, pp. 81–95. Springer, Cham (2019). https://doi.org/10.1007/978-3-030-05318-5_4
16. Masià, R.: First steps to automatic processing of ancient Greek mathematical texts (2013). https://www.academia.edu/8594347/DRAFT_First_steps_to_automatic_processing_of_ancient_Greek_mathematical_texts. Accessed 24 May 2022

17. Merlini, D., Rossini, M.: Text categorization with WEKA: a survey. Mach. Learn. Appl. **4** (2021). https://doi.org/10.1016/j.mlwa.2021.100033
18. Morrow, G.R.: Proclus. A Commentary on the First Book of Euclid's Elements. Princeton University Press, Princeton (1971). https://doi.org/10.2307/4347467
19. Netz, R.: Proclus' division of the mathematical proposition into parts: How and why was it formulated?, Class. Q. **49**(1), 282–303 (1999). https://www.jstor.org/stable/639502, https://doi.org/10.1093/cq/49.1.282
20. Netz, R.: The Shaping of Deduction in Greek Mathematics: A Study in Cognitive History. Cambridge University Press, Cambridge (1999)
21. Perseus Digital Library. http://www.perseus.tufts.edu/. Accessed 24 May 2022
22. Roughan, C.: Digital editions and diplomatic diagrams. In: ACM International Conference Proceeding Series, pp. 77–82. Association for Computing Machinery (2014). https://doi.org/10.1145/2595188.2595189
23. Schiefsky, M.: New technologies for the study of Euclid's Elements. Archimedes Project at Harvard University (2007). http://archimedes.fas.harvard.edu/euclid/euclid_paper.pdf. Accessed 24 May 2022
24. Schiefsky, M.: Beyond archimedes: the history and future of the arboreal software. In: Culture and Cognition: Essays in Honor of Peter Damerow (2019).https://scholar.harvard.edu/schiefsky/publications/beyond-arboreal-history-and-future-arboreal-software. Accessed 24 May 2022
25. Thornton, C., Hutter, F., Hoos, H.H., Leyton-Brown, K.: Auto-WEKA: Combined selection and hyperparameter optimization of classification algorithms. In: Proceedings of the 19th ACM SIGKDD International Conference on Knowledge Discovery and Data Mining, ACM, NY, USA, pp. 847–855 (2013). https://doi.org/10.1145/2487575.2487629
26. Zeng, M.L.: Semantic enrichment for enhancing LAM data and supporting digital humanities. Revi. Art. EPI 28 (2019). https://doi.org/10.3145/epi.2019.ene.03

Epigraphical Heritage Documentation via CIDOC CRM and CRMtex

Eleni Sfyridou[1], Georgios Papaioannou[1], Manolis Gergatsoulis[2(✉)], Eleftherios Kalogeros[2], and Konstantinos D. Politis[1,3]

[1] Museology Research Laboratory, Department of Archives, Library Science and Museology, Ionian University, Ioannou Theotoki 72, 49100 Corfu, Greece
{lena.sfyridou,gpapaioa}@ionio.gr

[2] Laboratory on Digital Libraries and Electronic Publishing, Department of Archives, Library Science and Museology, Ionian University, Ioannou Theotoki 72, 49100 Corfu, Greece
{manolis,kalogero}@ionio.gr

[3] Hellenic Society for Near Eastern Studies, Chalcis, Greece

Abstract. As the need for solid and interoperable heritage documentation models and systems becomes bigger, addressing aspects of representing archaeological and textual/epigraphical information adds special importance and value. Towards this end, this paper explores the use of CIDOC CRM and CRMtex to represent epigraphical heritage information. This paper aims to (1) describe, study and explain how ancient funerary inscriptions can be represented through CIDOC CRM and its extensions, (2) examine these archaeological and textual objects at two levels: (a) physical description, including size, shape, material, text and symbols, and b) interpretations, including chronology, text content, other archaeological interpretation. Our work consists of a case study based on a funerary inscription with a Greek inscription of the 5th century AD discovered in Ghor as-Safi (Byzantine Zoora or Zoara) in modern Jordan. This inscription is a typical example of funerary inscriptions in the area and the world, as it contains the basic information frequently found on similar object: name of the deceased, age, date of death, symbols. CIDOC CRM and CRMtex has been used to represent the production and the physical characteristics of a funerary inscription, its textual information (including ancient writing, transcription and translation) and cultural information content, its date, and its current condition and location. This case study initiates the work towards a model and an automated system for archaeological/epigraphical documentation and data integration.

Keywords: Epigraphy · cultural heritage documentation · archaeology · funerary inscriptions · CIDOC CRM · CRMtex · ontologies

1 Introduction

Developing a semantic model in the field of epigraphy and textual information has lately gained a continuous and growing interest [2,7,16] in the digital and

E. Garoufallou and A. Vlachidis (Eds.): MTSR 2022, CCIS 1789, pp. 65–76, 2023.
https://doi.org/10.1007/978-3-031-39141-5_6

information science world. In today's era of imperatives towards standardization, interoperability and integration, creating ontologies and conceptual models via advanced and efficient conceptual tools are of immense importance. CRMtex [9], the recent extension of CIDOC CRM [11], is the latest effort in this direction. In this effort, important questions emerge and persist: can models based on CIDOC CRM and CRMtex effectively represent epigraphical/textual data? To what extent can they provide a framework to support the documentation and interpretation of epigraphical data? How could they secure the integration of the archaeological and cultural information that inevitably accompanies epigraphical/textual data? We attempt to answer these questions and develop a model to assist scholars in the coding of inscriptions brought to light by archaeological research with the goal of developing an automated ancient inscription analysis system based on this model. In our endeavor, we case-study a funerary inscription of the 5th century AD from Ghor as-Safi (Byzantine Zoora or Zoara) in Jordan, with text in koine Greek and engraved symbols of crosses and a palm branch.

2 Related Work

Over the last 15 years, CIDOC Conceptual Reference Model (CIDOC CRM) has become the state-of-the-art formal ontology for modelling cultural heritage heterogeneous information. CIDOC CRM is appropriate for modelling interrelations and mappings between different heterogeneous sources [18] including EAD mappings to CIDOC CRM [14], VRA mappings in [17] and Dublin Core mappings in [22]. In the case of the archaeological data integration, ARIADNE [23] and ARIADNEplus [1] projects resulted to the CIDOC CRM extensions CRMarchaeo [8], and CRMba [6]. Documenting archaeological excavations and/or archaeological buildings can be found in the literature [12,13,19–21,25,28].

Regarding epigraphy, few attempts have been made to define the ontological level of the properties of a text. A first step towards representing epigraphy was made by the VBI-ERAT-LVPA project in 2004 which attempted to use CIDOC CRM to integrate epigraphic digital records using conceptual tools [15]. Another effort has been the EAGLE project [2], which explored the same field by trying to combine entities of EpiDoc and CIDOC CRM to harmonize the provided features (EAGLE Portal). The EAGLE metadata model uses CIDOC CRM to describe the physical aspects of an inscription, together with events related to its creation, finding and maintenance. It deals less with textual entities and their multifaceted nature in the context of epigraphy, despite the extra efforts by the TEI/EpiDoc model [10] that has also been created and used to describe epigraphic texts within EAGLE. Further research is yet to be undertaken to describe the relationships that exist between the physical and the conceptual aspects of textual entities, a very important element on which researches should focus, especially as scientific or methodological questions related to the analysis of "semiotic features" (EpiDoc:XML) are raised.

Another interesting research activity is the Menota project, which aimed to preserve and publish medieval texts in digital form by adapting, developing and maintaining coding standards. The standards proposed by Menota are so far limited to a model based on the TEI/EpiDoc project, but within this initiative efforts were made to include CIDOC CRM entities to provide richer semantic descriptions of manuscripts and their content [4].

The ARIADNE project, which is primarily focused on the integration of archaeological records, has also expanded into the area of epigraphy by developing a suite of tools based on CIDOC CRM to describe epigraphic entities in conceptual terms [1].

A tentative epigraphic extension, CRMepi, has been defined as an early attempt to define epigraphic entities within the CIDOC CRM model. All works on CRMepi is now fully integrated into the CRMtex extension. The inscriptional classes of CRMepi have been defined as specialized subclasses of CRMtex, as the new extension is designed to represent a broader conceptual level, i.e. ancient texts in general, not just inscriptions [16].

A project addressing digital epigraphy is the "Epigraphy.info A collaborative environment for Digital Epigraphy" [7], established in 2018. As clearly stated in the project's website, Epigraphy.info is "an international open community pursuing a collaborative environment for digital epigraphy, which facilitates scholarly communication and interaction". As per their mission statement, "it intends to be a hub for a fruitful exchange of epigraphic data and digital solutions that will benefit all epigraphers". The team has working groups on ontologies and vocabularies, and they have organized workshops. A milestone of the group's ongoing efforts is the document entitled "Modeling Epigraphy with an Ontology"[1]. In this document, contributors of the ontologies working group attempt to create a model that incorporates classes and properties of different systems. Our CIDOC CRM focused research will add to their work.

3 Preliminaries

3.1 Epigraphy

Although epigraphy is a scientific discipline with a long tradition and history, a single, unanimous and fully accepted definition of its object, the epigraph (or inscription), has not yet been formulated. Let us note that both the Greek verb "*ἐπιγράφειν*" and the corresponding Latin term "*inscribere*" indicate the action of writing 'on' something. The etymological route, although it is the one most frequently followed in handbooks, on the model of other disciplines, turns out in our case to be of little use, because it is clear that every manifestation of writing implies writing 'on' something, and our problem is precisely to understand in what respect epigraphic writing differs from writing that is not epigraphic.

The most complete definition has been proposed by Panciera [26] who defines an epigraph as "any particular type of written human communication of the sort that we would today call unidirectional, in the sense that it does not anticipate that a response will be provided to the sender, and which has the characteristic

[1] https://zenodo.org/record/4639508.

of not being addressed to a person or to a group but to a collectivity, and which for this reason is made with the location, writing technique, graphic form and impagination, mode and register of expression chosen because they are most suitable to the attainment of its intended goal, and which differentiates itself in this manner from other forms of contemporary verbal communication".

Epigraphic writing is therefore defined as writing that is divergent (according to time and place) in that it adopts a different form of writing in terms of medium and/or technique, depending on the intended purpose. At the same time, however, it highlights another essential and special characteristic of an inscription: it addresses a collective.

According to Felicetti et al. [16], an inscription can be analysed according to three main aspects: the text-bearing object or monument (obviously involving archaeological topics), the text (and the obvious correlations with content and linguistic aspects lato sensu) and the feature engraved on the support in the form of letters or other symbols, which is the central element that characterizes and differentiates an epigraph from any other manifestation of written communication.

The edition of ancient texts leads to one of the earliest and more consistent systems of standardisation in the field of Humanities, the Leiden Conventions, created by an international group of scholars gathered in Leiden in 1931 and is the standard still adopted in modern epigraphy. The Leiden Conventions or Leiden system is an established set of rules, symbols, and brackets used to indicate the condition of an epigraphic or papyrological text in a modern edition.

The need for an electronic format that could allow digital publishing, storage and exchange of epigraphic information in a consistent and shared format, results to EpiDoc, a collaborative format designed to transcode in digital format the Leiden-encoded printed editions using the Extensible Markup Language (XML). EpiDoc is an international, collaborative effort that provides guidelines and tools for encoding scholarly and educational editions of ancient documents. It uses a subset of the Text Encoding Initiative's (TEI) standard [3] for the representation of texts in digital form, which focuses on the history and materiality of the texts. The EpiDoc system, despite its undoubted advantages, it presents some issues, as it lacks the typical relational features that a database offers to describe the complex relationships that characterize the various aspects of epigraphy. Only ontologies i.e., CIDOC CRM, and similar semantic tools seem to be able to combine the advantages and flexibility that characterize XML with the characteristic relationality of databases.

3.2 CIDOC CRM and CRMtex

The CRMtex is an extension of the CIDOC CRM ontology model. It has been developed since 2018 to support the study of ancient documents by identifying relevant textual entities and modeling the scientific process related to the investigation of ancient texts and their characteristics in order to promote integration with other fields of cultural heritage research such as archaeology and history. CRMtex is intended to identify and define in a clear and unambiguous way the main entities involved in the study of ancient manuscript texts and then to describe them through appropriate ontological schemas under a multidimensional perspective. The expansion therefore aims to introduce new classes and properties that meet the specific needs of the various disciplines involved, including epigraphy. CRMtex allows the description of texts that:

1. they use alphabetic writing systems (such as Greek and Latin)
2. they use different non-alphabetic phonographic systems (such as Mycenaean script b and old Persian cuneiform inscriptions and Egyptian hieroglyphic texts).

This work is based on CIDOC CRM version 7.1.2 (June 2022) and CRMtex version 1.0 (June 2020).

4 The Zoara - Ghor as-Safi Excavations and the Discovery of Funerary Inscriptions

The Ghor as-Safi is located at the south-eastern end of the Dead Sea in the alluvial fan of the Wadi al-Hasa in modern Jordan. It is depicted as "Zoora" next to the Sanctuary of Agios Lot (Deir 'Ain 'Abata) on the late 6th century AD mosaic floor map in Madaba [24]. Ancient remains in the Ghor as-Safi were first recorded in the early 19th century and subsequently were sporadically and hastily explored during the 20th century. In 1999, a research project by the Hellenic Society for Near Eastern Studies under the direction of Dr Konstantinos D. Politis began surveys, followed by archaeological excavations for over 20 years. One of the main results has been the identification of a multi-period cemetery with Early Bronze Age, Early Byzantine and Islamic burials. It is estimated that over 500 funerary inscriptions (90% Greek and 10% Aramaic) from these graves originally existed, associated with Early Byzantine Zoara. Out of these, 488 have been published [24]. In addition, 31 inscriptions from adjacent Deir 'Ain 'Abata were published separately [27]. The importance of the Ghor as-Safi inscriptions, individually and as an assemblage, cannot be overestimated, since they provide us with a rare understanding into the 4th to 7th century society in Early Byzantine-period Jordan, as much as the 'Holy Land' in general.

5 Describing the Parthenios' Funerary Inscription

Among the more than 500 funerary inscriptions discovered in Ghor as-Safi, we have chosen to represent the Parthenios' funerary inscription (see Fig. 1). This funerary inscription can be characterized as most representative, as it contains content that is common to most funerary inscriptions in the area, i.e. name and age of the deceased, time of death and certain symbols (crosses and a palm branch). It received the inventory number Z-241 in the archaeological recording process. It is the funerary stone of the grave of the Parthenios who died at the age of 70 years in the early 5th century AD in the early Byzantine Zoara

Fig. 1. The Parthenios' Funerary Inscription (taken from [24, Plate XXVIII, inscr. 138]).

(or Zoora). The Parthenios funerary inscription is currently in Italy, part of a private collection.

To represent this artifact using CIDOC CRM and CRMtex, we followed a two-way approach. We start by representing what we see, i.e. the physical characteristics of the artefact (physical state, dimensions, material, shape, colour) as well as the text (five lines of text in koine Greek) and the symbols on it (crosses, palm branch). We continue by representing interpretations based upon the Parthenios' funerary inscription, such as its production and chronology.

5.1 The Physical Characteristics of Parthenios' Funerary Inscription

In epigraphy, text and material are in an essential and close relationship that tightly binds inscriptions with their physical support, i.e. the material base on which an inscription is. Physical materials (e.g. stone, metal, wood, et.c.), sizes and shapes, production techniques and all the attributes of the physical object/base hosting an inscription are fundamental towards our reading, understanding and interpreting an inscription. Note that epigraphical material may be on objects built specifically for accommodating an inscription (e.g. a tombstone, a traffic sign, an entrance tableau, et.c.), but also on objects on which inscriptions were added at a later stage. This is the case for rock carvings

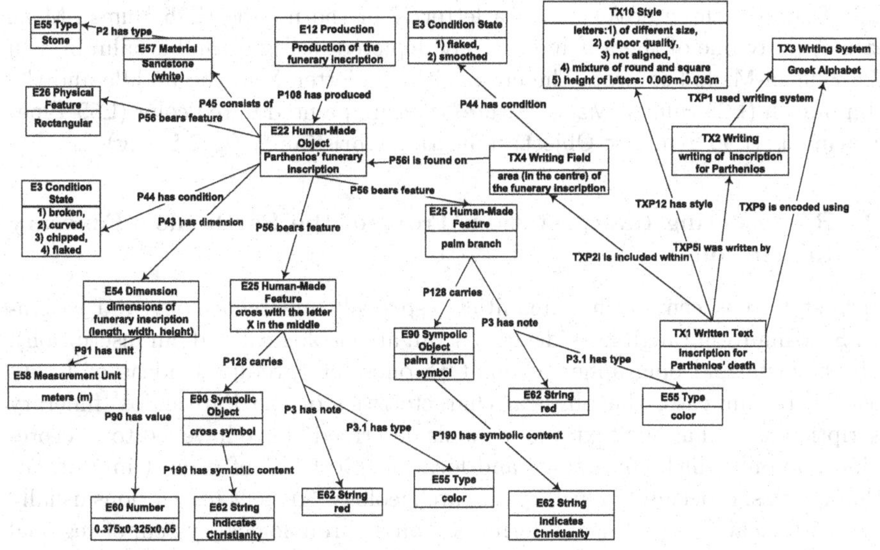

Fig. 2. The Physical Characteristics of Parthenios' Funerary Inscription.

and painted/engraved inscriptions on different smaller and bigger objects (from clothes and pots and to walls and vessels). In our case, we have an ancient funerary inscription. CIDOC CRM offers classes and properties with which we can describe the physical characteristics and the production of a funerary inscription, staring from E22 Human-Made Object.

Inscription consists of a textual part (i.e. letters, and therefore words and phrases) and symbols. Text and symbols, when interpreted, provide the cultural information content for epigrapher, archaeologists, historians and other scientists to study and interpret. In the case of the Parthenios inscription, we have textual information on the name of the deceased, his age, and the time of death. We also have the symbols of the cross and the palm leave. The CIDOC CRM representation of the physical characteristics of Parthenios' funerary inscription appears in Fig. 2.

For the creation (E12 Production) of the Parthenios' funerary inscription (E22 Human-Made Object), a type of stone (E55 Type) was used, namely the white Sandstone (E57 Material). The shape of the funerary inscription is rectangular (E26 Physical Feature). In terms of its condition, it is broken, curved, chipped, flaked (E3 Condition State). Its dimensions (length, width, height) (E54 Dimension), measured in meters (E58 Measurement Unit), have the values of $0.375 \times 0.325 \times 0.05$ m (E60 Number). On the funerary inscription there is a writing field (TX4 Writing Field) that is flaked and smoothed (E3 Condition State). This writing field (TX4 Writing Field) includes the text of the inscription for Parthenios' death (TX1 Written Text). Letters have different sizes, are of poor quality, not aligned, round and square (TX10 Style). Their height is of 0.008 - 0.035 m (TX10 Style). The funerary inscription also bears a cross (E25 Human-

Made Feature), three crosses with a letter X in the middle (E25 Human-Made Feature) (only one of them is indicatively depicted in Fig. 2) and a palm branch (E25 Human-Made Feature). The cross with the letter X in the middle and the palm branch (E25 Human-Made Feature) that are painted in red color (E55 Type) are symbols (E90 Symbolic Object) indicating Christianity (E62 String).

5.2 Representing Interpretations From/of the Parthenios' Funerary Inscription

Interpretation is central in humanities, especially in archaeology and epigraphy. Starting from tangible evidence (e.g. an archaeological find, an inscription), archaeologists and epigrapher attempt to offer interpretation, ideas and conclusions. In our case, the physical characteristics of the Parthenios' funerary inscription as well as the text and symbols described above have led to interpretations, among which chronology and location. Both are of utmost importance in humanities, especially in history and archaeology. Ancient inscriptions usually come with clear chronological information on a chronological system of regional status. Epigraphers, archaeologists, and historians transform this information to our chronological system, the so-called Gregorian calendar. The place were an ancient inscription has been discovered as well as its current hosting environment and/or its owners offer the grounds for archaeological reasoning and have implications at many levels: why the inscription was/is there? What does it mean, if we observe object mobility? In our case, we have an funerary inscription found in Safi, Jordan. However, the object is currently in a private collection in Italy.

The CIDOC CRM representation of the interpretations from/of the Parthenios' funerary inscription appears in Fig. 3. Note that the shaded instances of Fig. 3 also appear in Fig. 2.

The Parthenios' funerary inscription (E22 Human-Made Object) is a monument (E55 Type) that was created (E12 Production) for Parthenios' burial (E5 Event) at Zoora (E53 Place) in 326 E.P.A. (E52 Time-Span). Its current location is in Italy (E53 Place) in a private collection (E78 Curated Holding) and has preferred identifier inv.no.Z-241 (E42 Identifier).

Parthenios (E21 Person) died (E69 Death) in 326 E.P.A. (E52 Time-Span) according to the local chronological system of the region of Arabia (EPA = Era of the Province of Arabia). The corresponding date has alternative form in the Gregorian calendar 431 AD (E41 Appellation).

The text of the inscription for Parthenios' death (TX1 Written Text) lies on a specific area on the surface (TX4 Writing Field) of the stone of Parthenios' funerary inscription. It is encoded in Greek alphabet (TX3 Writing System), it has Greek alphabet characters (TX8 Grapheme) that are depicted by Greek alphabet characters (TX9 Glyph). Note that the Greek alphabet (TX3 Writing System) encodes the meaning of the inscription's text (E33 Linguistic Object).

The inscription for Parthenios' death (TX1 Written Text) was created by the activity of writing (TX2 Writing) using the specific technique of engraving (E29 Design or Procedure). The Greek alphabet (TX3 Writing System) encodes the

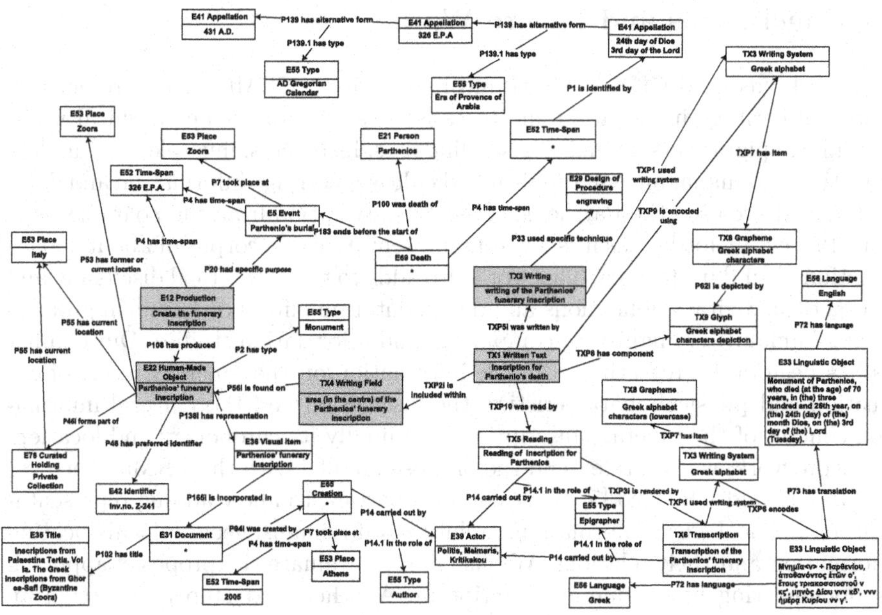

Fig. 3. Interpretations from/of the Parthenios' Funerary Inscription.

text of the inscription for Parthenios' (E33 Linguistic Object) which is written in Greek (E56 Language).

The process of reading (TX5 Reading) the inscription for Parthenios' death (TX1 Written Text) has been carried out by Politis (E39 Actor), Meimaris (E39 Actor), Kritikakou (E39 Actor) in the role of epigraphers (E55 Type). These (E39 Actor) are also in the role of authors (E55 Type) who have created (E65 Creation) a document (E31 Document) that has title (E35 Title) "Inscriptions from Palaestina Tertia Vol. Ia The Greek Inscriptions from Ghor es-Safi (Byzantine Zoora)" in which the photo of the funerary inscription (E36 Visual item) is incorporated. The creation (E65 Creation) of the book took place in Athens (E53 Place) in 2005 (E52 Time-Span). The process of reading (TX5 Reading) is rendered by the transcription (TX6 Transcription) of the Parthenios' funerary inscription. During the transcription process (TX6 Transcription), the Greek alphabet is used (TX3 Writing System) which consists of graphemes that are characters of Greek alphabet (TX8 Grapheme). The Greek alphabet (TX3 Writing System) encodes a linguistic object " Μνημῖα + ⟨ν⟩ Παρθενίου, ἀποθανόντος ἐτῶν ο′, ἔτους τριακοσσιοστοῦ ν κς′, μηνός Δίου ννν κδ′, ννν ἡμέρᾳ Κυρίου νν γ′. " (E33 Linguistic Object) in Greek language (E56 Language). This linguistic object (E33 Linguistic Object) has translated in another one linguistic object "Monument of Parthenios, who died (at the age) of 70 years, in (the) three hundred and 26th year, on (the) 24th (day) of (the) month Dios, on (the) 3rd day of (the) Lord (Tuesday)" (E33 Linguistic Object) in English language (E56 Language).

6 Conclusions and Future Work

This work has used CIDOC CRM and its extension CRMtex to represent epigraphical heritage information and to assist scientists of the epigraphical world (including epigraphers, archaeologists, linguists, historians, museologists) in documenting and managing epigraphical and cultural heritage information and data. To this end, we used the Parthenios funerary inscription from the Zoara Excavations Project in Jordan, as it is a good representative of a corpus of about 500 inscriptions found in the area. This work also adds to the theoretical discussion and to practical/digital applications and documentation efforts on common grounds among humanities, linguistics, computing, and information studies. Our emphasis has been on representing available information on the funerary inscription's creation and physical characteristics, the inscription and the cultural information content of the funerary inscription, and finally its chronology and location. As future work, we aim to extend the proposed model with the CRMarchaeo [8], CRMba [6] and CRMgeo [5] classes and properties, to allow adding representations of archaeological information, architectural remains, geographical/location information and their relations. We also aim to evaluate the proposed approach by documenting more funerary inscription. Another next step is to design an automated system for documenting excavation works as well as inscriptions and other epigraphical finds. This will provide epigraphers, archaeologists and historians with the capacity to document epigraphical information (inscriptions as objects/archaeological finds, text and other content, interpretation) and take advantage of the system's data entry and information searching and retrieving facilities as well as explore the relevant ontologies and their reasoning capabilities.

Acknowledgements. This research was supported by the project: "Activities of the Laboratory on Digital Libraries and Electronic Publishing of the Department of Archives, Library Science and Museology".

References

1. ARIADNEplus - a data infrastructure serving the archaeological community worldwide. https://www.ariadne-infrastructure.eu/. Accessed 12 Sept 2022
2. EAGLE Portal. https://www.eagle-network.eu/. Accessed 12 Sept 2022
3. TEI: Text Encoding Initiative. https://tei-c.org/. Accessed 12 Sept 2022
4. Medieval Nordic Text Archive (Menota) (2001). https://www.menota.org/. Accessed 12 Sept 2022
5. CRMgeo: a Spatiotemporal Model: An Extension of CIDOC-CRM to link the CIDOC CRM to GeoSPARQL through a Spatiotemporal Refinement. Version 1.2. Technical report (2015)
6. Definition of the CRMba: An extension of CIDOC CRM to support buildings archaeology documentation. Version 1.4. Technical report (2016)
7. Epigraphy.info A collaborative environment for Digital Epigraphy (2018). https://epigraphy.info/. Accessed 12 Sept 2022

8. Definition of the CRMarchaeo: An Extension of CIDOC CRM to support the archaeological excavation process. Version 1.4.8. Technical report (2019)
9. Definition of the CRMtex: An Extension of CIDOC-CRM to to Model Ancient Textual Entities Version 1.0. Technical report (2020)
10. EpiDoc: Epigraphic Documents in TEI XML (2021). https://epidoc.stoa.org/. Accessed 12 Sept 2022
11. Definition of the CIDOC Conceptual Reference Model (Vol. A). Version 7.1.2. Technical report (2022)
12. Binding, C., May, K., Souza, R., Tudhope, D., Vlachidis, A.: Semantic technologies for archaeology resources: results from the STAR project. In: Contreras, F., Farjas, M., Melero, F.J. (eds.) Proceedings 38th Annual Conference on Computer Applications and Quantitative Methods in Archaeology, BAR International Series, vol. 2494, pp. 555–561. BAR Publishing (2013)
13. Binding, C., Tudhope, D., Vlachidis, A.: A study of semantic integration across archaeological data and reports in different languages. J. Inf. Sci. **45**(3), 364–386 (2019)
14. Bountouri, L., Gergatsoulis, M.: The semantic mapping of archival metadata to the CIDOC CRM ontology. J. Arch. Organ. **9**(3–4), 174–207 (2011)
15. Doerr, M., Schaller, K., Theodoridou, M.: Integration of complementary archaeological sources. In: Proceedings of the Conference on Computer Applications and Quantitative Methods in Archaeology, CAA2004, Prato, Italy, pp. 13–17 (2004)
16. Felicetti, A., Murano, F., Ronzino, P., Niccolucci, F.: CIDOC CRM and epigraphy: a hermeneutic challenge. In: Ronzino, P. (ed.) Proceedings of the Workshop on Extending, Mapping and Focusing the CRM co-located with 19th International Conference on Theory and Practice of Digital Libraries, Poznań, Poland, 17 September 2015, vol. 1656 of CEUR Workshop Proceedings, pp. 55–68. CEUR-WS.org (2015)
17. Gaitanou, P., Gergatsoulis, M.: Defining a semantic mapping of VRA core 4.0 to the CIDOC conceptual reference model. Int. J. Metadata Semant. Ontol. **7**(2), 140–156 (2012)
18. Gergatsoulis, M., Bountouri, L., Gaitanou, P., Papatheodorou, C.: Query transformation in a CIDOC CRM based cultural metadata integration environment. In: Lalmas, M., Jose, J., Rauber, A., Sebastiani, F., Frommholz, I. (eds.) ECDL 2010. LNCS, vol. 6273, pp. 38–45. Springer, Heidelberg (2010). https://doi.org/10.1007/978-3-642-15464-5_6
19. Gergatsoulis, M., Papaioannou, G., Kalogeros, E., Carter, R.: Representing archeological excavations using the CIDOC CRM based conceptual models. In: Garoufallou, E., Ovalle-Perandones, M.-A. (eds.) MTSR 2020. CCIS, vol. 1355, pp. 355–366. Springer, Cham (2021). https://doi.org/10.1007/978-3-030-71903-6_33
20. Gergatsoulis, M., Papaioannou, G., Kalogeros, E., Mpismpikopoulos, I., Tsiouprou, K., Carter, R.: Modelling archaeological buildings using CIDOC-CRM and its extensions: the case of Fuwairit, Qatar. In: Ke, H.-R., Lee, C.S., Sugiyama, K. (eds.) ICADL 2021. LNCS, vol. 13133, pp. 357–372. Springer, Cham (2021). https://doi.org/10.1007/978-3-030-91669-5_28
21. Giagkoudi, E., Tsiafakis, D., Papatheodorou, C.: Describing and revealing the semantics of excavation notebooks. In: Proceedings of the CIDOC 2018 Annual Conference, Heraklion, Crete, Greece, 19 September–5 October 2018 (2018)
22. Kakali, C., et al. Integrating dublin core metadata for cultural heritage collections using ontologies. In: Proceedings of the 2007 International Conference on Dublin Core and Metadata Applications, DC 2007, Singapore, 27–31 August 2007, pp. 128–139 (2007)

23. Meghini, C., et al. ARIADNE: a research infrastructure for archaeology. ACM J. Comput. Cult. Herit. **10**(3), 18:1–18:27 (2017)
24. Meimaris, Y.E., Kritikakou-Nikolaropoulou, K.I.: Inscriptions from Palaestina Tertia. Vol Ia. The Greek Inscriptions from Ghor es-Safi (Byzantine Zoora). National Hellenic Research Foundation, Athens, Greece (2005)
25. Niccolucci, F.: Documenting archaeological science with CIDOC CRM. Int. J. Digital Libr. **18**(3), 223–231 (2017)
26. Panciera, S.: What is an inscription? problems of definition and identity of an historical source. Zeitschrift für Papyrologie und Epigraphik **183**, 1–10 (2012)
27. Politis, K.D.: Sanctuary of Lot at Deir 'Ain 'Abata in Jordan Excavations 1988–2003. Jordan Distribution Agency in association with the British Museum, Amman, Jordan (2012)
28. Vlachidis, A., Binding, C., May, K., Tudhope, D.: Automatic metadata generation in an archaeological digital library: semantic annotation of grey literature. In: Przepiórkowski, A., et al. (eds.) Computational Linguistics - Applications, vol. 458 of Studies in Computational Intelligence, pp. 187–202. Springer, Heidelberg (2013). https://doi.org/10.1007/978-3-642-34399-5_10

The "Comédie-Française" Registers as Linked Open Data: From Heterogeneity to Quantitative RDF Data

Charline Granger[1] and Fabien Amarger[2(✉)]

[1] Université Paris Nanterre, 200 avenue de la République, Nanterre, France
[2] Logilab, 104 avenue Auguste Blanqui, Paris, France
Fabien.Amarger@logilab.fr

Abstract. The registers of the Comédie-Française theatre company (Paris, France), kept since the 17th century, record the company's expenses. This data is particularly interesting for historical purposes. There is however currently no other way to study these expenses other than analysing the registers manually. This lack of easy access motivated us to create a database from the expenses registers transcription. The main objective is to address the registers' heterogeneity in order to translate it into a schema. The second challenge is to align these data with other transcription databases in order to obtain a single SPARQL endpoint, which can then be used to obtain quantitative information from initially heterogeneous data.

Keywords: archives · history of theatre · ontology · Linked Open Data · Digital Humanities

1 Introduction

The "Comédie-Française" is a theatre company created by Louis XIV in 1680 to centralize theatre actors: the company's status is ambiguous, since it is pensioned by the king, but run like a private company, with benefits shared among its members. For administration purposes (and to allow control by the royal power), the actors produced daily records from the company creation. Those records contain receipts and expenses for each day. Those accounting archives are, as far as we know, unique regarding their density and their continuity.

The Comédie-Français Registers Project[1] [5], a bilingual international research program, has been founded ten years ago to allow wider access to this precious archive [1].

The partners of this project include the library-museum of the Comédie-Française and several universities: Paris Nanterre (France), Sorbonne University (France), University of Rouen Normandie (France), Victoria University

[1] "Programme des registres de la Comédie-Française RCF" https://cfregisters.org.

E. Garoufallou and A. Vlachidis (Eds.): MTSR 2022, CCIS 1789, pp. 77–88, 2023.
https://doi.org/10.1007/978-3-031-39141-5_7

(Canada), New York University (U.S.A.) and the Massachusetts Institute of Technology (U.S.A.). The RCF project originated from the need to create a database of evenings' receipts from 1680 to 1793. This period represents 113 seasons and more than 30 000 programmed evenings: the receipt registers contain the evening's programming schedule (typically two representations each evening) and the number of entries sold per seat category. Two relational databases have then been created [4]. The first one is the receipts' database, which represents links between a representation date with a play title and an author name with a theatrical genre. The second one is the "feux" database (distribution by representation), which represents links, for the period 1765–1793, between a representation date with an actor name and a role, which is linked to a play, an author and a genre.

The two main objectives are: creating a third database containing the company expenses between 1680 and 1776, which completes the receipts and the "feux" databases; and deploying a SPARQL endpoint that contains all the data from the three databases, to contribute to the Linked Open Data and use the RDF versatility. The principal challenge is to model partially irregular data as faithfully as possible. The Logilab company, a computer science service provider, is responsible for the technical realization of these two parts of the project.

In this paper we present the registers, in order to observe the irregularities from the data, then the expenses' transcription application, and finally we describe how to merge the data from the three databases into an RDF triple store.

2 The "Comédie-Française" Registers

The challenge when creating these databases is multiple for the researcher community. First, this will give access to a wide audience (students, amateurs and of course academics and specialists) to data that is not easily accessible because it is consigned to the Comédie-Française library-museum funds. The digitized register facsimiles, to which the website give access, are the first step of this dissemination. But above all, the databases allow generating a kind of information that is inaccessible when consulting the registers of the digitized version: thanks to the data model allowed by the databases, a transversal reading is possible which leads to define constants or create long-term surveys. We can then make statistics on the plays that are the most profitable depending on the periods, on the spectator variation depending on the seat categories, on the actor specialization regarding the roles, etc. For the specific situation of the expenses' database, we hope we will be able to know which plays cost the most regarding the decor, the costumes and the additional staff, like musicians or extras (the "assistants" as was said at this time). Thanks to this database, we will understand better the theatre economy and the artist status. Then we will obtain valuable information about the beginnings of the history of staging.

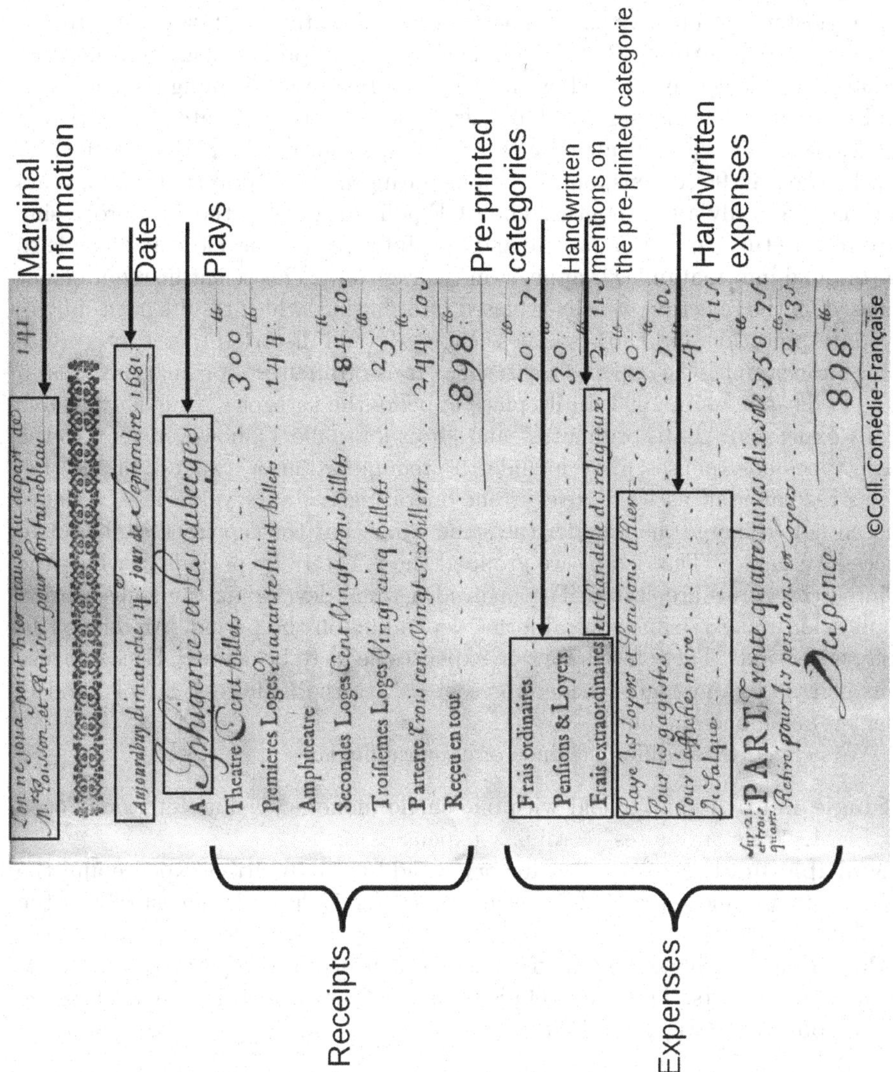

Fig. 1. Expense registry example

3 The Expenses Register Transcription Application

Register's data are, a priori, easily reconcilable with an automatic data processing since, actually, the daily registers contain systematic data because they are always dependent on a date (the "evening" when the representation took place) that generated the receipt or the expense. Especially for the expenses registers, in addition to this calendar regularity, we can observe that some expense categories are stable during several years, even decades, which allows us to consider these registers as "massive data". For example, the category of "parts d'acteurs" is present from 1680 to 1776. It corresponds to the profits made on the day's performance, which are shared by the actors and actresses forming the company.

However, from another point of view, the data is disparate. First, this is because a lot of expense categories are not stable during the period 1680–1776, which represent 96 seasons, but are stable during shorter periods, decades, years or sometimes only a few months. The RCF policy regarding the data processing is to restore the source in a precise and faithful way, to be as close as possible to the original information as it appears in the registers. This scientific requirement is based on the rejection to deliver biased information, which results from subjective interpretation and choices. These choices would distort the user interpretation. For example, the expense's category "frais ordinaires" (ordinary expenses) (Fig. 1) disappears in 1693. In its place appears the category "frais journaliers" (daily expenses). "Frais ordinaires" and "frais journaliers", however, refer to the same types of expenses: they include the remuneration or "wages" of the theatre's regular staff as well as recurrent operating costs. Nevertheless, we have chosen not to merge them under the same name, but to keep track of these two successive names. That's why we grouped the registers by periods in which the printed categories are stable. The main idea when developing the transcription application was to define several forms depending on the period. We defined 10 different periods. These forms contain expenses fields to be defined. Each expense is associated to an expense value represented with the **L** (livres), **S** (sols) and **D** (deniers) as monetary units.

We defined three different kinds of expense fields:

- **Single field.** A simple field with one single monetary value: for example, in Fig. 1, "frais ordinaires" (ordinary expenses).
- **Multiple field.** An expense category to add a handwritten expense and the monetary value associated: for example, in Fig. 1, "pour les gagistes" (for the staff).
- **Part field.** A single field with which we can define the part value and the number of parts. This part field is used to define the actor's payment, as we can observe in Fig. 1 ("PART").

Another disparate aspect of the expenses registers is the fact that these registers mix different status data. We need to distinguish between four different expense categories:

– The **pre-printed categories**: for example in Fig. 1, "frais ordinaires" (ordinary expenses).
– The **handwritten mentions on the pre-printed categories** (that can clarify or even replace them without any mention): for example in Fig. 1, "et chandelle des religieux" (candles for religious).
– The **marginal information** (always handwritten, that does not concern any expense but gives some precision about a "relâche"[2] or when someone

[2] "Relace" means "when the theatre must close".

prestigious is present). For example in Fig. 1, we can read "L'on ne joua point hier á cause du départ de Messieurs Poisson et Raisin pour Fontainebleau" (We did not play yesterday because of the departure of Messrs. Poisson and Raisin for Fontainebleau).
- The **handwritten expenses** which are added to the pre-printed categories. For example in Fig. 1, "pour l'affiche noire" (for the black poster).

The transcription application interface has been adapted to deal with this diversity. Thus, the transcriber can record these different mentions and pre-printed categories: each period contains the pre-printed expense categories and some are available to type a free label to name it. These free-label categories are always grouped in a super-category to try to regroup when it is possible. For example, the category "Frais extraordinaires" (extraordinary expenses) is used to group the expenses which concern this specific day, like, in Fig. 1, "pour l'affiche noire" (for the black poster) or, in other performances, *vin* (some wine) or *une robe de chambre* (a housecoat).

But the problem with these extraordinary expenses is that this accounting category, which defines irregular expenses, as opposed to ordinary expenses, does not have a fixed representation throughout the period. During some seasons, there is a printed category named "Frais extraordinaires" (extraordinary expenses), as we can observe in Fig. 1. But in other registers, we can observe several handwritten records which are not categorized. In this situation, it is difficult to define a category for these records: is this a real "extraordinary expense" or an uncategorizable expense? The problem here is twofold: how to transcribe these handwritten and uncategorized records and, on the other hand, define how we can, during a post-processing, find a way to categorize these records. This post-transcription categorization is important since it will orient the quantitative analysis afterwards. Depending on the accounting type defined during this step, the results may vary significantly. Since we do make some modelling choices or interpretations, we can diverge from the source and introduce a bias. For now, we have added the handwritten and uncategorized records as "Frais extraordinaires" without any further categorization. Here lies one of the most important challenge that we will discuss at the end of this article.

We can also identify a new problem to be solved: some expense categories partially overlap. In Fig. 1, we can observe that "frais extraordinaires" and "chandelles des religieux" (candles for religious) are represented as a single category. Then there is no way to define if the recorded 2 livres and 11 sols are about "frais extraordinaires", "chandelles des religieux" or both.

The Fig. 2 presents an example of what the application looks like. The left part of the web page is dedicated to render the page register to be transcribed. The right part contains the expense record fields, depending on the period. At the bottom, we can observe some metadata about the transcribe process, such as comments. In this metadata, there is the transcribe process state for this specific page. A page follows a workflow. At first the page is in state *to do*, then when

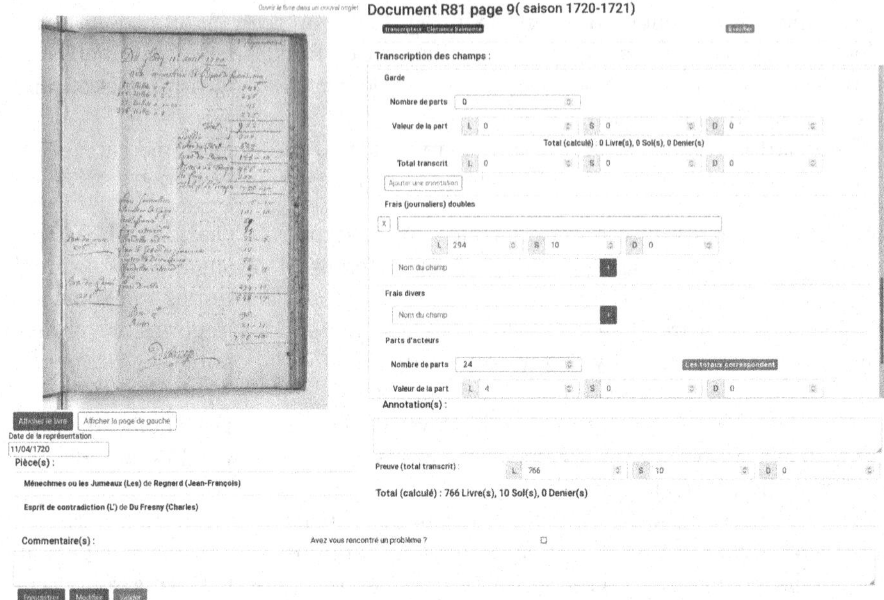

Fig. 2. Expenses transcribe application

the transcribe process is done the page state is changed to *to review* to let an expert review the data. Once the data is validated, the page goes to the state *validated.* At this moment the data can be analysed since it has been transcribed and validated. A page can be validated even if some errors appear. For example, one of the most common errors, is that the transcribed total is not equal to the computed total. Most of the time, this error appears in the page itself. We decided to keep the error in the data, but we flag the page as "erroneous". This gives researchers the possibility to study these errors, for example to study if this is a deliberate error or not, if it can be interpreted as money embezzlement. A very important field is the date definition, which appears under the page register image. This date is central information since it will be used to align data with the two other databases.

4 RDF Data to Merge the Three Databases

Once the three databases (*dépenses* (expenses), *recettes* (receipts) and *feux* (roles and actors)) were transcribed and validated, the problem was to merge them all. The alignment process was pretty simple, since each transcribed data contains the representation date. Then we can easily use this date as a pivot concept to link the three bases. Using RDF format and Semantic Web technologies was first the most appropriate idea since the main objective is to give access to as many people as possible. The Semantic Web technologies, and especially the Linked

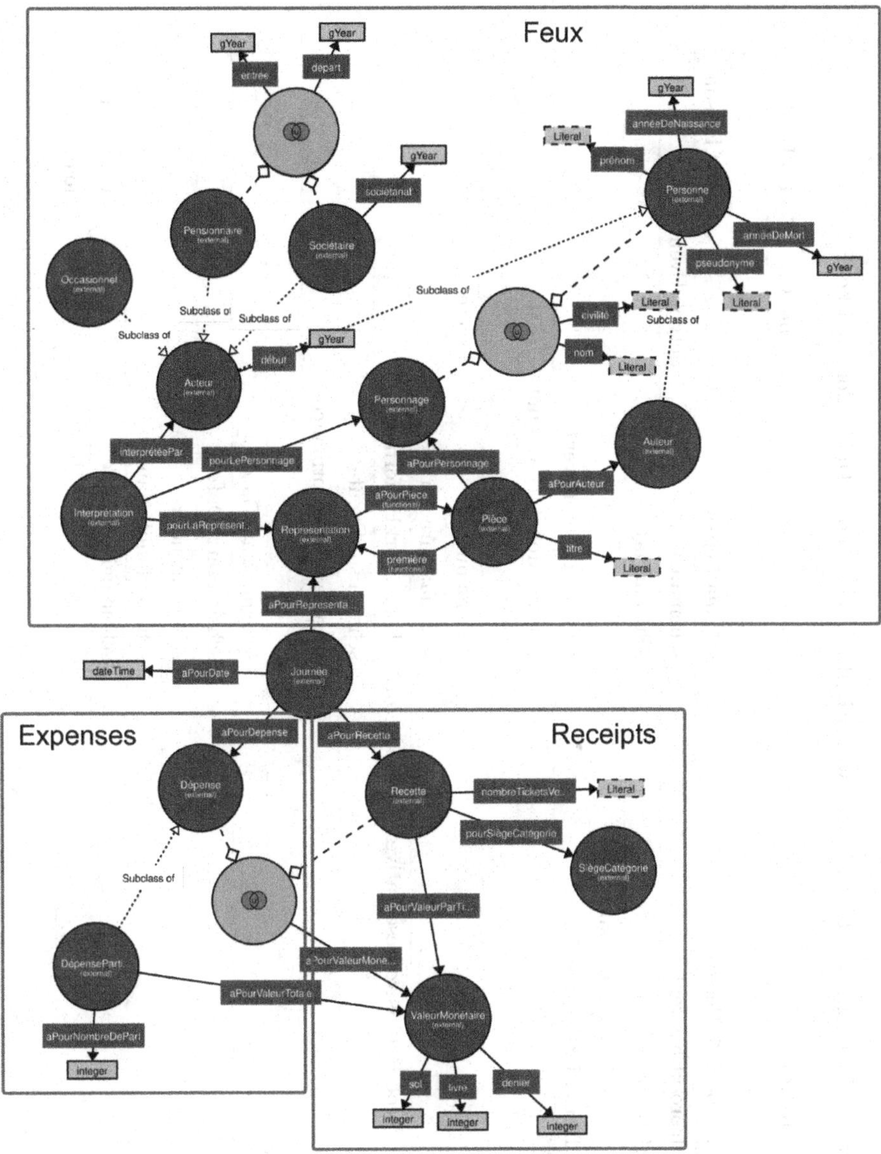

Fig. 3. RCF unified ontology

Open Data, are dedicated to that purpose [6]. But secondly, the RDF format has become a solution to the problem we described in Sect. 2. The data diversity is not easy to handle when dealing with relational databases, but there is no problem to not define some RDF attributes if they are not available during the transcribe process.

Table 1. Mapping from RCF ontology with FRBRoo, schema.org, DublinCore and FoaF

RCF	FRBRoo [2]	schema.org	DublinCore [7]	FoaF [3]
Class				
rcf:Personne	frbroo:E21_Person	schema:Person		foaf:Person
rcf:Journée	frbroo:E5_Event	schema:Event	dctype:Event	
rcf:Pièce	frbroo:F1_Work	schema:Play		
rcf:Inteprétation	frbroo:F31_Performance			
rcf:Représentation	frbroo:F2_Expression	schema:TheaterEvent		
rcf:ValeurMonétaire		schema:MonetaryAmount		
Object Properties				
rcf:aPourAuteur		schema:author	dce:creator	
rcf:aPourPersonnage		schema:character		
rcf:aPourPiece	frbroo:R40i_is_representative_expression_for.	schema:workPerformed		
rcf:aPourReprésentation		schema:subEvent		
rcf:première		schema:firstPerformance		
Data Properties				
rcf:annéeDeMort		schema:deathDate		
rcf:annéeDeNaissance		schema:birthDate		
rcf:civilité		schema:gender		
rcf:nom		schema:familyName		foaf:surname
rcf:prénom		schema:givenName		foaf:givenname
rcf:pseydonyme				foaf:nick

First, we needed to define a global ontology. We can observe the unified ontology in Fig. 3. The pivot concept to create links between all the others is the **Journée** (day) since all pages are specific to a date. All the upper part of the ontology is dedicated to the *Feux* (actors and roles); all the down part is dedicated to the *Recettes* (receipts—at the down left part) and the *Dépenses* (expenses—at the down right part). All the details (expenses categories, seat categories and so on) are not present in the initial ontology since these details are generated dynamically when exporting the data. To ease the readability of this schema, we do not render the whole ontology in detail. As you can observe, the expenses part do not deal with periods. We do consider only the domain specific and pertinent concepts for the domain.

Once the ontology is defined, we aligned the key concepts with some well-known ontologies. This alignment is a key feature since the ontology is defined using French words, because the domain and the concerned potential users are mostly French, but there is no reason to not let non-French speaking using this ontology, and the data. The alignment to well-known, and English, ontologies and vocabularies are as well the best way to ease the reusability of the ontology and the data, which is one of the main goals of the RCF project. If an ontology is already aligned with an upper ontology, then the alignment with the RCF ontology will be eased. This alignment can then be used to enrich data from other sources. For example, if a dataset contains actors information, such as birthdate, using an alignment can then be used to obtain all plays which contain actors born in a given date.

The Table 1 shows the mapping we made. We can see that we did not perform to use full FRBRoo ontology, even if this is one of the most famous ontology for this domain. This is mainly because of the main design choice for FRBRoo which put the events as the key concept for the whole ontology. We do have some events in the RCF ontology, but not everything is considered as events. For example, we do not have the "birth" event for a person, which is the case in the FRBRoo ontology (event inherited from Cidoc CRM). We want to avoid the complex alignments, then we let these kinds of alignment aside.

Once we had designed the ontology, we exported all the data from the three databases as RDF triples, considering the RCF ontology. All the data are exported in a public SPARQL endpoint[3] using Virtuoso Open-Source Edition[4]. This export can be used to obtain information such as "what is the cost of plays where a given actor played in and what the extraordinary expenses for these plays?" or compare the receipts for these plays to see if this actor is famous.

To help non-sparql friendly people to access the data, we developed a web application[5] using this SPARQL endpoint as backend data store. This application is dedicated to expose the expenses' data for now, but it would be interesting to extend the application to two other types of data.

---

3 https://rcf-sparql.demo.logilab.fr/.

4 https://vos.openlinksw.com.

5 https://upnd.pages.logilab.fr/rcf-ui-expense/.

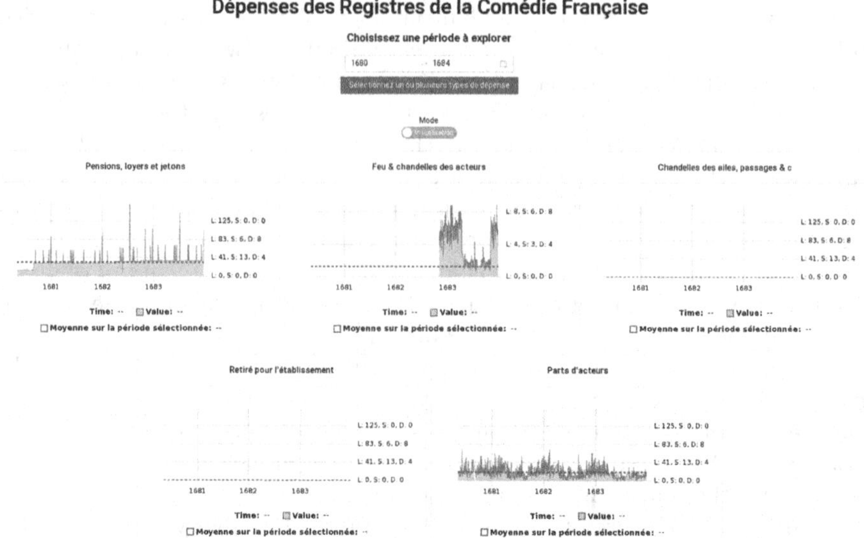

Fig. 4. Web application to visualize the expenses' data from the SPARQL endpoint

The Fig. 4 shows what this application looks like. We can see here that we can compare several kinds of expenses regarding a specific period of time. This is especially useful to determine which expense represents a huge amount regarding the other expenses, or during a period. This application let users compare the sum or the average of the selected expenses for some selected plays or authors on the selected period.

Developing this application is necessary to make the data available for a maximum of people. The problem is, the developers must make some choices during the developing process. Even if these choices have been made together with domain experts, these are still choices which consider only one point of view regarding the data interpretation. We can take a simple example: the partitioned expenses (part fields). For now, they are considered as simple expenses, and we compare only total values. If some people want to explore this kind of expenses and study the evolution of the part value, the application will be limited. This is why the SPARQL endpoint is crucial in our implementation, since the raw RDF data is available directly. But the user needs to know how to write some SPARQL queries, and this is why we are considering implementing Sparnatural[6].

5 Perspectives and Future Works

We have presented why the Comédie-Française registers are a very interesting and promising source for research in humanities. The transcribe process of

[6] https://sparnatural.eu/.

those registers is especially interesting since it allows a quantitative analysis of the registers. The expenses registers are particularly disparate because of the irregularities between periods, and handwritten records. We have seen how we have developed an application to transcribe the expenses from the registers, besides this irregularity. Then we have presented how we have merged the three databases into a dedicated RDF triple store to allow as many people as possible to access this data.

The data disparity observed in the RCF registers pushed us to alert the researcher about the quantitative approach limits. There is a bias regarding the observation of the data from visualization applications. Viewing a graph, one may believe in the objectivity of the delivered information. But this is a decoy: the quantitative aspect, which is only one way to read and understand the information, has been built through a long process of choices, discards and subjective renderings. This aspect needs the researcher interpretation, which will give meaning to the quantitative data and make visible all the choices that have led to its building. Contextualized data is therefore essential. We are starting the combined creation of a data dictionary and a documentary and encyclopedic space to enlighten our work and assure the scientific rigour of our approach[7]. Main defined terms to understand the registers, like "frais extraordinaires" (extraordinary expenses), "frais ordinaires" (ordinary expenses), "saisons" (seasons), "loges" (lodges), "preciput" (precipitate), etc. will be precisely defined since they are key to understanding and interpreting the numeric values that can be found in the data.

As discussed in Sect. 3, some records are uncategorized and handwritten. This is an issue since we create a new expense category, as a specialization of "Frais extraordinaires", for each different handwritten expense type. Since they are handwritten, the labels are, except for a few, different from one another, and we end up with a lot of single categories. This data is meant to help analysis and especially quantitative analysis. But if the records are not categorized at all, then there is no way to study this data efficiently. For this reason, we want to explore the use of the clustering algorithm applied to the "Frais extraordinaires" handwritten categories. The main idea is to use the RCF encyclopedia to detect named entities in the handwritten expense category labels and group them using this detection.

But, beyond this necessary data contextualization, the problem remains to access the raw data for the researchers. Since SPARQL is not easy to learn for humanities researchers, the pedagogic part will be central. Knowledge, even rudimentary, of SPARQL can allow researchers to avoid filters from visualization tools, which are necessarily subjective. How can we bring closer humanities researchers and a data funds as rich as the RCF registers? How can we capitalize on the OWL model to propose the most objective visualization tool? These questions will be central in our works for the next years.

---

[7] https://cfregisters.org/#!/encyclopedie/mots.

References

1. Burrows, S., Roe, G.: Digitizing Enlightenment: Digital Humanities and the Transformation of Eighteenth-Century Studies (2020)
2. Doerr, M., Bekiari, C., LeBoeuf, P.: FRBRoo, a conceptual model for performing arts. In: 2008 Annual Conference of CIDOC, Athens, pp. 15–18 (2008)
3. Graves, M., Constabaris, A., Brickley, D.: FOAF: connecting people on the semantic web. Cataloging Classif. Q. **43**(3–4), 191–202 (2007)
4. Guyot, S., Ravel, J.S.: Databases, Revenues, & Repertory: The French Stage Online, 1680–1793. MIT Press, Cambridge (2020)
5. Harvey, S., Sanjuan, A.: Le projet des registres journaliers de la comédie-française: Les humanités numériques, dialogue entre les mondes de la recherche et de la documentation. Bulletin des bibliothèques de France (9), 102–109 (2016)
6. Meroño-Peñuela, A., et al.: Semantic technologies for historical research: a survey. Semant. Web **6**(6), 539–564 (2015)
7. Weibel, S.L., Koch, T.: The Dublin core metadata initiative. D-lib Mag. **6**(12), 1082–9873 (2000)

Towards an Ontology of Pre-20th Century Scientific Instrument Types

Sarah Middle[1] and Alex Butterworth[2](✉)

[1] National Museums Scotland, Chambers Street, Edinburgh EH1 1JF, UK
[2] University of Sussex, Falmer, Brighton BN1 9RH, UK
A.Butterworth@sussex.ac.uk

Abstract. This paper introduces the project *Tools of Knowledge: Modelling the Scientific Instrument Trade, 1550–1914*, and focuses on our ongoing development of an ontology to represent knowledge about scientific instrument types produced during this period. After a brief introduction, we discuss the background to the project and a summary of previous work related to knowledge representation of scientific instrument types, particularly in the area of Linked Open Data. We continue with an explanation of the methods used to normalize and structure our data, as well as the vocabularies used to describe relationships between terms. Our interim findings comprise our reflections on the nature of these complex relationships and their semantic representation, alongside examples of analysis that has been facilitated through application of the ontology-in-progress to the project database. To conclude, we summarize our findings so far and provide an indication of how we might expand and enhance the ontology, as well as its contribution to the wider Linked Open Data ecosystem.

Keywords: scientific instruments · ontologies · cultural heritage

1 Introduction

Debates surrounding what constitutes a scientific instrument and where the boundaries of its definition should be drawn, as well as the often-complex relationships between instrument types, have thus far hindered development of a formal, widely used knowledge representation system in this domain. As part of the AHRC-funded *Tools of Knowledge* project[1], we seek to address these issues by developing an ontology of pre-20th century scientific instrument types. This work both serves the immediate and pragmatic imperatives of the project, starting from the normalisation of data from a legacy database, but in the process of integrating this core dataset with data from multiple museum collections the work also tests longer term value of the ontology for adoption in other academic and cultural heritage contexts. This paper provides a brief overview of work on the ontology to date, including the context within which it is being produced, methods and vocabularies used, and our interim findings. We will conclude by summarising our current insights and sharing our future plans.

[1] https://toolsofknowledge.org.

E. Garoufallou and A. Vlachidis (Eds.): MTSR 2022, CCIS 1789, pp. 89–94, 2023.
https://doi.org/10.1007/978-3-031-39141-5_8

2 Background

2.1 The Tools of Knowledge Project

Tools of Knowledge: Modelling the Scientific Instrument Trade in Britain, 1550–1914 is a thirty-month research project that is both reanimating an extraordinarily rich legacy database, developed over three decades, and augmenting its content with significant new data from diverse sources, including museum collections and text corpora. A collaboration between the Universities of Cambridge and Sussex, and National Museums Scotland, with the National Maritime Museum and Science Museum as partners, the project will transform the Scientific Instrument Makers, Notes and Observations (SIMON) database into a semantically modelled form (SEMSIM)[2], aligned to a combination of adopted and developed ontologies.

In parallel with this work of data development, the project team is undertaking a series of 'keyhole' case studies, conceived in part to demonstrate the analytical potential for Linked Open Data (LOD) [1] and the value of formal ontologies for enabling more fully implemented interoperability between historical datasets. These studies engage the 'historical scientific instrument ontology' at various levels. While the records generated by one strand of work, using X-Ray fluorescence (XRF) [2] to analyze the metallurgical composition of instruments in collections, reference the finest grain level of 'parts' in its recording, another will be more concerned with how the broadest historical concepts of 'philosophical', 'mathematical' and 'optical' instruments adjust their meaning over time, in relation to the specific instruments to which they allude. In further case studies, the ontology supports the necessary specificity around the repairs of chronometers under the Admiralty's maintenance regime, and enables a nuanced examination of the advertised self-presentation of maker trades.

2.2 Scientific Instruments and Knowledge Representation

There is much discussion over the meaning of the term "scientific instrument". Taub [3] identifies different approaches to its definition over time, from the separation between "mathematical", "optical" and "philosophical" instruments in the seventeenth and eighteenth centuries, to the overarching (but subtly different) term of "scientific instruments", introduced in the nineteenth century, and the varying interpretations that persist today. While some, such as James Clerk Maxwell, have preferred a narrow definition that restricts the term to describing instruments used to perform scientific experiments [4], others, such as Bud and Warner [5], take a broader approach by including objects such as navigational equipment and biological samples. This complexity and blurring of boundaries around what constitutes a "scientific instrument" has likely deterred large-scale attempts at formalizing knowledge representation in this domain. As such, any potential solution to this issue must be amenable to partial, context-specific use, with a structure that permits gradual expansion and enhancement over time.

[2] SEMSIM is currently under development and will be openly available from January 2024. It is not possible to share *Tools of Knowledge* data earlier due to agreements with IP holders.

As the result of a recent initiative, Morgan Bell and Steven Kruse at the Whipple Museum, University of Cambridge, have produced a taxonomy of objects in the museum catalogue. While this taxonomy represents significant progress in the area of knowledge representation, further expansion is required to accommodate the full range of instrument types included in SIMON. Additionally, a hierarchical structure does not convey the degree of nuance that it would be useful to represent. Some instrument types appear in more than one broader category: for example, many types could equally be described as astronomical and navigational, or meteorological and thermal. Elsewhere, some instrument types comprise part of other instruments, e.g. telescopes are incorporated to both sextants and theodolites. Similarly, many instrument types are often accompanied by others as accessories, e.g., microscope lamps or telescopic sights.

For this level of knowledge representation, a LOD structure is ideal, while there are several existing initiatives whose work might enhance such an ontology further. Examples include the Scientific Observation Model, CRMsci [6], an extension of the CIDOC CRM[3] that comprises a series of classes and properties to describe the various activities and relationships involved in making scientific observations, as well as the ongoing *Model SEN* project [7], which involves semantic modelling of socio-epistemic networks. A current Getty project, *Arches for Science* [8], promises additional resources in the heritage science data field.

More broadly, large-scale LOD vocabularies, such as the Getty Art and Architecture Thesaurus (AAT)[4] and Wikidata[5] provide persistent URIs for many scientific instrument types. Whilst key resources with which to align our ontology, neither provide the granularity or structural complexity required to represent the instrument types contained in SIMON, or the *Tools of Knowledge* partner institutions.

3 Method: Building the Tools of Knowledge Ontology

Development of the ontology has been organic, following a bottom-up approach, rather than strict adherence to a formal methodology, due to the derived nature of the legacy information that is detailed below, and the tightly integrated working of ontologists and historical scholars. However, our process has broadly approximated the specification, knowledge acquisition, conceptualization and integration components of Methontology [9], with evaluation by domain experts throughout.

As the instrument types contained within SIMON form the basis for the *Tools of Knowledge* ontology[6], we started by extracting all unique values from its Known and Advertised Instrument fields, then normalized them via various data cleaning processes using OpenRefine, to remove typographical errors, align spelling variants, and to ensure a consistent format throughout.

To introduce hierarchical structure and consolidate alternative names for particular types, we manually aligned each normalized instrument type to its equivalent in the Whipple Museum's taxonomy. Grouping types into broader categories provided a useful

3 https://cidoc-crm.org.

4 https://www.getty.edu/research/tools/vocabularies/aat/.

5 https://www.wikidata.org/wiki/wikidata:main_page.

6 Current version available at https://github.com/ddunc23/tok-ontology.

overview of the data, and alignment with an existing vocabulary further aided consistency in how the name of each type was expressed. However, as the Whipple taxonomy did not aim for the level of granularity we sought, we chose to maintain some distinct types that the Whipple had consolidated into one.

At this point, we also used OpenRefine's reconciliation services to align terms to Wikidata and the AAT, although only about half the terms in our ontology had an equivalent in either or both of these resources – further demonstrating the need for more extensive knowledge representation in this domain.

Simple relationships within the ontology are expressed using the Simple Knowledge Organization Format (SKOS)[7], including hierarchical structure (skos:broader and skos:narrower) and similarity (skos:closeMatch), as well as attaching scope notes (skos:scopeNote). Links to equivalent terms in external vocabularies are expressed using skos:exactMatch. Alternative names are represented using skos:altLabel. Our eventual interactive SEMSIM database will allow the user to enter any alternative name for an instrument type to retrieve the relevant entries.

As a further step, we sought to add relationships beyond simple hierarchy or equivalency. For example, we have used Dublin Core Terms[8] dct:isPartOf and dct:hasPart to represent part-whole relationships. More specific relationships are defined using CIDOC CRM[9] and include P62 "depicts" and P198 "holds or supports". Further complexity will be added by linking instrument types to usage types (E55 Type), using P101 "had as general use", and production events (E12 Production), using P125 "used object of type", and P186 "produced thing of product type". To achieve RDF representation, we converted our spreadsheet containing this information using the *SKOS Play*[10] tool.

Although this ontology is being built as part of *Tools of Knowledge* and is initially based on data from SIMON, our ultimate aim is for more widespread applicability and usefulness to other projects in the History of Science domain and beyond. As such, we are currently in the process of expanding it, by incorporating additional types from the Whipple taxonomy, as well as the vast number of terms listed in printed sources such as [10] and [11]. Unusual terms from the collections records of the National Museum of Scotland, the National Maritime Museum, the Science Museum and, possibly, the Oxford History of Science Museum will be similarly integrated.

Throughout the process of building the ontology, particularly with regard to implementing its structure and consolidating alternative types, we consulted with the domain experts on the project team, who provided insights into areas of nuance and ambiguity, as well as their knowledge of the historical context. For example, they confirmed that the instrument name "octant" can be considered equivalent to the historical term "Hadley's quadrant" and recommended that the two entries be combined. Their input has ensured a scholarly robustness that would not have been possible were the ontology constructed by information specialists alone.

---

[7] http://www.w3.org/2004/02/skos/core.

[8] Http://purl.org/dc/terms/.

[9] https://cidoc-crm.org/Version/version-7.1.1.

[10] https://skos-play.sparna.fr/play/.

4 Interim Findings

Having previously discovered that existing hierarchical taxonomies do not fully encapsulate the nuance and complexity of relationships between scientific instrument types, we have found that moving to an ontology structure has increased the scope for this representation. In doing so, the boundaries of what a "scientific instrument" is have become increasingly blurred. To fully represent instrument types in a structured format, it has been necessary to include parts and accessories alongside types that can be more unambiguously considered to be scientific instruments.

More practically, we have already found that aligning the instrument types contained in our interim SEMSIM database with their equivalent ontology terms has facilitated its navigation and discovery. For example, this enables makers to be filtered by the type of instrument they made, sold, supplied or wholesaled, as understood according to different classifications, with the user able to tune the level of granularity for their enquiry up or down, by selecting broader or narrower terms. The inclusion of instrument terms from the ontology as attributes of the Maker entity further allows for visual faceting within network or geospatial analytical tools (initially, Gephi and QGIS), with a similar flexibility in shifting the 'resolution' of the terms. How, for example, are the makers of optical instruments distributed in Scotland over time, compared to those making barometers; and how does the picture change if we narrow down to those making reflecting telescopes? Furthermore, it allows for a nuanced and historicized exploration of both the shifting semantics of instrument-related terms and those combinations of terms that were invoked by makers in their self-advertisement on trade cards.

5 Conclusions and Future Work

Our work in this area has demonstrated that a LOD ontology is the most effective format for representing knowledge about pre-20th century scientific instrument types. More complexity in this area has been revealed with each stage in the process of building the ontology, which has necessitated clear and regular communication between the domain experts and metadata specialists on the project team to ensure a credible resource with eventual uptake beyond the *Tools of Knowledge* project.

Future work on the ontology will continue its expansion using terms from other vocabularies and sources, as well as using it to integrate collections data from partner institutions into the SEMSIM database. To make the opportunities for inter-operation as broadly accessible as possible, we additionally hope to feed new terms back into Wikidata, which will enhance this already rich resource and provide an additional gateway to the scientific instrument types ontology, as well as optimizing the potential for alignment with upper ontologies, such as Cyc[11].

Already, by gathering data from multiple collections, linked through the ontology for the purposes of its case study analyses, the project is emulating and demonstrating the potential for dynamic linkage between instrument collections data. Furthermore, these 'keyhole' case studies present a persuasive example of the significant research

[11] https://cyc.com.

advantages to be derived from such interoperability of data. As the ontology is adopted and integrated into institutions' data management programmes, significant possibilities for intra-national and transnational study of the history of science through the material culture of its early instruments are likely to be enabled.

Acknowledgements. With thanks to Dr Gloria Clifton, creator of the SIMON database, the *Tools of Knowledge* advisory group, and team members who advised on the development and testing of the ontology: Professor Liba Taub, Dr Duncan Hay, Dr Rebekah Higgitt, Dr Boris Jardine and Dr Josh Nall. This work was supported by the Arts and Humanities Research Council [grant number AH/T-13400/1].

References

1. Berners-Lee, T.: Linked Data. https://www.w3.org/DesignIssues/LinkedData.html. Accessed 26 Oct 2022
2. Jardine, B., Nall, J.: The Lab in the Museum, or: Using New Scientific Instruments to Look at Old Scientific Instruments. Centaurus (forthcoming)
3. Taub, L.: What is a scientific instrument, now? J. Hist. Collections **31**(3), 453–467 (2019). https://doi.org/10.1093/jhc/fhy045
4. Warner, D.: What is a scientific instrument, when did it become one, and why? Br. J. Hist. Sci. **23**(1), 83–93 (1990). https://doi.org/10.1017/S0007087400044460
5. Bud, R., Warner, D.: Instruments of Science: An Historical Encyclopedia. Garland Publishing Inc, New York and London (1998)
6. Doerr, M., Kritsotaki, A., Rousakis, Y., Hiebel, G., Theodoridou, M.: CRMsci: the Scientific Observation Model, FORTH (2013). https://projects.ics.forth.gr/isl/CRMext/CRMsci/docs/CRMsci1.1.pdf. Accessed 23 Aug 2022
7. Model SEN. https://modelsen.mpiwg-berlin.mpg.de/de/. Accessed Aug 2022
8. Arches for Science. https://www.archesproject.org/arches-for-science/. Accessed 25 Aug 2022
9. Fernández, M., Gómez-Pérez, A., Juristo, N.: Methontology: From ontological art towards ontological engineering. In: Technical Report SS-97–06, pp. 33–40. The AAAI Press, Menlo Park, CA (1997). https://www.aaai.org/Papers/Symposia/Spring/1997/SS-97-06/SS97-06-005.pdf
10. Mollan, R.C.: Irish National Inventory of Scientific Instruments. Samton Ltd., Dublin (1995)
11. Holbrook, M.: Science Preserved: A Directory of Scientific Instruments in Collections in the United Kingdom and Eire. HMSO Books, London (1992)

Practical Application and Material Documentation of CIDOC – CRM (Conceptual Reference Model): A Scoping Review

Souzana Maranga(✉), Dimitrios Rousidis, Athanasios Gousiopoulos, and Emmanouel Garoufallou

International Hellenic University, Thessaloniki, Greece
smaranga27@gmail.com, mgarou@ihu.gr

Abstract. This paper aims to collect, critical study and present the research literature on practical applications and material documentation of CIDOC – CRM, from 2009 to 2019, in English language.The main objective of this study is the observation of semantic standard progress over the ten years of its using. The present scoping review used the methodological framework of Arksey and O'Malley (2005) and has followed by the rules of PRISMA – ScR. To conduct the research, Scopus/Elsevier, ScienceDirect, Springer, Semantic Scholar, CORE Aggregator, Google Scholar and MDPI Open Access Journals were searched to identify papers that were published in conference proceedings or in scientific journals, as well as through technical report papers that were developed by official bodies of CIDOC – CRM. From the 73 articles that we retrieved, 20 related to the topic of practical applications and material documentation with CIDOC – CRM semantic standard were selected for analysis. The majority of the included articles were published after 2010, from 2013 to 2019, equally distributed. Concluding this short scoping review indicates the importance of semantic ontology CIDOC – CRM for: a) solving semantic interoperability problems and ensuring information exchange and integration between heterogeneous sources of cultural heritage information, b) documenting the intangible cultural heritage, c) optimizing the documentation methods of digitizing products and representing provenance, and d) bringing spatiotemporal concepts and cultural heritage data.

Keywords: CIDOC – CRM · ISO21127 · scoping review · semantic standard · ontology · culture heritage management · interoperability · semantic integration

1 Introduction

The upgrowth of computer and information technology as well as the transition to semantic web lead galleries, libraries, archives and museums (GLAMs) redefined their role in the new semantic environment. The aforementioned cultural institutions as *memory institutions* preserve the global cultural memory through a well-building process which includes the collection, documentation, preservation, exhibition and sharing of cultural heritage, tangible or intangible.

E. Garoufallou and A. Vlachidis (Eds.): MTSR 2022, CCIS 1789, pp. 95–106, 2023.
https://doi.org/10.1007/978-3-031-39141-5_9

Nowadays, the cultural heritage management is a multidimensional, elaborate and interdisciplinary domain where the GLAMs have to handle a plethora of heterogeneous material, like archaeological findings, archaeological monuments and places, artworks, photographs, works of folk art, printed or digital media (*databases, moving images, audio, graphics, software and web pages*) etc. (UNESCO Charter on the Preservation of the Digital Heritage 2003). In addition to the digital evolution, the large amount of data produced daily and the need of storage have created the need for a new framework in which its primary role is the large – scale databases and repositories, the usage of semantic technologies and the collaboration between professionals from different scientific disciplines (Lusenet 2007). Archaeologists, museologists, historians, anthropologists, architects, restorers, and computer scientists should work together in order to protect and give prominence to global cultural heritage. All these professionals should meet different demands of a multitudinous public and users. Thus, they should create cultural heritage information management systems that cover a range of tasks, such as collection management, conservation process, the research and display of cultural objects (Doerr 2009). The problem comes up when each memory organization documents its collections with different metadata standards and uses different information management systems. Therefore, this diversity of standards, systems and resources augment the matter of interoperability and integration at various levels, such as system, schematic, syntactic and mainly at semantic level (Stasinopoulou et al. 2007). As Cruz and Xiao (2005) described in detail "*semantic heterogeneity is caused by different meanings or interpretations of data in various contexts*".

A possible solution to the problem became apparent with the emergence of the new notion of *data integration* that refers to the combination of data from different sources and providing the users with a unified view of these data (Lenzerini 2002). Nowadays, the interest is moving to the new notion of *semantic integration* because of the development of Semantic Web and semantic web technologies. Semantic integration "*is a process of using a conceptual representation of the data and of their relationships to eliminate heterogeneities*" (Cruz and Xiao 2005). A fundamental principle of semantic data integration is the notion of *ontology* that semantic web uses in order to provide vocabulary (concepts and relationships) and describe the background of a specific domain of knowledge. In addition, ontologies with their concrete, syntactic structure, model the semantics of a given domain in a machine understandable language that offer rich expression of meanings and the ability of reasoning (Jacob 2005; Stasinopoulou et al. 2007).

In this way, the ICOM/CIDOC Documentation Standards Group developed the CIDOC Conceptual Reference Model, an event – oriented model, on September 2000. Since September 2006, it has been accepted as ISO21127. It focuses on promoting the communication between different computer information systems in various cultural institutions (GLAMs), operating as the "*semantic glue*" to mediate different sources of cultural heritage information (CIDOC – CRM, n.d.).

In our study, we focused on practical applications and material documentation of CIDOC – CRM. Firstly, we describe the methodology of this study, in particular the terms of searching and the data sources from which the results were retrieved. Then, we present the available published works on topic to observe the development of the semantic standard over the years. We conclude with interesting findings about the use of CIDOC – CRM from different cultural institutions around the world, the new ways of preserving cultural heritage and the effective interchange between museums, libraries, archives and the other cultural institutions of bibliographic, museum and cultural information.

2 Methodology

2.1 Data Collection and Study

In this short paper we present a scoping review that has followed the Arksey and O'Malley (2005) rules on scoping review studies and it was enriched by the rules of PRISMA – ScR Checklist. We focused on articles published as conference and journals articles regarding the practical applications and material documentation of CIDOC – CRM. The articles were searched in the following bibliographic databases and open access journals: 1) Scopus/Elsevier, 2) ScienceDirect, 3) Springer, 4) Semantic Scholar, 5) CORE Aggregator, 6) Google Scholar, and 7) MDPI Open Access Journals. The exact term "CIDOC – CRM" was mainly preferred as search term, but "CIDOC", "Conceptual Reference Model", "ISO 21127", "semantic ontology" were also included. Due to the large number of retrieved articles in the preliminary stage of searching the following limitations were imposed: 1) the searching terms should be included in the title and/or in the abstract of the articles, 2) the review's time period should be in the decade from 2009 until 2019, 3) the language of the paper should be English, and 4) duplicated titles of articles from different databases were deleted.

3 CIDOC – CRM in Practice

The semantic standard, CIDOC – CRM, was applied in many cultural heritage information cases, both for documentation needs and for covering the users' information needs. It aims to promote the semantic interoperability between different cultural sources of cultural heritage domain and support the semantic data integration residing in heterogeneous data sources. In this way, galleries, libraries, archives, and museums can be identified as a unified whole that preserves, document, manages and shares cultural heritage information in the most effective way.

In the context of data collection, we collected, twenty articles according to the limitations set.

3.1 CIDOC – CRM and CRMdig

Five of the included articles referred both to the usage of CRMdig (CRM digitazation) extension related to the representation and the data documentation of digital objects and the optimization of information retrieval, data mining and provenance propagation processes.

In particular, Amico et al. (2013) applied CIDOC – CRM and its extension CRMdig in order to support the design and the creation of 3D models of cultural objects and to manage the quality of the replicas. Based on the above mentioned semantic standards they modelled all the various stages of digitization process, such as the aim definition, the team group, the location survey, the design and the creation of the repository, the decisions about digitization devices, the scanning procedures and other field operations.

In the same year, Tzompanaki et al. (2013) created and presented a powerful reasoning mechanism based on property propagation and metadata integration as a means to help scientists to search effectively a semantic repository. This mechanism based on CIDOC standard and CRMdig extension in the cultural heritage domain. Moreover, some of the advantages of this implementation are the following: firstly, scientists can find and understand their data sources and secondly, they can reproduce the searching results and enable the quality control of results and processes.

Similarly, Strubulis et al. (2014) presented a case study concerning the provenance information of digital objects through CIDOC – CRM and CRMdig usage. They defined some provenance – based inference rules in order to establish in what way the information propagation can be disseminated over a core conceptual model for provenance representation.

CIDOC – CRM was also used for classification and indexing of complex digital objects, as demonstrated by Enge and Lurk (2014). They presented two case studies, specifically, the film "*Sintel*" (2010) by Colin Levys which can be found in many varied copies in the web and the network-based artwork *"Summer"* (2003) by Olia Lialina. A semantic MediaWiki system was created, known as "*CRM – Wiki*" in which they transferred entities organized in hierarchical wiki categories.

Another study that indicated the practical application of CIDOC – CRM and its CRMdig and CRMinf extension is that of Guillem et al. (2015). They used the aforementioned formal ontologies to model a virtual argumentation reconstruction schema alongside the use of an open – source Drupal database. The purpose of this effort was the optimal access in 3D virtual representations of archaeological monuments giving users, especially in scientific community, the ability to scholarly criticism, knowledge mining and tracing of knowledge provenance in reconstruction of cultural heritage.

3.2 CIDOC – CRM and Intangible Cultural Heritage

Four articles focused on the documentation of intangible cultural heritage. In particular, Tan et al. (2009) applied the CIDOC – CRM ontology in order to document, preserve and bequeath to next generations a kind of a traditional dance, named "Funeral dance", of Tujia, an ethnic minority that used it in their funeral ceremonies. For the knowledge representation, an event – centric approach was selected to describe the entities and properties of "Funeral dance". After that, a modeling and semantic description tool was created, a reasoning tool, namely a plugin inference engine to verify the efficiency of the ontology. In the same way, Hu et al. (2014) based on CIDOC – CRM to create a semantic ontology for documentation of folk customs of Yao ethnic group as it takes place at "Pan Wang Festival" in China. The process involved three main stages: 1) the analysis of concepts, 2) the construction of an ontology, and 3) data storage. The construction of semantic ontology based on five main entities: E2 Temporal Entity, E39 Actor, E52 Time – Span, E53 Place, and E70 Thing. Sharma and Singh (2018) used the semantic standard in order to achieve the cultural mapping of Indian villages with heterogeneous cultural background. In the ontology framework, suitable entities and properties were selected to represent both tangible and intagible views of Indian culture, such as folk dances, music, theatre and rituals. In the same year, Araújo et al. (2018) presented an ontology named OntoMP referred to the Museum of the Person (Museu da Pessoa, MP), a virtual museum that keeps heterogeneous collections of various interviews by people who want to preserve their life stories in perpetuity. The usage of CIDOC – CRM refined with FOAF and DBpedia ontologies contributed to create a conceptual navigation over collections in which museum visitors can navigate in museum's virtual rooms.

3.3 CIDOC – CRM and Archaeology Discipline

Four of the total twenty articles were concerning the archaeology domain and the use of CIDOC – CRM. Binding (2010), at his detailed paper titled *"Implementing archaeological time periods using CIDOC CRM and SKOS"* presented how the semantic ontology can be used to model and represent temporal concepts and relations between archaeological time periods. This effort is included in the STAR (Semantic Technologies for Archaeological Resources) project giving emphasis to the extraction and representation of time period information. Deicke (2016) presented a modeling based on CIDOC – CRM for a standard archaeological catalogue object. An archaeological object can be anything, from an archaeological finding to a location. The contribution of semantic ontology is that it provides to all researchers in the field a common base to document and model archaeological catalogue data. Niccolucci (2017) presented an extension of CIDOC – CRM, the CRMas for research data documentation and mainly for various processes documentation in the archaeology domain. Specifically, CRMas was used to analyze a painted picture in carnivorous discovered in 2008, near Larnaka of Cyprus, during excavation works. The metadata recording of the analysis process in whole was held with CRMas. Lastly, Cantone et al. (2019) presented the semantic ontology named EpiONT based on the CIDOC – CRM and SKOS vocabulary of the EAGLE project (European network of Ancient Greek and Latin Epigraphy). As a practical application, they applied the above ontology to model the *peculiar* features of 580 epigraphs collected from the Castle Ursino Civic Museum in Catania, Sicily.

3.4 CIDOC – CRM and World Cultural Heritage

The ISO standard CIDOC – CRM has a wide range of use in cultural heritage domain in general. Seven papers demonstrated this claim. Scholz (2013) proposed the use of semantic ontology event classes, especially the class *"E5 Event"* and its sub-classes in order to detect events mentioned as free – text in german sources concerning cultural heritage documentation. More specifically, a mapping of event classes to GermaNet, a German wordnet was held, and from this mapping a list of words was compiled, which formed the basis for the creation of an event detection algorithm.

Another semantic standard application comes from Russia and Cherny et al. (2015) who presented the CIDOC – CRM applied as CRM/OWL. They semantically represented the *rmgallery.ru* website, which contains selected artworks choosen for the official mobile application in the context of *"Russian Heritage Cloud project"*. The basic information has coded in RDF triples, the concepts represented in CIDOC – CRM and the authors were connected with links from DBpedia. In addition, the Thesaurus, developed by British Museum and based on SKOS ontology, was re-used.

In the same year, a very interesting study came to be added to the practical application by Haubt (2015), concerning the larger *"Rock Art Database"* (RADB) project. The paper focused on the development of a conceptual reference model for the rock art heritage which was used for the design of a global online platform. In particular, three main systems were created: 1) the Rock Art Database (RADB), a virtual organization that brings together professionals and simple members of rock art in order to share information on this art, 2) the RADB Management System which provides a conceptual Rock Art Reference Model (RARM) with international implementation over all rock art works and use of CIDOC – CRM, 3) the RADB Management System, an online portal of Database which allows users to collect, chat and share information about rock art. Although several problems remain and should be resolved, the study indicated that CIDOC – CRM provides flexibility, so that individual needs can be addressed within a global system.

An extremely interesting implementation of CIDOC – CRM was conducted by Mäkelä et al. (2016) concerning an application which was able to gather a set of different data as Linked Data of persons, events and historical places during the First World War (WW1). This work, named WW1LOD, provided the opportunity to observe how a semantic standard can cover a wide range of materials from different types. The dataset is comprised of 63,807 RDF triples and served as a controlled vocabulary that linked together disparate historical collections and data publications related to WW1. The data organized around the Event (E5) concept underlined the importance of CIDOC – CRM as an event – centric semantic ontology.

Another application that came from Portugal was the case study of the Portuguese National Archives presented by Koch et al. (2019). It concerned the *"ArchOnto"*, a CIDOC – CRM ontology – based model for Archives. In particular, ArchOnto, the new semantic ontology was the result of merging and mapping five different ontologies in which CIDOC – CRM had the primary role. Its flexibility and extensibility decided its selection. The semantic standard documented a great diversity of records, semantically enriched them without losing their meaning. The dataset, also organized over the *"Event"* concept, such as baptism, death and marriage, underlined the event – centric character of CIDOC – CRM.

Morales-del-Castillo et al. (2019) from Mexico presented the development of the *"Mexican Cultural Heritage Data Model"* (MDM), an ontology for the Mexican national cultural aggregator mainly based on CIDOC – CRM.The Mexican "cultural Renaissance" in cultural management and documentation sector was based on the new semantic web technologies and new semantic standard, which created the essential context for cultural heritage object description and information integration.

In the same way, Padfield et al. (2019) worked on documenting, representing and semantic modeling of cultural heritage information and location provenance data from the National Gallery Collection, in London, based on CIDOC – CRM and CRMba. This attempt was one of the four in total cross-cultural pilot projects, which all together, constitute the *CrossCult* project. In particular, the National Gallery of London presents a huge multi – thematic collection consisting of 66 rooms and 2 floors that has been seen as a "Venue" where correlations were made between the museum spaces and the entire museum as a building. In addition, movements of paintings, their previous and current location were semantically recorded providing a location provenance of its collection information.

4 Results

The original searches, outlined in the methodology, produced around 4,949 results, that were initially extracted from the large volume of Google Scholar results, that were around 7,630, that were searched with the exact term "CIDOC – CRM" selecting the option anywhere in the article, without any other restrictions. After refining the process in all sources, 223 articles were retained, in total. After deleting duplicates and imposing date restrictions (2009–2019) and language restrictions (English), we ended up with a set of 73 articles focused on CIDOC – CRM in general. The identified literature was further analyzed and seven themes emerged based on each paper's expressed aim and objectives. The seven themes were the following: 1) theoretical framework of CIDOC – CRM, 2) extensions of CIDOC – CRM, 3) CIDOC – CRM's mappings with other metadata standards and ontologies, 4) CIDOC – CRM and Linked Data, 5) CIDOC – CRM and matter of querying and searching, 6) CIDOC – CRM in digital libraries and museums, and 7) practical applications and material documentation with CIDOC – CRM. Finally, a set of 20 from those articles were selected for our scoping review focused on the last of the abovementioned themes, as shown in Table 1.

Table 1. Selected papers and publication categories according to limitations set and theme.

Kind of paper	Paper	Specific Source	Country
Journal paper	Cantone et al. (2019)	*Archeologia e Calcolatori*	Italy
	Hu et al. (2014)	*Journal of U- and e-Service, Science and Technology*	China
	Mäkelä et al. (2016)	*International Journal on Digital Libraries*	Finland/USA
	Morales-del-Castillo et al. (2019)	*Heritage*	Mexico
	Niccolucci, F. (2017)	*International Journal on Digital Libraries*	Italy
	Padfield et al. (2019)	*Heritage*	UK

(*continued*)

Table 1. (*continued*)

Kind of paper	Paper	Specific Source	Country
	Strubulis et al. (2014)	*International Journal on Digital Libraries*	Greece
Proceedings Paper	Amico et al. (2013)	*CEUR Workshop Proceedings: Workshop Practical Experiences with CIDOC CRM and Its Extensions, CRMEX 2013*	Italy
	Binding (2010)	*ESWC 2010: The Semantic Web: Research and Applications. Lecture Notes in Computer Science*	UK
	Cherny et al. (2015)	*ADBIS 2015: New Trends in Databases and Information Systems. Part of the Communications in Computer and Information Science book series (CCIS, volume 539)*	Russia/Finland/ Germany
	Deicke (2016)	*CEUR Workshop Proceedings: Proceedings of the First Workshop on Digital Humanities and Digital Curation (DHC 2016)*	Germany
	Enge and Lurk (2014)	*Final Program and Proceedings. Archiving*	Germany/Switzerland
	Guillem et al. (2015)	*2015 DigitalHeritage*	Slovenia/Greece
	Haubt (2015)	*ISPRS Annals of the Photogrammetry, Remote Sensing and Spatial Information Sciences*	Australia

(*continued*)

Table 1. (*continued*)

Kind of paper	Paper	Specific Source	Country
	Koch et al. (2019)	*TPDL 2019: Digital Libraries for Open Knowledge*	Portugal
	Scholz (2013)	*CEUR Workshop Proceedings: Workshop Practical Experiences with CIDOC CRM and Its Extensions, CRMEX 2013*	Germany
	Sharma and Singh (2018)	*CEUR Workshop Proceedings: Proceedings of the Third International Workshop on Semantic Web for Cultural Heritage*	India
	Tan et al. (2009)	*2009 s International Symposium on Knowledge Acquisition and Modeling*	China
	Tzompanaki et al. (2013)	*CEUR Workshop Proceedings: Workshop Practical Experiences with CIDOC CRM and Its Extensions, CRMEX 2013*	Greece
Bookchapter	Araújo et al. (2018)	*Developments and Advances in Intelligent Systems and Applications. Studies in Computational Intelligence*	Portugal

5 Conclusion

This scoping review presents some of the applications of CIDOC – CRM in cultural heritage domain during a span of ten years, from 2009 to 2019. The importance of the semantic standard lies on solving semantic interoperability problems and ensuring information exchange and integration between heterogeneous sources of cultural heritage information. Furthermore, the included papers cover a variety of fifteen countries around the world, a fact that demonstrates the potential of the semantic ISO standard and the dissemination of its reputation, due to its flexibility and extensibility with other metadata standards and ontologies. In this context, new paths are opened for cultural heritage documentation, now including both the *digital* and *intangible* cultural heritage documents. Specifically, *intangible* cultural heritage refers to the oral history memories documentation, while *digital* refers to the *traditions, performing acts, social practices, rituals, festive events, knowledge and practices concerning nature and the universe or the knowledge and skills to produce traditional crafts* (UNESCO, Article 2, 2003). Furthermore, the advent and application of CIDOC – CRM optimizes both the querying process and searching results quality, based on reasoning rules and provenance information. Last but not least, the high usefulness of the present semantic standard is underlined by linking spatio – temporal concepts with archaeological or museum space, historical events and cultural heritage domain, in general.

References

Amico, N., Ronzino, P., Felicetti, A., Niccolucci, F.: Quality management of 3D cultural heritage replicas with CIDOC-CRM. In: Alexiev, V., Ivanov, V., Grinberg, M., (eds.) CEUR Workshop Proceedings: Workshop Practical Experiences with CIDOC CRM and Its Extensions, CRMEX 2013, vol. 1117, pp. 61–69. CEUR Workshop Proceedings (2013). http://ceur-ws.org/Vol-1117/

Araújo, C., Martini, R.G., Henriques, P.R., Almeida, J.J.: Annotated documents and expanded CIDOC-CRM ontology in the automatic construction of a virtual museum. In: Rocha, Á., Reis, L.P. (eds.) Developments and Advances in Intelligent Systems and Applications. SCI, vol. 718, pp. 91–110. Springer, Cham (2018). https://doi.org/10.1007/978-3-319-58965-7_7

Arksey, H., O'Malley, L.: Scoping studies: towards a methodological framework. Int. J. Soc. Res. Methodol. **8**(1), 19–32 (2005). https://doi.org/10.1080/1364557032000119616

Binding, C.: Implementing archaeological time periods using CIDOC CRM and SKOS. In: Aroyo, L., et al. (eds.) ESWC 2010. LNCS, vol. 6088, pp. 273–287. Springer, Heidelberg (2010). https://doi.org/10.1007/978-3-642-13486-9_19

Cantone, D., Nicolosi-Asmundo, M., Santamaria, D.F., Cristofaro, S., Spampinato, D., Prado, F.: An EpiDoc ontological perspective: the epigraphs of the Castello UrsinoCivic Museum of Catania via CIDOC CRM. Archeologia e Calcolatori **30**, 139–157 (2019). https://doi.org/10.19282/ac.30.2019.10

Cherny, E., Haase, P., Mouromtsev, D., Andreev, A., Pavlov, D.: Application of CIDOC-CRM for the Russian heritage cloud platform. In: Morzy, T., Valduriez, P., Bellatreche, L. (eds.) ADBIS 2015. CCIS, vol. 539, pp. 448–457. Springer, Cham (2015). https://doi.org/10.1007/978-3-319-23201-0_45

CIDOC – CRM Conceptual Reference Model. What is the CIDOC CRM? https://www.cidoc-crm.org/. Accessed 13 May 2022

Cruz, I.F., Xiao, H.: The role of ontologies in data integration. J. Eng. Intell. Syst. 13(4), 1–18 (2005). https://citeseerx.ist.psu.edu/viewdoc/download?doi=10.1.1.60.4933&rep=rep1&type=pdf

Deicke, A.: CIDOC CRM-based modeling of archaeological catalogue data. In: de Luca, E.W., Bianchini, P., (eds.) CEUR Workshop Proceedings: Proceedings of the First Workshop on Digital Humanities and Digital Curation (DHC 2016), vol. 1764, pp. 37–47 (2016). http://ceur-ws.org/Vol-1764/

Doerr, M.: Handbook on Ontologies. In: Staab, S., Studer, R., (eds.) Handbook on Ontologies. 2nd edn, pp. 463–486. Springer, Heidelberg (2009). https://doi.org/10.1007/978-3-540-92673-3

Enge, J., Lurk, T.: Classification and indexing of complex digital objects with CIDOC CRM. Final Program Proc. Arch. **2014**, 58–62 (2014)

Guillem, A., Zarnic, R., Bruseker, G.: Building an argumentation platform for 3D reconstruction using CIDOC-CRM and Drupal. In: 2015 Digital Heritage, pp. 383–386 (2015). https://doi.org/10.1109/digitalheritage.2015.7419529

Haubt, R.A.: The global rock art database: developing a rock art reference model for the RADB system using the CIDOC CRM and Australian heritage examples. In: Yen, Y.N., Weng, K.H., Cheng, H.M. (eds.) ISPRS Annals of the Photogrammetry, Remote Sensing and Spatial Information Sciences, pp. 89–96. Copernicus GmbH (2015). https://doi.org/10.5194/isprsannals-ii-5-w3-89-2015

Hu, J., Lv, Y., Zhang, M.: The ontology design of intangible cultural heritage based on CIDOC CRM. Int. J. u- and e- Serv. Sci. Technol. **7**(1), 261–274 (2014). https://doi.org/10.14257/ijunesst.2014.7.1.24

Jacob, E.K.: Ontologies and the semantic web. Bull. Am. Soc. Inf. Sci. Technol. **29**(4), 19–22 (2005). https://doi.org/10.1002/bult.283

Koch, I., Freitas, N., Ribeiro, C., Lopes, C.T., da Silva, J.R.: Knowledge graph implementation of archival descriptions through CIDOC-CRM. In: Doucet, A., Isaac, A., Golub, K., Aalberg, T., Jatowt, A. (eds.) TPDL 2019. LNCS, vol. 11799, pp. 99–106. Springer, Cham (2019). https://doi.org/10.1007/978-3-030-30760-8_8

Lenzerini, M.: Data integration: a theoretical perspective. In: Proceedings of the Twenty-First ACM SIGMOD-SIGACT-SIGART Symposium on Principles of Database Systems – PODS 2002 (2002). https://doi.org/10.1145/543613.543644

Lusenet, Y.D.: Tending the garden or harvesting the fields: digital preservation and the UNESCO charter on the preservation of the digital heritage. Libr. Trends **56**(1), 164–182 (2007). https://doi.org/10.1353/lib.2007.0053

Mäkelä, E., Törnroos, J., Lindquist, T., Hyvönen, E.: WW1LOD: an application of CIDOC-CRM to World War 1 linked data. Int. J. Digit. Libr. **18**(4), 333–343 (2016). https://doi.org/10.1007/s00799-016-0186-2

Morales-del-Castillo, J., Ángeles Jiménez, P., Molina Salinas, C.: Mexico's tradition and culture entering the digital age: the Mexican cultural heritage repository project. Heritage **2**(1), 356–365 (2019). https://doi.org/10.3390/heritage2010024

Niccolucci, F.: Documenting archaeological science with CIDOC CRM. Int. J. Digit. Libr. **18**(3), 223–231 (2017). https://doi.org/10.1007/s00799-016-0199-x

Padfield, J., Kontiza, K., Bikakis, A., Vlachidis, A.: Semantic representation and location provenance of cultural heritage information: the national gallery collection in London. Heritage **2**(1), 648–665 (2019). https://doi.org/10.3390/heritage2010042

Scholz, M.A.: Mapping of CIDOC CRM events to German Wordnet for event detection in Texts. In: Alexiev, V., Ivanov, V., Grinberg, M., (eds.) CEUR Workshop Proceedings: Workshop Practical Experiences with CIDOC CRM and Its Extensions, CRMEX 2013, vol. 1117, pp. 1–10 (2013). http://ceur-ws.org/Vol-1117/

Sharma, T., Singh, N.: Cultural mapping of villages in India using CIDOC-CRM. In: Bikakis, A., Jean, S., Markhoff, B., Mosca, A., (eds.) CEUR Workshop Proceedings: Proceedings of the Third International Workshop on Semantic Web for Cultural Heritage, vol. 2094 (2018). http://ceur-ws.org/Vol-2094/

Stasinopoulou, T., et al.: Ontology-based metadata integration in the cultural heritage domain. In: Goh, D.-L., Cao, T.H., Sølvberg, I.T., Rasmussen, E. (eds.) ICADL 2007. LNCS, vol. 4822, pp. 165–175. Springer, Heidelberg (2007). https://doi.org/10.1007/978-3-540-77094-7_25

Strubulis, C., Flouris, G., Tzitzikas, Y., Doerr, M.: A case study on propagating and updating provenance information using the CIDOC CRM. Int. J. Digit. Libr. **15**(1), 27–51 (2014). https://doi.org/10.1007/s00799-014-0125-z

Tan, G., Sun, C., Zhong, Z.: Knowledge representation of "funeral dance" based on CIDOC CRM. In: 2009 Second International Symposium on Knowledge Acquisition and Modeling, pp. 39–42 (2009). https://doi.org/10.1109/kam.2009.163

Tzompanaki, K., Doerr, M., Theodoridou, M., Fundulaki, I.: Reasoning based on property propagation on CIDOC-CRM and CRMdig based repositories. In: Alexiev, V., Ivanov, V., Grinberg, M., (eds.) CEUR Workshop Proceedings: Workshop Practical Experiences with CIDOC CRM and Its Extensions, CRMEX 2013, vol. 1117, pp. 37–47(2013). http://ceur-ws.org/Vol-1117/

UNESCO Charter on the Preservation of the Digital Heritage (2003). https://unesdoc.unesco.org/ark:/48223/pf0000179529. Accessed 21 Sept 2022

UNESCO Basic Texts of the 2002 Convention for the Safeguarding of the Intangible Cultural Heritage. Cultural heritage (2003). https://ich.unesco.org/doc/src/2003_Convention_Basic_Texts-_2020_version-EN.pdf. Accessed 21 Sept 2022

Track on Digital Libraries, Information Retrieval, Big, Linked, Social & Open Data, and Metadata, Linked Data, Semantics and Ontologies - General Session

Towards Addressing the Cultural Snapshot Phenomenon in Cultural Mapping Libraries

Spiridon Mousouris(✉) and Evangelia Kavakli

Department of Cultural Technology and Communication, University of the Aegean, Mitilini, Greece

{spirosmousouris,kavakli}@aegean.gr

Abstract. This paper focuses on Digital Libraries that geovisualize cultural data, highlighting the need to define them as a separate category termed "Cultural Mapping Libraries", based on the culture-location connection to represent cultural data on a map. An exploratory analysis of Digital Libraries conforming to that definition brought forward the observation that existing Digital Libraries fail to geovisualize the entirety of cultural data per point of interest, resulting in a phenomenon we termed Cultural Snapshot. This phenomenon was confirmed by the results of a systematic bibliographic research. To address it, this paper proposes the use of the Semantic Web principles to efficiently interconnect spatial cultural data through time, per geographic location. This way, points of interest transform into scenery where culture evolves over time. This evolution is expressed as events over time, in an event-oriented manner, endorsed by the CIDOC Conceptual Reference Model (CRM). We posit the use of CIDOC CRM as the baseline for defining the logic of Cultural Mapping Libraries as part of the Culture Domain in accordance with the Digital Library Reference Model, in order to define the rules of cultural data management by the system. Our future goal is to transform this conceptual definition in to inferencing rules that resolve the Cultural Snapshot, supporting a more complete geovisualization of cultural data.

Keywords: Digital Libraries · Semantic Web · Geovisualization · Cultural Informatics · CIDOC-CRM

1 Introduction

Maps help us understand the "where" of Cultural Heritage. Braudel in [2] emphasizes the dependence of culture to the benefits of a geographical area, while noting that the challenges of the latter characterize human habits. Marking data on a map traces how people interact with an area [1]. According to [4], digital interactive maps are transformed into ergocentric spaces, focusing on actions instead of consuming data, realizing a plethora of scenarios. In addition, a map supports knowledge extraction by assisting visual thinking and conveying the creator's message by revealing patterns because of its graphic nature [5]. Users of the same map can extract different meanings, depending on their perspectives and skills [5]. Thus maps topologically re-organize narration, a claim also supported by [4].

E. Garoufallou and A. Vlachidis (Eds.): MTSR 2022, CCIS 1789, pp. 109–121, 2023.
https://doi.org/10.1007/978-3-031-39141-5_10

Digital Libraries (DLs) play an important role in managing cultural data. They have evolved from traditional libraries with the integration of information technologies. This evolution varies, depending on their audience. As a result, terms such as digital archive, digital collection and repository are used interchangeably to describe organised collections of digital information that share common functions, such as "search" and "browse".

Yet, by combining the definitions provided in [10, 16] and the working definition of Digital Library provided in [19], a set of common characteristics is outlined. DLs are defined as online platforms, providing knowledge for a subject or subjects, offering at least search and information accessing functionalities. They are charged with gathering, preserving, visualizing and disseminating data. Providing a complete picture of their subject, is an essential service of DLs and to this end, they often rely on multiple external sources for collecting data. Lastly, DLs offer means to extract knowledge or interpret the data.

We focus on DLs that contain data about culture. We define "cultural data" as data referring to all human material and spiritual achievements [3], as well as testimonies of the tangible and intangible cultural heritage [17, 18]. Since culture is related to location which can be depicted on maps, we define "geographic cultural data" as cultural data that also refer to geospatial elements and include at least a set of coordinates that comply with a universal geospatial standard.

Since everyone can publish on the Internet [6], DLs move to the centre of information publishing and archiving. They are the medium between identity, memory and research, ensuring social sustainability. DLs motivate communities to archive their cultural data, while guiding and providing infrastructure for knowledge interpretation. The above, along with the popularity of geospatial tools, led DLs that contain geographical cultural data to use maps to present and categorize them in a structured way [9].

In a DL we define Points of Interest (POIs) as the locations contained in geographical cultural data. We argue that the evolution of culture over time for a POI is represented by different geographical cultural data, referring the same location. These data represent different POI states over time. In most DLs, POIs are identified and represented in their current state or one that is considered important. This creates an incomplete geovisualization, as other states are not rendered. Such incomplete data modelling hides the relationships between the different states of the same POI or between states of different POIs. The POI states which are not located on the map are either found as secondary information in secondary elements in the interface or are completely absent. We term this phenomenon as "Cultural Snapshot". It has a negative impact on a maps' ability to visualize knowledge and actualize interactions. It stands in contrast with the need for DLs to present their content unbiased, as opposed to other apps that by definition have to favour a part of their data in order to narrate.

In a previous study we studied DLs that geovisualize geographical cultural data and proposed the definition of Cultural Mapping Libraries (CMLs) [7]. CMLs were defined as DLs that geovisualize and interpret geographical cultural data, using an interactive map as the main interface element. The definition of a CML is based on the Digital Library Reference Model (DLRM) [16], a modular reference model that defines interconnected domains that describe a DL and their relationships. For a complete CML description, we proposed the introduction of the Cultural Domain, as a complementary domain, summarizing the concepts describing the geographical cultural data, and the mechanisms for their interconnection and visualization.

This paper focuses on the "Cultural Snapshot" phenomenon, and puts forward an approach towards its resolution based on the semantic web principles. The rest of the paper is organized as follows: Sect. 2 presents the bibliographic research conducted, whose results confirm the existence of the Cultural Snapshot. Section 3 discuss how the outcomes of the research affect the CML and the Cultural Domain definitions. The latter is further elaborated as a CML-specific domain. It is suggested that incorporating Semantic Web principles in it will resolve the Cultural Snapshot phenomenon. This event-centric idea is aligned with the CIDOC-CRM model [20], which is used to express the CML logic and detect Cultural Snapshot phenomena. Section 4 concludes this paper and briefly discusses the next stages of our research.

2 Research for Geovisualizing Geographical Cultural Data in Digital Libraries

2.1 Research Methodology

To confirm the existence of the Cultural Snapshot we performed an exploratory review, in order to discover relevant DL literature and identify key concepts that inform current practice, adapting the "Systematic mapping study" process described in [26]. Based on this process, the first step has been the "Definition of Research Questions", aiming to focus on the Cultural Snapshot phenomenon and reflect how DLs treat geographical cultural data and communicate them to their users. These research questions are: RQ1: "What the geographical cultural data contained in the DL are about?", RQ2: "When geovisualized, are the geographical cultural data interconnected?", RQ3: "Are there different states for each POI?", RQ4: "Are different states for each POI interconnected?", RQ5: "Do the maps and their data follow universal geospatial standards?", Research Question 6: "Is the map the main element of the UI from which users get answers for their questions?".

RQ1 explores the type of cultural data that is managed and geovisualised by the DLs. RQ2, RQ3 and RQ4 help us identify the Cultural Snapshot phenomenon. If the answer in all three questions is "no" then that phenomenon exists in that DL. If the answer in all three questions is "yes" then that phenomenon does not exist in that DL. If the answers in these three questions vary between "yes" and "no", then there is an attempt to address it. RQ5 helps us understand if it is possible to perform geospatial queries in a DL, creating a more effective interaction and geovisualization and an effective representation of knowledge. RQ6 checks if the map is the main UI element, a basic characteristic of CMLs.

During the next step "Conduct Search for Primary Studies", we performed a keywords-based search in indexed online scientific repositories (namely IEEE, ACM, Science Direct, Springer) since they have high impact factors and contain a large volume of articles and publications, constantly updated, relevant to information technology, web applications, (geo) visualization, digital libraries and semantic data. The combination of keywords aimed to identify published papers about DLs that geovisualize and interconnect geographical cultural data, so that we can extract information about their technologies and logic. Since the space-time cube visualization presents a continuum of data per location, we also searched for publications that discussed it. We avoided general terms such as "map" or "GIS" that resulted to publications from other fields and domains. The outcomes of this step are available in Table 1 and Table 2.

Table 1. Search strings

Repository	Filters	Keyword combinations
IEEE	In all metadata, 2011–2021	semantic web, library, map
		linked open data, cultural heritage, map
		cultural heritage, semantic web, linked open data, web maps
ACM	from: The ACM Guide to Computing Literature, Search Within: anywhere, 2011–2021	geohumanities, digital library, semantic web
Springer	with all of the words, 2011–2021	digital libraries, cultural heritage, linked data, geovisualization
		digital libraries, culture, linked data, GIS (within Conference Papers)
Science Direct	Quick search form field Find articles with these terms, 2011–2021	digital humanities, linked data, library, GIS

Table 2. Search strings including space-time cube

Repository	Filters	Keyword combinations
ACM	from: The ACM Guide to Computing Literature, Search Within: anywhere, 2011–2021 (sort by relevance)	space time cube, library, cultural heritage, semantic web, linked data
Springer	with all of the words, 2011–2021 (within Chapters)	space-time cube, digital cultural heritage, semantic web, linked data
Science Direct	Quick search form field Find articles with these terms, 2011–2021, Social Sciences and Computer Science as Subject areas	space-time cube, library, cultural heritage, semantic web, linked data
IEEE	search terms in all metadata, 2011–2021	space time cube, library, digital humanities, semantic web, linked data

For the next step "Screening of Papers for Inclusion and Exclusion", we selected articles based on their relevance reflected in their title, keywords and abstract. If in doubt the paper's introductions and conclusions were also screened. To conduct further examination, a paper had to discuss a DL geovisualizing geographical cultural data, interconnecting them using semantic web principles, analyzing or presenting an implementation, otherwise it was excluded. The numerical results of paper screening are shown in Table 3[1].

Table 3. Search results

Repository	Results	Selected
IEEE	28	0
ACM	45	2
Springer	120	3
ScienceDirect	82	0

The "Classification Scheme", in the next step was built in accordance to whether the selected studies address or not the Cultural Snapshot phenomenon (as discussed in step 1). Finally, during the next and last step "Data Extraction and Mapping of Studies", we extracted information related to our research questions. With respect to RQ5, if an implementation link was provided in the publication, we visited it and explored it as end users, to examine the UI. If there was no implementation, we studied the concept presented.

In addition, to the above research articles we also studied DLs that geovisualize geographical cultural data, that we found using online search engines. These are the following: Ariadne Portal, Pluggy Pins, Arches (Demo), Historypin and Map your heritage. We examined those as end users, studying their UI and UX, aiming to discover the Cultural Snapshot phenomenon and if and how it is addressed.

2.2 Results

An initial observation is that there is a growing number of DLs proposing new ways of organizing and presenting cultural data through the geographical context, supporting the need to define CMLs as a separate DL category. At the same time research in the area is fragmented, something that is reinforced by the fact that we had to search with various sets of keywords to find DLs that geovisualize geographical cultural data.

For each of the ten included DLs we analysed them according to the 6 research questions defined in the previous section. The results are summarized in Table 4. As shown in this Table all the DLs that were studied use a map as the main UI element (RQ6) allowing users to explore data using geospatial queries (RQ5). Regarding the cultural focus of the DLs (RQ1) we can observe that the majority (7/10) focus on cultural heritage, whilst less (3/10) focus on historical data. Finally, 4/10 explicitly address the temporal aspect of geographical cultural data.

[1] An indicative list can be found here: https://docs.google.com/spreadsheets/d/12JKXskMV42B7oUkhmM5ELbZCzxVMd-A4D-EPY7lt-hM/edit?usp=sharing.

Regarding the Cultural Snapshot phenomenon, our findings support the observation that independent of their geographical cultural data, how they model them, interconnect and geovisualize them, the entirety of the POIs states is not geovisualized, since none of the studied DLs has Yes in all three relevant questions (RQ2, RQ3 and RQ4). Indicatively, only Space-Time Cube, A Visualization Tool for Landscape Changes [12] and SILKNOWViz: Spatio-Temporal Data Ontology Viewer [15] have Yes in research questions RQ2 and RQ4. We thus conclude, that that the Cultural Snapshot phenomenon is not fully resolved.

Table 4. Comparative analysis of DLs

Digital Library	RQ1	RQ2	RQ3	RQ4	RQ5	RQ6
Ariadne Portal [21]	Archaeological datasets	No	No	No	Yes	Yes
Pluggy Pins [22]	European cultural heritage	No	No	No	Yes	Yes
Arches [23]	Worldwide natural and cultural heritage	Yes	No	No	Yes	Yes
Historypin [24]	Crowdsourced stories linked to tangible or intangible elements of cultural heritage	No	Yes	No	Yes	Yes
Map your heritage [25]	Cultural heritage in European coastal and maritime regions	Yes	No	No	Yes	Yes
Milano Attraverso [11, 28]	Cultural heritage of Milan	No	No	No	Yes	Yes
Space-Time Cube-A Visualization Tool for Landscape Changes [12]	Spatiotemporal data of cultural heritage sites	Yes	Yes	No	Yes	Yes
Semantically geo-annotating an ancient Greek "travel guide" [13, 27]	Spatiotemporal archaeological data	Yes	No	No	Yes	Yes
Linked Places in World Historical Gazetteer [14]	Historical place data	No	No	No	Yes	Yes
SILKNOWViz: Spatio-Temporal Data Ontology Viewer [15]	Spatiotemporal data of silk heritage	Yes	Yes	No	Yes	Yes

2.3 Discussion

The results of our study confirm the existence of the Cultural Snapshot phenomenon. DLs do not take full advantage of the geographical cultural data interconnections and the ability of maps to extract knowledge and reveal patterns. Whilst, some DLs support the interconnection of geographical cultural data based on the principles of the semantic web (e.g., [13, 14]), it is expected that each implementation determines its own way of presenting geographical cultural data. Therefore, a common logic upon which different implementations will base the geovisualization and effective interconnections of geographical cultural data, is still missing.

Regarding the representation of cultural data some DLs propose the use of a specific conceptual model, such as the CIDOC-CRM (e.g., [15]) for the representation of cultural data, but even then, the evolution of states over time for each POI is not considered, limiting the opportunities for user exploration, making geovisualization insufficient, as the cultural and geographical layers connection is not fully presented.

For example, the geovisualization of different states for each POI could be used in the Ariadne Portal [21] to show the evolution of archaeological data over time per location. Accordingly, Milano Attraverso [11] could geovisualize the related POIs it displays in text. In addition, we notice that there is no common way of presenting the time axis in relation to geographical cultural data, while in many cases it is not presented at all (e.g., in Map your Heritage [25]). We usually find time as a search filter or slider that defines a timespan (Milano Attraverso [11]) but it is rarely depicted with the geographical cultural data of a POI.

With respect to inter-POI relationships, the majority of the DLs we have studied, each connects the POIs according to its own internal logic or not at all, while multiple readings offered by the maps are ignored since there is only one state per POI. In particular, the platforms we have studied simply present on the map POIs related to a selected onebased on specific features (Ariadne Portal [21]). Even in these cases, simply presenting additional POIs on the map, without any other visual clue or symbol, does not give to the end user a complete context of how or why POIs are connected. For example, Arches [23] could also combine the data graphs it contains, along with its maps, to geovisualize the connections contained in the graphs, geospatially charging them. We also find connections in the case of routes and tours (Pluggy Pins [22], Map your Heritage [25]), but it is a choice based on the needs of the routes to connect geospatially close POIs, rather than based on POI relevance.

Nevertheless, there exist attempts to model the spatio-temporal context and present interconnections of geographical cultural data, either conceptually, geographically or both. Milano Attraverso [11] based on the assertion that "spatial representation is not neutral" and commenting that maps suggest a social interpretation for an area, provides layers with older maps. Historypin [24] presents different states over time for a POI, combining Google Street View with historical photos, but this is limited to two states, while it does not interconnect states from different POIs. By using the Space-time cube approach, [12] manages to present more states over time but only for one POI. While the interconnections are not based on linked data, it is an interesting attempt to render change over time. SILKNOWviz [15], based on CIDOC-CRM is interested in presenting changes over time per POI with a method similar to space-time cube. It contains 3 elevated maps representing different time intervals. End users click on a POI, and relationships with other POIs are visualized. Periegesis [13] geovisualizes the journey of Pausanias, focusing on the relationships between space and time. Aiming at finding references of different time periods and locations in the Pausanias corpus, their examination and understanding can be based on the chosen point of view by the end user.

Finally, we note a tendency to use "event" or "snapshot" as a unit of measurement of the evolution of geographical cultural data over time in order for them to be geovisualized. This is observed in [12] and Periegesis [13], where "event" is used to analyse space-time and in the World Historical Gazetteer [14], where connections are based on historical phenomena, objects and events. The aforementioned observations suggest that the way DLs that geovisualize geographical cultural data evolve, is at a point that a common logic for interconnecting cultural data is needed and can be supported.

3 Extending the Definition of CMLs

The above observations for detecting and resolving the Cultural Snapshot phenomenon, has motivated the extension of the previous definition of CMLs and to the re-examination of the objectives of the Culture Domain as defined in [7]. The new CML definition is: "a DL that contains geographical cultural data about tangible and/or intangible culture and uses an interactive map based on universal geospatial standards, as the main channel and interface element for the geovisualization of the entirety of the states every POI has over time, based on the entirety of interconnections between geographical cultural data".

Based on the DLRM reference model [16], a CML can be described as a set of connected Organization Domains that are common to all DLs and they focus on a specific aspect of a DL such as the Functionality Domain, the Architecture Domain and the User Domain. Considering the characteristics of CMLs, the Functionality and Architecture Domain must include a map, based on a universal projection system and a geospatial standard, that are used to design a CML supporting geospatial queries and calculations. Those support the interpretation of geographical cultural data. These Domains together with the User Domain determine how a CML UI and UX are designed. CMLs do not dictate the use of a specific implementation technology, since CMLs introduce a common logic and not technical restrictions. Each CML contains different geographical cultural data with different implementation needs.

The DLRM model allows the definition of Complementary Domains, which are necessary for studying a system, being the point where extensions can be added, depending on the nature of the system into consideration. The CML Complementary Domain is the Culture Domain. It is the set of geographical cultural data contained in a CML together with the set of mechanisms that visualize them and the mechanisms that interconnect them. Since all the Domains influence each other [16], we argue that the Cultural Domain changes per CML and influences its character, according to the data it contains, and their geovisualization needs. This is also supported by our research results, since each DL has its own characteristics, but the need for sufficient geographical cultural data interconnection based on a common logic is a common need for all. This also agrees with Roth's argument [5] that a specific, universal geovisualization solution does not make sense.

As in any DLRM Domain, the concepts and objects of the Culture Domain are related to those of other Domains. For example, it brings together the Architectural Components of the Architecture Domain and the Functions of the Functionality Domain that relate to the interconnection and geovisualization of geographical cultural data. Similarly, it relates to the Information Objects of the Content Domain that are geographical cultural data and the Actor's Actions of the User Domain related to geographical cultural data, their searching and browsing. The Culture Domain determines how all the above elements are interconnected, containing the CML way of thinking.

3.1 Cultural Domain and the Semantic Web

The Cultural Snapshot phenomenon is part of the Cultural Domain, as it relates to geographical cultural data and the way their states and interconnections are geovisualized. Since CMLs define and refer to DLs that geovisualize geographical cultural data, they can introduce a common solution to address the Cultural Snapshot phenomenon.

By incorporating Semantic Web principles in CMLs through the Culture Domain we can address the Cultural Snapshot phenomenon. The semantic web introduces a way to reason based on data relationships, offering a way to extract knowledge about culture, rooted in meaning and context. Semantic web is flexible enough so as not to enforce a single solution or implementation. Its principles help to establish a common way of thinking on how to define cultural data interconnections based on the entirety of POI states. Semantic web deals with the massiveness of data, an attribute also commented in [9] and [6]. Semantic web also establishes a way to manage a plethora of interconnections and introducing stability in data interconnections, so reasoning is always achieved [8].

3.2 POIs as Scenery

From a CML end user's perspective, the Cultural Snapshot phenomenon can be characterized as a gulf of evaluation issue, as defined in [5]: difference between what gets presented to the end user and what the user expected to receive, after submitting a query. Even if we accept that the end user cannot always know the richness of a CML's content, cultural snapshot limits its geovisualization abilities, limiting user's interpretation. This is rooted in the lack of a unified CML way of thinking to support the connection and presentation of its data. It also supports our intention to utilize semantic web reasoning to answer user questions and resolve the Cultural Snapshot phenomenon. This could erase the gulf of evaluation, by suggesting a universal way to present and interconnect data.

Based on the discussion so far, we argue that the solution is the Culture Domain to view POIs as a scenery for cultural events over time. Event-oriented data capture moments in time and transmit processes, as [8] also discusses about archival records. Each event is a new POI state, connected to others, either in the same POI or in others. Events can be enablers of other events, creating an event chain for each POI, a scenery of actions. This transforms POIs from simple elements to interactive and interconnected objects, an active part of the UI that carries the CML mindset. The semantic web, specifically Linked Data reasoning, manages the connections between events deducing facts where needed. It is a common structure where cultural data from different sources can complement each other, to make a rich geovisualization. By combining those facts with the remarks about event-oriented records in [8], the event-centered CML logic makes geographical cultural data independent from their initial captured form and creator. They do not carry the specifics of a form, the focus is now on their meaning, their structure and their relationships network.

In addition, the event-centered CML logic can be mapped onto the CIDOC-CRM a widely accepted model for the definition and formal description of the implicit and explicit concepts and relationships used in cultural heritage information. CIDOC-CRM can help us describe events, since it allows one to view data from a perspective based on events, actors, space and time. It is a tool for ensuring interoperability at the semantic level and the first step for introducing CML logic to researchers. The diagram in Fig. 1 is a first approach to depict the CML logic using the CIDOC-CRM model.

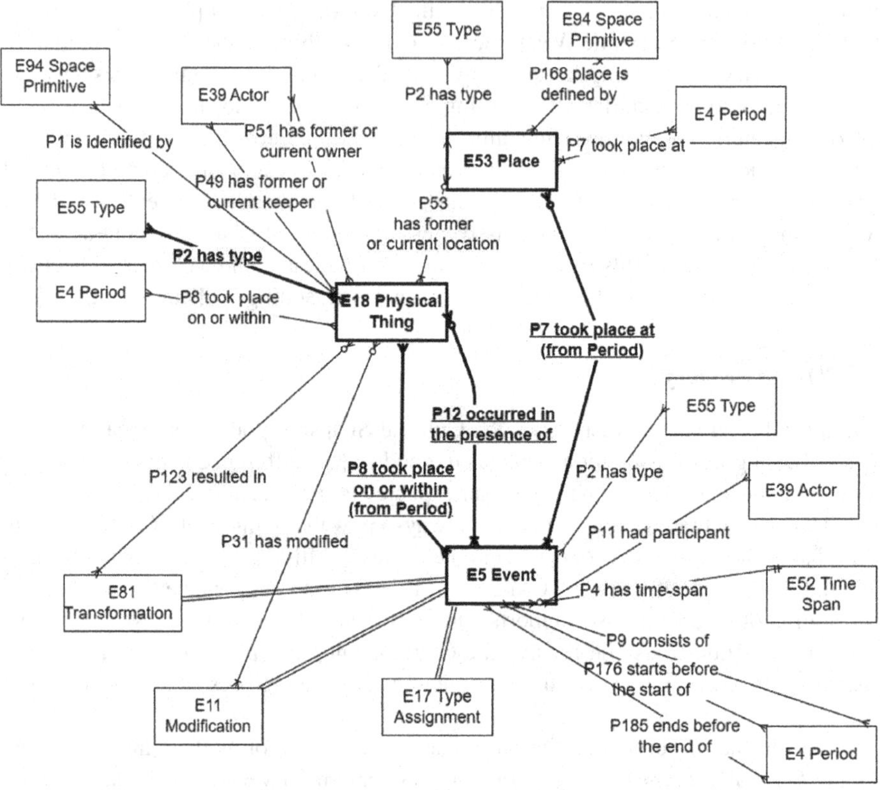

Fig. 1. Conceptual description of the CML geographical cultural data

The basic classes are the E5 Event which happened either in an E53 Place or in an E18 Physical Thing, for example a building or construction. The properties between these classes define their relationships. Through properties and inheritance, we define the relationship between event and space for each POI. E53 Place and E18 Physical Thing are characterized by an E94 Space Primitive containing coordinates. Actors (E93 Actors) are participants in Events. E5 Events that happened during an E4 Period can change the E55 Type of an E53 Place or an E18 Physical Thing. This also marks the change of state in a POI. For example, an E81 Transformation that is a subclass of the E5 Event may have occurred in a building (E18 Physical Thing) and changed its Architectural Type (E55 Type), signalling a new use, and thus a new POI state. E81 Transformation inherits

its properties through E5 Event, so it took place in an E4 Period, it has its own E55 Type and an E39 Actor participated in it. This is how we capture in CIDOC-CRM the POI as scenery logic.

CIDOC-CRM also helps us capture the cultural snapshot: if an application does not store the multiple events that occurred in a POI or does not save the changes in its properties, such as the Type, then the cultural snapshot phenomenon appears, because not all POI states are stored. Based on CIDOC-CRM as a guide for semantic compatibility between data, we can identify Events, Actors, Space and Time, to identify the appropriate interconnections and arrive at a more efficient geovisualization.

4 Conclusions

This paper focuses on the field of digital libraries and aims to improve the way they interconnect and geovisualize their geographical cultural data. In particular, it proposes how to address the Cultural Snapshot phenomenon occurring when DLs that geovisualize geographical cultural data do not interconnect and successfully geovisualize the entirety of geographical cultural data a Point Of Interest contains.

In this context, it reconsiders the definition of Cultural Mapping Libraries as a specific category of DLs containing geographical cultural data, as well as the logic of the Culture Domain describing the mechanisms of interconnection and geovisualization of geographical cultural data based on the Semantic Web. We argue that a CML-wide, Semantic Web reasoning-based logic will support the CML research, proposing new ways of organizing and presenting geographical cultural data, regardless of the technology of implementation of each CML.

A common logic among CMLs focuses on finding the events contained in a data set. The events include both the place and the time that were observed, thus representing the cultural evolution for each POI. This logic turns a POI into a scenery of cultural evolution over time. To describe events in geographical cultural data, we propose the use of CIDOC-CRM, a conceptual model for event-focused semantic interoperability. As the events can refer to both the tangible and the intangible culture, they expand the possibilities of CMLs to present a representative picture of the culture of an area.

The present work focused on conceptually addressing the cultural snapshot phenomenon through the semantic interconnection of the "POIs as scenery" logic, that determines the modelling of the geographical cultural data of CMLs. In the next stages of our research, we will focus on semantic web reasoning, composing rules that will help us inference facts about the CML data, in order to interconnect POI states. Those rules must be applicable to all CMLs, without being too restrictive to enforce one solution.

References

1. Eagleton, T.: The Idea of Culture. Polis Publications, Athens (2003). Translated by Magklinis H
2. Braudel, F.: Grammaire des Civilisations, pp. 52–72. National Bank of Greece Cultural Foundation, Athens (2005). Translated by Aleksakis A., 4th reprint

3. Pessoa, J., Deloumeaux, L., Ellis, S.: UNESCO Framework for Cultural Statistics (FCS). UNESCO Institute for Statistics (UIS), Montreal (2009)
4. Abend, P., Harvey, F.: Maps as geomedial action spaces: considering the shift from logocentric to egocentric engagements. GeoJournal **82**(1), 171–183 (2015). https://doi.org/10.1007/s10708-015-9673-z
5. Roth, R.E.: Interactive maps: "what we know and what we need to know." J. Spatial Inf. Sci. **6**, 59–115 (2013). https://doi.org/10.5311/JOSIS.2013.6.105
6. Stogner, M.B.: Searching for Aristotle in the digital age: creating cultural narrative with 21st century media technologies. Int. J. New Media Technol. Arts **8**(1), 11–21 (2014). https://doi.org/10.18848/2326-9987/CGP/v08i01/11-21
7. Mousouris, S., Styliaras, G.: The research development of cultural mapping libraries. In: 2018 9th International Conference on Information, Intelligence, Systems and Applications (IISA), Zakynthos, Greece, pp. 1–6 (2018). https://doi.org/10.1109/IISA.2018.8633684
8. Anderson, K.: The footprint and the stepping foot: archival records, evidence, and time. Arch. Sci. **13**(4), 349–371 (2012). https://doi.org/10.1007/s10502-012-9193-2
9. Manovich, L.: Cultural data: possibilities and limitations of the digital data universe. In: Museum and Archive on the Move. Changing Cultural Institutions in the Digital Era, pp. 259–276. De Gruyter, Berlin, Boston (2017)
10. Candela, L., et al.: The DELOS Digital Library Reference Model. Foundations for Digital Libraries. DELOS: A Network of Excellence on Digital Libraries (2007)
11. Bollini, L.: Representing a space-based digital archive on historical maps: a user-centered design approach. In: Luigini, A. (ed.) EARTH 2018. AISC, vol. 919, pp. 599–607. Springer, Cham (2019). https://doi.org/10.1007/978-3-030-12240-9_62
12. Bogucka, E.P., Jahnke, M.: Space-time cube—a visualization tool for landscape changes. J. Cartogr. Geogr. Inf. **67**, 183–191 (2017)
13. Foka, A., et al.: Semantically geo-annotating an ancient Greek "travel guide" itineraries, chronotopes, networks, and linked data. In: Proceedings of the 4th ACM SIGSPATIAL Workshop on Geospatial Humanities (GeoHumanities 2020), pp. 1–9. Association for Computing Machinery, New York (2020). https://doi.org/10.1145/3423337.3429433
14. Grossner, K., Mostern, R.: Linked places in world historical gazetteer. In: Proceedings of the 5th ACM SIGSPATIAL International Workshop on Geospatial Humanities (GeoHumanities 2021), pp. 40–43. Association for Computing Machinery, New York (2021). https://doi.org/10.1145/3486187.3490203
15. Sevilla, J., Portalés, C., Gimeno, J., Sebastián, J.: SILKNOWViz: spatio-temporal data ontology viewer. In: Rodrigues, J.M.F., et al. (eds.) ICCS 2019. LNCS, vol. 11540, pp. 97–109. Springer, Cham (2019). https://doi.org/10.1007/978-3-030-22750-0_8
16. Candela, L., et al.: DL.org The Digital Library Reference Model. DL.org (2011). http://bscw.research-infrastructures.eu/pub/bscw.cgi/d222816/D3.2b%20Digital%20Library%20Reference%20Model.pdf. Accessed 27 Apr 2021
17. UNESCOa, Convention for the Protection of Cultural Property in the Event of Armed Conflict, 14 May 1954: UN Educational, Scientific and Cultural Organisation (UNESCO). https://unesdoc.unesco.org/ark:/48223/pf0000082464. Accessed 31 Jan 2021
18. UNESCOb, Text of the Convention for the Safeguarding of the Intangible Cultural Heritage: UN Educational, Scientific and Cultural Organisation (UNESCO) (2003). https://ich.unesco.org/doc/src/2003_Convention_Basic_Texts-_2018_version-EN.pdf. Accessed 31 Jan 2021
19. Digital Library Federation: A working definition of digital library (1998). https://old.diglib.org/about/dldefinition.htm. Accessed 31 Mar 2021
20. CIDOC CRM Special Interest Group: CIDOC CRM: Volume A: Definition of the CIDOC Conceptual Reference Model. http://www.cidoc-crm.org/sites/default/files/cidoc_crm_v.7.1.1_0.pdf. Accessed 22 Sept 2021

21. Ariadne Portal. https://portal.ariadne-infrastructure.eu/. Accessed 15 Sept 2021
22. Pluggy Pins. https://www.pluggy-project.eu/pluggypins/. Accessed 15 Sept 2021
23. Arches Project. http://v5demo.archesproject.org/. Accessed 15 Sept 2021
24. Historypin. https://www.historypin.org/en/. Accessed 15 Sept 2021
25. Map your heritage. https://mapyourheritage.eu/. Accessed 15 Sept 2021
26. Petersen, K., Feldt, R., Mujtaba, S., Mattsson, M.: Systematic mapping studies in software engineering. In: Proceedings of the 12th International Conference on Evaluation and Assessment in Software Engineering (EASE 2008), pp. 68–77. BCS Learning & Development Ltd., GBR, Swindon (2008)
27. Digital Periegesis. https://gis.periegesis.org/. Accessed 15 Sept 2021
28. Milano Attraverso. https://www.milanoattraverso.it/. Accessed 15 Sept 2021

Finding Closeness Between EHRMDS and Open-Source Electronic Health Record Systems: An Analytical Approach

Biswanath Dutta[1(✉)] and Debanjali Bain[1,2]

[1] Documentation Research and Training Centre (DRTC), Indian Statistical Institute, Bangalore, India
{bisu,debanjali}@drtc.isibang.ac.in

[2] Department of Library and Information Science, Calcutta University, Kolkata, India

Abstract. The use and adoption of electronic health records (EHR) are growing rapidly around the world. To drive the implementation of EHR in healthcare, the Ministry of Health and Family Welfare of the Government of India published recommendations for EHR standards including EHRMDS (Electronic Health Record Minimum Data Set) in September 2013 and revised in 2016. EHRMDS is a recommendation for adopting EHR for data capture, storage, visualization, presentation, transmission, and interoperability in clinical records. The current work investigates the closeness of EHRMDS to the available open-source electronic health record systems (OS-EHRS). The results of this study reveal the most suitable OS-EHRS for India in terms of clinical metadata coverage as required by EHRMDS. The current study also develops EHRMDS-ext, an extension of the current EHRMDS. The EHRMDS-ext is aligned with the clinical data exchange standards, such as SNOMED-CT and UMLS terms, which support meaningful communication, cooperation, and decision-making in the clinical process.

Keywords: Electronic Health Record · Open-Source · EHRMDS · Reference Model · Metadata · ontology · Metadata profile

1 Introduction

Metadata has been acknowledged as a method for managing, maintaining, preserving, and exchanging Electronic Health Records (EHR) of patients. It helps in capturing a patient's record at the "granular" or data element level [1]. This allows sharing of some parts of the health record while preventing sharing of other areas. According to ISO 18308:2011 [2], EHR is "the repository(s), physically or virtually integrated, of information in computer processable form, relevant to the wellness, health, and healthcare of an individual, capable of being stored and communicated securely and of being accessible by multiple authorized users, represented according to a standardized or commonly agreed logical information model. Its primary purpose is the support of lifelong, effective, high-quality, and safe integrated healthcare."

E. Garoufallou and A. Vlachidis (Eds.): MTSR 2022, CCIS 1789, pp. 122–134, 2023.
https://doi.org/10.1007/978-3-031-39141-5_11

The use and adoption of EHR are rapidly leveraging worldwide. In the United States of America (USA), the first EHR guideline came in February 2009 entitled "Health Information Technology for Economic and Clinical Health (HITECH) Act" [3]. In France, the first guideline arrived in January 2011 entitled "Dossier Medical Personnel (DMP)" [4]. As a developing country, with the second-largest population in the world, India has an ever-increasing need for quality health care. The Ministry of Health and Family Welfare (MoHFW) of the Government of India published an EHR standard in September 2013, entitled "Electronic Health Record Standards of India" [5]. The aim is to establish a uniform system for the maintenance of EHR by hospitals and healthcare providers in India. Among others, the standard consists of a set of recommendations on the Electronic Health Record Minimum Data Set (EHRMDS) to adopt EHR for data capture, storage, visualization, presentation, transmission, and interoperability in clinical records. A brief overview of EHRMDS has been provided in Sect. 2.1.

The EHR systems (EHRS) are designed to capture and store data accurately and provide the state of patients across time. There is a wide range of Open-Source Electronic Health Record Systems (OS-EHRS) in use around the world. Most of the Northern European countries have adopted OpenEHR. GNU Health is popular in China, USA, Argentina, Germany, and Spain. OpenMRS is quite famous in Africa, India, and Southeast Asia [6]. OpenEMR has implementations in the USA, Brazil, the United Kingdom, and South Korea [7].

In this paper, we study EHRMDS in the context of OS-EHRS. We design a systematic approach to find the resemblance between the elements of EHRMDS and OS-EHRS. Any organization is interested in the adoption of an OS-EHRS, especially in India, the findings of this study will provide helpful information regarding the coverage of OS-EHRS when compared with EHRMDS. The study will assist in the selection of an OS-EHRS in an organization. On the other hand, any organization already using an EHR system, from this analysis, can identify missing elements that they could add from the EHRMDS. This study also possesses additional items found in OS-EHRS and not in EHRMDS. Stakeholders can judge whether they need these additional elements. This work can be helpful in achieving interoperability and supporting data exchange between EHR systems.

The main contributions of this work are (1) investigates the closeness between the EHRMDS and the OS-EHRS; (2) provides a systematic methodology for the closeness study; (3) provides a crosswalk between EHRMDS and OS-EHRS; (4) develops an extended EHRMDS, namely EHRMDS-ext. The EHRMDS-ext can be called a comprehensive metadata vocabulary and can be used as an EHR metadata profile.

The rest of the paper is organized as follows: Section 2 describes the EHRMDS and discusses the related works. Section 3 illustrates the entire study in step-by-step. It discusses the selection process of OS-EHRS for the current study, the crosswalk, and the closeness analysis between EHRMDS OS-EHRS. It also provides an extended EHRMDS. Section 4 concludes the paper with a note for study.

2 Background

2.1 EHRMDS

The Electronic Health Record Minimum Data Set (EHRMDS) is introduced by the Ministry of Health and Family Welfare, Government of India as part of the guidelines initiated and published in September 2013 entitled "Recommendations on Standards of electronic medical records in India" [5] to be adopted in the EHR for data capture, storage, visualization, presentation, transmission, and interoperability in clinical records. EHRMDS consists of a minimal but necessary set of data elements to implement in EHR systems for efficient retrieval and exchange of clinical information at the time of clinical encounter. The EHRMDS is primarily derived from the Continuity of Care Record (CCR), a health record standard specification developed jointly by ASTM International, the Massachusetts Medical Society (MMS), and others. According to the above-mentioned guidelines, an EHR system in India should cover all mandatory elements mentioned in EHRMDS. However, an EHR system may include additional elements in accordance with the clinical need. The EHRMDS provides a total of 91 elements covering the various aspects of health data, for example, demographics, insurance, diagnosis, medications, allergies, and care plans. Table 1 provides an overview of the EHRMDS elements arranged by their types and the number of elements in each category.

Table 1. Categorized elements of EHRMDS

Sl. no.	Category	Description	# of Elements	Example Elements
1	Identifiers	include the identity of the entity.	3	UHID, Alternate UHID, Insurance ID
2	Demographics	include identifying information.	42	Patient name, Age, Address
3	Status	establishes the state of particulars.	3	Organ Donor Status, Insurance Status, Allergy Status
4	Episode	is a distinctive healthcare event.	2	Episode type, Episode Number
5	Encounter	is a casual healthcare contact between patient and healthcare provider.	4	Encounter Type, Encounter Date & Time, Reason for Visit
6	History	is the aggregate of occurred or ongoing medical events.	8	Present History, Personal History, Immunization History, Allergy History
7	Clinical examination	establishes the nature, implications, and result of the clinical findings.	13	Clinical Exam Vitals Systolic BP, Clinical Exam Pulse Rate, Clinical Exam Temperature (°C), Clinical Exam Height (cms)
8	Diagnosis	is a decision on the clinical condition identifying the nature or cause	4	Diagnosis Type, Diagnosis (Description)
9	Treatment Plan	is a detailed plan on the patient's disease, goal and options of treatment, and approximate duration of treatment.	6	Treatment Plan Investigations, Treatment Plan Medication, Treatment Plan Procedure, Treatment Plan Referral
10	Medication	is for alleviating or treating the illness with medicine	6	Medication Name, Strength, Dose, Route, Frequency

2.2 Related Work

This section represents various works undertaken to find the similarity between EHR metadata elements and various standards. It also discusses the many studies that have been made on the approaches of overlapping and crosswalking between metadata elements of EHR standards.

Chen, et al. [8] studied the similarity between the elements of Cambio COSMIC, a Sweden-based EHR system, and OpenEHR, an EHR standard. A semantic mapping between the Reference Model (RM) and Archetype Model (AM) of OpenEHR and the COSMIC has been provided. The study found many similarities between the COSMIC model and OpenEHR AM. Ferranti, et al. [9] have critically evaluated two EHR standards: the Clinical Document Architecture (CDA) of Health Level 7 (HL7) and the Continuity of Care Record (CCR) of the American Society for Testing and Materials (ASTM International). CDA is used for radiology reports, progress notes, clinical summaries, and discharge summaries [9, 10]. The CCR is a minimal data set that contains information about the provider, insurance, and patient's health status including allergies, medications, vital signs, diagnoses, problems, recent procedures, etc. Ferranti, et al. have proposed a strategy for harmonizing CDA and CCR with a solution to define a set of common data elements using content and knowledge from both.

Muller, et al. [11] have developed a Hospital Information System (HIS) for electronic data transfer based on CDA. CDA elements have been mapped to their corresponding HIS terms. Automatic mapping was performed using a mapping engine developed in Microsoft Excel.

The HL7 International Electronic Health Record Technical Committee [12] has done a crosswalk between key criteria between the Lifecycle Model, CDA R2 Header, and RM-ES Profile to determine related metadata terms and has developed a single list of metadata concepts and term definitions. They have proposed an overlap of concepts between the Interoperability Model and CDA R2.

Cucchiara [13] has generated a crosswalk and alignment between the Patient-Centered Medical Home (PCMH) model and Meaningful Use (MU). This work has concluded many areas of overlap between PCMH and MU. Coffin, et al. [14] have discovered that an intersection or crosswalk can accurately explain how specific MU criteria can meet PCMH requirements. As can be observed from the above discussion, none of the existing works, study EHRMDS India and investigate its closeness to the OS-EHRS.

3 Closeness Analysis and EHRMDS-ext

The entire study is conducted in three phases as shown in Fig. 1. In phase I, we identify the open-source EHR systems and their respective metadata elements; in phase II, we select the metadata elements from EHRMDs; and in phase III, we study the closeness of EHRMDS to each OS-EHR system. In this phase, we also produce an extended EHRMDS i.e., EHRMDS-ext. The phases are detailed in the following subsections.

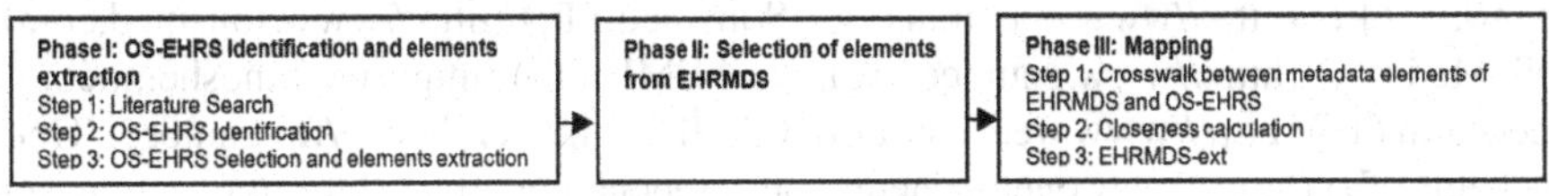

Fig. 1. Overview of methodology

3.1 Phase I: OS-EHRS Identification for Elements Selection

The identification and selection of OS-EHRS for the current study have been conducted in three steps as follows.

Step 1: Literature Search - In order to select the OS-EHRS, scholarly publications are studied. They have been retrieved from PubMed, ScienceDirect, Springer, IEEE Xplore, and Google Scholar. For the selection of relevant literature, we have used the PRISMA flow diagram [15] shown in Fig. 2. The articles were retrieved from the databases using the following keywords – "electronic patient records", "computerized patient record", "computer-based patient record", "computerized health record", "computer-based health record", "open-source electronic health record systems", "comparison of open-source electronic health record tools", "best electronic health record system", "analysis of open-source EHR system", "electronic health record system free", "rank list of OS-EHRS". We have considered the articles in English, original articles published during 2013–2021, and discuss open-source EHR systems.

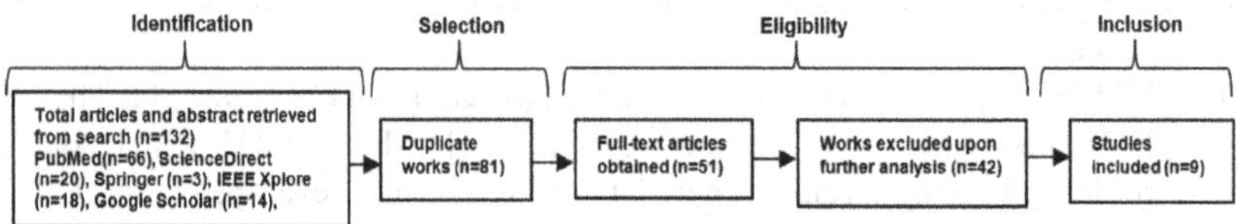

Fig. 2. The PRISMA flowchart describing the systematic search process for the selection of relevant literature

Initially, we found a total of 132 publications. From this list, duplicates were removed. The literature was reduced to 81. But then we had access only to 51 full-text literature of the 81. 42 works were again excluded based on articles published in English, between 2013 and 2021, dealing with only open-source EHR systems. This process yielded 9 core literatures as provided in Table 2 for the identification of EHR systems.

Step 2: OS-EHRS identification - From the selected 9 literature, 70 EHRS were identified as shown in Table 2. After removing the duplicates, 40 OS-EHRS were identified.

Step 3: OS-EHRS selection and element extraction – Studying the metadata elements of all 40 OS-EHRS is beyond the scope of the work. To select the EHR systems for the current study, the criteria such as frequency of occurrence in the literature (FOiL) and Online Demo Availability (ODA) were applied. FOiL has allowed in gauging the popularity of the EHR tools. From 40 tools, we selected 10 tools for the study. They are: 75Healh (T_1) (http://www.75health.com), OpenEMR (T_2) (http://www.open-emr.org), OpenMRS(T_3) (http://www.openmrs.org), Solismed (T_4) (http://www.solismed.com), GNUMed (T_5) (http://www.gnumed.org), NoshEMR (T_6) (http://www.noshemr.com), Freehealth (T_7) (http://www.freehealth.io), GNUHealth (T_8) (https://ftp.gnu.org), Onetouchemr (T_9) (http://www.onetouchemr.com), Openclinic (T_{10}) (http://openclinic.sourceforge.net). Table 3 provides the selected OS-EHRS and their corresponding number of elements. For example, the EHRS, such as 75Health provides 48 elements and OpenEMR provides 41 elements to describe the clinical data. For the elements from each tool, see Table 5. The elements were extracted manually by vising each system.

Table 2. Referred EHR tools in selected literature

Ref. No.	Description	Tools referred
[16]	Studied the functionalities of free and open source EHRs.	CHITS, GNUmed, Open-EMR, OpenMRS, OSCAR, and PatientOS
[17]	Evaluated multiple EMR systems by considering, acceptance in the healthcare community, inpatient and outpatient support, community support, and frequency of updates.	OpenVistA, WorldVistA, Astronaut, ClearHealth, VistA, WebVista, OpenMRS, Care2x, OpenEMR, OSCAR, Patient OS, GNUHealth, GNUmed, THIRRA, FreeMED.
[18]	This study analyses open-source EHRs based on a set of criteria.	HOSxp, OpenEMR, and OpenVistA
[19]	This study analyses available open-source EHRS.	FreeMED, GNUmed, OSCAR, GNU Health, Hospital OS, Solismed, OpenEMR, THIRRA, OpenMRS, WorldVista, ZEPRS, ClearHealth, MedinTux.
[20]	This study evaluates open-source EHRs based on a set of criteria.	GNUmed, OpenEMR, and OpenMRS ZEPRS
[21]	This study discusses the top 26 FREE and Open-source EMR-EHR for Windows, Linux, and Mac OSX.	HospitalRun, Open-MRS, Bahmni, FreeMed, OpenEMR, Cottage Med, GNU med, Open-Clinic, OpenEyes, World-VistA, OpenMAXIMS, GNUHealth, FreeMed-Forms, ZEPRS, SMARTPediatric Growth, OpenHospital, Libre-HealthEHR, THIRPA, FreeHealth.io, Medin-Tux, DoliMed EMR, NoshEMR, ODOO EMR, Chikitsa.
[6]	This study identifies the most popular OS-EHRS based on Alexa web ranking and Google trends.	OSHERA VistA, GNU Health, the Open Medical Record System (Open-MRS), Open Electronic Medical Record (Open-EMR), and OpenEHR
[22]	This study analyses and lists the 3 best open source EHRs solutions listed on Capterra.	75Health, OpenEMR, OpenMRS
[23]	This study analyses and compare between best free and open source EHRs	TalkEHR, 75Health, OpenEMR, One-TouchEMR, OpenMRS.

Table 3. Shows the OS-EHRS and their corresponding number of elements

OS-EHRS	75Health (T1)	OpenEMR (T2)	OpenMRS (T3)	Solismed (T4)	GNUMed (T5)	NoshEMR (T6)	Freehealth (T7)	GNUHealth (T8)	Onetouchemr (T9)	Openclinic (T10)
# of elements	48	41	28	49	26	38	28	31	38	21

3.2 Phase II: Selection of Elements from EHRMDS

In the current study, we have selected all the mandatory elements from EHRMDS related to clinical data. The total number of metadata elements in EHRMDS is 91. We have selected 42 elements (provided in Table 5) and excluded the rest 49. The reasons for the exclusion and inclusion of elements are as follows.

Reason for Exclusion- excluded metadata that specifies demographic details (i.e., patient age, name, address, contacts), care provider details, insurance details, and patient's unique number (i.e., UHID, Aadhar, etc.) as all fields are mostly present across all the EHR tools.

Reason for Inclusion- included all the EHRMDS elements marked as mandatory to include in any EHR tool.

3.3 Phase III: Mapping

In this phase, we study the closeness between EHRMDS and OS-EHRS. Also, develops EHRMDS-ext. This phase consists of three steps as follows.

Step 1: Crosswalk between metadata elements of EHRMDS and OS-EHRS – Following the extraction of metadata elements from OS-EHRS (see phase II, step 3) and EHRMDS (phase II), we perform the crosswalk to study the closeness. For the crosswalk, we consider the EHRMDS minimum data set as a reference model (RM). We tally each metadata element of the OS-EHRS, both syntactically and semantically against the EHRMDS. The Syntactic analysis helps to signify the structure of terms without considering their meaning. It basically emphasizes the structure, layout, or morphology of the terms with their appearance or lexicographical similarity. For example, the terms "Temp", "T", "temps" and "Temperature" are syntactically the same. The Semantic analysis helps us to find out the terms bearing the same meaning and not necessarily lexicographically similar. For example, "HPI" and "Present history" are semantically the same (abb. HPI = History of Present Illness). For the purpose of mapping, Microsoft Excel has been used. Mapping is basically a mathematical intersection process [24], and can be represented as follows:

$$\bigcap_{i=0}^{n} Tool_i$$

where $Tool_0$ is EHRMDS data elements and $Tool_1$ to $Tool_{10}$ are data elements of ten OS-EHRS. In this process, we have taken not only the syntactically same but also semantically the same elements. Suppose, the intersection of two data sets T_1 and T_2 denoted by ($T_1 \cap \mathrm{T}_2$) consists of all the elements that are both in T_1 and T_2. Therefore, the intersection of the set of terms for tool T_1 and tool T_2 is $(T_1) \cap (T_2) =$ {Allergy Name, Allergy Type, Allergy Note, Severity, Allergic reaction} ∩ {Allergen, Allergy Type, Severity, Reaction} = {Allergy Name OR Allergen, Allergy Type, Severity, Allergic Reaction OR Reaction}. We have included both *AllergyName* from (T_1) and *Allergen* from (T_2). *AllergyName* is semantically the same as *Allergen. AllergyType* is present in both the tools (T_1 and T_2), and they are *syntactically* the same. Similarly, *AllergicReaction* and *Reaction.* Similarly, *AllergicReaction* is semantically the same as *Reaction.* Like this, Immunization and Vaccine have been placed together since both of them are semantically the same. Table 5 shows the mapping.

Step 2: Closeness calculation - Following the above step 1 Crosswalk, we find the closeness of EHRMDS to each OS-EHR system. For this purpose, we count at what percentage the EHRMDS elements match with an EHR system. The finding of this closeness calculation will reveal which EHR system is more suitable for India in terms of clinical metadata coverage as mandated by EHRMDS. Figure 3 shows the closeness in terms of overlapping and non-overlapping EHRMDS elements with respect to each OS-EHRS. As can be seen from the figure that EHRMDS is closer to T_2, i.e., OpenEMR. Of the 42 EHRMDS elements, 31 elements (73.81%) are available in T_2 and only 11 elements (26.19%) elements are not available. On the other hand, T_{10}, i.e., Openclinic has the least number of EHRMDS elements i.e., 33.33%. It can be observed from this analysis that there are many clinical elements still there that are considered by the EHR tools but not available in EHRMDS. In the following step, we develop an extended EHRMDS, namely EHRMDS-ext.

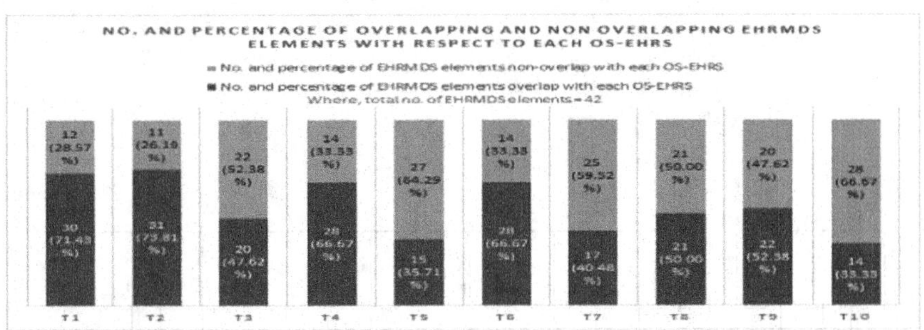

Fig. 3. Shows the number of overlapping and non-overlapping EHRMDS elements with respect to each OS-EHRS

Step 3: EHRMDS-ext – Following the crosswalk, we develop the extended EHRMDS, namely EHRMDS-ext. The EHRMDS-ext can be considered for an enriched clinical metadata set. It is prepared by extending the present EHRMDS and by adapting the elements from the OS-EHR systems. Table 4 shows the total number of elements of each tool, and out of which how many are found and not-found in EHRMDS. For example, T_1 i.e., 75Health has a total of 42 elements, out of which 30 elements are found in EHRMDS and 12 elements are not found in EHRMDS. These uncovered elements are adapted from OS-EHRS in preparing the EHRMDS-ext. For this purpose, we first analyse the non-found elements of OS-EHRS to prepare a unique list of elements. This unique list was then merged with EHRMDS to produce EHRMDS-ext. The extended EHRMDS consists of 89 elements as listed in the second last column of Table 5. The 89 elements include 42 existing elements of EHRMDS and 47 unique elements derived from OS-EHRS. The 47 unique elements that have come from OS-EHRS are highlighted in bold. The last column of the table provides the UMLS CUI Ids for the EHRMDS-ext elements. The corresponding UMLS terms, SNOMED CT terms, and Ids for the EHRMDS-ext elements can be found in the extended table available from https://figshare.com/s/b606590c3e4bd6d2b722. \

Table 4. Shows the number of OS-EHRS elements found and not-found in EHRMDS

	T1 (48)	T2 (41)	T3 (28)	T4 (49)	T5 (26)	T6 (38)	T7 (28)	T8 (31)	T9 (38)	T10 (21)
# of elements found in EHRMDS	30	31	20	28	15	28	17	21	22	14
# of elements not found in EHRMDS	18	10	8	21	11	10	11	10	16	7

Table 5. Shows crosswalk between EHRMDS and OS-EHRS. It also provides the extended EHRMDS i.e., EHRMDS-ext

EHRMDS	OS-EHRS										EHRMDS-ext	UMLS CUI
	75Health	OpenEMR	OpenMRS	Solismed	GNUMed	NoshEMR	Freehealth	GNUHealth	Opentouchemr	Openclinic		
Encounter Type	Encounter type	Encounter type	Encounter type	Encounter	Encounter type	Encounter	Encounter type	Encounter type	Encounter type	Encounter	Encounter Type	C0586016
Encounter Number	Encounter no	Patient Encounter no	Patient Encounter number	Encounter number	Encounter no	Encounter Number		Encounter Number			Encounter Number	C4086434
Encounter Date & Time	Encounter Date	Encounter Date	Encounter Date		Encounter Date			Encounter Date			Encounter Date	C4087739
Reason for Visit	Visit Reasons	Visit Reason		Reason		Reason		Indication		Reason	Reason for Visit	C1704447
	Physical Examination			Physical Exam							**Physical Examination**	C0031809
				Review of Systems							**Review of Systems**	C0489633
Present History		Present History	History and Examination	HPI		Present Medical History			Present Medical History		Present History	C1827596
									Conservative Therapy		**Conservative Therapy**	C0459914
				Surgical History		Surgical History	Patient Overview: Surgical		Surgical History		**Surgical History**	C0455610
Past History		General History		Past Medical History			Patient Overview: Past				Past History	C0455458
Personal History		Life Style					Patient Overview: Personal	Individuals, lifestyle		Personal Antecedents	Personal History	C0585172
Family History	Family Health	Family History		Family History		Family History	Patient Overview: Family	Families	Family History	Family Antecedents	Family History	C0241889
Menstrual & Obstetric History			Obstetrics Gynecology				patient overview: obstetric	OB/GYN	Last Menstrual		Menstrual & Obstetric History	C0425963
Socio-economic Status	Social History			Social History		social history		Socioeconomics	Social History	Social Data	Social History	C0424945
Immunization History	Vaccine & Immunization			Immunizations		Immunizations		vaccine	Imm/ Injections		Immunization History	C0552506
Clinical Exam Vitals Systolic BP	Patient Health Record vital: Blood Pressure	BP Systolic	Blood Pressure	Blood Pressure	BP Systolic	Systolic	BP		Blood Pressure		Systolic Blood Pressure	C0871470
Clinical Exam Vitals Diastolic BP	Patient Health Record vital: Blood Pressure	BP Diastolic			BP Diastolic	Diastolic					Diastolic Blood Pressure	C0428883
Clinical Exam Pulse Rate	Patient Health Record vital: Heart rate/ pulse	Pulse	Pulse	Pulse	Heart Rate	Pulse			Pulse		Pulse Rate	C0577836
Clinical Exam Temperature (°C)	Patient Health Record vital: Temperature	Temperature	Temperature (C)	Temperature	Body Temp (degree c)	Temperature	T	Temperature	Temperature		Temperature	C0039476
Clinical Exam Temperature Source		Temp Location			Rectal temp						Temperature Source	C0204688
Clinical Exam Respiration Rate	Patient Health Record vital: Respiratory rate	Respiration	Respiratory rate	Respiratory	RR	RR			Respiratory Rate		**Respiratory Rate**	C0231832
				Breathing Pattern							Breathing Pattern	C0517987
Clinical Exam Height (cms)	Patient Health Record vital: height & Patient Health Record vital: Height at > 25	Height/Length	Height (cm)	Height	Height	Height	Height	Height	Height	Height	Height	C0005890
Clinical Exam Weight (kgs)	Patient Health Record vital: weight	Weight	Weight (kg)	Weight	Weight	Weight	Weight	Weight	Weight	Weight	Weight	C0005910
Blood Group											Blood Group	C0800103

(continued)

Table 5. *(continued)*

Clinical Exam Observation			Latest observation	Observation						Observation	Clinical Exam Observation	C1274016
Investigation Results				Lab Result	Lab Results	Results	Consultation reports Lab test report		Labs		Investigation Results	C0587081
Clinical Summary	Problems	Medical Problems		Problem list		Problem list		Problem	Problem list	Medical Problem	Clinical Summary	C0033213
			Health Maintenance therapy	Health Maintenance summary							**Health Trend Summary**	C0677908
Diagnosis Type	Diagnosis Type	Diagnosis Type		Diagnosis Type			Diagnosis Type				Diagnosis Type	C0332131
Diagnosis Code Name	Diagnosis Code Name	Diagnosis Code Name		Diagnosis Code Name		Diagnosis Code Name				Diagnosis Code Name	Diagnosis Code Name	C2985803
Diagnosis Code	Diagnosis Code	Diagnosis Code		Diagnosis Code		Diagnosis Code				Diagnosis Code	Diagnosis Code	C1550350
Diagnosis (Description)	Diagnosis (Description)	Diagnosis (Description)	Diagnosis	Diagnosis (Description)	Diagnosis	Diagnosis (Description)			Diagnosis	Diagnosis Description	Diagnosis (Description)	C0011900
Treatment Plan Investigations											Treatment Plan Investigations	
Treatment Plan Medication	Plan of Treatment	Treatment Plan		Treatment	Treatments	Medical Action Plan		Treatments	Health Maintenance Plans		Treatment Plan Medication	C4545837
Treatment Plan Procedure	Procedure	Procedure		Procedures			Programs	Procedures	Procedure		Treatment Plan Procedure	C0237403
Treatment Plan Referral	Referral	Referral		Referrals							Treatment Plan Referral	C0814457
Other Treatment Plan Type											Other Treatment Plan Type	
Other Treatment Plan Details											Other Treatment Plan Details	
Current Clinical Status			Conditions: Active Conditions: History Of Conditions: Inactive		Conditions	Condition					Current Clinical Status	C3899485
Medication Name	Medication: Medicine name	Medication	Medication	Medication List: Drug		Medication RXNorm	Long-term Medication	Medicaments	Medication RxNorm	Drugs	Medication Name	C2360065
Drug Code	Drug code	Drug Code	Drug Code			Drug code			Drug code		Drug Code	C54185
Strength	Medication: Medicine Strength	Strength	Strength			Strength	Strength	Strength	Strength		Strength	C1705922
Dose	Dose	Dose	Dose	Medication List: Direction Dose		Dosage	Dose	Dose			Dose	C0178602
Route	Route	Route	Route			Route	routes	Administration Route			Route	C0013153
	Medication: Instructions			Narration & Instruction		Special Instructions					Special Instructions	C1442085
Frequency	Frequency	Frequency				Frequency	Duration	Frequency			Frequency	C89081
	Medication: Refills	Refills		Refills			refill	Refills	Refill Allowed		Refills	C4289665
	Medication: Start Date						Date and time	Start: Date and time	Start Date		**Medication: Start Date**	C5141805
	Medication: End Date						limits	End: Date and time	End Date		**Medication: End Date**	C5141806
	Medication: Company Name			Medication List: Package Description							**Medication: Company Name**	C0815266
Allergy Status	Allergy: Status	Allergies		Allergy status		Allergies		Patients: Patient allergies and Critical Information	Allergies: Status	Allergy	Allergy: Status	C4521222
Allergy History	Allergy: Allergen Name		Allergies	allergy: agent					Allergies: Agent		Allergy: Allergen Name	C0002092
	Allergy: Type		Allergy type	Allergy: type			Drug Allergies		Allergies: Type	Allergy type	**Allergy: Type**	C1550403
	Allergy: Reactions		Reactions	Allergy: reactions		Reaction			Allergies: Reaction		**Allergy: Reactions**	C1527304

(continued)

Table 5. (*continued*)

	Allergy: Severity		severity	Allergy: severity		Severity			Severity		**Allergy: Severity**	C1550404
	Allergy: From Date		Allergy Date	Allergy date recorder					Start Date, End Date		**Allergy: From Date**	C2209280
									Allergies: Source		**Allergies: Source**	C1690571
						Substance or Medication					**Substance or Medication**	C3266231
				Allergy: conditions							**Allergy: conditions**	C0851444
	Patient Health Record vital: Oxygen Saturation	Oxygen Saturation	Blood oxygen saturation	SpO2	SPO2				SpO2	Spo2	**SpO2**	C0513686
	Blood Glucose										**Patient Health Record vital: Glucose by Glucometer**	C3669205
	Patient Health Record vital: BMI	BMI	(Calculated) BMI	BMI	BMI	BMI Status	BMI		BMI	BMI	**BMI**	C0578022
		Head Circumference		Head Circumference		Head Circumference	Head Circumference		Head Circ		**Head Circumference**	C0262499
		Waist Circumference		Waist Size	Waist Circum				Waist		**Waist Circumference**	C0455829
	Test order	Past Test Order		Lab Order Status		Orders	Lab Order Fulfillments				**Lab Order**	C4302923
	Implantation process										**Implantation procedure**	C0021107
	Goals										**Goals**	C0557971
		Surgeries						Surgeries			**Surgeries**	C0543467
		Dental treatment									**Dental procedure**	C0011331
					Posture						**Posture**	C1262869
		Diagnostic Imaging			Pacs orders			Imaging		Imaging	**Imaging**	C0011923
				Pathology Order	Pathology Orders						**Pathology order**	C4302922
				Radiology Order	Radiology Orders						**Radiology Order**	C4302924
				Radiology Result	Radiology				Radiology	Radiology	**Radiology**	C1290916
					Disposition						**Disposition**	C0743223
					followup						**Follow-up**	C0589120
						sensitive level					**sensitive level**	C1455667
						Supplement				Supplements	**Supplement**	C0242295
					Urine Sugar						**Urine Sugar**	C1456823
							Drug Intolerance				**Drug Intolerance**	C0277585
								Pediatrics History			**Pediatrics History**	C0587599
								Pediatrics Growth Charts			**Pediatrics Growth Charts**	C2718056
								Recreational Drugs			**Recreational Drugs**	C1318616
								Medical Specialities			**Medical Specialities**	C0037778
								Pages of Life: Genetics			**Genetics**	C3887703
							Patient overview: Risk factors				**Risk factors**	C0035648
	Advance Directive: Assessment								Advance Directive		**Advance Directive**	C0587820
	Medication: Directions for use or SIG CODE	SIG code	SIG code				SIG code			SIG	**Medication: Directions for use or SIG CODE**	C3476380

4 Conclusion

From the current study, we can observe the diversity that exists in the present health record-keeping tools. Therefore, it is the basic need of clinicians to find reliable EHR tools among all available options [25, 26]. Among others, it is the similarity between the elements specific to a tool and the minimum requirements, which measure the effectiveness of such a tool. If a tool sufficiently expresses all patient's health data, the tool would be expected to have more users. Based on the closeness calculation, it is found that of the ten OS-EHRS, the OpenEMR adequately meets the minimum data set requirements as prescribed in EHRMDS. It is also found that the Openclinic does not sufficiently satisfy the EHRMDS. Thus, the current study has the potential to assist the stakeholders (e.g., hospitals) in making informed decisions in selecting OS-EHR tools. The designed approach used in the current study can be applied to similar studies. The current study also developed EHRMDS-ext, an enriched set of medical metadata that has come after a thorough analysis of elements of EHRMDS and OS-EHRS, and their crosswalk. The EHRMDS-ext can be considered an enriched medical dataset for acquiring effective clinical information exchange among healthcare providers. Our future work will focus on the semantic representation of EHRMDS-ext using the technologies, such as RDF and OWL followed by the evaluation.

Acknowledgment. This work is executed under the research project entitled "Integrated and Unified Data Model for Publication and Sharing of prolonged pandemic data as FAIR Semantic Data: COVID-19 as a case study", funded by Indian Statistical Institute Kolkata.

References

1. AHIMA. Rules for Handling and Maintaining Metadata in the EHR. J. AHIMA **84**, 50–54 (2013)
2. ISO 18308:2011(en), Health informatics — Requirements for an electronic health record architecture. https://www.iso.org/obp/ui/#iso:std:iso:18308: ed-1:v1:en
3. Rights (OCR), O. for C. HITECH Act Enforcement Interim Final Rule. HHS.gov (2009). https://www.hhs.gov/
4. DMP: Shared Medical Record. https://www.dmp.fr/
5. EHR Standards – National Health Portal of India. https://www.nhp.gov.in/
6. Purkayastha, S., Allam, R., Maity, P., Gichoya, J.W.: Comparison of open-source electronic health record systems based on functional and user performance criteria. Healthc. Inform. Res. **25**, 89–98 (2019). https://doi.org/10.4258/hir.2019.25.2.89
7. Abajo, B.S. de Ballestero, A.L.: Overview of the most important open source software: analysis of the benefits of OpenMRS, OpenEMR, and VistA. In: Telemedicine and E-Health Services, Policies, and Applications: Advancements and Developments, pp. 315–346 (2012)
8. Chen, R., Klein, G.O., Sundvall, E., Karlsson, D., Ahlfeldt, H.: Archetype-based conversion of EHR content models: pilot experience with a regional EHR system. BMC Med. Inform. Decis. Mak. **9**, 33 (2009). https://doi.org/10.1186/1472-6947-933
9. Ferranti, J.M., Musser, R.C., Kawamoto, K., Hammond, W.E.: The clinical document architecture and the continuity of care record: a critical analysis. J. Am. Med. Inform. Assoc. JAMIA **13**, 245–252 (2006). https://doi.org/10.1197/jamia.M1963

10. Dolin, R.H., et al.: HL7 clinical document architecture, release 2. J. Am. Med. Inform. Assoc. JAMIA **13**, 30–39 (2006). https://doi.org/10.1197/jamia.M1888
11. Müller, M.L., Ückert, F., Bürkle, T., Prokosch, H.U.: Cross-institutional data exchange using the clinical document architecture (CDA). Int. J. Med. Inform. **74**(2–4), 245–256 (2005). https://doi.org/10.1016/j.ijmedinf.2004.09.005
12. Crosswalk Results: Minimum Metadata Set & Crosswalk Between EHR Interoperability Model/Life Cycle Model – CDA R2 – RM-ES Functional Profile. (n.d.). https://wiki.hl7.org/w/images/wiki.hl7.org/9/92/Crosswalk_EHRInterop_CDAr2_RMES_Final_2009-10-12.doc
13. Cucchiara, P.A.: crosswalk and an alignment: PCMH and MU (2014)
14. Coffin, J., Duffie, C., Furno, M.: The patient-centered medical home and meaningful use: a challenge for better care. J. Med. Pract. Manage. MPM **29**, 331–334 (2014)
15. Moher, D., Liberati, A., Tetzlaff, J., Altman, D.G.: Preferred reporting items for systematic reviews and meta-analyses: the PRISMA statement. BMJ **339**, b2535 (2009). https://doi.org/10.1136/bmj.b2535
16. Flores, A.E. Vergara, V.M.: Functionalities of open electronic health records system: a follow-up study. In: 2013 6th International Conference on Biomedical Engineering and Informatics, pp. 602–607 (2013). https://doi.org/10.1109/BMEI.2013.6747011
17. Multak, N.L., Khazraee, E., Rogers, M. Dalrymple, P.W.: Implementing an open source EMR in a nursing informatics course (2013)https://doi.org/10.9776/13445
18. de la Torre, I., Mart´ınez, B. Lo´pez-Coronado, M.: Analyzing open-source and commercial EHR solutions from an international perspective. In: 2013 IEEE 15th International Conference on e-Health Networking, Applications and Services (Healthcom 2013), pp. 399–403 (2013). https://doi.org/10.1109/HealthCom.2013.6720708
19. Kiah, M.L.M., Haiqi, A., Zaidan, B.B., Zaidan, A.A.: Open source EMR software: profiling, insights and hands-on analysis. Comput. Methods Programs Biomed. **117**, 360–382 (2014). https://doi.org/10.1016/j.cmpb.2014.07.002
20. Zaidan, A.A., et al.: Evaluation and selection of open-source EMR software packages based on integrated AHP and TOPSIS. J. Biomed. Inform. **53**, 390–404 (2015). https://doi.org/10.1016/j.jbi.2014.11.012
21. Mo, D.: Top 26 FREE & Open Source EMR - EHR for Windows, Linux and Mac OSX. MEDevel.com: Open-source Guide to Healthcare and Medical Software (2018). https://medevel.com/top-20-free-and-open-source-emr-ehr/
22. Kumar, R.: 3 Best Free and Open Source EMR Software (2019). https://blog.com/top-7-free-open-source-emr-software-products/
23. Hedges, L.: 5 Easy Steps to Pick the Ideal Free or Open-Source EMR (2019). https://www.softwareadvice.com/resources/free-ehr-vs-open-source/
24. Concept Maps. Learning Center https://learningcenter.unc.edu/tips-and-tools/using-concept-maps/
25. Neal, D.: Choosing an electronic health records system. Innov. Clin. Neurosci. **8**, 43–45 (2011). https://www.ncbi.nlm.nih.gov/pmc/articles/PMC3140898/
26. Ajami, S. Bagheri-Tadi, T.: Barriers for adopting electronic health records (EHRs) by physicians. Acta Inform. Medica AIM J. Soc. Med. Inform. Bosnia Herzeg. Cas. Drustva Za Med. Inform. BiH **21**, 129–134 (2013). https://doi.org/10.5455/aim.2013.21.129-134

An Architecture for Generating Questions, Answers, and Feedback from Ontologies

Toky Raboanary(✉) and C. Maria Keet

Department of Computer Science, University of Cape Town, Cape Town, South Africa
{traboanary,mkeet}@cs.uct.ac.za

Abstract. Automatically generating questions, answers, and feedback from ontologies and conceptual models is crucial for learning activities and knowledge validation. Existing proposals are limited to predefined types of questions and the modelling style that they are tailored to, lack feedback generation, and their core algorithm are dependent on those characteristics, therewith hampering maintainability and reusability. We designed a new architecture where the question, answer and feedback specifications, the core algorithm for selecting the contents from the ontology, and the verbaliser are modularised for resolving these problems. We instantiated the architecture as a proof-of-concept, examined three test cases, and showed that it compares favourably to related work.

Keywords: Ontology-based Question Generation · Ontology-based Feedback Generation · Architecture · Natural Language Generation · Template-based Question Generation · Ontologies for Education

1 Introduction

Natural Language Generation (NLG) is increasingly being used for daily consumption of information; e.g., the automatic generation of weather forecasts and reports (e.g., [17]) and generating articles about soccer matches. NLG also provides benefits for educational technologies, such as automating question generation and marking for computer-assisted language learning exercises [6,10], generating quizzes from DBpedia [18] and improving student learning in the Biology domain [3,4] by means of 'intelligent textbooks'. We focus on generating questions with their answers and feedback from structured knowledge, namely ontologies and conceptual models, i.e., from the TBox (terminological knowledge) rather than ABox (assertional knowledge). These systems are developed for different purposes, including education [2–4,11,16,19,20] and ontology (knowledge base) validation [1,13], and they offer different types of questions, being mainly Multiple Choice Questions (MCQs), but also similarity, yes/no, and short answer questions. They generally focus on controlling MCQ question difficulty and generating distractors [2,11,19]. Nevertheless, some look at the verbalisation of the questions (rendering the questions in a natural language) and the feedback generation (e.g., [11]).

E. Garoufallou and A. Vlachidis (Eds.): MTSR 2022, CCIS 1789, pp. 135–147, 2023.
https://doi.org/10.1007/978-3-031-39141-5_12

Existing approaches are based on predefined types of questions and tested or/and evaluated with one or few ontologies, not considering the different modelling styles (e.g., [1,11,19]). Then, it is still being determined how they can be reused for other types of questions (if possible). In addition, their axiom prerequisites, i.e., the prerequisites that an ontology should satisfy, for generating questions for a particular type of question, are not clear. A partial disentanglement was proposed by [16], where question preconditions were specified that further provide control on question generation, but those axiom prerequisites and their mappings with the templates[1] are embedded in the core algorithm, which limits the maintainability, extensibility, reusability and generalisability of the approach.

Also, in the educational environment, providing feedback to learners is crucial. Leo et al. [11] developed an ontology-based multi-term MCQs question for the medical domain. They provided an explanation for the correct and incorrect options as feedback. However, they only consider four fixed types of questions and only use one ontology. Hence, it may not support other ontologies with different modelling styles, naming schemes and types of questions.

To the best of our knowledge, existing proposals are limited to predefined types of questions and the modelling style that they are tailored to, and lack feedback generation. To address these problems, we aim to develop a new architecture for generating questions, answers and feedback so that it can flexibly support different types of questions with their axiom prerequisites and different modelling styles, deal with complex answer types and provide feedback explaining the answer of the question, while using a unique core algorithm.

The principal concept of the designed architecture is to modularise the question, answer and feedback specifications, the core algorithm for selecting the contents from the ontology, and the verbaliser to produce the sentences. These specifications are structured in so-called *question card* with manageable subparts. Our results show that 1) one can generate questions, answers and feedback by adopting the architecture by only defining the specifications externally, such that the whole architecture does not have to be modified for more types of questions or considering more modelling styles; and 2) our analysis shows that this new architecture is better than existing studies in terms of flexibility and functionality. The instances of the question card, algorithms, source code and results are available at https://github.com/mkeet/AQuestGO.

The remainder of this paper is structured as follows: Sect. 2 presents the architecture for the question, answer and feedback generation, Sect. 3 illustrates the proof-of-concept implementation, presents test cases and compares it to related work, and we conclude in Sect. 4.

2 Architecture

The description of the architecture, as depicted in Fig. 1, is divided into four categories: the inputs, the content selection algorithm (CSA), the verbaliser and the outputs for generating the questions, answers and feedback from an ontology.

[1] A template is a linguistic structure containing slots, which are intended to be replaced by relevant words to construct a sentence.

We present the different components and the decision choices for obtaining a flexible architecture.

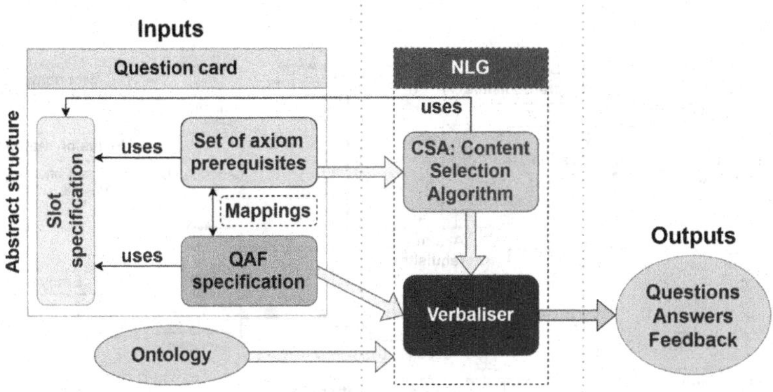

Fig. 1. The proposed architecture (QAF = Questions, Answers and Feedback)

2.1 Inputs

There are two types of input: the ontology and so-called *question card*, the latter of which can be subdivided into the abstract content for the ontology, slot and QAF (Questions, Answers and Feedback) specifications. The architecture requires a well-formed instance of the question card and a consistent ontology.

Ontology or Conceptual Model. This is the structured knowledge to be fed into the NLG process without changing its structure and contents.

Question Card. The question card, which is presented in Fig. 1 and Fig. 2, comprises three main elements for a given type of question, such as 'yes/no question containing 2 classes and one property': the slot specification, the set of axiom prerequisites and the QAF specification. Essentially, the latter concerns the 'linguistic templates' formalising the questions, answers and feedback (be they basic or grammar-infused templates [12]). The slot specification describes the different slots intended to be used in the axiom prerequisites and the linguistic templates. The set of axiom prerequisites is the set of preconditions that need to be satisfied by the ontology to be able to generate questions for that type of question. The linguistic templates are the linguistic structures to be filled in from the selected ontology vocabulary elements to generate the sentences. Listing 1.1 presents an example of an instance of the question card, which also illustrates in lines 11 and 12 that it can deal with different modelling styles.

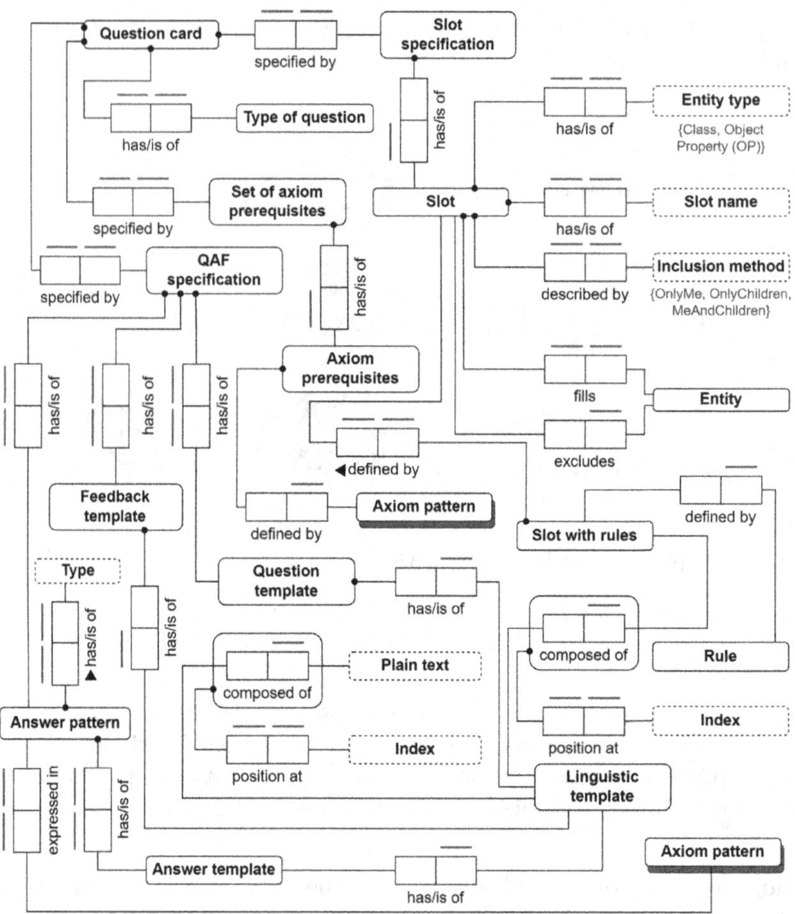

Fig. 2. An ORM model of the components of 'Question card' with the other entities

Listing 1.1. Example of a *qCard1* question card instance that deals with two different modelling styles, represented in an abstract specification (see online supplementary material for the equivalent XML representation). C and OP are the sets of classes and object properties (OPs), respectively.

question card name: qCard1 *(a question card instance)*
type of question: Which X prop Y?
begin {slot specification}
  slot (1, 2, 3): '[X]', '[Y]' and '[Z]' representing a class in $\mathsf{C}_1 = \{\forall \mathsf{c} \in \mathsf{C} : \mathsf{c} \sqsubset \mathsf{Thing}\} - \{\mathsf{SocialObject}, \mathsf{PhysicalObject}\}$
  slot (4): '[Soc]' representing the class SocialObject
  slot (5): '[Phy]' representing the class PhysicalObject
  slot (6): '[inheresIn]' representing the OP inheresIn
  slot (7): '[prop]' representing an OP in $\mathsf{OP}_1 = \{\forall \mathsf{p} \in \mathsf{OP} : \mathsf{p} \sqsubset \mathsf{TopObjectProperty}\}$
end {slot specification}
begin {set of axiom prerequisites}

```
11    axiom prerequisites (1) (first modelling style): (a) [X] ⊑ [Phy], (b) [Y] ⊑ [Soc],
      (c) [Phy]¬[Soc], (d) [Soc] ⊑ ∃[inheresIn].[Phy], (e) [Y] ⊑ ∃[inheresIn].[X], (f) [Y] ⊑ ∃
      [prop].[Z], (g) [X]¬[Y]
12    axiom prerequisites (2) (second modelling style): (a) [Y] ⊑ [X], (b) [Y] ⊑ ∃[prop].[Z]
13  end {set of axiom prerequisites}
14  begin {QAF specification}
15    begin {question template (qt)}
16      qt(1): What type of [X/noArticle] [prop/*OP_Verb-third] [Z]? ('noArticle' and
        'OP_Verb-third' mean that the class X should be written without any article, and the
        template qt(1) can only be used if the OP prop is classified as a verb (see [16]) and will
        be conjugated in the third person, respectively.)
17      qt(2): What type of [X/noArticle] [prop/*OP_VerbPrep-third] [Z]?
18      qt(3): What type of [X/noArticle] [prop/*OP_HasNouns-third] that is [Z]?
19      qt(4): What type of [X/noArticle] is [prop/*OP_IsNounsPrep] [Z]?
20      qt(5): What type of [X/noArticle] is [prop/*OP_IsPastParticipleBy] [Z]?
21      qt(6): What type of [X/noArticle] is [prop/*OP_IsPastParticiplePrep] [Z]?
22    end {question template (qt)}
23    begin {answer pattern}
24      answer template: The answer is [Y].
25      axiom pattern: [Y]
26    end {answer pattern}
27    feedback template: The answer is [Y] since it is [X] that [prop] [Z].
28  end {QAF specification}
```

Slot Specification. The slot specification (e.g., lines 3–9 in Listing 1.1) permits defining and restricting the tokens' scope. A token can be either a class or an object property (OP). This may be a single class or OP, only subclasses or sub-OPs thereof or both (Inclusion method in Fig. 2). Also, it allows the exclusion of classes or OPs that are unfavourable for the generation of questions (e.g., in Listing 1.1, line 4). Leo et al. [11] also considered this exclusion process, but the flexibility of the axiom prerequisites and the linguistic templates were missing.

Set of Axiom Prerequisites. A type of question has a set of axiom prerequisites to be able to deal with the fact that there are different ways to represent the same piece of knowledge. As an illustration, one may adopt a top-down ontology development and reuse a foundational ontology, or a bottom-up approach . Following that, there may be different axiom patterns that are similar [5] and they would be verbalised in the same way. For instance, one may represent 'A student is a person.' with a subsumption relation or represent 'student' as a role that a person plays (see [5]). Thereby, we designed the question card to support several axiom prerequisites for a given type of question. In our example in Listing 1.1, the two axiom prerequisites in lines 11 and 12 are defined in the instance *qCard1* for dealing with the two different modelling styles: a role representation and a subsumption relation representation, respectively.

QAF Specification. (e.g., lines 14–28 in Listing 1.1) A type of question has sets of questions, answers and feedback templates. More than one linguistic template is required since the verbalisation of the axiom patterns may differ depending on the specifications of the entities involved in the sentence generation, e.g., Part-Of-Speech (POS) tagging and the OP naming scheme. For instance, the adequate template from the axiom Book $\sqsubseteq \exists$isBorrowed-by.Student is "*Is* [X : Noun][P : OP_Is_Past_Part_By] [Y : Noun]*?*"[2], with X and Y are classes and P is an OP, and a valid question is "Is a book borrowed by a student?" rather than "Does a book borrowed by a student?". Thereby, we design the question card to accommodate several linguistic templates so that the verbalisation approach may implement a strategy to select the appropriate one.

One may combine ontology element-based and natural language-driven templates (strategy chosen in Listing 1.1) by constraining the entities in the slot specification and the axiom prerequisites definitions (e.g., X $\sqsubseteq$ Document for, say, an ontology about libraries). Furthermore, for grammar-infused templates [12] for languages with complex grammars, one can go a step further to reusability and interoperability with the task ontology ToCT for declaring templates [14]. Either way, the ontology elements must be mentioned in the linguistic templates for the mappings between them and the axiom prerequisites.

The axiom pattern is also considered in the answer pattern of the question card to ease the automatic marking of the responses provided by learners in an educational setting. In addition, this could be useful for the generation of MCQs.

Mappings between the Axiom Prerequisites and Linguistic Templates. The mappings connect what is stated in the axiom prerequisites and stated in the linguistic templates for generating the sentences. The two above structures share the same slot names defined in the slot specification, which serve as mappings. Thereby, the places of the slots only depend on the definitions of the linguistic templates. For instance, in Listing 1.1 line 16, the slot [X] in the linguistic template represents a class that is defined in the axiom prerequisites in line 11, and the slot specification in line 4.

Linguistic Template used in the Question Card. The question card is abstract. Its principle is that one may use it for different types of linguistic templates, such as 'grammar-infused template' [12], since the verbaliser is not embedded in the main algorithm (CSA). In this study, the chosen linguistic template is accommodated to the verbalisation approach of AQuestGO [16] (We shall discuss the choice of this question generation approach in Subsect. 2.3.). Thereby, we select ontology element-based and natural language-driven templates as linguistic templates, and the rest of the paper is based on that.

2.2 Content Selection Algorithm

The algorithm finds all instances satisfying the abstract specifications in a given instance of the question card and an ontology, and the results are used for the verbalisation. The first step is to parse the instance of the question card. Then, the algorithm processes it with the ontology to get the valid axioms for the generation of the questions, answers and feedback based on the specifications in the

[2] In this example, Noun means that the POS of a class (X, Y) is a noun. [OP_Is_Past_Part_By] indicates that the OP is composed of 'is', a verb in a past participle form and 'by' (i.e., passive voice).

considered instance of the question card, namely, the set of axiom prerequisites and the slot specification. After reducing the research space from the latter, it recursively searches all semantically and logically valid forms of axioms based on the definitions of the axiom prerequisites. Then, CSA associates each selected ontology vocabulary element with the adequate slot. Thereafter, it outputs the set of pairs of slot and ontology element for the generation of the questions, answers and feedback. As an illustration, by using the instance of the question card in Listing 1.1 and the African Wildlife Ontology (AWO) that we used in earlier work [16], one can obtain the following output: $\{([\mathsf{Y}], \mathsf{CarnivosoursPlant}), ([\mathsf{X}], \mathsf{Plant}), ([\mathsf{Z}], \mathsf{Animal}), ([\mathsf{prop}], \mathsf{eats})\}$, satisfying the second axiom prerequisites in the instance of the question card. And the explanation of the selection is the following axioms: $\mathsf{CarnivorousPlant} \sqsubseteq \exists \mathsf{eats.Animal}$, $\mathsf{CarnivorousPlant} \sqsubseteq \mathsf{Plant}$.

One may define different axiom prerequisites to express different modelling styles in a unique or different instance(s) of the question card. Either way, the algorithm just needs to receive the necessary slot specification with adequate axiom prerequisites.

The algorithm and the source code can be found in supplementary materials.

2.3 Verbaliser

Apart from the linguistic templates in the question card and the ontology, the verbaliser only receives the set of pairs of slot and ontology element selected by CSA. Thereby, one may use any ontology verbaliser here. Practically for the realisation of the architecture, we will reuse and extend the one of [16] because it 1) explicitly incorporates axiom prerequisites for generating questions from the TBox of ontologies, 2) has shown to generate good questions with respect to the syntactic and semantic quality thereof, and 3) it is open source. Their approaches only work with natural language-driven or ontology element-based templates. Our verbaliser can combine them because of the mappings, offering more flexibility.

2.4 Outputs

There are three main categories of outputs: the questions, answers and feedback in natural language. Moreover, the explanation of the results is also provided by CSA. The explanation is the concrete valid axioms satisfying the axiom prerequisites for a given ontology. For instance, with AWO, the axioms: $\mathsf{CarnivorousPlant} \sqsubseteq \exists \mathsf{eats.Animal}$, $\mathsf{CarnivorousPlant} \sqsubseteq \mathsf{Plant}$ explains the generation of the results from the axiom prerequisites: a) $[\mathsf{Y}] \sqsubseteq [\mathsf{X}]$, (b) $[\mathsf{Y}] \sqsubseteq \exists [\mathsf{prop}].[\mathsf{Z}]$ in Listing 1.1 line 12. The answers can also be axioms, a class or an OP, and/or Boolean format, and/or a set of pairs of slot and ontology element.

There are different outputs so that one can exploit the results depending on the objectives. Thereby, it offers flexibility for the question, answer and feedback generation approaches.

3 Implementation And Evaluation

For validating the feasibility of the architecture, a particular instantiation was implemented. This was then tested on three examples to verify that it can indeed generate questions, answers and feedback. We will report on this first. Second, we compare the architecture to other systems and architectures, demonstrating its more comprehensive functionality and flexibility.

3.1 Implementation And Test Cases

We briefly present the implementation of the architecture. We choose the XML language to represent instances of the question card for reusability and interoperability. We implemented the question, answer and feedback generation with JAVA since we make use of OWL API [9] for manipulating the ontology and HermiT reasoner [8] for implementing CSA. The syntax of the axiom prerequisites is based on Manchester syntax; slots are used instead of ontology elements. Regarding the verbalisation, WordNet [15] was used for basic POS tagging, and SimpleNLG [7] resolved agreement of subject and verb, gerund form generation and article checking.

The test cases were carefully selected to show that one can generate results and deal with i) complex types of questions, ii) different modelling styles and iii) the types of questions that AQuestGO is designed for [16] by adopting the architecture. An extended version of the AWO is used for the first test, which was also used by [16], and two test ontologies for the second test (see supplementary materials), containing the following:

1. $ontology_a$, with: $\mathsf{Person} \sqsubseteq \mathsf{PhysicalObject}$, $\mathsf{Student} \sqsubseteq \mathsf{SocialObject}$, $\mathsf{SocialObject} \sqsubseteq \exists \mathsf{inheresIn.PhysicalObject}$, $\mathsf{Student} \sqsubseteq \exists \mathsf{inheresIn.Person}$, $\mathsf{PhysicalObject} \sqsubseteq \neg \mathsf{SocialObject}$ and $\mathsf{Student} \sqsubseteq \exists \mathsf{borrows.Book}$ (a subsumption relation representation); and
2. $ontology_b$, with: $\mathsf{Student} \sqsubseteq \mathsf{Person}$ and $\mathsf{Book} \sqsubseteq \mathsf{Document}$ (a role representation), where $ontology_b$ is semantically similar to $ontology_a$.

Complex Types of Questions. We chose AWO and *qCard2* in Listing 1.2 for the first test case, where two different questions (lines 18 and 19) were defined for the same answer. And all questions that can be asked for the same answer will be generated if the axiom prerequisites in line 14 are satisfied. One can remark that the two different linguistic templates can use different slots.

Listing 1.2. Example of a *qCard2* question card instance that deals with a complex type of question, represented in an abstract specification (see online supplementary material for the equivalent XML representation). C and OP are the sets of classes and object properties (OPs), respectively.

1 **question card name**: qCard2 *(a question card instance)*
2 **type of question**: Which X prop Y?
3 **begin** {slot specification}

4 **slot (1, 2, 3, 4, 5)**: '[X]', '[Y]', '[Z]', '[W]' and '[S]' representing a class in $\mathsf{C}_1 = \{\forall \mathsf{c} \in \mathsf{C} : \mathsf{c} \sqsubseteq \mathsf{Animal}\}$

5 **slot (6, 7)**: '[P1]' and '[P3]' representing a class in $\mathsf{C}_2 = \{\forall \mathsf{c} \in \mathsf{C} : \mathsf{c} \sqsubseteq \mathsf{PlantParts}\}$

6 **slot (8, 9, 10)**: '[P2]', '[P4]' and '[P5]' representing a class in $\mathsf{C}_3 = \{\forall \mathsf{c} \in \mathsf{C} : \mathsf{c} \sqsubseteq \mathsf{Plant}\}$

7 **slot (11, 12, 13, 14)**: '[prop1]', '[prop2]', '[prop3]' and '[prop4]' representing an OP in $\mathsf{OP}_1 = \{\forall \mathsf{p} \in \mathsf{OP} : \mathsf{p} \sqsubseteq \mathsf{eats}\}$

8 **slot (15, 16)**: '[prop5]' and '[prop6]' representing an OP in $\mathsf{OP}_2 = \{\forall \mathsf{p} \in \mathsf{OP} : \mathsf{p} \sqsubseteq \mathsf{part\text{-}of}\}$

9 **slot (17)**: '[prop8]' representing the OP live-on

10 **slot (18)**: '[Omni]' representing the class Omnivore

11 **slot (19)**: '[L]' representing the class Land

12 **end** {slot specification}

13 **begin** {set of axiom prerequisites}

14 **axiom prerequisites (1)**: (a) $[\mathsf{X}] \sqsubseteq [\mathsf{Z}]$, (b) $[\mathsf{X}] \sqsubseteq [\mathsf{Omni}]$, (c) $[\mathsf{S}]\neg[\mathsf{Omni}]$, (d) $[\mathsf{X}] \sqsubseteq \forall[\mathsf{prop8}].[\mathsf{L}]$, (e) $[\mathsf{X}] \sqsubseteq \exists[\mathsf{prop1}].[\mathsf{Z}] \sqcap \exists[\mathsf{prop2}].[\mathsf{P1}] \sqcap \exists[\mathsf{prop3}].[\mathsf{P2}] \sqcap \exists [\mathsf{prop3}].[\mathsf{P3}]$

15 **end** {set of axiom prerequisites}

16 **begin** {QAF specification}

17 **begin** {question template (qt)}

18 **qt(1)**: What [Z/noArticle], which is not [S] and [prop8/third] [L], [prop1/third] some [Y] and the following plants or parts of plants: [P1], [P2] and [P3]?

19 **qt(2)**: What is the mysterious object? It is [Z]. It is not [S] and [prop8/third] [L]. It is [Omni], and [prop1/third] some [Y] and the following plants or parts of plants: [P1], [P2] and [P3].

20 **end** {question template (qt)}

21 **begin** {answer pattern}

22 **answer template**: The answer is [X].

23 **axiom pattern**: [X]

24 **end** {answer pattern}

25 **feedback template**: The answer is [X], since [X] is [Omni], which means that [X] can eat animals and plants.

26 **end** {QAF specification}

The instantiation of the architecture can generate, for example, the two following questions 1) "What animal, which is not a carnivore and lives on land, eats some animal and the following plants or parts of plants: a root, grass and a fruiting body?" (Linguistic template in Listing 1.2, line 18) and 2) "What is the mysterious object? It is an animal. It is not a herbivore and lives on land. It is an omnivore, and eats some animal and the following plants or parts of plants: a fruiting body, grass and a root." (Linguistic template in Listing 1.2, line 19). It can then generate the following answer: "The answer is a warthog." (Linguistic template in Listing 1.2, line 22) and feedback: "The answer is a warthog, since a warthog is an omnivore, which means that a warthog can eat animals and plants." (Linguistic template in Listing 1.2, line 25). The axiom-based explanation can also be provided as discussed previously in Subsect. 2.4.

Table 1. Comparison of the approach to existing studies; predef. = predefined; TQ = type of question, TA = type of answer, SA = short answer, CA = complex answer, FC = feedback on correct answer, FI = feedback on incorrect answer, DF = dynamic feedback, MS = considering modelling styles, AP = considering axiom prerequisites, RV = replaceable verbaliser and LR = language restriction.

Criteria	[1]	[16]	[13]	[19]	[4]	[11]	our architecture
TQ	predef	predef	predef	predef	predef	predef	**flexible**
TA	predef	predef	predef	predef	predef	predef	**flexible**
MCQs	**yes**	no	no	**yes**	**yes**	**yes**	no
Yes/No	**yes**	**yes**	**yes**	no	**yes**	no	**yes**
SA	**yes**	**yes**	**yes**	no	**yes**	no	**yes**
CA	no	no	no	no	no	no	**yes**
FC	no	no	no	no	no	**yes**	**yes**
FI	no	no	no	no	no	**yes**	no
DF	no	no	no	no	no	no	**yes**
MS	no	no	no	no	no	no	**yes**
AP	no	**yes**	no	no	no	no	**yes**
RV	no	no	no	no	no	no	**yes**
LR	less than $\mathcal{ALC}$	$\mathcal{ALC}$	n/c	$\mathcal{SHIQ}$	n/c	n/c	**none**

Different Modelling Styles. We used *ontology*$_a$ and *ontology*$_b$ and the question card presented in Listing 1.1 to show that the architecture can deal with different modelling styles. When using *ontology*$_a$, the first axiom prerequisites (Listing 1.1, line 11) are selected by CSA since they are conformed to the content of the ontology. And the verbaliser generates the question: "What type of person borrows a book?" (Linguistic template in Listing 1.2, line 16) and the answer: "The answer is a student.". The generated axiom-based explanation is: $\mathsf{Person} \sqsubseteq \neg\mathsf{Student}$, $\mathsf{Student} \sqsubseteq \exists\mathsf{borrows.Book}$, $\mathsf{Student} \sqsubseteq \exists\mathsf{inheresIn.Person}$, $\mathsf{Document} \sqsubseteq \mathsf{PhysicalObject}$, $\mathsf{SocialObject} \sqsubseteq \exists\mathsf{inheresIn.PhysicalObject}$, $\mathsf{PhysicalObject} \sqsubseteq \neg\mathsf{SocialObject}$, and $\mathsf{Student} \sqsubseteq \mathsf{SocialObject}$. And with the same instance of the question card and *ontology*$_b$ as input, CSA selects the second axiom prerequisites for generating the same results with a different explanation: $\mathsf{Student} \sqsubseteq \exists\mathsf{borrows.Book}$ and $\mathsf{Student} \sqsubseteq \mathsf{Person}$.

Types of Questions Defined in AQuestGO. Raboanary et al. [16] investigated ten types of useful educational questions. We were able to represent all these types of questions in instances of the question card, and we did the generation by using AWO. As an illustration, from the type of question: yes/no with one class and one property, one can generate the question: "Does a bumble bee fly?", the answer: 'yes' and the explanation: $\mathsf{BumbleBee} \sqsubseteq \exists\mathsf{Participate\text{-}In.Fly}$, with $\mathsf{BumbleBee} \sqsubseteq \mathsf{Endurant}$ and $\mathsf{Fly} \sqsubseteq \mathsf{Perdurant}$. All results are available online.

3.2 Comparing the New Architecture to the Existing Studies

We compare and discuss the new architecture with the relevant existing studies [1,4,11,13,16,19] considering the following criteria: the dynamic aspect of the types of questions and answers, the generation of feedback, the consideration of the modelling styles and the axiom prerequisites, the replaceability of the verbaliser and the language restriction. The comparison is presented in Table 1.

Existing studies only deal with predefined types of questions. Their architecture is rigid and cannot support flexibility. This limits their approach's maintainability, extensibility, reusability and generalisability. The newly designed approach does not suffer this problem since all specifications are defined externally in instances of the question card, which offers flexibility. The types of answers are flexible in our architecture, whereas it is not the case for the others. Our architecture can specify the answer as a very complex axiom or a very long text, while [1,13,16] are only limited to yes/no and short answer questions, for instance. Leo et al. [11] consider feedback generation. However, since their types of questions are predefined, they are not dynamic. They took into account generating feedback for incorrect answers, a feature our architecture does not have, and it does not generate the distractors of MCQs. However, one may use Alsubait's findings [2] to adapt our study for MCQs generations, for instance. Then, only our architecture considers dealing with different modelling styles, and apart from our study, only [16] considers the axiom prerequisites for the types of questions. Also, our approach does not have language restrictions when expressing the axiom prerequisites.

Further, observe that other verbalisers with different verbalisation techniques can be attached to the architecture since the output of the content selection algorithm is a set of pairs of slot and ontology element. It is also amenable to generating questions for other languages, such as French or Malagasy, provided the ontology has such vocabulary and the templates are in said language.

4 Conclusion

We designed a new architecture for generating questions, answers and feedback from ontologies that is able to deal with non-predefined types of questions and different modelling styles. The test cases from an instantiation of the architecture show that the new architecture offers flexibility since all processes can be done by only instantiating the question card externally for defining the necessary specifications for generating the questions, answers and feedback. Further, our analysis shows that our study compares favourably to existing proposals in terms of flexibility and functionality. This architecture is a step to generalising the generation of questions, answers and feedback from ontologies. As future work, we plan to automatically create instances of the question card to reduce manual efforts as well as human-in-the-loop control mechanisms.

Acknowledgements. TR acknowledges support from the Hasso Plattner Institute for Digital Engineering through the HPI Research School at UCT.

References

1. Abacha, A.B., Dos Reis, J.C., Mrabet, Y., Pruski, C., Da Silveira, M.: Towards natural language question generation for the validation of ontologies and mappings. J. Biomed. Semant. **7**(1), 1–15 (2016)
2. Alsubait, T.: Ontology-based multiple-choice question generation. Ph.D. thesis, University of Manchester, Manchester, England (2015)
3. Chaudhri, V.K., Clark, P.E., Overholtzer, A., Spaulding, A.: Question generation from a knowledge base. In: Janowicz, K., Schlobach, S., Lambrix, P., Hyvönen, E. (eds.) EKAW 2014. LNCS (LNAI), vol. 8876, pp. 54–65. Springer, Cham (2014). https://doi.org/10.1007/978-3-319-13704-9_5
4. Chaudhri, V., et al.: Inquire biology: a textbook that answers questions. AI Mag. **34**(3), 55–72 (2013)
5. Fillottrani, P.R., Keet, C.M.: Patterns for heterogeneous TBox mappings to bridge different modelling decisions. In: Blomqvist, E., Maynard, D., Gangemi, A., Hoekstra, R., Hitzler, P., Hartig, O. (eds.) ESWC 2017. LNCS, vol. 10249, pp. 371–386. Springer, Cham (2017). https://doi.org/10.1007/978-3-319-58068-5_23
6. Gardent, C., Perez-Beltrachini, L.: Using FB-LTAG derivation trees to generate transformation-based grammar exercices. In: Proceedings of the TAG+11, pp. 117–125. ACL (2011). sep 2012, Paris, France
7. Gatt, A., Reiter, E.: SimpleNLG: a realisation engine for practical applications. In: Krahmer, E., Theune, M. (eds.) Proceedings of the 12th European Workshop on Natural Language Generation, ENLG 2009, pp. 90–93. Association for Computational Linguistics (ACL), Athens, Greece, March 2009
8. Glimm, B., Horrocks, I., Motik, B., Stoilos, G., Wang, Z.: HermiT: an OWL 2 reasoner. J. Autom. Reason. **53**(3), 245–269 (2014)
9. Horridge, M., Bechhofer, S.: The OWL API: a java API for OWL ontologies. Semant. Web **2**(1), 11–21 (2011)
10. Lange, H., Ljunglöf, P.: Putting control into language learning. In: Davis, B., Keet, C.M., Wyner, A. (eds.) Proceedings of Controlled Natural Language Workshop (CNL'18). FAIA, vol. 304, pp. 61–70. IOS Press (2018)
11. Leo, J., et al.: Ontology-based generation of medical, multi-term MCQs. Int. J. Artif. Intell. Educ. **29**(2), 145–188 (2019)
12. Mahlaza, Z., Keet, C.M.: A classification of grammar-infused templates for ontology and model verbalisation. In: Garoufallou, E., Fallucchi, F., William De Luca, E. (eds.) MTSR 2019. CCIS, vol. 1057, pp. 64–76. Springer, Cham (2019). https://doi.org/10.1007/978-3-030-36599-8_6
13. Mahlaza, Z., Keet, C.M.: OWLSIZ: An isiZulu CNL for structured knowledge validation. In: Proceedings of the 3rd International Workshop on Natural Language Generation from the Semantic Web (WebNLG+), pp. 15–25 (2020)
14. Mahlaza, Z., Keet, C.M.: ToCT: a task ontology to manage complex templates. In: Proceedings of the 12th International Conference on Formal Ontology in Information Systems, FOIS 2021. CEUR, Bolzano, Italy (2021)
15. Miller, G.A.: WordNet: a lexical database for English. Commun. ACM **38**(11), 39–41 (1995)
16. Raboanary, T., Wang, S., Keet, C.M.: Generating answerable questions from ontologies for educational exercises. In: Garoufallou, E., Ovalle-Perandones, M.-A., Vlachidis, A. (eds.) MTSR 2021. CCIS, vol. 1537, pp. 28–40. Springer, Cham (2022). https://doi.org/10.1007/978-3-030-98876-0_3
17. Ramos-Soto, A., Bugarin, A.J., Barro, S., Taboada, J.: Linguistic descriptions for automatic generation of textual short-term weather forecasts on real prediction data. IEEE Trans. Fuzzy Syst. **23**(1), 44–57 (2014)

18. Rodríguez Rocha, O., Faron Zucker, C.: Automatic generation of quizzes from DBpedia according to educational standards. In: Lahoud, I., Cardoso, E., Matta, N. (eds.) Proceedings fo the 3rd Educational Knowledge Management Workshop, EKM 2018, pp. 1035–1041. Lyon, France, 23–27 April 2018
19. Venugopal, V.E., Kumar, P.S.: A novel approach to generate MCQs from domain ontology: considering DL semantics and open-world assumption. J. Web Semant. **34**, 40–54 (2015)
20. Venugopal, V.E., Kumar, P.S.: Automated generation of assessment tests from domain ontologies. Semant. Web **8**(6), 1023–1047 (2017)

Process-Level Integration for Linked Open Data Development Workflows: A Case Study

Manuel Fiorelli[1](✉), Armando Stellato[1], Ilaria Rosati[2], and Nicola Fiore[3]

[1] Department of Enterprise Engineering, University of Rome Tor Vergata, Via del Politecnico 1, 00133 Rome, Italy
{manuel.fiorelli,stellato}@uniroma2.it

[2] Institute of Research on Terrestrial Ecosystems (IRET), National Research Council (CNR), 73100 Lecce, Italy
ilaria.rosati@cnr.it

[3] LifeWatch ERIC Service Centre, Lecce, Italy
nicola.fiore@lifewatch.eu

Abstract. Dataset maintenance and development is a complex endeavor that necessitates the use of different systems through the dataset lifecycle. The semantic web succeeded in setting common standards that enable data interchange between these systems. Still, there is often a lack of interoperability and integration at the process level, indispensable to use different systems in a single, combined workflow. In this regard, we considered use cases concerning the interaction of dataset editors with content publication/fruition systems, which provide a linked data interface, and dataset catalogs, which meet the FAIR principle of findability and persistency. As a case study, we considered ShowVoc and OntoPortal as examples of these two classes of systems. Having committed to the collaborative knowledge editor VocBench 3, we contributed extensions for it that address the defined use cases. Evaluating our contributions, we identified some aspects of future improvement in the relevant subset of VocBench 3.

Keywords: linked open data · workflow · integration · catalogs · publication · OntoPortal · ShowVoc · VocBench

1 Introduction

The semantic web [1] was conceived as an extension of the traditional document web, aimed at enabling machines to better understand and process resources on the web through the explication of their intended semantics. Although the original vision has not been delivered yet, research on semantic web – renewed by the linked open data paradigm [2] – succeeded in the definition of common standards for data publication, reuse, and integration [3], towards the realization of a web of data, evolving the current document web into a global data space [4]. Unsurprisingly, a lot of systems have been developed to cover the different stages of the data lifecycle on the semantic web, including – but not limited to – (collaborative) editing, linking, and publication. Related to the latter,

E. Garoufallou and A. Vlachidis (Eds.): MTSR 2022, CCIS 1789, pp. 148–159, 2023.
https://doi.org/10.1007/978-3-031-39141-5_13

the semantic web has traditionally relied on decentralization and, with the advent of link open data, data publishers are in charge of setting up HTTP servers so that resource IRIs resolve into different representations (e.g., HTML for humans and different RDF serializations for machines), while the primary mechanism to find information is link traversal – often called "follow your nose". Search engines (e.g., Google, Bing, Yahoo, Baidu), which have become the entry point to the web, are still not widely established on the semantic web (nor have existing actors provided large support for it, having developed their own internal "knowledge graphs"); nonetheless, some forms of centralization have already made their way to the semantic web through data catalogs [5–7], which address a variety of needs, not least persistency against failure of the original data sources. In fact, catalogs acquire primary importance at the intersection of the semantic web and the open data movement. The latter has promoted data accessibility as a means to increase accountability and transparency of governments and organizations as well to speed up scientific progress. The scientific open data community eventually formulated the FAIR principles [8] for data management and stewardship with the idea of reducing obstacles to data reuse. Metadata and catalogs play a critical role in this, as they facilitate the discovery of relevant datasets through keyword search and other criteria. Showing their closeness to the semantic web aims, the FAIR guidelines actually value machine-actionability, defined as "the capacity of computational systems to find, access, interoperate, and reuse data with none or minimal human intervention"[1]. As an example, metadata and catalogs have been used to orchestrate ontology matching processes [9, 10].

Dataset development and publication according to the practices and principles just described require a complex workflow, which inevitably relies on different systems. The common standards set by the semantic web may support data interchange between these systems; still, there is often a need for better interoperability and integration at the process level – as required to use them in a single, combined workflow. In this regard, our contribution is a set of bridges between different systems that address data editing, publication/fruition, and cataloging.

In this study, we committed to VocBench 3 [11] as the editing system, and then exploited its extensible data loading and export facilities, as well as its support for dataset catalogs in order to enable interoperability with other relevant tools. As a case study, we developed concrete extensions for ShowVoc[2] – a new read-only companion to VocBench 3 for data publication/fruition – and OntoPortal[3] – a software for data catalogs originated from the BioPortal repository of biontologies. Thanks to our contributions, these two disparate systems have been successfully integrated into a cohesive ecosystem centered on VocBench 3.

The paper is structured as follows. Section 2 discusses related work. Section 3 defines our use cases. Section 4 describes our contribution in the context of VocBench 3 architecture. Section 5 describes the extensions that we developed for our case study. Section 6 is about evaluation. Section 7 contains the conclusions.

[1] https://www.go-fair.org/fair-principles/.

[2] https://showvoc.uniroma2.it/.

[3] https://ontoportal.org/.

2 Related Work

There is a large number of editors for the semantic web addressing different concerns.

Protégé [12] is a renowned, long-standing open-source ontology editor. Extensibility is one of Protégé strong points, which contributed to its adoption as a de facto standard development platform for ontology-related research. WebProtégé [13] is a recent companion to the original software (now called Protégé Desktop) providing a collaborative, web-based ontology development environment. Generic ontology development tools may not be so effective to support dataset development conforming to specific modeling vocabularies, say SKOS(-XL) [14, 15] for thesauri or OntoLex [16] for lexicons, requiring dedicated software [17–19].

PoolParty Semantic Suite [20] is a family of proprietary systems addressing data management, data ingestion – including acquisition form textual sources – and exploitation in semantic search. PoolParty features dedicated support for SKOS thesauri. TopQuadrant Enterprise Data Governance [21] is another propriety system with a strong focus on data governance, lineage-tracking, etc.

VocBench 3 is an open-source web-application for collaborative editing of ontologies, thesauri, lexicons, and RDF-datasets in general, complying with all relevant semantic web standards. Multi-model editing and compliance with standards are two tenants of VocBench 3 together with its several extensibility features (ranging from very complex plugins to implementations of predetermined extension points).

Most editing systems support data extraction from a variety of sources and loading the edited data onto diverse destinations. The latter includes publication of data. PoolParty integrates UnifiedViews [22], which can source raw data from downloads, HTTP API and PoolParty Concept Extraction, while allowing loading data onto a SPARQL endpoint. TopQuadrant Enterprise Data Governance can export data to files and, optionally, upload them to AWS S3 [23]. Both editors can export a dataset to a service for content fruition, respectively, TopBraid Explorer, and the Wiki Frontend (also supporting lightweight editing) or the Linked Data Frontend. A special use case of data input/output is related to tabular data (e.g., CSV files, spreadsheets, etc.) for which editing systems often have dedicated facilities [24]. As an example, VocBench 3 provides a dedicate tool, called Sheet2RDF [25], which builds upon the knowledge acquisition platform CODA [26].

Protégé has a plugin [27] to import data from BioPortal. It enables to reference entities found in ontologies hosted on BioPortal, and to import their definitions into the dataset being edited: indeed, bioontologies often combine concepts from different ontologies/namespaces. Similarly, PoolParty enables enriching a dataset with information fetched from (previously connected) Linked Data sources[4].

We conclude with a brief discussion of linked data publication software. Pubby[5] is the progenitor of a lineage of tools that implement HTTP resolution (requested by the

4 https://help.poolparty.biz/en/user-guide-for-knowledge-engineers/advanced-features/linked-data-management---overview/linked-data-enrichment-with-poolparty.html.

5 https://github.com/cygri/pubby.

linked data paradigm) on top of a SPARQL endpoint. More recent solutions include LodView[6] and Loddy[7], not to mention the ones integrated into editing tools or triple stores. Skosmos[8] combines traditional subject pages (i.e., the result of content negotiation) for SKOS thesauri with more sophisticated visualizations (e.g., alphabetic index over the dataset), search and multi-thesaurus management. ShowVoc extends this approach beyond thesauri to ontologies, lexicons, and datasets in general: it focuses on content fruition and cross-dataset operations (e.g., global search), and it also supports content negotiation.

3 Use Cases

We set the requirements for our contributions through the identification of the following use cases. They define different interaction scenarios between VocBench 3 – chosen as editing system – and dataset catalogs and content publication/fruition systems.

3.1 Pull

The first scenario concerns with the need to *pull* a dataset from a catalog. We can further distinguish between i) *loading data* and ii) *importing ontologies*, depending on whether the pulled data is being put in the editable part of the dataset or just available as read-only.

3.2 Pull-Push

The second scenario extends the previous one with the subsequent upload of the pulled data to another different system, using VocBench 3 as a pivot. This is probably a less common use case, dealing with the re-publication of already existing datasets.

3.3 Push-Push

The third scenario is related to an integrated workflow for dataset development. VocBench 3 enables collaborative editing of a dataset, which is then pushed to a system for data publication/fruition (e.g., ShowVoc) and another system for cataloging (e.g., an OntoPortal instance).

4 Architecture

VocBench 3 is very flexible in both exporting and loading data, thanks to extension points that allow different destinations and data sources to be linked, respectively.

Figure 1 illustrates the export of a dataset to a i) a triple store, ii) a downloadable file, iii) a custom destination. In fact, the export chain is introduced by an optional chain of *RDF transformers* that can process the data before being exported. These transformers are defined by an *extension point* that enables to plug diverse implementations.

[6] https://github.com/LodLive/LodView.

[7] https://bitbucket.org/art-uniroma2/loddy.

[8] https://skosmos.org/.

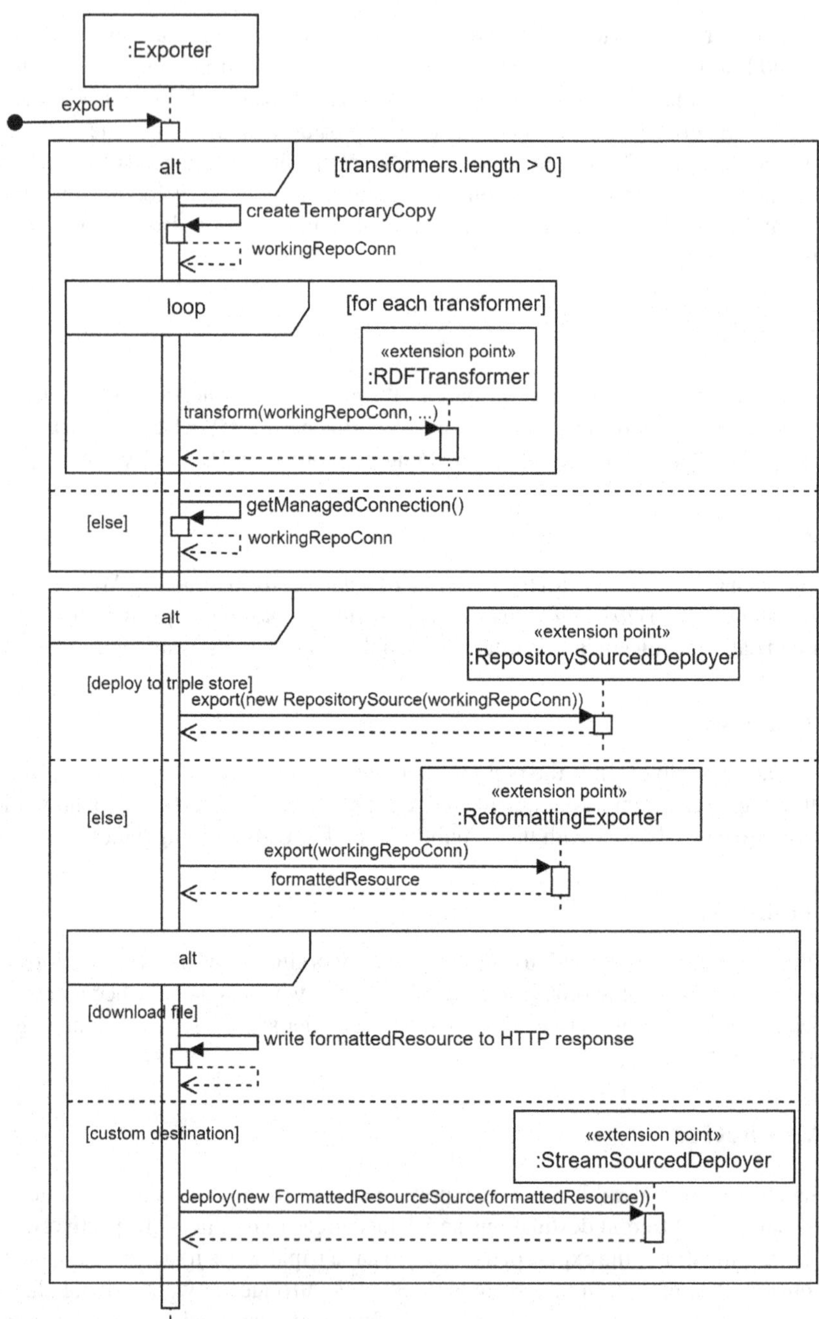

Fig. 1. Execution of the data export pipeline (UML2 sequence diagram)

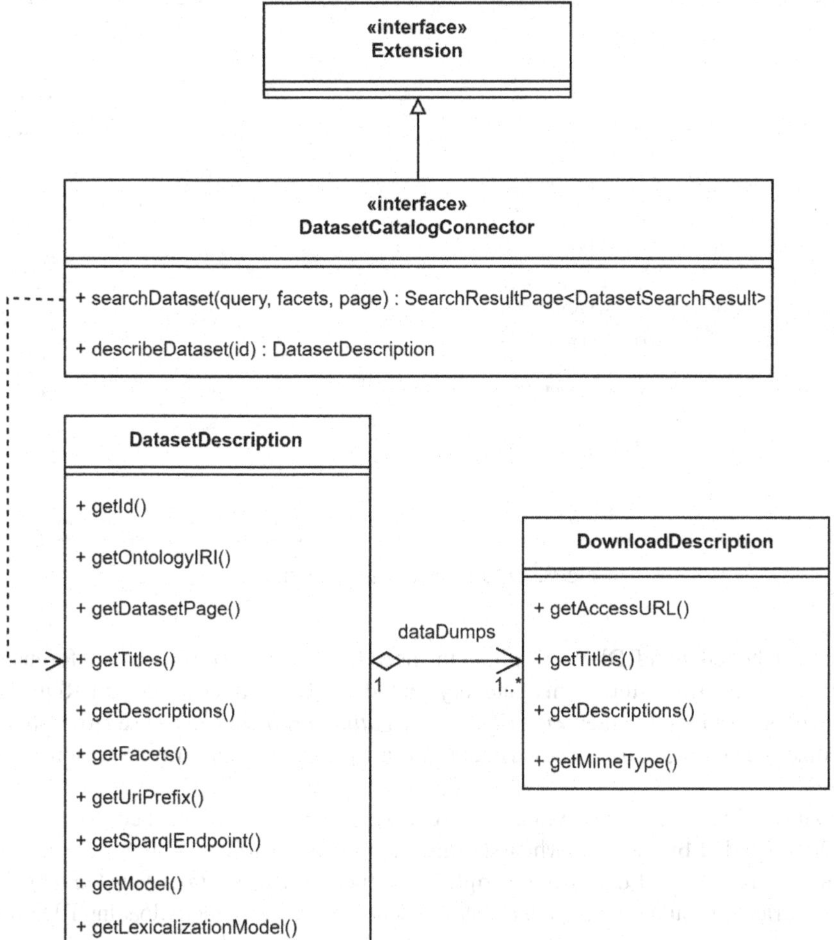

Fig. 2. Simplified UML class diagram for the extension point dataset catalog connector

Prepackaged transformers include one for simple property value update and another utilizing SPARQL to specify the transformation. These transformers are executed on a temporary copy of the dataset being exported, as they could perform potentially destructive changes that should not be applied to the original dataset. The rest of the export pipeline will use a working connection to this temporary copy; alternatively, when no transformation is necessary, no temporary copy is created, avoiding the (unnecessary) costs associated with that, while directly working with a (read-only) connection to the dataset being exported.

The export pipeline continues differently depending on the destination type. Unless the exported data is to be downloaded, a *deployer* is invoked ultimately. Again, this is an extension point, which is further specialized into *repository sourced deployer* (for deploying to a triple store) and *stream sourced deployer* (for deploying to a stream-oriented destination). In this context, triple store is broadly intended as any destination

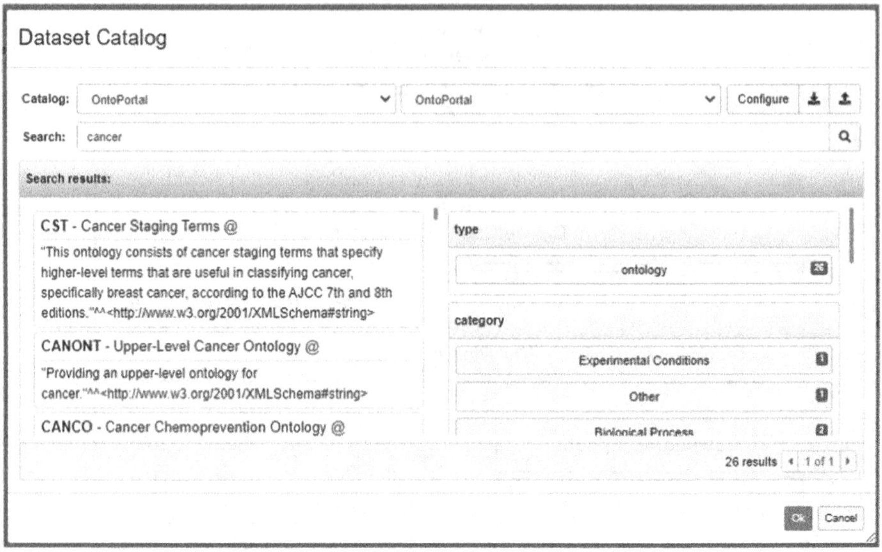

Fig. 3. Dataset catalog user interface

which can be fed with RDF data without the need for an explicit conversion beforehand. Beyond actual triple stores, this category includes RDF data catalogs and RDF data publication services. In other scenarios, a *reformatting exporter* can be used to explicitly serialize the (possibly transformed) data into a byte stream conforming to some data format.

Data loading is somehow symmetric to the export mechanism described so far. Unless data is uploaded by the user when starting the process, a *loader* – another extension point – is used to pull data from a triple store (i.e., *repository targeting loader*) or a stream-oriented source (i.e., *stream targeting loader*). Unless directly loading RDF data from a triple store, it is necessary to use an *RDF lifter* – another extension point – to convert the pulled byte stream into actual RDF data. At the end of the loading pipeline, a transformation chain can be used to implement data massaging.

Another requirement lifted from the use cases is the need for accessing a data catalog to lookup for datasets. We addressed it using the extension point *dataset catalog connector* (see Fig. 2). A connector provides an operation to *search for a dataset* (returning a paginated list of results) and an operation to *obtain a description of a dataset*. The latter is modeled with a class that includes general metadata (e.g., titles and descriptions) mostly targeted at humans, as well as other more machine actionable metadata, such as *model* (telling the difference between an OWL ontology, SKOS thesaurus, etc.), *lexicalization model* (telling how lexical information is represented), and the *data dumps*. These are described in turn with actionable metadata such as the *access URL* (to fetch the dump) and *MIME-type* (telling the data format and charset).

Data catalogs are presented as another option for importing an ontology or loading data. In fact, they just provide the ontology IRI or the data dump access URL to the already existing machinery for ontology import – from an (alternative) URL – or data loading – from an URL. Figure 3 illustrates the dialog for searching a dataset on a catalog. The first step is to select a connector implementation (e.g., the contributed connector for OntoPortal) and, if required, configure it. At this point, it is possible to issue a query based on some search terms. The results are presented as a list, complemented on the right by catalog-specific facets to refine the query. When a dataset is chosen, its description is shown on the right.

5 Case Study: ShowVoc and OntoPortal

Our case study for the architecture discussed in Sect. 4 is the use of VocBench 3 to integrate (at the process level) both ShowVoc (for data publication and fruition) and OntoPortal (for data cataloging).

Looking at use cases in Sect. 3, all but the pull scenario require the ability to deploy data to either system. We thus implemented a *deployer* for each application, which have been considered as *triple store destinations*. The ShowVoc deployer works by communicating with the backend server (Semantic Turkey [28]) of ShowVoc, while the OntoPortal deployer uses the REST API originally developed by BioPortal.

In the pull scenario, we need to look up a dataset in one of these applications. To this end, we implemented a *dataset catalog connector* for each system.

6 Evaluation

We compiled Table 1 to ascertain that our contributions satisfy the needs associated with the scenarios discussed in Sect. 3.

The response time of dataset catalog connectors and deployers is mostly determined by the performance of the backing service. This holds true, in particular, when the extension is implemented through a single request to the backing service with a minimal overhead. We consider uninformative any performance discussion in this case, since there is little that can be ascribed to our implementation. In fact, the OntoPortal connector does not fall into such scenario, since the OntoPortal API does not have a dedicated ontology search endpoint – while offering some for concept-lookup.

We followed the example of the OntoPortal web application, which implements a searchable catalog in the *ontologies* page. In absence of a dedicated search API, the web application first retrieves all ontologies (metadata), and all categories and groups, which can be used to classify ontologies: the description of an ontology just references the IRI of a group or category, thus necessitating the description of the latter to obtain their human-friendly names. In fact, the description of an ontology does not contain metadata used (in the user interface) as search facets (i.e., modification date, data format), nor does it include the textual description of the ontology. These missing attributes are, indeed, derived from the latest submission for the ontology. Consequently, the web application also fetches the latest submissions for all ontologies (through a single request). All the retrieved information is then incorporated into the *ontologies* page, which implements search completely client-side (without further requests to the backend).

Given the complexity of the implementation of the search functionality for OntoPortal, it is worth evaluating its performance through some experiments (see Table 2). We

Table 1. Requirements traceability matrix

Scenario	Features
pull – i) loading data	use of data catalogs in data loading, or in preloading when creating a project
pull – ii) importing ontologies	use of data catalogs when importing an ontology
pull - push	those in the first row, together with the use of deployers to "triple stores"
push - push	use of deployers to "triple stores"

made these experiments against BioPortal, which is the largest installation of OntoPortal to date. The first two rows describe the (minimum, maximum, and average) response time of a search using our dataset catalog connector with the term "cancer". The difference between these two is whether we perform the additional step of retrieving the list of all latest submissions. The third row is the time required to download just the HTML of the *ontologies* pages (which embeds all information for doing a search). The fourth row is the time required to retrieve all ontologies using the API (including just the required attributes in the obtained objects).

Our measures are consistent with the fact that the third and fourth rows should be an upper and lower bound of our connector runtime, respectively: without a search API it is not possible to be quicker than a listing of all ontologies, and the implementation should not be slower than the ontologies page, which contains all required information. The difference between the first and second row is 1.2 s on average, justifying our decision to let users decide which configuration to use.

We conclude the evaluation with a discussion of the VocBench 3 architecture, highlighting some aspects that could require future improvements.

Dataset catalog connectors must be stateless (by design); therefore, current service processing cannot benefit from the work done for previous requests. This is not a problem when the actual work is done by the connected service. Conversely, the OntoPortal connector implements the search locally, against metadata about all ontologies retrieved on the fly. In this scenario, it makes sense to enable storing this metadata at least on the session, avoiding the need to repeat the costly API invocation that would most likely return exactly the same results in the short term. The problem with caching as obvious is the strategy to evict the cache, in order to guarantee the freshness of the result.

As discussed about the VocBench 3 architecture, dataset catalog connectors are loosely coupled to the data loading and ontology import machinery as a mere provider of the data access URL. However, this could be problematic when the location of a resource is not sufficient. For example, when accessing a protected resource, we need to authorize the data access. For OntoPortal, we addressed this use case, by embedding the API key as a query parameter – a controversial practice, which is also used in some parts of the OntoPortal web application. A possible solution is to let the data loading and ontology import machinery to directly invoke the dataset catalog connector when downloading the data, in order to delegate to it authentication concerns.

Table 2. Response time evaluation related to the OntoPortal connector (using 50 repetitions)

	Min (s)	Max (s)	Avg (s)
OntoPortal Dataset Catalog connector w/o submissions	2.306785	3.182033	2.425709
OntoPortal Dataset Catalog connector w/ submissions	3.364919	8.696316	3.59604518
BioPortal "ontologies" page	3.365554	5.761266	3.752337
BioPortal API ontologies collection	1.232167	2.841468	1.557863

7 Conclusions

Dataset development for the semantic web unavoidably requires the use of different tools, which have to be integrated into a unified workflow at the process level. Assigning a pivotal role to the editing environment, we committed to the use of VocBench 3 and identified some use cases concerning its interaction with dataset catalogs and fruition/publication systems. We considered an actual case study using OntoPortal and ShowVoc as concrete examples of these two categories of systems. We addressed the defined use cases through extensions to VocBench 3 related to data load and export processes, and the support for dataset catalogs. The evaluation of our contributions then allowed us to identify possible future improvements to the VocBench 3 architecture.

Acknowledgements. This work has been supported by the European e-science infrastructure for biodiversity and ecosystem research LifeWatch Eric and by LifeWatch Italy through the project "LifeWatchPLUS" - PIR01_00028. It also received support from the KATY project, which has received funding from the European Union's Horizon 2020 research and innovation programme under grant agreement No 101017453.

References

1. Berners-Lee, T., Hendler, J.A., Lassila, O.: The semantic web: a new form of web content that is meaningful to computers will unleash a revolution of new possibilities. Sci. Am. **284**(5), 34–43 (2001)
2. Berners-Lee, T.: Linked data. In: Design Issues (2006). https://www.w3.org/DesignIssues/LinkedData.html
3. Shadbolt, N., Berners-Lee, T., Hall, W.: The semantic web revisited. IEEE Intell. Syst. **21**(3), 96–101 (2006)
4. Heath, T., Bizer, C.: Linked data: evolving the web into a global data space. Synth. Lect. Semant. Web: Theory Technol. **1**(1), 1–136 (2011)
5. Vandenbussche, P.-Y., Atemezing, G.A., Poveda-Villalón, M., Vatant, B.: Linked open vocabularies (LOV): a gateway to reusable semantic vocabularies on the web. Semant. Web **8**(3), 437–452 (2017)

6. Whetzel, P.L., et al.: BioPortal: enhanced functionality via new Web services from the national center for biomedical ontology to access and use ontologies in software applications. Nucleic Acids Res. **39**(suppl_2), W541–W545 (2011)
7. Jackson, R. et al.: OBO foundry in 2021: operationalizing open data principles to evaluate ontologies. Database **2021**, baab069 (2021)
8. Wilkinson, M.D., et al.: The FAIR guiding principles for scientific data management and stewardship. Sci. Data **3**(160018) (2016)
9. Fiorelli, M., et al.: Metadata-driven semantic coordination. In: Garoufallou, E., Fallucchi, F., William De Luca, E. (eds.) MTSR 2019. CCIS, vol. 1057, pp. 16–27. Springer, Cham (2019). https://doi.org/10.1007/978-3-030-36599-8_2
10. Mochol, M., Jentzsch, A.: Towards a rule-based matcher Selection. In: Gangemi, A., Euzenat, J. (eds.) EKAW 2008. LNCS (LNAI), vol. 5268, pp. 109–119. Springer, Heidelberg (2008). https://doi.org/10.1007/978-3-540-87696-0_12
11. Stellato, A., et al.: VocBench 3: a collaborative semantic web editor for ontologies, thesauri and lexicons. Semant. Web **11**(5), 855–881 (2020). https://doi.org/10.3233/SW-200370
12. Musen, M.A.: The protégé project: a look back and a look forward. AI Matters **1**(4), 4–12 (2015)
13. Tudorache, T., Nyulas, C., Noy, N.F., Musen, M.A.: WebProtégé: a collaborative ontology editor and knowledge acquisition tool for the web. Semant. Web **4**(1), 89–99 (2013)
14. World Wide Web Consortium (W3C): SKOS Simple Knowledge Organization System Reference. In: World Wide Web Consortium (W3C), 18 August 2009. http://www.w3.org/TR/skos-reference/. Accessed 22 Mar 2011
15. World Wide Web Consortium (W3C): SKOS Simple Knowledge Organization System eXtension for Labels (SKOS-XL). In: World Wide Web Consortium (W3C), 18 August 2009). http://www.w3.org/TR/skos-reference/skos-xl.html. Accessed 22 Mar 2011
16. Cimiano, P., McCrae, J.P., Buitelaar, P.: Lexicon model for ontologies: community report, 10 May 2016. Community Report, W3C (2016). https://www.w3.org/2016/05/ontolex/
17. Jupp, S., Bechhofer, S., Stevens, R.: A flexible API and editor for SKOS. In: Aroyo, L., et al. (eds.) ESWC 2009. LNCS, vol. 5554, pp. 506–520. Springer, Heidelberg (2009). https://doi.org/10.1007/978-3-642-02121-3_38
18. Fiorelli, M., Pazienza, M.T., Stellato, A.: Semantic turkey goes SKOS managing knowledge organization systems. In: I-SEMANTICS '12 Proceedings of the 8th International Conference on Semantic Systems, Graz, Austria, pp.64–71 (2012). https://doi.org/10.1145/2362499.2362509
19. Mochón, G., Méndez, E.M., Bueno de la Fuente, G.: 27 pawns ready for action: a multi-indicator methodology and evaluation of thesaurus management tools from a LOD perspective. Libr. Hi Tech **35**(1), 99–119 (2017)
20. PoolParty Semantic Suite - Semantic Technology Platform. https://www.poolparty.biz/
21. TopBraid Enterprise Data Governance. https://www.topquadrant.com/products/topbraid-enterprise-data-governance/
22. Knap, T., et al.: UnifiedViews: an ETL tool for RDF data management. Semant. Web **9**(5), 661–676 (2018)
23. AWS: Amazon S3. In: Amazon Web Services. https://aws.amazon.com/s3/
24. Fiorelli, M., Stellato, A.: Lifting tabular data to RDF: a survey. In: Garoufallou, E., Ovalle-Perandones, M.-A. (eds.) MTSR 2020. CCIS, vol. 1355, pp. 85–96. Springer, Cham (2021). https://doi.org/10.1007/978-3-030-71903-6_9
25. Fiorelli, M., Lorenzetti, T., Pazienza, M.T., Stellato, A., Turbati, A.: Sheet2RDF: a flexible and dynamic spreadsheet import & lifting framework for RDF. In: Ali, M., Kwon, Y.S., Lee, C.-H., Kim, J., Kim, Y. (eds.) IEA/AIE 2015. LNCS (LNAI), vol. 9101, pp. 131–140. Springer, Cham (2015). https://doi.org/10.1007/978-3-319-19066-2_13

26. Fiorelli, M., Pazienza, M.T., Stellato, A., Turbati, A.: CODA: computer-aided ontology development architecture. IBM J. Res. Dev. **58**(2/3), 14:1–14:12 (2014). https://doi.org/10.1147/JRD.2014.2307518
27. Nair, J., Tudorache, T., Whetzel, T., Noy, N., Musen, M.: The BioPortal import plugin for protégé. In: Bodenreider, O., Martone, M.E., Ruttenberg, A. (eds.) Proceedings of the 2nd International Conference on Biomedical Ontology, Buffalo, NY, USA, 26–30 July 2011, p. 299 (2011)
28. Pazienza, M.T., Scarpato, N., Stellato, A., Turbati, A.: Semantic Turkey: a browser-integrated environment for knowledge acquisition and management. Semant. Web J. **3**(3), 279–292 (2012). https://doi.org/10.3233/SW-2011-0033

Track on Agriculture, Food and Environment, and Metadata, Linked Data, Semantics and Ontologies - General Session

FAIRification of Multidimensional and Tabular Data by Instantiating a Core Semantic Model with Domain Knowledge: Case of Meteorology

Cassia Trojahn[1(✉)], Mouna Kamel[1], Amina Annane[2], Nathalie Aussenac-Gilles[1], Bao Long Nguyen[1], and Christophe Baehr[3]

[1] IRIT, CNRS, Université Toulouse 2, Toulouse, France
prenom.nom@irit.fr
[2] Geotrend, Toulouse, France
amina.anane@geotrend.fr
[3] CNRM, Météo-France, France
christophe.baehr@meteo.fr

Abstract. Open data is exposed in several formats, including tabular format. However, the meaning of columns, that can also be seen as dimensions, is not always explicit what makes difficult the reuse of this data for data consumers. This paper presents the FAIRification process of tabular and multidimensional datasets that relies on a (FAIR) core semantic model that is able to represent different kinds of metadata, including the data schema and the internal structure of a dataset. We describe how the instantiation of such a model offers in addition the possibility to describe the semantics of columns using domain ontologies. Once instantiated, this model forms a set of formal metadata that documents the dataset and facilitates understanding by data consumers. This process is then applied to three metereological datasets, for which the degree of improvement of the FAIRness ("I" and "R") has been evaluated.

Keywords: Meteorological data · FAIR principles · Semantic metadata

1 Introduction

Large volumes of Open data, in particular, scientific data shared for an open science, or government and statistical data, are now available on the web. They can be accessed under open licenses from different portals, such as governmental portals for public data (e.g., data.gouv in France[1] or data.gov[2] in the US, European portals like the European Data Portal[3]), portals of public services (e.g., the French National Library[4]), or portals of scientific data (e.g. data-

[1] https://www.data.gouv.fr/fr/.
[2] https://www.data.gov/.
[3] https://ec.europa.eu/info/statistics/eu-open-data-portal_en.
[4] https://data.bnf.fr/.

E. Garoufallou and A. Vlachidis (Eds.): MTSR 2022, CCIS 1789, pp. 163–174, 2023.
https://doi.org/10.1007/978-3-031-39141-5_14

terra.org[5] for Earth Sciences). This data is usually structured in tables, available in various formats, mainly CSV or JSON. Not only the schema of these tables is not always provided or made explicit, but it is also described with properties (in particular the meaning of columns) labelled in a relevant way for domain experts (data producers) but that are not properly understood and reusable by other scientific communities than the one of the authors. For the latter, one of the challenges is to find relevant data among the increasingly large amount of continuously generated data, by moving from the point of view of data producers to the point of view usages. One way to overcome these weaknesses is to guarantee compliance of data to the FAIR principles [22]. These principles correspond to a set of 15 recommendations that aims to facilitate data reuse by humans and machines. The first step towards the fulfilment of FAIR principles is to define precise metadata schemes. Indeed, 12 out of the 15 FAIR principles refer to metadata [22]. To go a step further in improving data FAIRness, several authors have shown that metadata schemes should be based on semantic models (i.e., ontologies) for a richer and more metadata representation [10]. Thanks to their ability to make data types explicit, in a format that can be processed by machines, ontologies are essential to make data FAIR [11]. While most efforts in data FAIRification are limited to specific kinds of metadata, mainly those describing the overall features of datasets and data catalogues, this description is not enough to fully address all FAIR principles [14], in particular for promoting data reuse by other scientific communities.

This paper presents the FAIRification process of tabular and multidimensional datasets using a (FAIR) core semantic model. We describe how the instantiation of such a model additionally provides the ability to describe the semantics of columns using domain ontologies. Once instantiated, this model forms a set of formal metadata (including those describing the data schema and the internal structure of a dataset) that documents the dataset and facilitates understanding by data consumers. We illustrate this process in the meteorological domain. The contributions of the paper are the following: (1) an extension of the work in [21] by describing the late stages of the FAIRification process, i.e. how the core model can be instantiated to generate a domain specific knowledge base (here meteorology) to used as a metadata schema. (2) an extension of the work in [2] by improving the FAIRness of three metereological datasets provided by Météo-France (the official French weather agency) that share the same features. Here, we use a new version of the semantic model [21] that was generalised to accommodate any kind of tabular data together with new notions required to represent dataset collections. (3) an evaluation of the FAIRness degree of different datasets annotated either with existing metadata (most of which are not machine readable) or with semantic metadata using our semantic model, showing how the proposed model improves their interoperability and reusability.

The rest of this paper is organised as follows. Section 2 discusses the main related work. Section 3 shortly presents the used core semantic model and details its instantiation. We expose in Sect. 4 how this process is performed to describe three datasets in the domain of Meteorology. Section 5 reports the FAIRness

[5] https://www.data-terra.org/.

evaluation of these datasets with or without the semantic metadata resulting from the instantiation process. Finally Sect. 6 concludes the paper.

2 Related Work

(FAIR) Metadata Vocabularies. A number of vocabularies has been proposed to represent metadata in general (Dublin core, VoID, Schema.org, DCAT, DCAT-AP)[6], with extensions for accommodating specific kinds of data, such as geo-spatial data (GeoDCAT-AP) or statistical data (StatDCAT-AP). In [17], the authors expose their own way of representing metadata on spatial and temporal data identification, content, distribution and presentation forms. In a different way, [8] extend the existing VoID vocabulary to cover datasets that are not RDF ones. Another group of works and initiatives has addressed the problem of representing domain-specific metadata using domain vocabularies. For instance, in the context of social sciences and humanities, the Data Documentation Initiative[7] (DDI) proposes two XML schemes for metadata, reusing vocabularies like Prov-O[8], DC-terms, Data Cube[9] or CSVW[10]. Targeting tabular data as we do, several proposals have combined the use of RDF Data Cube (qb) with other vocabularies to represent observational data, as in [16] or [24]. Close to our goal, the Semantic Government Vocabulary is dedicated to the annotation of Open Government Data, notably CSV distributions [15]. Thanks to these vocabularies, these authors annotate data in CSV format at different levels of detail and show how this improves the discovery of datasets [15].

FAIR Principles and FAIRness Evaluation. Several frameworks assess the degree of FAIRness of digital objects[11]. The reader can refer to [20] for a recent survey on the topic. In many of them, the evaluation is performed by answering a set of questions – also called metrics or indicators – or by filling a checklist such as the "FAIR Data Maturity Model" [7] or "FAIRshake" [4]. This evaluation can be automated, as proposed by [6,23], based on web applications that test digital resources against predefined metrics. Recently, in addition to the FAIRness degree of data, the FAIRness of vocabularies and ontologies used as metadata schemas was also evaluated [5,9]. FOOPS! [18] and O'FAIRe (Ontology FAIRness Evaluator) [1]) are some of the few tools automating this task.

3 FAIRification Process

Making data FAIR (FAIRification) can be devided into several steps, such as those of the generic step-by-step FAIRification workflow in [12]: 1) identify the

[6] https://www.dublincore.org/, https://www.w3.org/TR/void/, https://www.w3.org/TR/vocab-dcat/, https://op.europa.eu/en/web/eu-vocabularies/dcat-ap.
[7] https://ddialliance.org/learn/what-is-ddi.
[8] https://www.w3.org/TR/prov-o/.
[9] https://www.w3.org/TR/vocab-data-cube/.
[10] http://www.w3.org/ns/csvw#.
[11] most of which are listed here: https://fairassist.org/.

FAIRification objective, 2) analyze data, 3) analyze metadata, 4) define semantic model for data (4a) and metadata (4b), 5) make data (5a) and metadata (5b) linkable, 6) host FAIR data, and 7) assess FAIR data. As part of a generic methodology, here we use the generic semantic model for metadata proposed in [21]. For an easier understanding of the instantiation process, we briefly present in the following this model and how we instantiate it.

3.1 Core Dataset Metadata Ontology

We defined the Dataset Metadata Ontology Core to represent data schema and the internal structure of tabular datasets using several FAIR vocabularies. Here we briefly recall the main concepts and the reader can refer to [21] for a detailed description. The notion of *Catalog* is a curated collection of metadata about *Datasets*, which in turn can be described with different types of metadata and may have associated *Distributions*. Distributions may be in a tabular format, where each *Table* is described by its *Schema*. A schema specifies the various *Columns*. Each column has an associated *Measure* or *Dimension*. While the model in [2] focused on the representation of spatio-temporal data (using GeoDCAT-AP and qb4st), *dmo-core* forms a more generic core semantic model for representing any kind of tabular data for any domain by adopting DCAT and qb. Improving the FAIRness of domain datasets requires to instantiate this model, as introduced in the following.

3.2 Model Instantiation

The main idea behind our FAIRification process is to associate meaning to the data, in particular the columns of the tabular data. To that extent, domain ontology concepts are associated to that columns. We made the choice of instantiating the model instead of extending it, as there is no need for introducing new concepts or relations, as recommended when reusing the standard vocabularies (CSVW and qb), as detailed in the following.

This process can be viewed in two stages: the instantiation of the core model, and the association of domain-specific concepts to the instances. The first stage

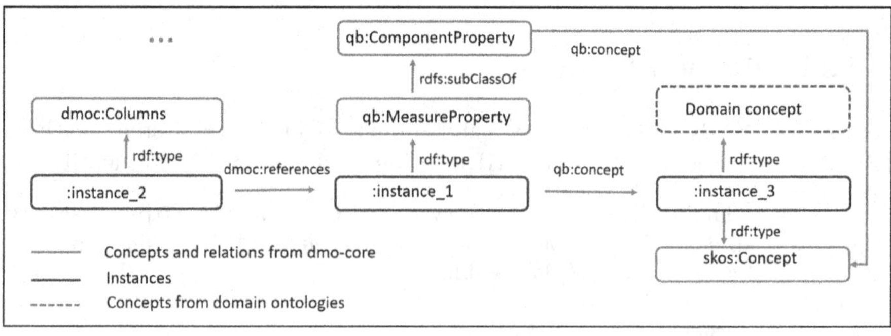

Fig. 1. Instantiation model.

concerns the description of the tabular dataset as a whole, and reference can be made to [21]. The latter concerns the more specific description of table columns using relevant domain ontologies and is carried out in the following steps:

1. Selecting Relevant Domain Ontologies. Several ontology repositories can be queried, such as: Linked Open Vocabularies (LOV) (https://lov.linkeddata.es/dataset/lov/), vocab.org (http://purl.org/vocab/), ontologi.es (http://ontologi.es/), SOCoP+OOR (https://ontohub.org/socop), AgroPortal (https://agroportal.lirmm.fr), BioPortal (https://bioportal.bioontology.org/), OntoHub (https://ontohub.org/), COLORE (http://stl.mie.utoronto.ca/colore/), OOR (Open Ontology Repository) (http://www.oor.net/), ONKI service (https://onki.fi/).

2. Choosing Appropriate Concepts in these Ontologies. This step requires the intervention of domain experts. In fact, the core model instantiation must be carried out in collaboration between a domain expert and semantic web experts. This collaboration aims to present the domain to the semantic web expert, who is responsible for creating the instantiation files. At this stage, ontology editors such as Protégé[12] can be useful.

3. Associating* dmo-core *to Domain Concepts. Tabular columns (instances of `csvw:Column`) are linked to a dimension, attribute or measure (represented as a `qb:ComponentProperty`). A `qb:ComponentProperty` has a `qb:concept` property whose default range is a `skos:Concept` to which is added a domain concept, as illustrated in Fig. 1. More specifically, for each column $\texttt{COL}_i$, the process consists in creating the following instances: (a) $\texttt{INST\_COL}_i$ of `csvw:Column`; (b) an anonymous instance of both `skos:Concept` and the domain concept; (c) $\texttt{COMPONENT\_PROPERTY\_COL}_i$ of `qb:ComponentProperty` (i.e., a dimension, attribute or measure). Then (d) $\texttt{COMPONENT\_PROPERTY\_COL}_i$ is linked to the blank node with the `qb:concept` property. Finally (e) the `dmo-c:references` property links $\texttt{INST\_COL}_i$ to $\texttt{COMPONENT\_PROPERTY\_COL}_i$.

In the example below, to help understanding the meaning of column `t` (:t_col) (Fig. 2), from one of the meterological CSV files we evaluate here (Sect. 4), (:t_col) is associated to the measure :t. This measure is then linked to the `ENVO:ENVO_09200001` concept which represents the `air temperature`.

```
:t rdf:type qb:MeasureProperty;
   qb:concept [
      rdf:type <http://purl.obolibrary.org/obo/ENVO_09200001>,
               <http://www.w3.org/2004/02/skos/core#Concept>
         ] .
:t_col rdf:type csvw:Column;
       dmo-c:references :t.
```

[12] https://protege.stanford.edu/ (accessed on 28th July 2022.).

4 Metereological Datasets FAIRification

Meteorological open data is essential in many applications, including weather forecast, climate change, environmental studies, agriculture, and risk management. Its production is based on mathematical models that assimilate different data from several sources including sensors located on weather stations, satellites and weather radars. While this data has been made available as open data, through different portals, its exploitation is rather limited. Not only the schema of these tables is not always provided or made explicit, but it is also described with properties (in particular the meaning of columns) labelled in a relevant way for meteorology data producers but that are not properly understood and reusable by other scientific communities. For the latter, one of the challenges is to find relevant data among the increasingly large amount of continuously generated data, by moving from the point of view of data producers to the point of view of data usages.

Thus meteorological data is a good experimental ground to test the benefits brought by the addition of semantic metadata based on dmo-core to the dataset reusability by other scientific communities. To this end, we instantiate the *dmo-core* model to describe three collections of tabular datasets (SYNOP, NIVO and SWI) provided by Météo-France. These datasets were chosen because, in the context of the Semantics4FAIR[13] project, the biologist partners needed to access and reuse such (understandable) weather data for identifying the meteorological conditions that favor the germination and flowering of ragweed. Currently, on the Météo-France website, these datasets are presented with few metadata in natural language, which prevents dataset search engine crawlers from finding them, and hence minimises the dataset discoverability.

A search for domain ontologies on the above mentioned repositories led us to choose the following ones: SWEET (http://sweetontology.net/), ENVO (http://purl.obolibrary.org/obo/), QUDT (http://qudt.org/1.1/vocab/unit), qb4st (http://www.w3.org/ns/qb4st/) and SOSA (http://www.w3.org/ns/sosa/). SWEET [19] is a collection of ontologies conceptualizing knowledge for the Earth sciences, a part of which models meteorological parameters such as humidity, wind speed, pressure at sea level or rainfall. ENVO [3] represents environmental entities. It is used in addition to SWEET to better describe environmental processes, for example by offering the possibility to specify the extremes of a temperature (minimum and maximum). QUDT defines the classes, properties, and restrictions for modelling physical quantities, units of measure, and their dimensions in various measurement systems. For our purpose, QUDT allows to specify units of measure for measurements. SOSA [13] is a reference ontology to describe sensors (such as thermometer, barometer, etc.) and their observations (measures), the involved procedures, the studied features of interest, the samples used to do so, and the observed properties, as well as actuators. Finally, qb4st is a qb extension for spatio-temporal components.

[13] https://www.irit.fr/semantics4fair/.

SYNOP Dataset. The SYNOP data archive consists of a set of monthly generated files (since January 1996) where each file covers only the observations made in one month. Generated files are freely available online[14]. These files share the same structure (1 table with 59 colums). Figure 2 shows an excerpt of one SYNOP file. DMO-SYNOP corresponds to the instantiation of *dmo-core* to describe the SYNOP dataset. Part of the instantiation is presented below and the whole DMO-SYNOP instantiation is available online[15].

numer_sta	date	pmer	tend	cod_tend	dd	ff	t	td	...
7005	2,02E+13	103180	-80	8	120	1.800000	274.350000	272.750000	...
7015	2,02E+13	103320	0	5	80	4.700000	275.250000	275.150000	...
7020	2,02E+13	102870	-70	8	80	1.300000	280.550000	279.450000	...
7027	2,02E+13	103080	0	0	100	4.200000	275.750000	275.750000	...
7037	2,02E+13	103190	-30	8	130	2.200000	272.250000	272.250000	...
7072	2,02E+13	103320	-20	8	60	1.100000	270.650000	269.550000	...
7110	2,02E+13	102740	10	0	180	0.600000	282.750000	282.650000	...
7117	2,02E+13	102760	-20	8	130	0.500000	281.550000	280.950000	...
7130	2,02E+13	102940	-90	8	110	3.100000	278.350000	278.050000	...
...	...	...	...	...	...	...	...	...	...

Fig. 2. Excerpt of SYNOP data.

Representing Metadata of SYNOP Dataset. SYNOP dataset is represented by an instance of `dmoc:Dataset`. SYNOP is a collection of monthly files, that, in turn, can be considered as datasets themselves. Using the concepts linked to a dataset in DMO-core, `:SYNOP_dataset` is given the following metadata values: `dct:publisher` is Météo-France; `dct:provenance` is made explicit with the label value "The measurements were provided by the meteo_France stations"; `dct:spatial` points to France in Geonames (<https://www.geonames.org/countries/FR/>); etc. To represent the structure of the dataset, which is shared by all SYNOP files, we use `:SYNOP_dataset_structure`, an instance of `qb:DataStructureDefinition`. `:SYNOP_dataset_structure` is linked to an instance of `qb:ComponentSpecification` for each of the 59 columns, each measure unit (1) and each measuring method (1), i.e. 61 instances in total. For example, the instances `:pmer_Component` and `:month_Component` correspond respectively to "pmer" and "month" columns. Then each of these instance was linked to instances of `qb:MeasureProperty`, `qb:DimensionProperty` or `qb:AttributeProperty` depending on the nature of the component. Finally, these instances are also linked to concepts of domain ontologies (we mainly used SWEET) via the `qb:concept` property. For example, `:pmer_Component` is linked to `sweet:SeaLevelPressure` (<http://sweetontology.net/propPressure/SeaLevelPressure>). The property `dmo:requires` makes explicit the dependency between `:SYNOP_dataset` and `:Meteo_Station`, the characteristics (longitude, latitude, etc.) of the weather station generating the measures being stored in the Weather Station file.

[14] https://donneespubliques.meteofrance.fr/?fond=produit&id_produit=90&id_rubrique=32.

[15] https://gitlab.irit.fr/melodi/semantics4fair/synop/ (DMO-core-SYNOP.ttl).

Representing Metadata of SYNOP Dataset (February, 2020). The dataset stored in each file of the SYNOP collection is represented as an instance of `dmo:Slice`. For instance, `:SYNOP_dataset_Feb_20` is an instance of `dmo:Slice` linked to `:SYNOP_dataset` via the property `qb:slice`. `:SYNOP_dataset_Feb_20` is associated with several metadata (`dct:created`, `dct:creator`), including structural metadata via the `qb:structure` property (`:SYNOP_dataset_structure`). Representing the metadata of a `qb:Slice` also requires the definition of dimensions with fixed values, which are specified using the `qb:SliceKey` concept. In our case, the fixed dimensions for a monthly dataset are year and month, with values `month:FEB` and `year:2020`.

Representing Metadata of a SYNOP Dataset Distribution (February 2020). The CSV file itself is represented as a distribution (`dmo:TabularDistribution`) of `:SYNOP_dataset_Feb_20` with identifier `:SYNOP_distribution_Feb_20`. Several metadata associated with this distribution were specified: the format (CSV), the URL from which the CSV file can be downloaded, the kind of license (open license), the description, etc. The distribution schema is represented by `:SYNOP_Schema` (to be reused across distributions), an instance of `csvw:Schema`. It includes all the columns of the CSV file (e.g., `numer_sta` and `pmer`). For each column, we represent its name (`csvw:name`), its label (`csvw:title`), its data type (`csvw:datatype`), etc. The foreign key `:SYNOP_ForeignKey` which connects the column "numer_sta" of the SYNOP data, to the column "ID" of the station data (`:Distribution_Stations_Météo`) is represented by the instance `:SYNOP_Stations_Table_Reference` of `csvw:TableReference`.

NIVO Dataset. This dataset refers to meteorological observation data from mountain stations operated by partners under agreement with Météo-France for monitoring the snowpack in winter. The generated files, containing data measured since January 1996, are available free of charge online[16], in CSV format. Documentation is available on a PDF file. Each CSV file contains 45 columns (temperature, dew point, snow state, predominant type of surface grains, etc.). DMO-NIVO corresponds to the instantiation of *dmo-core* for describing the NIVO dataset. The instantiation rules are the same as those applied when instantiating DMO-SYMOP. ENVO [3], a knowledge representation of environmental entities, has been used as domain ontology. The whole DMO-NIVO instantiation is available online[17].

SWI Dataset. The (uniform) SWI dataset represents the Soil Wetness Index (SWI) calculated by the Safran-Isba-Modcou (SIM) model for measuring complex interactions between meteorological data. This kind of index is used by Météo-France in the reports to commission responsible for the management of natural disasters in France. Generated files are freely available online[18], in CSV

[16] https://donneespubliques.meteofrance.fr/?fond=produit&id_produit=94&id_rubrique=32.

[17] https://gitlab.irit.fr/melodi/semantics4fair/nivo (DMO-core-NIVO.ttl).

[18] https://donneespubliques.meteofrance.fr/?fond=produit&id_produit=301&id_rubrique=40.

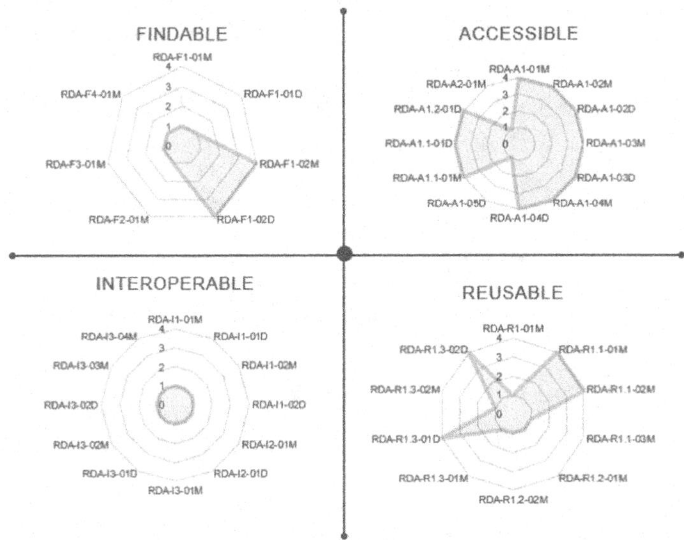

Fig. 3. Dataset FAIRness progress per indicator (without semantic MD)

format. Each file contains 5 columns: grid cell number, geographic x and y coordinates (Lambert format), date, SWI value. Each monthly value integrates the current month and the two previous months: average of the three of daily SWI values. DMO-SWI corresponds to the instantiation of *dmo-core* for describing the SWI dataset. The instantiation rules and the domain ontology are the same as those applied when instantiating DMO-SYNOP. The whole DMO-SWI instantiation is available online[19].

5 Evaluation

We evaluated the degree of FAIRness of the datasets before and after they are described with *dmo-core*, thanks to the framework *FAIR data maturity model* proposed by the Research Data Alliance (RDA) [7]. This model is based on three components: i) 41 indicators measure the state or level of a digital resource according to a FAIR principle; ii) priorities (*essential*, *important*, *useful*) are associated with the indicators; iii) two evaluation methods: the first assigns each indicator a maturity level between 0 and 4 so that data providers have indications about how to improve the FAIRness degree of their data; the second consists of verifying whether the criterion carried by the indicator is true or false. The indicators were applied first to the original dataset description, and then to the dataset described with metadata (MD) instantiating *dmo-core*. The evaluation was manually carried out and guided by the RDA Excel form.

[19] https://gitlab.irit.fr/melodi/semantics4fair/swi ((DMO-core-SWI.ttl).

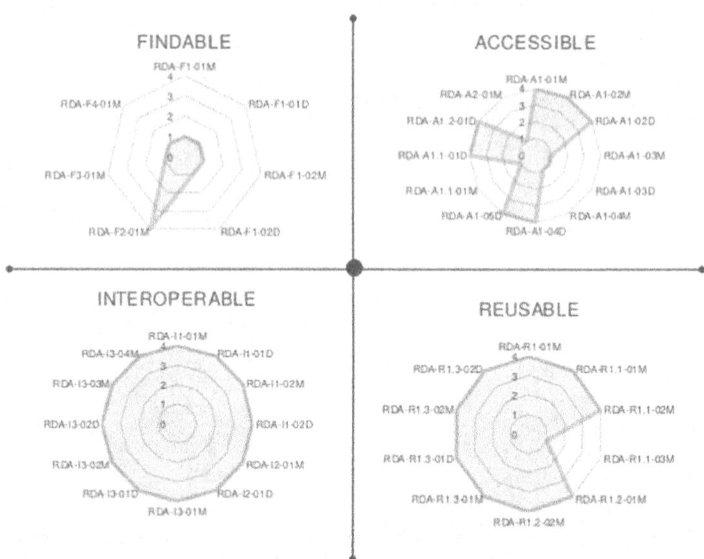

Fig. 4. Dataset FAIRness progress per indicator (with semantic MD)

We first evaluated the original description of the datasets (without semantic metadata). The datasets share the same conditions of access and lack of metadata. Their evaluation confirmed that they were not FAIR: i) level 0 for principles **F**, **A** and **R**, because at least one essential indicator was not satisfied for each of them; ii) level 1 for principle **I**, because no indicator is essential for this principle (Fig. 3). The datasets were **re-evaluated** after generating the semantic metadata that describe them. These semantic metadata significantly contribute to improve their FAIRness level, especially for the **I** and **R** principles (Fig. 4). In fact, one of the main concerns when proposing the dataset annotation with semantic metadata was to improve their exploitation by non-experts from other scientific communities which would consequently improve their interoperability. Indeed, the proposal meets the main **I** criteria: *metadata and data schemes are expressed in standardised and machine-understandable format, using FAIR-compliant vocabularies; metadata and data refer to other (open) data (here, domain ontologies) and links with these files are made explicit.* Although the re-evaluation of the **F** principle did not show any gain, the model does allow for the representation of "rich" indexing metadata that satisfy **F2** principle. However, higher **F** and **A** degrees would require satisfying essential indicators that are beyond the capabilities of any semantic model e.g., the generation of persistent and unique identifiers (**F1**), persistent metadata (**A2**), publication of metadata on searchable resources (**F4**), which must be managed by the data publisher (Meteo-FR). We also observe that the FAIRness degree is preserved with the generic instantiation model with respect to the results obtained with the specific dmo model in [2].

6 Conclusion and Future Work

This paper presented the FAIRification process of tabular and multidimensional datasets. It detailed how we defined the metadata of each dataset as instances of the DMO-core ontology and domain-specific ontologies. Three meterological collections of datasets were annotated in that way. The paper finally reported the evaluation of the approach on these meteorological datasets. An evaluation of the FAIRness of the datasets with their semantic metadata proves the relevance of the proposal in the FAIRification process, improving in particular criteria **I** and **R**. Yet we have planned several improvements and additional evaluations in other domains than meteorology. A first goal is to extend *dmo-core* to tabular datasets with other format than CSV, such as XML or JSON (which can be done quite easily by integrating dedicated vocabularies as done for CSVW). In fact, the combination of RDF Data Cube and DCAT is suitable for describing any kind of general metadata. A second one is to write SHACL constraints for the DMO-core ontology and implement a form generated from the SHACL file to make it easier for domain expert to annotate their datasets. a third one could be to test our proposal in other domains (such as health) using other domain ontologies. Finally, we plan to complement our evaluation using other frameworks such as F-uji[20] and Fairshake[21].

References

1. Amdouni, E., Jonquet, C.: FAIR or FAIRer? an integrated quantitative FAIRness assessment grid for semantic resources and ontologies. In: Garoufallou, E., Ovalle-Perandones, M.-A., Vlachidis, A. (eds.) MTSR 2021. CCIS, vol. 1537, pp. 67–80. Springer, Cham (2022). https://doi.org/10.1007/978-3-030-98876-0_6
2. Annane, A., Kamel, M., Trojahn, C., Aussenac-Gilles, N., Comparot, C., Baehr, C.: Towards the fairification of meteorological data: a meteorological semantic model. In: Garoufallou, E., Ovalle-Perandones, M.-A., Vlachidis, A. (eds.) MTSR 2021. CCIS, vol. 1537, pp. 81–93. Springer, Cham (2022). https://doi.org/10.1007/978-3-030-98876-0_7
3. Buttigieg, P.L., Morrison, N., Smith, B., et al.: The environment ontology: contextualising biological and biomedical entities. J. Biomed. Semant. **4**, 43 (2013)
4. Clarke, D., et al.: Fairshake: toolkit to evaluate the fairness of research digital resources. Cell Syst. **9**(5), 417–421 (2019)
5. Cox, S.J.D., Gonzalez-Beltran, A.N., Magagna, B., Marinescu, M.-C.: Ten simple rules for making a vocabulary fair. PLOS Comput. Biol. **17**(6), 1–15 (2021)
6. Devaraju, A., et al.: FAIRsFAIR data object assessment metrics 0.5. Technical report, Research Data Alliance (RDA), October 2020. https://zenodo.org/record/6461229. Accessed 3 May 2022
7. FAIR Data Maturity Model Working Group RDA. FAIR Data Maturity Model. Specification and Guidelines, June 2020. https://doi.org/10.15497/rda00050. Accessed 6 May 2022

[20] https://www.f-uji.net/.
[21] https://fairshake.cloud/.

8. Frosterus, M., Hyvönen, E., Laitio, J.: DataFinland—a semantic portal for open and linked datasets. In: Antoniou, G., et al. (eds.) ESWC 2011. LNCS, vol. 6644, pp. 243–254. Springer, Heidelberg (2011). https://doi.org/10.1007/978-3-642-21064-8_17
9. Garijo, D., Poveda-Villalón, M.: Best practices for implementing FAIR vocabularies and ontologies on the web. CoRR, abs/2003.13084 (2020). https://arxiv.org/abs/2003.13084. Accessed May 2022
10. Guizzardi, G.: Ontology, ontologies and the "I" of FAIR. Data Intell. **2**(1–2), 181–191 (2020)
11. Jacobsen, A., et al.: FAIR principles: interpretations and implementation considerations. Data Intell. **2**(1–2), 10–29 (2020)
12. Jacobsen, A., et al.: A generic workflow for the data fairification process. Data Intell. **2**(1–2), 56–65 (2020)
13. Janowicz, K., Haller, A., Cox, S.J., Le Phuoc, D., Lefrançois, M.: Sosa: a lightweight ontology for sensors, observations, samples, and actuators. J. Web Semant. **56**, 1–10 (2019)
14. Koesten, L., Simperl, E., Blount, T., Kacprzak, E., Tennison, J.: Everything you always wanted to know about a dataset: studies in data summarisation. Int. J. Hum. Comput. Stud. **135** (2020)
15. Kremen, P., Necaský, M.: Improving discoverability of open government data with rich metadata descriptions using semantic government vocabulary. J. Web Semant. **55**, 1–20 (2019)
16. Lefort, L., Bobruk, J., Haller, A., Taylor, K., Woolf, A.: A linked sensor data cube for a 100 year homogenised daily temperature dataset. In: Proceedings of the 5th International Workshop on Semantic Sensor Networks, vol. 904, pp. 1–16 (2012)
17. Parekh, V., Gwo, J., Finin, T.W.: Ontology based semantic metadata for geoscience data. In: Arabnia, H.R. (ed.), Conference on Information and Knowledge Engineering, pp. 485–490 (2004)
18. Poveda-Villalón, M., Espinoza-Arias, P., Garijo, D., Corcho, O.: Coming to terms with FAIR ontologies. In: Keet, C.M., Dumontier, M. (eds.) EKAW 2020. LNCS (LNAI), vol. 12387, pp. 255–270. Springer, Cham (2020). https://doi.org/10.1007/978-3-030-61244-3_18
19. Raskin, R.: Development of ontologies for earth system science. In: Geoinformatics: Data to Knowledge. Geological Society of America, January 2006
20. Sun, C., Emonet, V., Dumontier, M.: A comprehensive comparison of automated fairness evaluation tools. In: SWAT4HCLS 2022, vol. 3127, pp. 44–53 (2022)
21. Trojahn, C., Kamel, M., Annane, A., Aussenac-Gilles, N., Nguyen, B.L.: A FAIR core semantic metadata model for FAIR multidimensional tabular datasets. In: Corcho, O., Hollink, L., Kutz, O., Troquard, N., Ekaputra, F.J. (eds.) Knowledge Engineering and Knowledge Management. EKAW 2022. LNCS, vol. 13514. Springer, Cham (2022). https://doi.org/10.1007/978-3-031-17105-5_13
22. Wilkinson, M., Dumontier, M., et al.: The FAIR guiding Principles for scientific data management and stewardship. Sci. data **3**(1), 1–9 (2016)
23. Wilkinson, M., Dumontier, M., et al.: Evaluating FAIR maturity through a scalable, automated, community-governed framework. Sci. Data **6**(1), 1–12 (2019)
24. Yacoubi, N., Faron, C., Michel, F., Gandon, F., Corby, O.: A model for meteorological knowledge graphs: application to Météo-France observational data. In: 22nd International Conference on Web Engineering, ICWE 2022, Bari, Italy, July 2022

Toward a Flexible Metadata Pipeline for Fish Specimen Images

Dom Jebbia[1,2,3(✉)], Xiaojun Wang[2], Yasin Bakis[2], Henry L. Bart Jr.[2], and Jane Greenberg[1]

[1] Drexel University Metadata Research Center, Philadelphia, PA 19104, USA
jg3243@drexel.edu

[2] Tulane University Biodiversity Research Institute, Belle Chasse, LA 70037, USA
{xwang48,ybakis,hbartjr}@tulane.edu

[3] Carnegie Mellon University, Pittsburgh, PA 15213, USA
djebbia@andrew.cmu.edu

Abstract. Flexible metadata pipelines are crucial for supporting the FAIR data principles. Despite this need, researchers seldom report their approaches for identifying metadata standards and protocols that support optimal flexibility. This paper reports on an initiative targeting the development of a flexible metadata pipeline for a collection containing over 300,000 digital fish specimen images, harvested from multiple data repositories and fish collections. The images and their associated metadata are being used for AI-related scientific research involving automated species identification, segmentation and trait extraction. The paper provides contextual background, followed by the presentation of a four-phased approach involving: 1. Assessment of the Problem, 2. Investigation of Solutions, 3. Implementation, and 4. Refinement. The work is part of the NSF Harnessing the Data Revolution, Biology Guided Neural Networks (NSF/HDR-BGNN) project and the HDR Imageomics Institute. An RDF graph prototype pipeline is presented, followed by a discussion of research implications and conclusion summarizing the results.

Keywords: Metadata pipelines · Open data · Metadata workflows · FAIR data · Digital images · Biodiversity Collections

1 Introduction

Digital technology, cyberinfrastructure, and the full open research movement have enabled new pathways for scientific research. This is particularly true with digital images of scientific specimens. Scientists are able to examine and compare samples on a scale that was not possible in the analog world. Moreover,

Supported by NSF-HDR-OAC: Biology-guided Neural Networks for Discovering Phenotypic Traits: 1940233 and 1940322m, NSF HDR-OAC: Imageomics: A New Frontier of Biological Information Powered by Knowledge-Guided Machine Learning: 2118240, and the Institute of Museum and Library Services (IMLS) RE-246450-OLS-20.

E. Garoufallou and A. Vlachidis (Eds.): MTSR 2022, CCIS 1789, pp. 175–190, 2023.
https://doi.org/10.1007/978-3-031-39141-5_15

computational methods enable new modes of inquiry. Although the research opportunities seem endless, researchers face obstacles as they try to sample the correct type of scientific specimen, or develop efficient pipelines to support their work. Many of these challenges stem from metadata quality issues, or simply the absence of metadata, associated with the life-cycle of the digital specimen [24,29,41,53].

A range of metadata challenges in this area became quite apparent as a group of researchers associated with the NSF supported Harnessing the Data Revolution, Biology Guided Neural Networks (HDR-BGNN) project began their work. A key goal of this research is to examine images of fish specimens and their morphological traits via segmentation followed by feature extraction to determine differences among images representing fish from different taxonomic groups. Combining state-of-the-art image segmentation techniques with Phenoscape ontologies for algorithmic analysis [5,21,23,38,39], researchers could potentially identify undescribed species grouped within currently described species. The collections of images for training neural networks and developing an image-processing workflow revealed many metadata challenges, which led BGNN collaborators at Drexel University's Metadata Research Center (MRC) and Tulane University's Biodiversity Research Institute (TUBRI) to develop a flexible, extensible metadata pipeline.

This paper reports on the efforts of the MRC-TUBRI collaboration. The next section of the paper provides background context, followed by the underlying goals and objectives. The four-phased approach that framed the work is explained, along with the current RDF-graph prototype model. Finally, the discussion addresses the extensibility of the current model, and the conclusion summarizes the key results.

2 Background Context

Digital technology and data sharing have motivated the development of national and global repositories that provide global access to digital images of biological specimens. Even so, connecting to these repositories and taking advantage of this new infrastructure can be obstructed by a range of challenges associated with metadata and pipeline models [13,33].

2.1 Open Science Repositories

Over the past two decades, researchers have supported the proliferation of digital repositories. The growth of these collections has been motivated by a number of key factors, including the open science movement and, most recently, the international embrace of the Findable, Accessible, Interoperable, and Reusable (FAIR) [60] data principles. For the purposes of this paper, it is important to note the role of government policy, which first encouraged and now requires publicly funded data to be made available. These evolving mandates can take several forms.

Europe. The European Union was the first major government body to develop policy regarding the availability of publicly funded research. It first did so through the Public Sector Information Directive in 2003 [6], and later by its 2019 amendment as the Open Data Directive [8]. The European Commission (EC) has supported these directives by developing infrastructure such as OpenAIRE and Europeana [7,27,28,32,33,40,51].

United States of America. Similarly, in 2013 the U.S. Office of Science and Technology Policy (OSTP) mandated that federal agencies with more than $100 million in research and development should make their data available within one year of publication [12]. Most recently, in August 2022 the same agency issued a White House supported memo stating that all federally funded research should be available without delay [45].These policies and similar developments worldwide have created an imperative for academic organizations to make researchers' data available. They have also encouraged the development of metadata standards that support open data and data interoperability on a global scale.

2.2 Metadata for Open Science and Digital Scientific Specimens

Open science and open data sharing have motivated the development of many metadata standards, and the adaptation of existing standards. At the general domain level, researchers can apply the Dublin Core (DC) metadata following the extensive list of metadata properties registered at the DCMI Terms namespace [9]. Researchers may also develop a Dublin Core Metadata application profile by integrating metadata properties from other standards with Dublin Core properties. Two well-known examples include the Virtual Open Access Agriculture & Aquaculture Repository Project (VOA3R) metadata application profile [22] developed to support the description and reuse of research results in the fields of agriculture and aquaculture as part of a larger federation of open access repositories; and the Dryad metadata application [31], which underlies a global repository that publishes research data underlying scientific publications. On a more specific level, there are hundreds of metadata schemes developed for different research domains and types of scientific data. Examples include the Ecological Metadata Language (EML) [42] for ecology data, the Darwin Core [59] (DWC) for scientific museum specimens, and the Data Document Initiative (DDI) [61] for social science research. There are also a wide array of metadata standards associated with the type (e.g., static image, X-ray, moving image), preservation status, and rights specifying data access and usage.

The overabundance of metadata standards that can be used to describe scientific data can be both exciting and overwhelming for scientists trying to determine which standards support their data needs. In response to this challenge, various communities have developed directories and registries to help inform decision making and pipeline design. Key examples include the Digital Curation Center's Disciplinary Metadata Directory [14,15], the Research Data Alliance's Metadata Standard Directory [15,50], the National Consortium of Biological

Ontologies Bioportal [4], and the FAIR Sharing Standards Registry [1]. These are significant efforts; however, these extensive resources require human examination, which can be daunting. This challenge is quite evident when looking specifically at the metadata for individual specimens. The 'Life Sciences' class in the RDA directory includes 32 sub-topic areas. Most of the sub-topics identify five or more metadata standards, and a number of subtopics refer to ten or more applicable metadata standards for any given area. This is also simply within the 'Life Sciences' class, and does not include the applicable metadata standards listed in the 'Physical Sciences & Mathematics' and 'Social & Behavioral Science' classes–both of which may include metadata standards that are applicable to physical or other types of scientific specimens. The challenges associated with identifying an appropriate metadata standard further impact metadata pipeline development, data sharing, and the FAIR principles.

The FAIR principles motivated this work. FAIR establishes that data should be findable, accessible, interoperable, and reusable. Scientific images, particularly images of specimens housed in digital repositories may be findable and accessible, but the data associated with them is not always interoperable or reusable. These limitations are grounded in metadata [16,18,20,37,43,58]. Moreover, they interfere with being able to leverage rich resources for scientific research. One key solution is to develop better metadata pipelines to support FAIR, which is key to the work presented here.

2.3 Metadata Pipelines

The concept of pipelines denotes a workflow or systems approach to how materials, information, or other types of resources flow from one place to the next, and the stops along the way. Computing and informatics frequently refer to data pipelines to describe the flow of data throughout an information system. A metadata pipeline is, essentially, a type of data pipeline. Metadata pipelines are key to supporting reproducible computational research [11], and the overall execution of the FAIR principles. A metadata pipeline frequently begins with the harvesting of existing metadata or creation of new metadata in the absence of metadata, followed by the transport of the metadata, often with the associated object, through a series of operations. While a metadata pipeline is intended to support a workflow, the operation is frequently inhibited by inconsistent application of metadata, the absence of key metadata, and conflicting metadata — all of which impact metadata quality [47,48,56]. Finally, the identification and implementation of a metadata workflow model presents challenges. Researchers can work with the common workflow language and look at developments, such as the metadata underlying the Open Archival Information System (OAIS) reference model, Digital Asset Management System (DAMS) workflows, or potentially more sophisticated developments, such as the Unified Modeling Language (UML) information model. Another way that may be more comprehensible to researchers is the Resource Description Framework (RDF) model, which underlies the Semantic Web and linked data. All of this has informed the work reported in this paper.

3 Goals and Objectives

Metadata challenges along with associated metadata model complexities impact the development of successful metadata pipelines. The current circumstance has helped shape the overall goals and objectives that inform our work, the overall goal of which is to develop a flexible and extensible metadata pipeline to support the HDR-BGNN effort. The flexibility allows TUBRI to align the final output of the pipeline with FAIR principles, increasing the impact of the data. Furthermore, the work is also necessary for BGNN to interconnect with the recently established HDR Imageomics Institute. Key objectives shaping our work include:

1. Understanding the scope of TUBRI's data flow and metadata needs to accommodate AI research across the BGNN project and the connected Imageomics Institute.
2. Designing a plan to improve the current metadata pipeline.
3. Implementing, assessing, and modifying the metadata pipelines as needed.
4. Demonstrating a proof-of-concept using RDF to align data pipelines and their outputs with FAIR principles.

Our work is presented in the next section.

4 Designing a Flexible, Extensible Metadata Pipeline

Our approach to addressing the above objectives and our overall goal was carried out in four phases, identified and discussed here.

4.1 Phase 1: Assessment of the Problem

The process started by evaluating the BGNN metadata lifecycle. First, we determined potential sources of future image collections and what associated metadata elements could potentially be included. Then we considered the future internal needs at TUBRI. Throughout the process, we weighed how these workflows could be restructured to make the dataset useful to the largest audience.

This was explored by evaluating the previous data pipelines, workflows, and internal practices at TUBRI and BGNN. Figure 1 demonstrates the fish specimen image pipeline developed by BGNN, as well as the challenges to creating fully automated computational workflows. We contextualized these observations through interviews and collaboration with researchers in the groups. This information was then compared with the practices of other organizations that contribute to the HDR Imageomics Institute [10], oceanographic data organizations [2,3], and open science repositories. This assessment identified several deficiencies within the data pipeline. The two most significant were the number of organizations providing collection event metadata and the sparse, irregular conditions of the raw datasets. This created difficulties adapting the ingestion process to normalize metadata with recognized standards (DC, DWC, Exchangeable Image File (EXIF), etc.) communicating those choices to users of the dataset. Many organizations have developed various approaches for making their data FAIR, unfortunately those solutions are generally project specific and not often shared in the literature. It was clear that workflows for making datasets FAIR needed to be made more FAIR.

4.2 Phase 2: Investigation of Solutions

TUBRI researchers determined that there were two approaches to improving the flexibility of the new database structure for BGNN. One is to modify the database schema based on the relational (table-based) database. The other is to switch from the relational database to a document-oriented NoSQL database. Table 1 details the solutions identified during the investigation.

The second option is a document-oriented NoSQL database, which is a non-tabular database structure to store the data like a relational database. It offers a fast and flexible schema that enables data models to evolve with frequent changes. The database can use JSON, XML, BSON, and YAML formats to define and manage data.

The first approach was chosen because it built upon the relational database structure in use, rather than conceptually redesigning the database structure. Furthermore, this builds upon the semantic interoperability work pursued by earlier collaboration between the MRC and TUBRI on the BGNN project [25, 35, 36, 49]. Of the identified techniques, the EAV model was the most adaptable as a database design pattern to restructure the relational databases containing BGNN data. There were also concerns that the JSON and XML data types solutions may cause problems such as poor performance or making the database structure difficult to manage. EAV model was the most abstract of the solutions, but offered methods to redesign the databases to make it more adaptable to new workflows and extensible when ingesting new metadata elements. There are also numerous ways to implement EAV using JSON or XML. EAV implementation can may use an XML column in a table to capture the incomplete information or variable information, while similar principles apply to databases that support JSON-valued columns.

RDF was chosen to implement EVA because:

- It offers an extensible solution to the ongoing ingestion of new data from disparate sources.
- Major repositories have already adopted some form of RDF, for instance many cultural heritage organizations have adopted it built on the Europeana Data Model, or science data through OpenAIRE.
- It makes FAIR principles foundational to the design of data pipelines.

4.3 Phase 3: Implementation

Two methods were examined to create an RDF graph to represent the metadata. One is an implementation using Python libraries; the other uses the desktop version of Protégé. Python libraries offer numerous applications and workflows, but

Protégé was chosen to create the prototype because the graphical user interface (GUI) provides an interface to directly interact with the graph. Moreover, the Protégé-OWL batch import plug-in offered an efficient, if limited, way to transform spreadsheet data into RDF schema.

Team members evaluated the standards in use and chose new control schemes to more accurately describe the metadata. Selected standards are described in Table 3. This included the removal of duplicated, redundant, or deprecated elements. The remaining elements were checked for accurate usage and adjusted accordingly, such as changing <dwc:AccessConstraints> to <dc:accessRights>. Finally, new schemes were chosen to align the image data with standards used in other photographic applications, for instance, the adoption of standard maintained by Adobe, the International Press Telecommunications Council, and the PLUS Registry, amongst others. The RDF model theoretically allows for the adoption of any standard to normalize data. A rights statement and IRI was also included as an `rdfs:comment` in the graph.

Figure 2 represents the RDF graph prototype that was generated. Table 2 lists the previous data containers and the updated database structure and the sources from which the metadata were derived. In the new structure, metadata is grouped into classes based on the kind of metadata in use. For example, `Multimedia` represents the administrative metadata related to the raw image and its capture event. `IQ metadata` refer to the elements generated by BGNN through computational workflows; the training dataset was created by humans and then metadata was generated through segmentation and trait extraction. The `ExtendedImageMetadata` class encompasses image quality metadata for processed images. `Collection event` metadata refers to the specimen data gathered by researchers in the field. `Bach` contains administrative metadata for the final dataset. Each of the top-level updated nodes is assigned an Archival Resource Key (ARK) that serves as a persistent identifier. The ARK associated with `Multimedia` is the parent identifier for the set of images and metadata generated from the workflow.

4.4 Phase 4. Refinement

Phase 1 assessed the metadata ecosystem at TUBRI and identified pipeline features that create data bottlenecks and barriers for image processing and segmentation masking. Phase 2 investigated the potential solutions to these identified problems. Phase 3 implemented a prototype RDF model to restructure the BGNN databases. As of this writing, the project is in Phase 4, which synthesizes the results of the previous stages to design more robust and sustainable workflows.

Some of the barriers identified in the previous phases include:

- Determining which technology or approach is effective and scalable to different collections.
- Creating an RDF structure that will enhance the metadata pipeline and make the final datasets more FAIR.

- Designing processes and techniques that are applicable to many different fields, rather than domain specific solutions.

Phase 4 seeks to further investigate and resolve these challenges by:

- Creating programmatic workflows that make it easier to create and maintain RDF graphs.
- Employing the prototype RDF schema to implement a system that accesses the relational databases as virtual RDF graphs. This allows the query a non-RDF database using SPARQL, access the content of the database as Linked Data over the Web, create custom dumps of the database in RDF formats for loading into an RDF store, and access information in a non-RDF database using the Apache Jena API.
- Using a Python wrapper to make the data more accessible to researchers through an application programming interface (API).

(a) A raw image with a ruler and specimen label.

(b) A bounding box image is created from the raw image.

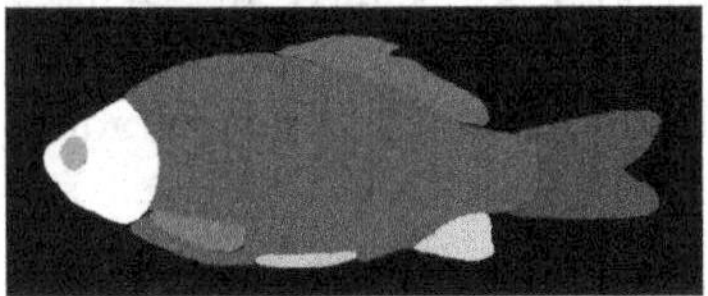

(c) A segmentation mask is generated from the bounded image.

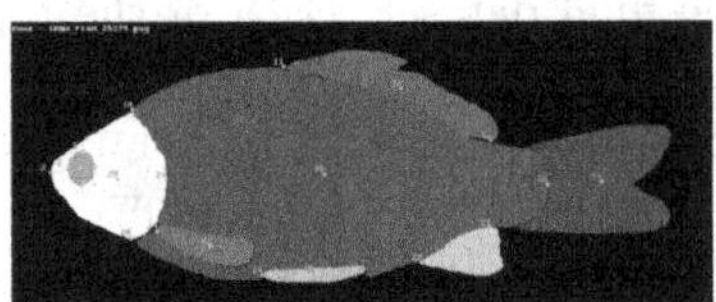

(d) Trait features are labeled on the segmentation mask.

Fig. 1. The BGNN image processing pipeline featuring a *Carassius auratus* specimen image. Optical character recognition (OCR) is used to extract metadata from the specimen label and validate against the collection event metadata associated with the raw image.

5 Discussion

5.1 RDF

This paper demonstrates how RDF's flexibility and extensibility can be used to streamline the (meta)data creation process, in addition to providing a database

Table 1. Relational database solutions.

Solution	Description
Add columns to tables	Extend existing database
Entity-Attribute-Value (EAV)	Restructure database using EAV model
JSON data type	Convert database structure to JSON/XML
XML data type	Convert database structure to XML

Table 2. Changes in the database structure.

Original data containers	Updated RDF nodes	Metadata source
Media	Multimedia	Raw image
Collection event	Collection event	Specimen
ImageQualityMetadata	IQ metadata	Bounding box image
	ExtendedImageMetadata	Labeled segmentation mask
	Batch	Administrative

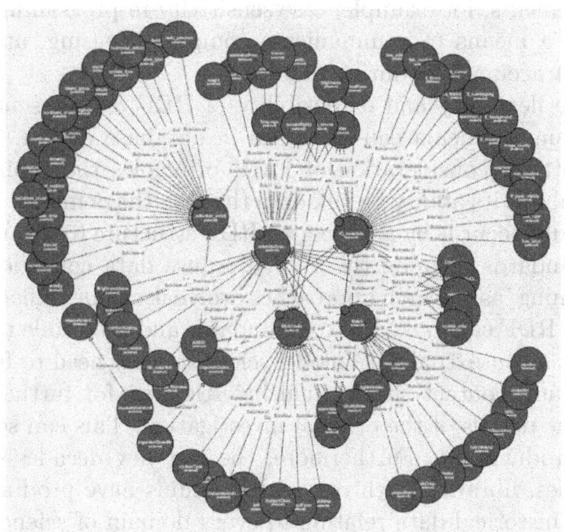

Fig. 2. A visualization of the RDF prototype created with Protege.

design pattern that can adapt to the changing needs of research investigations. The framework makes research output more FAIR by providing the foundational infrastructure for computational analysis. Specifically, RDF provides a means to express the metadata elements in relation to the resources they describe and to each other, rather than the arbitrary location of the information in a database structure. Investigators spend most of their research time cleaning data [57], so pipeline design is an important part of making the final output of a project

Table 3. Standards added to the RDF prototype.

Standard	Namespace prefix	IRI
Audobon Core	ac	http://rs.tdwg.org/ac/terms/
Camera Raw	crs	http://ns.adobe.com/camera-raw-settings/1.0
Darwin Core	dwc	http://rs.tdwg.org/dwc/terms/
Darwin Core	dwciri	http://rs.tdwg.org/dwc/iri/
Exchangeable Image File	exif	http://ns.adobe.com/exif/1.0/
IPTC* Core	Iptc4xmpCore	http://iptc.org/std/Iptc4xmpCore/1.0/xmlns/
Photoshop	photoshop	http://ns.adobe.com/photoshop/1.0/
Picture Licensing Universal System	plus	http://ns.useplus.org/ldf/xmp/1.0/
Extensible Metadata Platform	xmp	http://ns.adobe.com/xap/1.0/
Basic Job Ticket	xmpBJ	http://ns.adobe.com/xap/1.0/bj/
XMP Media Management	xmpMM	http://ns.adobe.com/xap/1.0/mm/

* International Press Telecommunications Council

reusable and ultimately affects the results of later machine learning and neural networks. RDF provides a means of rapidly responding to the changing technical and structural parameters of a project. One major reason for this RDF implementation was to make the database structure able to respond to changing technical requirements, for example, case sensitivity in programming languages. It also provides a means to communicate complex licensing, attribution, and usage rights that accumulate during data reuse.

However, the flexibility and extensibility of RDF can present a number of challenges. Although schema can be useful in database design [34], if RDF is implemented without consideration of FAIR principles the resulting database structure may inhibit its ability to link data through the Semantic Web [44]. One way that this could occur is by applying an RDF structure to a database without curating the standards defining the data. Because data collection is laborious and time-consuming, as research approaches evolve it can be difficult to maintain structured data. RDF can make this data findable and accessible to some degree, however without a contextual data model scientists may need to further analyze and clean the data, contact the original investigators for further information, or guess as to the details of the original investigation. This can severely impact quality and reproducibility. Furthermore, the last few decades of digitization efforts by galleries, libraries, archives, and museums have produced corpora of semi-structured historical data relating to every domain of science documented before the digital age. These datasets are important to climate and biological scientists as they attempt to understand climate change and biodiversity [26,46,52,54]. However, the people who created these early datasets had no idea how the data they were collecting could be used by others in the future. The cost of data management and geopolitical remnants of colonialism are also significant barriers to making data FAIR [17,46,55]. RDF can help make these datasets findable and accessible if the circumstances allow, however significant curation is necessary to make them interoperable and reusable by machines.

5.2 FAIR Pipelines for Open Science Repositories

One of the desired outputs of the BGNN project is a dataset of processed images, segmented masks, and rich metadata for others to reuse in future studies. The RDF database structure makes it easy to manage and update data structures, resulting in the ability to accept new metadata elements and adjust them as the requirements of the project evolve. The workflows that RDF makes possible improve the quality and quantity of metadata associated with the images in the dataset. This helps align the research output with FAIR, while also designing pipelines that can be adopted by other studies interested in building FAIR aligned workflows. Although researchers conceptually understand metadata, it is difficult to stay up-to-date with the technical and practical nuances of metadata creation, even among metadata professionals [19]. As technology becomes more sophisticated and metadata standards proliferate, there is a growing need for researchers to use adaptable schemes in their pipelines to make their data interoperable with machines. Open science mandates from governments and funders will further encourage scholars to house research datasets in open repositories. Data repositories have a role encouraging the adoption of RDF schemes that will make curated data more FAIR.

5.3 Future Research

As discussed in Sect. 4.4, the Phase 4 Refinement will continue to refine the RDF protype. The prototype has already been used to construct a demo REST API to interact with the BGNN dataset [30]. The API provides both a GUI to search the dataset by genus or ARK identifier, as well as command line access using `cURL` and `Wget`. An API call will download a zip file that contains:

- CSV files containing the metadata associated with each image.
- XML files containing he metadata associated with each image.
- A text document with the preferred citations.
- An OWL file containing the RDF graph.

The future focus of the MRC-TUBRI collaboration is to continue refining the RDF model and testing the API. Further investigation into different modes of RDF adoption for data management and metadata creation is needed to understand other database implementations using RDF automatic workflows for creating and managing knowledge graphs.

6 Conclusion

This paper reports on an initiative targeting the development of a flexible metadata pipeline through a collaborative effort involving the MRC-TUBRI. A key contribution is a four-phased approach covering the 1. Assessment of the Problem, 2. Investigation of Solutions, 3. Implementation, and 4. Refinement. The other key contribution is the presentation of the RDF graph prototype. The work presented has been applied to over 300,000 digital images of scientific specimens, specifically fish images, drawn from multiple collections. While we are in the early stage of the RDF graph prototype, the biologist and computer scientists are finding that the workflow and the model expedites their work to service the larger BGNN team in seeking image samples for training the bio-generated neural network. Our next steps include extending our model to other images in the Imageomics institute, given the broad applicability of this work.

As already stated, open data sharing has motivated development of many metadata standards, and a range of metadata models. Indeed these standards aim to ensure smooth operations, whether the goal is resource discovery, support for other aspects of FAIR, or integrating into an AI operation. Metadata is a form of data intelligence, and significant time and money are involved in developing, reviewing, endorsing and implementing standards. With respect to the work reported on in this paper, the initial metadata spreadsheet reviewed was loosely structured around the database containers where the various elements were stored as a result of the pipeline structure. This metadata was roughly organized by metadata creation or modification date. Our four-phased approach and adoption of RDF presents a proof of concept for expressing the metadata elements and their relationship to each other rather than the specific location of the data. This work has helped the team achieve a flexible and extensible metadata pipeline. Our overall conclusion is that the RDF graph prototype and our 4-phased approach is flexible and extensible to the wider variety of analysis of a full range of images being examined in the Imageomics institute. In addition, the proof-of-concept is applicable to other metadata pipelines, and supports computational analysis.

Acknowledgments. We thank the Integrated Digitized Biocollections (iDigBio), Global Biodiversity Information Facility (GBIF) and MorphBank data repositories, and the curators of the fish collections in the Great Lakes Invasives Network – Field Museum of Natural History, Illinois Natural History Survey, J. F. Bell Museum of Natural History, Ohio State University Museum of Biological Diversity, University of Michigan Museum of Zoology, and University of Wisconsin-Madison Zoological Museum - for sharing images of their fish specimens with us. We also thank Anuj Karpatne and team at Virginia Tech University who developed and trained the fish feature segmentation ANN component of the workflow, Joel Pepper for automated image quality feature extraction workflow and Bahadir Altintas for developing automated landmark extraction workflow.

References

1. FAIR Sharing Standards Registry. https://fairsharing.org/search?fairsharingRegistry=Standard
2. Introduction to BCO-DMO | BCO-DMO. https://www.bco-dmo.org/
3. Marine Environmental Research Infrastructure for Data Integration and Application Network, https://meridian.cs.dal.ca/
4. National Center for Biomedical Ontology BioPortal. https://bioportal.bioontology.org/

5. Phenoscape. https://phenoscape.org
6. Directive 2003/98/EC of the European Parliament and of the Council of 17 November 2003 on the re-use of public sector information (2003). http://data.europa.eu/eli/dir/2003/98/oj
7. EU-funded projects go public www.openaire.eu. MRS Bull. **37**(8), 714 (2012). https://doi.org/10.1557/mrs.2012.193
8. Directive (EU) 2019/1024 of the European Parliament and of the Council of 20 June 2019 on open data and the re-use of public sector information (recast) (2019), http://data.europa.eu/eli/dir/2019/1024/oj/eng
9. DCMI Metadata Terms (2020). https://www.dublincore.org/specifications/dublin-core/dcmi-terms/
10. Imageomics Institute (2021). https://imageomics.osu.edu/
11. Arencibia, E., Martinez, R., Marti-Lahera, Y., Goovaerts, M.: On metadata quality in Sceiba, a platform for quality control and monitoring of Cuban scientific publications. In: Garoufallou, E., Ovalle-Perandones, M.-A., Vlachidis, A. (eds.) MTSR 2021. CCIS, vol. 1537, pp. 106–113. Springer, Cham (2022). https://doi.org/10.1007/978-3-030-98876-0_9
12. Atkins, D.E., et al.: Revolutionizing science and engineering through cyberinfrastructure: report of the national science foundation blue-ribbon advisory panel on cyberinfrastructure. Technical report, National Science Foundation (2003). https://www.nsf.gov/cise/sci/reports/atkins.pdf
13. Bailey, C.B., Balakirev, F.F., Balakireva, L.L.: Closing the gap between FAIR data repositories and hierarchical data formats. Code4Lib J. (52) (2021). https://journal.code4lib.org/articles/16223
14. Ball, A.: Metadata standards directory (2016). https://www.youtube.com/watch?v=Lh8w2_TpFP8
15. Ball, A., Chen, S., Greenberg, J., Perez, C., Jeffery, K., Koskela, R.: Building a disciplinary metadata standards directory. Int. J. Digit. Curat. **9**(1), 142–151 (2014). https://doi.org/10.2218/ijdc.v9i1.308
16. Batista, D., Gonzalez-Beltran, A., Sansone, S.A., Rocca-Serra, P.: Machine actionable metadata models. Sci. Data **9**(1) (2022). https://doi.org/10.1038/s41597-022-01707-6
17. Brunet, M., Gilabert, A., Jones, P., Efthymiadis, D.: A historical surface climate dataset from station observations in Mediterranean North Africa and Middle East areas. Geosci. Data J. **1**(2), 121–128 (2014). https://doi.org/10.1002/gdj3.12
18. Child, A.W., Hinds, J., Sheneman, L., Buerki, S.: Centralized project-specific metadata platforms: toolkit provides new perspectives on open data management within multi-institution and multidisciplinary research projects. BMC. Res. Notes **15**(1), 106 (2022). https://doi.org/10.1186/s13104-022-05996-3
19. Chuttur, M.Y.: Perceived helpfulness of Dublin core semantics: an empirical study. In: Garoufallou, E., Greenberg, J. (eds.) MTSR 2013. CCIS, vol. 390, pp. 135–145. Springer, Cham (2013). https://doi.org/10.1007/978-3-319-03437-9_14
20. Courtot, M., Gupta, D., Liyanage, I., Xu, F., Burdett, T.: BioSamples database: FAIRer samples metadata to accelerate research data management. Nucleic Acids Res. **50**(D1), D1500–D1507 (2022). https://doi.org/10.1093/nar/gkab1046
21. Dececchi, T.A., Balhoff, J.P., Lapp, H., Mabee, P.M.: Toward synthesizing our knowledge of morphology: using ontologies and machine reasoning to extract presence/absence evolutionary phenotypes across studies. Syst. Biol. **64**(6), 936–952 (2015). https://doi.org/10.1093/sysbio/syv031

22. Diamantopoulos, N., Sgouropoulou, C., Kastrantas, K., Manouselis, N.: Developing a metadata application profile for sharing agricultural scientific and scholarly research resources. In: García-Barriocanal, E., Cebeci, Z., Okur, M.C., Öztürk, A. (eds.) MTSR 2011. CCIS, vol. 240, pp. 453–466. Springer, Heidelberg (2011). https://doi.org/10.1007/978-3-642-24731-6_45
23. Edmunds, R.C., et al.: Phenoscape: identifying candidate genes for evolutionary phenotypes. Mol. Biol. Evol. **33**(1), 13–24 (2016). https://doi.org/10.1093/molbev/msv223
24. Elberskirch, L., et al.: Digital research data: from analysis of existing standards to a scientific foundation for a modular metadata schema in nanosafety. Part. Fibre Toxicol. **19**(1) (2022). https://doi.org/10.1186/s12989-021-00442-x
25. Elhamod, M., et al.: Hierarchy-guided neural networks for species classification. Preprint Evol. Biol. (2021). https://doi.org/10.1101/2021.01.17.427006
26. Fordham, D.A., et al.: Using paleo-archives to safeguard biodiversity under climate change. Science **369**(6507), eabc5654 (2020). https://doi.org/10.1126/science.abc5654
27. Freire, N., Meijers, E., de Valk, S., Raemy, J.A., Isaac, A.: Metadata aggregation via linked data: results of the Europeana common culture project. In: Garoufallou, E., Ovalle-Perandones, M.-A. (eds.) MTSR 2020. CCIS, vol. 1355, pp. 383–394. Springer, Cham (2021). https://doi.org/10.1007/978-3-030-71903-6_35
28. Freire, N., Voorburg, R., Cornelissen, R., de Valk, S., Meijers, E., Isaac, A.: Aggregation of linked data in the cultural heritage domain: a case study in the Europeana network. Information **10**(8), 252 (2019). https://doi.org/10.3390/info10080252
29. Gallas, E.J., Malon, D., Hawkings, R.J., Albrand, S., Torrence, E.: An integrated overview of metadata in ATLAS. J. Phys: Conf. Ser. **219**(4), 042009 (2010). https://doi.org/10.1088/1742-6596/219/4/042009
30. tubri github: tubri-github/bgnn_api (2022). https://github.com/tubri-github/bgnn_API. Original-date: 2022-10-12T14:03:39Z
31. Greenberg, J., White, H.C., Carrier, S., Scherle, R.: A metadata best practice for a scientific data repository. J. Libr. Metadata **9**(3–4), 194–212 (2009). https://doi.org/10.1080/19386380903405090
32. Houssos, N., Stamatis, K., Banos, V., Kapidakis, S., Garoufallou, E., Koulouris, A.: Implementing enhanced OAI-PMH requirements for Europeana. In: Gradmann, S., Borri, F., Meghini, C., Schuldt, H. (eds.) TPDL 2011. LNCS, vol. 6966, pp. 396–407. Springer, Heidelberg (2011). https://doi.org/10.1007/978-3-642-24469-8_40
33. Houssos, N., Stamatis, K., Koutsourakis, P., Kapidakis, S., Garoufallou, E., Koulouris, A.: Enhanced OAI-PMH services for metadata sharing in heterogeneous environments. Libr. Rev. **63**(6/7), 465–489 (2014). https://doi.org/10.1108/LR-05-2014-0051
34. Kalogeros, E., Gergatsoulis, M., Damigos, M.: Document-based RDF storage method for parallel evaluation of basic graph pattern queries. Int. J. Metadata Semant. Ontol. **14**(1), 63 (2020). https://doi.org/10.1504/IJMSO.2020.107798
35. Karnani, K., et al.: Computational metadata generation methods for biological specimen image collections (2022). https://doi.org/10.21203/rs.3.rs-1506561/v1
36. Leipzig, J., et al.: Biodiversity image quality metadata augments convolutional neural network classification of fish species (2021). https://doi.org/10.1101/2021.01.28.428644
37. Leipzig, J., Nüst, D., Hoyt, C.T., Ram, K., Greenberg, J.: The role of metadata in reproducible computational research. Patterns **2**(9), 100322 (2021). https://doi.org/10.1016/j.patter.2021.100322

38. Mabee, P.M., Balhoff, J.P., Dahdul, W.M., Lapp, H., Mungall, C.J.: Reasoning over anatomical homology in the Phenoscape KB. In: Proceedings of the 9th International Conference on Biological Ontology (ICBO 2018), Corvallis, Oregon, USA, p. 2 (2018)
39. Manda, P., Balhoff, J.P., Lapp, H., Mabee, P., Vision, T.J.: Using the phenoscape knowledgebase to relate genetic perturbations to phenotypic evolution. Genesis **53**(8), 561–571 (2015). https://doi.org/10.1002/dvg.22878
40. Manghi, P., Houssos, N., Mikulicic, M., Jörg, B.: The data model of the OpenAIRE scientific communication e-infrastructure. In: Dodero, J.M., Palomo-Duarte, M., Karampiperis, P. (eds.) MTSR 2012. CCIS, vol. 343, pp. 168–180. Springer, Heidelberg (2012). https://doi.org/10.1007/978-3-642-35233-1_18
41. Margaritopoulos, M., Margaritopoulos, T., Mavridis, I., Manitsaris, A.: Quantifying and measuring metadata completeness. J. Am. Soc. Inform. Sci. Technol. **63**(4), 724–737 (2012). https://doi.org/10.1002/asi.21706
42. Michener, W.K.: Creating and managing metadata. In: Recknagel, F., Michener, W.K. (eds.) Ecological Informatics, pp. 71–88. Springer, Cham (2018). https://doi.org/10.1007/978-3-319-59928-1_5
43. Mons, B.: Data Stewardship for Open Science: Implementing FAIR Principles, 1 edn. Chapman and Hall/CRC, New York (2018). https://doi.org/10.1201/9781315380711
44. Mons, B., Neylon, C., Velterop, J., Dumontier, M., da Silva Santos, L.O.B., Wilkinson, M.D.: Cloudy, increasingly FAIR; revisiting the FAIR data guiding principles for the European open science cloud. Inf. Serv. Use **37**(1), 49–56 (2017). https://doi.org/10.3233/ISU-170824
45. Nelson, A.: Desirable characteristics of data repositories for federally funded research. Technical report, Executive Office of the President of the United States (2022). https://doi.org/10.5479/10088/113528
46. Nordling, L.: Scientists struggle to access Africa's historical climate data. Nature **574**(7780), 605–606 (2019). https://doi.org/10.1038/d41586-019-03202-2
47. Park, J.R.: Metadata quality in digital repositories: a survey of the current state of the art. Catalog. Classif. Q. **47**(3–4) (2009). https://doi.org/10.1080/01639370902737240
48. Park, J.R., Tosaka, Y.: Metadata quality control in digital repositories and collections: criteria, semantics, and mechanisms. Catalog. Classif. Q. **48**(8) (2010). https://doi.org/10.1080/01639374.2010.508711
49. Pepper, J., Greenberg, J., Bakiş, Y., Wang, X., Bart, H., Breen, D.: Automatic metadata generation for fish specimen image collections (2021). https://doi.org/10.1101/2021.10.04.463070
50. Perez, C.I.: The RDA's metadata standards directory: information gathering. Master's thesis, University of North Carolina at Chapel Hill (2013). https://www.rd-alliance.org/sites/default/files/CPerez-RDA-Metadata.pdf
51. Rettberg, N., Schmidt, B.: OpenAIRE: supporting a European open access mandate. Coll. Res. Libr. News **76**(6), 306–310 (2015). https://doi.org/10.5860/crln.76.6.9326
52. Rockembach, M., Serrano, A.: Climate change and web archives: an Ibero-American study based on the Portuguese and Brazilian contexts. Rec. Manage. J. **31**(3) (2021). https://doi.org/10.1108/RMJ-11-2020-0039
53. Schöpfel, J.: Adding value to electronic theses and dissertations in institutional repositories. D-Lib Mag. **19**(3/4) (2013). https://doi.org/10.1045/march2013-schopfe

54. Soltis, P.S.: Digitization of herbaria enables novel research. Am. J. Bot. **104**(9), 1281–1284 (2017). https://doi.org/10.3732/ajb.1700281
55. Sterner, B., Elliott, S.: The FAIR and CARE data principles influence who counts as a participant in biodiversity science by governing the fitness-for-use of data (2022). http://philsci-archive.pitt.edu/21039/
56. Tsiflidou, E., Manouselis, N.: Tools and techniques for assessing metadata quality. In: Garoufallou, E., Greenberg, J. (eds.) MTSR 2013. CCIS, vol. 390, pp. 99–110. Springer, Cham (2013). https://doi.org/10.1007/978-3-319-03437-9_11
57. Virkus, S., Garoufallou, E.: Data science from a perspective of computer science. In: Garoufallou, E., Fallucchi, F., William De Luca, E. (eds.) MTSR 2019. CCIS, vol. 1057, pp. 209–219. Springer, Cham (2019). https://doi.org/10.1007/978-3-030-36599-8_19
58. Vlachidis, A., Antoniou, A., Bikakis, A., Terras, M.: Semantic metadata enrichment and data augmentation of small museum collections following the FAIR principles. In: Information and Knowledge Organisation in Digital Humanities, pp. 106–129. Routledge (2021). https://doi.org/10.4324/9781003131816-6
59. Wieczorek, J., et al.: Darwin core: an evolving community-developed biodiversity data standard. PLoS ONE **7**(1), e29715 (2012). https://doi.org/10.1371/journal.pone.0029715
60. Wilkinson, M.D., et al: The FAIR guiding principles for scientific data management and stewardship. Sci. Data **3**(1), 160018 (2016). https://doi.org/10.1038/sdata.2016.18
61. Wong, E.Y.: Data documentation initiative. Tech. Serv. Q. **33**(1) (2016). https://doi.org/10.1080/07317131.2015.1093852

Thesaurus Enrichment via Coordination Extraction

Anna Chepaikina[1], Robert Bossy[2](✉), Catherine Roussey[3,4], and Stephan Bernard[3]

[1] Inria, 2 rue Simone Iff, 75012 Paris, France
anna.chepaikina@inria.fr

[2] Université Paris-Saclay, INRAE, UR MAIAGE, 78350 Jouy-en-Josas, France
robert.bossy@inrae.fr

[3] Université Clermont Auvergne, INRAE, UR TSCF, 63000 Clermont-Ferrand, France
{catherine.roussey,stephan.bernard}@inrae.fr

[4] INRAE, UMR MISTEA, Montpellier, France

Abstract. We advance a method of thesaurus enrichment, based on the extraction of coordinations in a domain-related corpus. Our hypothesis is that there is a semantic homogeneity between the conjuncts located in a coordination. We conducted an experiment that allowed us to evaluate the effectiveness of our method. This experiment aims to enrich the concept hierarchy of a French agricultural thesaurus named French Crop Usage (FCU), thanks to the texts of the Plant Health Bulletins (PHB). The FCU thesaurus is published on the Web using the SKOS model.

Keywords: thesaurus enrichment · agricultural thesaurus · SKOS model · term extraction · coordination · hyperonym · text mining

1 Introduction

The thesaurus French Crop Usage (FCU) normalises crop names in French. Moreover, it organises these crop names in categories according to their uses in France territory. The uses represent the agricultural sectors. This thesaurus is not complete and evolves according to related projects. FCU was first built to annotate French agricultural alert bulletins in the Vespa project [14]. It is also reused to identify crops when French agricultural reference datasets are published on the Web using semantic Web technologies, like the plant phenological scales [15]. Previously, thesaurus enrichment was based on a manual review of reference agricultural documents. Enrichment goal identifies new crop names or new categories that should be added to the thesaurus. To improve the completeness of FCU, we propose a semi-automatic method which is based on the extraction of coordinations in a corpus of agricultural alert bulletins. Our hypothesis is that

Supported by the French ANR D2KAB Project.

E. Garoufallou and A. Vlachidis (Eds.): MTSR 2022, CCIS 1789, pp. 191–202, 2023.
https://doi.org/10.1007/978-3-031-39141-5_16

there is a semantic homogeneity between elements in an coordination structure. We also conducted an experiment that allowed us to evaluate the effectiveness of our method.

The paper is organised as follows: Sect. 2 presents the content of FCU, the manual update method and access methods. Section 3 describes the method we advance, as well as the corpus used for the extraction. Section 4 describes the evaluation setting and results. In Sect. 5 we review existing works on automatic acquisition of new terms, using in particular coordination structures. Finally, in Sect. 6 we conclude and provide insights for future work.

2 French Crop Usage Thesaurus

The FCU thesaurus organises plants based on their roles in agriculture, or in other words, agricultural plant uses. The thesaurus hierarchy has two main branches as shown in Fig. 1. The branch named *Multiusages* contains all the cultivated plants that have several uses in agriculture. For example, *carotte* (carrot) may be used as vegetable or as fodder. When a cultivated plant has several uses, it is represented by several crop names. First a crop name represents all uses. For example, *carotte* at the top of Fig. 1 represents all the uses of carrot. Another crop name represents the specific use of the plant in agriculture.

As shown in Fig. 1, *carotte potagère* (vegetable carrot) represents the human consumption of carrot and *carotte fourragère* (fodder carrot) represents animal fodder. Thus, *carotte* is linked to *carrote potagère* and *carrote fourragère* by a hierarchical relationship. The branch *Usages_plantes_cultivees* organises cultivated plants according to their uses and represents agricultural sectors. In this branch the crop name *carotte potagère* is linked to the crop category *légume racine* (root vegetable).

2.1 Content Description

The FCU thesaurus is formalized using the Simple Knowledge Organisation System (SKOS) vocabulary proposed by W3C [8]. The thesaurus is published on the Web using Linked Data principles. Each crop or crop category is represented by an instance of *skos:Concept* as shown in Fig. 2.

This work has been developed using the 2.1 version of FCU which contains 521 instances of *skos:Concept*. The maximum depth of the hierarchy is 6 levels. Each *skos:Concept* is defined by several properties as shown in Fig. 2. The description of a crop or crop category contains the following:

- *skos:prefLabel* property contains the crop label name in French. The term is the common name of the crop or crop category. To avoid ambiguity in the case of cultivated plant with different uses, the crop label name is the combination of the common name of the plant and its use. For example in Fig. 2, the crop label name is "carotte potagère".

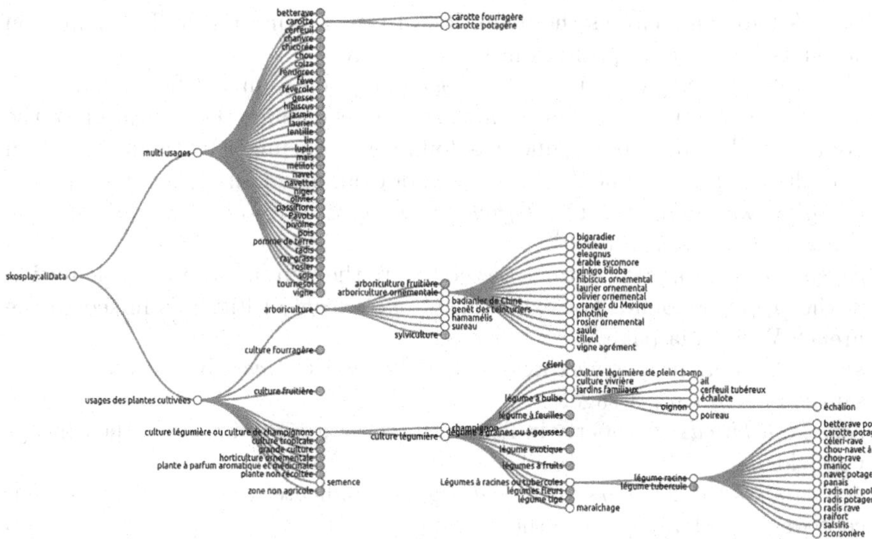

Fig. 1. An extract from the FCU thesaurus, visualised with the SKOS Play tool. Blue node means that the branch can be extended. White node means that the branch is already extended. (Color figure online)

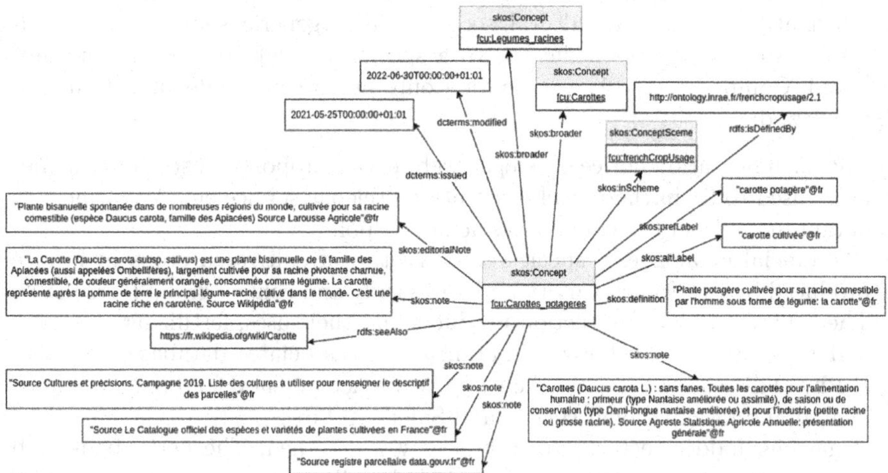

Fig. 2. The instance of *skos:Concept* that describes the *carotte potagère* crop (vegetable carrot)

- *skos:altLabel* property contains other possible label names that can be used for the crop. For example in Fig. 2, an alternative crop label name is "carotte cultivée".

- *skos:definition* contains the definition of the crop in French. The definition accounts for the crop position in the hierarchy.
- *skos:note* property contains at least one definition from another source, such as the French Wikipedia. The definition always ends by the indication of the Source. If the crop label name was found in a document without definition only the document name is mentioned. For example in Fig. 2, the crop *carotte potagère* was found in The *Official Catalogue of Species and Varieties of Cultivated Crops in France*[1].
- *rdfs:seeAlso* property contains a Web link to the web site where one definition of the crop was found. For example, *skos:Concept* of Fig. 2, is linked to the French Wikipedia page.
- *skos:inScheme* property expresses that the *skos:Concept* belongs to the thesaurus French Crop Usage.
- *rdfs:isDefinedBy* property indicates the thesaurus version when the concept was added.
- *dcterms:issued/dcterms:modified* property indicates the date when the concept was added/modified in the thesaurus.
- *skos:broader/skos:narrower* property links the crop to its parent category.

2.2 Sources

To build the thesaurus, we have studied the terms contained in reference sources of information in the agricultural sectors. First, generic sources were studied. More specific sources dedicated to a specific agricultural sector were also reviewed. Compared to [14], we mention only new reference documents manually reviewed:

- The documentation notice of telepac web service proposes a list of crop names to be used to fill in the parcel description. Telepac service enables farmers to obtain funds from the common agricultural policy[2].
- The official catalogue of species and varieties of cultivated crops in France produced by the French variety and seed study and control group (GEVES)[3].
- The catalog of plant protection products and their uses, fertilizing materials and growing media authorized in France[4]. The associated database is entitled E-Phy. This catalog is published by the French Agency for Food, Environmental and Occupational Health and Safety (ANSES).
- Regarding fodder sector, two web sites were studied: The herbe-book web site[5] and the plantesfourrageres web site[6] describe different varieties of fodder crops. Those web sites are published by the French interprofession of seeds and seedling named SEMAE.

[1] https://www.geves.fr/catalogue-france/.
[2] https://www1.telepac.agriculture.gouv.fr/telepac/pdf/tas/2019/Dossier-PAC-2019_notice_cultures-precisions.pdf.
[3] https://www.geves.fr/catalogue-france/.
[4] https://ephy.anses.fr/.
[5] https://www.herbe-book.org.
[6] http://www.plantesfourrageres.org/pages/caracteristiques.htm.

- Regarding vegetables there is no crop reference documentation. Thus, the common crops between several data sources were sought: Wikipedia, Bonduelle, FranceAgriMer, Encyclopedia Universalis, the Bec Hellouin organic farm.

2.3 Manual Update Method

The RDF file of the FCU thesaurus is updated using Protégé ontology editor v5.1.0 [9] with Cellfie plugin[7]. When a new reference source of information is identified, the thesaurus manager creates a new CSV file dedicated to this source. Cellfie is used to generate individuals of *skos:Concept* class using transformation rules applied on the CSV file. To improve the consistency of the final RDF dataset, we used some SWRL rules to infer all inverse properties using SWRL Protege Tab. A final check is performed using the SKOS Play! tool[8] it enables to visualise and control the SKOS model and detects errors.

The thesaurus is published in a Git repository[9], the Agroportal repository[10] and a dedicated SPARQL endpoint[11] The Git repository is a reference storage system divided into branches. The *master* branch contains the last version published on the web. Each old version has a dedicated branch. Note that the branch named *enrichissementThesaurus* contains the files and documentation, used for the method proposed in this paper.

3 Automatic Detection of New Terms

For the moment the information sources, used to update the FCU thesaurus, are all agricultural reference documents that somehow define crops. We decide to use another type of information sources: a corpus of french agricultural alert bulletins. This corpus can be categorised as usage documents, not reference documents. Due to the fact that it contains a large number of files, we need an automatic extraction process to identify new crop names.

3.1 Corpus Description

In France, the Grenelle Environment and Ecophyto 2018 program strengthened national surveillance networks of crops and agricultural practices. Plant Health Bulletins are one of the modalities established by these surveillance networks in all regions and French overseas departments. A Plant Health Bulletin (PHB)[12] is an agricultural alert document, both technical and regulatory in nature, written under the responsibility of a regional epidemiological surveillance committee.

[7] https://github.com/protegeproject/cellfie-plugin.
[8] http://labs.sparna.fr/skos-play:.
[9] https://gitlab.irstea.fr/copain/frenchcropusage.
[10] http://agroportal.lirmm.fr/ontologies/CROPUSAGE.
[11] http://ontology.inrae.fr/frenchcropusage/sparql.
[12] PHB are named Bulletin de Santé du Végétal (BSV) in French.

A PHB gathers information about the health status of crops. It first presents pest risk analyses, and it is also used to disseminate regulatory information (mandatory control order, national notes, regulation evolution, etc.) and non-regulatory information (description of pest biology or prophylactic methods, such as management of intercropping, tillage, choice of cultivars, etc.). Since the beginning of their publication, PHBs are freely available in PDF format on the websites of the Regional Chambers of Agriculture or the websites of the regional agency of the French Ministry of Food and Agriculture (DRAAF). Therefore, PHBs are disseminated on different websites (one per region). Depending on the health issues or crop development, the frequency of PHB publications is variable, ranging from monthly to weekly. Nearly 15,000 plots are observed each year to edit approximately 3400 PHBs per year [14].

3.2 Method Description

Corpus Preprocessing. We rely on a test corpus of the PHBs for automatic extraction of new crop concepts and label names. Our test corpus holds 880 PHB files with an average of 2,548 tokens per file, each covering different sectors of French agriculture. The PHB files have been collected during various periods from 2009[13] and transformed from their initial PDF format into an HTML format using a conversion tool named `pdf2blocks`[14]. Our system applies on standard methods of text preprocessing (sentence segmentation, word tokenization, part-of-speech tagging) and also takes into account issues after the conversion from PDF.

Assumption. In our method, we focus on detecting coordination structures in paragraphs of the bulletins. Coordinations are complex syntactic structures composed of several conjuncts, one or more of which are preceded by a coordinator (e.g. "et") or a comma [6]. Coordinations are often used to enumerate, exemplify and compare. [4] observes that the conjuncts share the same semantic relations with their environment. Hence, the assumption at the heart of our method is that if a term which is already present in the thesaurus appears to be a conjunct of a coordination, then the other conjuncts from the same coordination can share similar semantic relations, and serve therefore as candidates for enrichment of this resource. For instance, a coordination "pittospore, acacia, eucalyptus et eleagnus" consists of 4 conjuncts. One of them, namely "eucalyptus", is already featured in the FCU thesaurus. Therefore, the other conjuncts are to be considered as candidate terms for the enrichment. Our method is decomposed into three parts : extraction of coordinations, selection of candidate crop label names, suggestion of hyperonyms and similar label names.

[13] https://gitlab.irstea.fr/copain/d2kab/.
[14] https://doi.org/10.5281/zenodo.4067965.

Extraction of Coordinations. To detect coordinations, we use the latest[15] version of `Stanza` [12], a natural language processing toolkit that provides a neural pipeline for text analysis. Stanza offers a state-of-the-art performance for a wide spectrum of languages, including French, in regards to tokenization, lemmatization, part-of-speech, morphological feature labelling, and dependency parsing. We use its default lemmatization model for French with adjustments on a few domain-specific words. For example "radis", a french crop name for radish, should be lemmatized as "radis" and not "radi" (a form proposed by the default model) and thus adjusted by our system.

Regarding coordination structures, Stanza treats them as symmetric relations and uses the relation *CONJ* to connect the first conjunct of the coordination to all subsequent conjuncts. The language model used by Stanza is based on Universal Dependencies v2 [11]. According to this version, the coordinators *CC* and punctuation marks *PUNCT* of the coordination are attached to the conjunct *CONJ*, mentioned right afterwards. Figure 3 shows a dependency analysis of a sentence containing a coordination structure.

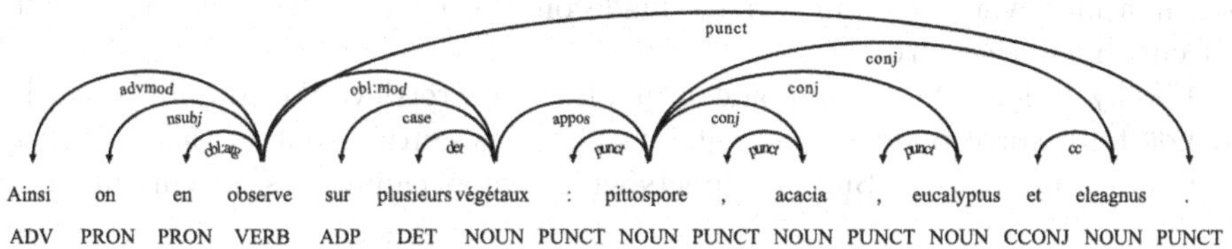

Fig. 3. Stanza's Dependency Analysis

The extraction process starts with a dependency parsing of the sentences, obtained from the corpus. In particular, we look for coordinations whose conjuncts have *NOUN* as a part-of-speech tag. These conjuncts may be accompanied by one or more expansions such as determiners, qualifying adjectives, prepositions or noun complements. Due to frequent mentions of phenological stages of plants inside the coordinations, we impose that a conjunct must not contain any digit (e.g. the conjunct equal to *"BBCH55"* would represent a phenological stage in the BBCH scale [7] rather than a crop label name). Moreover, names of pests, plant parts, tools and scientific names of plants are filtered. Those terms are very common in the text of the bulletins but are not useful for enrichment.

Selection of Candidates. As already mentioned, we assume that conjuncts share same semantic relations with their environment. In order to find candidates for enrichment, we need to find at least one conjunct that already corresponds to a crop label name from the thesaurus. The other conjuncts from the same coordination can share similar semantic relations and serve as potential candidates for enrichment.

[15] https://github.com/stanfordnlp/stanza/releases/tag/v1.4.0.

So, firstly, we search for crop concepts inside the coordination. We align each conjunct of each coordination with existing crop label names (*skos:prefLabel*, *skos:altLabel*) and link this conjunct to the respective crop concept. The alignment is done by comparing lemmatized forms of a conjunct and of a crop label name, with no regard for their case or punctuation marks. By the end of the alignment, we characterise conjuncts into the following groups:

- **exact match**: if the comparison between the conjunct and the crop label name is exact (e.g.: "choux chinois" is a label name of the crop concept *Choux_chinois* and is also found in the text).
- **partial match**: if the comparison between the conjunct and the crop label name is partial (e.g. "cerise de Cayenne" is found in the corpus and the crop concept *Cerise* has a label name "cerise").
- **null match**: if the comparison between the conjunct and the crop label name has not been made.

Secondly, we filter out coordinations which are out of topic, such as the coordinations whose conjuncts have made only null matches. We also remove coordinations whose conjuncts have made only exact matches, since they will not enrich the thesaurus.

Finally, among the remaining coordinations, we retrieve the conjuncts which do not fully correspond to the entries of the thesaurus, that is those with a partial or a null match. Such conjuncts will serve as candidates for enrichment.

Suggestion of Hyperonyms and Similar Label Names. We anticipate that some candidates will be considered as new crop concepts and that subsequently they will need to be placed in the hierarchical structure of the thesaurus. Therefore, we suggest a set of hyperonym concepts for each candidate, hoping that this will help to determine the best position for their integration. Hyperonyms are computed by extracting *skos:broader* concepts for conjuncts from the same coordination as the candidate, once these conjuncts have been linked to a crop concept.

On the other hand, we presume that some candidates will be added as new label names for already existing crop concepts. In this case, we suggest a set of similar label names which would help to update an associated concept. Similar label names are retrieved by computing the cosine similarity between the vector of an existing label name and the vector of a candidate. In order to establish a vector, either for a label name or a candidate, we chunk their respective word sequence and find the average of all word embeddings in the chunk. We train a `fastText` [1] model on the test PHB corpus to determine these word embeddings.

On average, we suggest 3 hyperonyms and 5 similar label names for a candidate. The choice of the most appropriate suggestion is ultimately made by the thesaurus manager.

4 Evaluation

The evaluation of the candidates is conducted manually by the thesaurus manager. We provided a document containing candidate terms, their respective coordination, context, linked crop concepts, suggested hyperonym concepts and similar label names. The first part of the evaluation concerned the relevance of the candidate terms and their typifying. The second part was focused on the accuracy of the suggested hyperonyms for those candidates, typified as new concepts, and on the accuracy of the suggested similar label names for those, typified as new label names. In addition, the coordinations were also examined for their well-formedness.

As a result, we have obtained 138 coordinations in our test corpus. 70% of coordinations are well-formed. For example, our system helped to find a coordination "saule, tilleul, marronnier, platane, cerisier, éléagnus" inside the sentence: "De façon moins fréquente les espèces suivantes ont aussi été touchées : le saule (Salix babylonica) , le tilleul (Tilia sp), le marronnier (Aesculus hippocastanum), le platane (Platanus sp,) le cerisier (Prunus cerasus), l'éléagnus (Eleagnus sp)". This coordination contains two conjuncts that were identified as the crop concepts (*Tilleuls*, *Cerisiers*) and the rest of the conjuncts were proposed as candidates for enrichment.

Regarding badly formed coordinations, they either lack conjuncts or at least one of the conjuncts is incomplete or grammatically incorrect. For example, in the sentence "Des taches sporulantes sont observées sur les feuilles de la couronne extérieure des laitues rouges et des laitues iceberg", we found a coordination "laitue rouge, laitue". It has all two conjuncts, nevertheless one of them lacks its nominal modifier "iceberg". This would be considered as an example of an incomplete extraction and a potential source of improvement.

Table 1. Candidate terms

Relevency	*relevant*			*irrelevant*		
Type	new concepts	new label names	already existing label names	scientific names	ill-formed	unspecified
Count	54 45 %	32 26 %	4 3 %	13 11 %	12 10 %	6 5 %
Total	90 74 %			31 26 %		

With the help of the retrieved coordinations, we have submitted a set of 121 unique candidate terms, most of which have been considered relevant by the thesaurus manager (Table 1). The irrelevant candidates were generally either ill-formed or outside the scope of the thesaurus, representing scientific names of plants. The thesaurus manager also concluded that approximately two-thirds of the relevant candidates have been added as new concepts and one-third as new label names. In regards to the integration of these relevant candidates, in 67%

of cases the suggested hyperonyms have been considered helpful for placing a new crop concept in the hierarchy. The same goes for the suggested similar label names (84% of cases).

Note that the detection of a new term can lead to the creation of three new crop concepts: one in the branch *Multiusages* (*Frênes*) and two in the branch *Usages_plantes_cultivees* (*Frênes forestiers*, *Frênes ornementaux*). Thanks to this experiment the version 3.0 of the FCU thesaurus was build.

5 Related Work

Our work pertains to the field of automatic acquisition or enrichment of lexicons from text. The acquisition of new labels is typically divided into two sub-tasks: the extraction of candidate labels from the text, and the prediction of the relation between candidate labels and existing labels in the lexicon. The two tasks can be tackled either in sequence, or jointly.

In the present work, we focus on noun phrase candidates, and on hypernym/hyponym relations. On the one hand, terminology labels are rarely adjectival or verbal phrases. On the other hand, the hierarchy of hyponyms is the most common denominator in lexical resources, such as terminologies or ontologies.

Since [5], hand crafted syntactic patterns have been used for automatically extracting information from text, in particular the extraction of hyperonyms. The syntactic patterns take form of regular expressions with placeholders for the extracted labels. Typical hyperonymy extraction patterns look like "$Label_{NP}$ *is a* $Hyper_{NP}$" or "$Hyper_{NP}$ *such as* $Label_{NP}$".

The SEXTANT system [3] introduced the use of distributional semantics for extracting labels from corpora. The core hypothesis of distributional semantics is that words that occur in similar contexts must have similar meanings. This family of methods have received a lot of attraction with the availability of word embeddings trained on very large corpora [10,16].

However [13] showed that pattern-based methods provide better and more robust results than embeddings-based methods. [18] demonstrates that patterns based on coordination structures are particularly powerful to extract new hyponym labels for domain-specific lexicons. Other works, like [2] demonstrated that coordination structures may be used to improve supervised extraction of hyponyms.

[17] is a method that aims at extracting a taxonomy in a specific domain (medical) from text using coordination. This system is also based in the *Lowest Common Ancestor* in WordNet of coordinated nouns, which is very similar to our strategy for suggesting candidate hyperonyms.

To the best of our knowledge all methods extract coordination structures using lexical patterns. Our system uses the result of automatic parsing. We believe that parsers have reached sufficient performance to point to coordinations without limitations on the cardinality (number of elements) or the complexity of each element (noun phrases).

6 Conclusion and Perspectives

This paper presents an experiment of enriching French Crop Usage thesaurus by extracting coordinations in a corpus of Plant Health Bulletins. This experiment has improved the FCU thesaurus by adding 54 new crop concepts and update 32 crop concepts with new label names. The improvement concerns mainly arboriculture sector, which was poorly represented in FCU. All the results are available on a Git repository.

We believe this method can be applied to fill holes in any vocabulary. Nevertheless the use of coordinations requires two resources. The first resource is a corpus of relatively well-formed documents on the same topic as the thesaurus. Our experiment shows that the "cleanliness" of documents is decisive to produce relevant candidates. Indeed, we spent a considerable amount of effort in fixing the text extracted from PDF documents. The second requirement is a set of computational linguistics resources for the language of the documents and thesaurus in order to extract noun phrases and coordination structures. The software we used, `Stanza` proposes models for more than 60 languages, including regional and dead languages.

In the future, we plan to improve our extraction system to reduce the number of badly formed coordinations. We also plan to repeat this experiment on a regular basis in order to update regularly the FCU thesaurus, and other agricultural resources like plant phenological scales or pest lists.

References

1. Bojanowski, P., Grave, E., Joulin, A., Mikolov, T.: Enriching Word Vectors with Subword Information. Trans. Assoc. Comput. Linguist. **5**, 135–146 (2017). https://doi.org/10.1162/tacl_a_00051
2. Cederberg, S., Widdows, D.: Using LSA and noun coordination information to improve the recall and precision of automatic hyponymy extraction. In: Proceedings of the Seventh Conference on Natural Language Learning at HLT-NAACL 2003, pp. 111–118 (2003). https://aclanthology.org/W03-0415
3. Grefenstette, G.: Exploration in Automatic Thesaurus Discovery. Kluwer Academic Publishers (1994). https://doi.org/10.1007/978-1-4615-2710-7
4. Haspelmath, M.: Coordination. In: Shopen, T. (ed.) Language Typology and Syntactic Description, vol. 2, pp. 1–51. Cambridge University Press (2007). https://doi.org/10.1017/CBO9780511619434.001
5. Hearst, M.A.: Automatic acquisition of hyponyms from large text corpora. In: COLING 1992 Volume 2: The 14th International Conference on Computational Linguistics (1992). https://aclanthology.org/C92-2082
6. Maier, W., Kübler, S., Hinrichs, E., Krivanek, J.: Annotating coordination in the Penn Treebank. In: Proceedings of the Sixth Linguistic Annotation Workshop, Jeju, Republic of Korea, pp. 166–174. Association for Computational Linguistics (2012). https://aclanthology.org/W12-3624
7. Meier, U., et al.: The BBCH system to coding the phenological growth stages of plants-history and publications. J. für Kulturpflanzen **61**, 41–52 (2009). https://doi.org/10.5073/JfK.2009.02.01

8. Miles, A., Bechhofer, S.: SKOS Simple Knowledge Organization System Reference. W3C Recommendation, World Wide Web Consortium, United States (2009)
9. Musen, M.A.: The protégé project: a look back and a look forward. AI Matters **1**(4), 4–12 (2015)
10. Nguyen, K.A., Köper, M., Schulte im Walde, S., Vu, N.T.: Hierarchical embeddings for hypernymy detection and directionality. In: Proceedings of the 2017 Conference on Empirical Methods in Natural Language Processing, Copenhagen, Denmark, pp. 233–243. Association for Computational Linguistics (2017). https://doi.org/10.18653/v1/D17-1022. https://aclanthology.org/D17-1022
11. Nivre, J., et al.: Universal dependencies v2: an evergrowing multilingual treebank collection. In: Proceedings of the 12th Language Resources and Evaluation Conference, Marseille, France, pp. 4034–4043. European Language Resources Association (2020). https://aclanthology.org/2020.lrec-1.497
12. Qi, P., Zhang, Y., Zhang, Y., Bolton, J., Manning, C.D.: Stanza: a Python natural language processing toolkit for many human languages. In: Proceedings of the 58th Annual Meeting of the Association for Computational Linguistics: System Demonstrations (2020). https://nlp.stanford.edu/pubs/qi2020stanza.pdf
13. Roller, S., Kiela, D., Nickel, M.: Hearst patterns revisited: automatic hypernym detection from large text corpora. In: Proceedings of the 56th Annual Meeting of the Association for Computational Linguistics (Volume 2: Short Papers), Melbourne, Australia, pp. 358–363. Association for Computational Linguistics (2018). https://doi.org/10.18653/v1/P18-2057. https://aclanthology.org/P18-2057
14. Roussey, C., et al.: A methodology for the publication of agricultural alert bulletins as LOD. Comput. Electron. Agric. **142**, 632–650 (2017). https://doi.org/10.1016/j.compag.2017.10.022. https://www.sciencedirect.com/science/article/pii/S0168169917306361
15. Roussey, C., Delpuech, X., Amardeilh, F., Bernard, S., Jonquet, C.: Semantic description of plant phenological development stages, starting with grapevine. In: Garoufallou, E., Ovalle-Perandones, M.-A. (eds.) MTSR 2020. CCIS, vol. 1355, pp. 257–268. Springer, Cham (2021). https://doi.org/10.1007/978-3-030-71903-6_25
16. Shwartz, V., Santus, E., Schlechtweg, D.: Hypernyms under siege: linguistically-motivated artillery for hypernymy detection. In: Proceedings of the 15th Conference of the European Chapter of the Association for Computational Linguistics: Volume 1, Long Papers, Valencia, Spain, pp. 65–75. Association for Computational Linguistics (2017). https://aclanthology.org/E17-1007
17. Widdows, D., Toumouh, A., Dorow, B., Lehireche, A.: Ongoing developments in automatically adapting lexical resources to the biomedical domain. In: Proceedings of the Fifth International Conference on Language Resources and Evaluation (LREC 2006), Genoa, Italy. European Language Resources Association (ELRA) (2006). https://www.lrec-conf.org/proceedings/lrec2006/pdf/489_pdf.pdf
18. Ziering, P., van der Plas, L., Schütze, H.: Bootstrapping semantic lexicons for technical domains. In: Proceedings of the Sixth International Joint Conference on Natural Language Processing, Nagoya, Japan, pp. 1321–1329. Asian Federation of Natural Language Processing (2013). https://aclanthology.org/I13-1188

Scoring Ontologies for Reuse: An Approach for Fitting Semantic Requirements

Sabrina Azzi[1(✉)], Ali Assi[1], and Stéphane Gagnon[2]

[1] The House of Commons, Ottawa, Canada
{sabrina.azzi,ali.assi}@parl.gc.ca
[2] Université du Québec en Outaouais, Gatineau, Canada
stephane.gagnon@uqo.ca

Abstract. The process of reusing ontologies is still challenging for the ontological community. One of the challenging efforts is to select the most relevant ontology from a set of candidates that needs a deep consideration. After the step of finding the candidates, many of them can be more appropriate than others as they fit better to the ontology requirements expressed by competency questions. First, we develop a mathematical formalisation based on Set Theory and we design the problem as an optimization problem to assist the knowledge engineer in selecting ontologies. Then, we provide formal steps to make well-founded comparison across a set of candidate ontologies. At last, we propose metrics to quantify the decision during the selection step.

Keywords: Competency questions · Ontology engineering · Ontology reuse · PNADO · Semantic requirements

1 Introduction

An ontology is *a formal and explicit specification of a shared conceptualization* [1]. It consists of resources (see Sect. 3) that describe a domain of interest (*e.g.*, finance, parliament, pneumonia diagnosis, *etc.*).

Ontology building process includes the definition of its domain and its scope. Indeed, the knowledge engineer must identify the functional requirements that the ontology must satisfy. Therefore, Competency Questions (CQs) were first introduced in [2] for ontology engineering and formulated in natural language.

Ontology reuse is the process of selecting existing ontologies that meet some of the requirements defined in the conception [3]. This process significantly reduces the development time and effort.

Reusing ontologies is not a trivial process. It can be applied either in hard or soft mode. While, the former reuses the whole selected ontology. The latter imports only a set of its concepts. This process starts by selecting the candidate ontologies according to four main criteria [4]. These ontologies could be found in public repositories. Then, by pruning them to select the most appropriate ones.

Supported by the House of Commons of Canada.

E. Garoufallou and A. Vlachidis (Eds.): MTSR 2022, CCIS 1789, pp. 203–208, 2023.
https://doi.org/10.1007/978-3-031-39141-5_17

To choose the most relevant ontology, [5] presents an approach based on the notion of preference between candidate ontologies. However, the approach omits cases of reuse and which reuse to consider, *i.e*, soft or hard. As well, in the context of selecting foundational ontologies as starting points for ontology engineering, [6] implements a selection algorithm scoring ontologies by number of categories and end-user CQs they can satisfy. Then, the authors formulate a representative description along preset ontology attributes, such as Ontological Commitments. However, this approach presupposes that CQs are formulated within the scope of the ontology, and that ontology attributes are the end-users decision criteria.

In this paper, we propose an approach that facilitates the ontology reuse. This approach has been applied during the project about developing an ontology covering pneumonia diagnosis (PNADO) [7] and has proven its efficiency. In contrast to the existing approaches, ours permits to guide the knowledge engineer to select relevant ontologies for reuse. Indeed, it covers all the cases of reuse and recommend the corresponding mode. We develop a mathematical formalisation based on Set Theory and we design the problem as an optimization function. The novelty of our approach is to refine the decision criteria for ontology reuse objectives. To the best of our knowledge, there is no approach that leverages the decision criteria during ontology selection for reuse.

2 Related Work

Selecting the appropriate ontology for reuse from a set of candidates is still challenging. Many works have recognized the challenge of making a well-founded comparison with a reasonable amount of effort [3,8]. [9] affirms that choosing ontology for reuse is a highly subjective task carried out by experienced ontology engineers, who choose ontologies that intuitively respond to the requirements. Whether implemented as a tool or presented as a guideline, most works used some kind of calculation over a set of subjectively-weighted criteria conducting to approaches that are too superficial to account for the candidates' semantics.

Among the aspects affecting the reusability of an ontology is the perception of its quality according to some evaluation criteria. The only work that has tackled this challenge and addressed the assessment the candidates' semantics was done by Katsumi and colleagues [5]. This work introduced for the first time the notion of preference between ontologies and provided a definition that allows the knowledge engineer to make a well-founded comparison between ontologies, with respect to their semantic requirements. One of the major limitations of this work is not considering all the cases of comparison between candidate ontologies. Also, the approach does not provide any measures that allow to select accurately the ontologies.

In our approach, we consider more than two ontology candidates and compare them based on the semantic requirements of the ontology expressed by CQs. We take into account all the cases of reuse and recommend the corresponding mode. We provide a mathematical formalisation based on Set Theory and we design the problem as an optimization problem.

3 Preliminaries and Definitions

In this section, we present preliminary definitions about ontologies and the order set between the candidate ontologies.

Definition 1 *(Ontology). An ontology is a set of triplets in the form of* *<subject, predicate, object>* $\in \mathbf{R} \times \mathbf{P} \times (\mathbf{R} \cup \mathbf{L})$ *where R is the set of resources, P is the set of predicates and L is the set of literals.*

In the following, we refer to the set of *relevant* concepts (*i.e.*, those that respond to the CQs) by *intended models*, denoted by R. This set is defined by a domain experts during the first phase of the ontology development.

Indeed, we refer to the set of candidate ontologies by $O = \{i : 1 \leq i \leq n\}$. An ontology $i \in O$ consists of a set concepts denoted by O_i. According to the CQs, we split the concepts for each candidate ontology $i \in O$ into two sets R_i and $\bar{R}_i$, *i.e.*, $O_i = R_i \cup \bar{R}_i$ where $R_i \cap \bar{R}_i = \emptyset$. R_i represents the set of concepts in i that also belongs to R, *i.e.*, $R_i \subseteq R$. Thus, R_i represents the relevant concepts in ontology i. Similarly, $\bar{R}_i$ consists of the remaining concepts in O_i *i.e.*, $O_i - R_i$. Thus, $\bar{R}_i \not\subset R$ which means that $R \cap \bar{R}_i = \emptyset$.

Based on R_i and $\bar{R}_i$, we measure the *meaningful* of each ontology $i \in O$ by the number of concepts in $R - R_i$ and $\bar{R}_i$. The former quantifies the concepts corresponding to the one CQ that are omitted in i. The latter measures the number concepts included in i which are not relevant to any CQ. We call such concepts by superfluous concepts or noisy concepts. The more the number of the omitted concepts in i is small, the more i covers the needed concepts defined by the CQs. Indeed, the more the number of the concepts in $\bar{R}_i = O_i - R_i$ is small, the more i does not include concepts related to any CQ.

Definition 2 *(Optimal Ontology). An ontology $j \in O$, where O is the set candidate ontologies, is called optimal if j verifies: $R \cap R_j = R$ (which means that $R_j = R$) and $\bar{R}_j = \emptyset$.*

We define the following objective function that globally scores the suitability of an ontology $i \in O$:

$$score(i) = |R - R_i| + |\bar{R}_i| \tag{1}$$

Our approach is motivated by the minimization problem:

$$\arg\min_{i^* \in O} score(i^*) = |R - R_{i^*}| + |\bar{R}_{i^*}| \tag{2}$$

where O is the set of candidate ontologies and $i^* \in O$ is the ontology that has the smallest meaningful *score* value.

Definition 3 *(Meaningful Ontology). We call an ontology $i \in O$ more meaningful than ontology j, denoted by $i \preceq j$, when $|R - R_i| \leq |R - R_j|$ and $|\bar{R}_i| \leq |\bar{R}_j|$ where O is the set of candidate ontologies.*

Definition 4 ***(Meaningfully Equivalent Ontology).*** *We call an ontology i is meaningfully equivalent to ontology j, denoted by $i = j$, iff $|R - R_i| = |R - R_j|$ and $|\bar{R}_i| = |\bar{R}_j|$.*

Lemma 1. *$\preceq$ is a partial ordering over the set of candidates O.*

Proof. We need to prove that $\preceq$ is reflexive, transitive and antisymmetric.

- **$\preceq$ is reflexive.** We must prove that $O_1 \preceq O_1$ where $O_1 \in O$. Since $O_1 \preceq O_1$, we have $|R - R_1| = |R - R_1|$ and $|\bar{R}_1| = |\bar{R}_1|$ where R_1 is the set of the relevant concepts in O_1. Hence, $\preceq$ is reflexive.
- **$\preceq$ is transitive.** Let $O_1 \in O$, $O_2 \in O$ and $O_3 \in O$. We need to prove that if $O_1 \preceq O_2$ and $O_2 \preceq O_3$ then $O_1 \preceq O_3$. Since $O_1 \preceq O_2$, we have $|R - R_1| \leq |R - R_2|$ and $|\bar{R}_1| \leq |\bar{R}_2|$. Similarly, since $O_2 \preceq O_3$ then $|R - R_2| \leq |R - R_3|$ and $|\bar{R}_2| \leq |\bar{R}_3|$. Therefore, $|R - R_1| \leq |R - R_3|$ and $|\bar{R}_1| \leq |\bar{R}_3|$. Hence, $O_1 \preceq O_3$.
- **$\preceq$ is antisymmetric.** We need to prove that if $O_1 \preceq O_2$ and $O_2 \preceq O_1$, then $O_1 = O_2$. Since $O_1 \preceq O_2$ and $O_2 \preceq O_1$ then $|R - R_1| \leq |R - R_2|$ and $|R - R_2| \leq |R - R_1|$ then $|R - R_1| = |R - R_2|$. Similarly, $|\bar{R}_1| \leq |\bar{R}_2|$ and $|\bar{R}_2| \leq |\bar{R}_1|$ then $|\bar{R}_2| = |\bar{R}_1|$. Therefore, $|R - R_1| = |R - R_2|$ and $|\bar{R}_1| = |\bar{R}_2|$. Hence, $O_1 = O_2$.

Based on the Lemma 1, the candidate ontologies in O are now comparable. Thus, the best ontology that can be used from O is simply the ontology that has the smallest meaningful score value. If two ontologies $i \in O$ and $j \in O$ posses the same meaningful score, we prioritize i over j and vice-versa. If i has more relevant concepts than j, *i.e.*, $|R_i| > |R_j|$, then i is more precise than j. Formally:

Definition 5 ***(Precise Ontology).*** *An ontology $i \in O$ is more precise than ontology $j \in O$ if for score(i) = score(j) we have $|R - R_i| < |R - R_j|$ where O is the set candidate ontologies. We denote this relation between i and j by $i \rhd j$.*

Lemma 2. *$\rhd$ is a strict order over the set of candidate ontologies O.*

Proof. We need to prove that $\rhd$ is irreflexive, transitive and asymmetric.

- **$\rhd$ is irreflexive.** We must prove $i \rhd i$ does not hold for any i in O. Let say that $i \rhd i$ holds. That means $|R - R_i| < |R - R_i|$ which is incorrect since $R_i = R_i$. Therefore, $\rhd$ must be irreflexive.
- **$\rhd$ is transitive.** Let $O_1 \in O$, $O_2 \in O$ and $O_3 \in O$. We need to prove that if $O_1 \rhd O_2$ and $O_2 \rhd O_3$ then $O_1 \rhd O_3$. Since $O_1 \rhd O_2$, we have $|R - R_1| < |R - R_2|$. Similarity, since $O_2 \rhd O_3$, we have $|R - R_2| < |R - R_3|$. Thus, $|R - R_1| < |R - R_2| < |R - R_3|$. Therefore, $\rhd$ must be transitive.
- **$\rhd$ is asymmetric.** We need to prove that if $i \rhd j$, then $j \rhd i$ does not hold. Let consider that $i \rhd j$ (*i.e.*, $|R - R_i| < |R - R_j|$) and $j \rhd i$ (*i.e.*, $|R - R_j| < |R - R_i|$) hold for $i \neq j$. Thus, $|R - R_i| = |R - R_j|$. This equality leads to a contradictory since $|R - R_i| \neq |R - R_j|$ for $i \neq j$.

Algorithm 1. Selecting relevant ontologies

Input: $O = \{o_1, o_2 \ldots, o_n\}$ set of (n) candidate ontologies that respond to one QC.
R set of relevant concepts.
Output: $O_s = \{o_i, o_j \ldots, o_k\}$ set of ontologies $(m \leq n)$ to be reused.

1: $O_s \leftarrow \{\}$;
2: **for all** $o_i \in O$ **do**
3: $score(o_i) \leftarrow |R - R_{o_i}| + |\bar{R}_{o_i}|$
4: **end for**
5: Rank $o_i \in O$ by their meaningful $score(o_i)$.
6: Select the most meaningful ontologies $o_i^* \in O$ with the minimum $score(o_i^*)$.
7: $O_s \leftarrow \cup\{o_{i^*}\}$
8: **if** $|O_s| = 1$ **then**
9: **if** $R_{o_i} = 0$ **then**
10: **return** O_s ▷ Hard reuse of o_i
11: **else**
12: **return** O_s ▷ Soft reuse of o_i
13: **end if**
14: **else if** $|O_s| > 1$ **then** ▷ More than 1 ontology has the same score
15: $O_p \leftarrow \{\}$;
16: Rank $o_j \in O$ by their precise score $|R - R_{o_j}|$.
17: Select ontology o_j with the minimal precise value $|R - R_{o_j}|$.
18: $O_p \leftarrow \cup\{o_j\}$
19: **if** $|O_p| = 1$ **then**
20: **if** $R_{o_j} = 0$ **then**
21: **return** O_p ▷ Hard reuse of o_j
22: **else**
23: **return** O_p ▷ Soft reuse of o_j
24: **end if**
25: **end if**

4 Our Approach

The proposed approach focuses on reuse of ontologies that best respond to some of semantic requirements or intended models. Its main idea is to use CQs to select only the ontologies that would be interesting for the knowledge engineer (*i.e.*, the relevant ontologies). In following, we present an algorithm that returns these ontologies based on Definitions 3 and 5. For each ontology chosen and according to its meaningfulness score, we recommend hard of soft reuse.

For each CQ, we calculate the score of its $o_j \in O$ candidate ontologies (line 3). Then, we rank the candidates according to their meaningful scores (line 5). Two cases are considered. The first one is where only one ontology is returned (line 8). In this case, the ontology is considered as the most meaningful ontology and it is selected for reuse. Then, its precision score is calculated. Based on this score, the hard or soft mode will be recommended. If is a precise ontology, *i.e*, no superfluous models then we recommend hard reuse. Otherwise, soft reuse is considered. The second case is where many ontologies are returned (line 14). In this case, we rank them according to their precise score $|R - R_{o_j}|$ and we select the most precise ontology having the minimal precise score.

5 Conclusion

We presented in this paper a new formalized approach for selecting relevant ontologies to be reused during ontology development. The approach was drawn from lessons learned during the project of developing a pneumonia diagnosis ontology (PNADO). We developed a mathematical formalisation based on Set Theory and we designed the problem as an optimization problem. In this perspective, we proposed an efficient algorithm based on this formalisation. We also proposed metrics to quantify the decision during selection ontologies.

An important future work would be to implement this algorithm and evaluate it in real use cases. It also be interesting to propose an extension of this approach that leverages parallel computation frameworks to handle ontology reuse in big data era.

References

1. Studer, R., Benjamins, V.R., Fensel, D.: Knowledge engineering: principles and methods. Data Knowl. Eng. **25**(1–2), 161–197 (1998)
2. Grüninger, M., Fox, M.S.: The role of competency questions in enterprise engineering. In: Rolstadås, A. (ed.) Benchmarking—Theory and Practice. IAICT, pp. 22–31. Springer, Boston, MA (1995). https://doi.org/10.1007/978-0-387-34847-6_3
3. Katsumi, M., Grüninger, M.: What is ontology reuse? In: FOIS, pp. 9–22 (2016)
4. Azzi, S.: Nouvelle méthodologie de construction d'ontologies médicales: cas d'étude: diagnostic de la pneumonie. Ph.D. thesis, Université du Québec en Outaouais (2021)
5. Katsumi, M., Grüninger, M.: Choosing ontologies for reuse. Appl. Ontol. **12**(3–4), 195–221 (2017)
6. Khan, Z., Keet, C.M.: ONSET: automated foundational ontology selection and explanation. In: ten Teije, A., et al. (eds.) EKAW 2012. LNCS (LNAI), vol. 7603, pp. 237–251. Springer, Heidelberg (2012). https://doi.org/10.1007/978-3-642-33876-2_22
7. Azzi, S., Michalowski, W., Iglewski, M.: Developing a pneumonia diagnosis ontology from multiple knowledge sources. Health Inform. J. **28**(2), 14604582221083850 (2022)
8. Alharbi, R., Tamma, V., Grasso, F.: Characterising the gap between theory and practice of ontology reuse. In: Proceedings of the 11th on Knowledge Capture Conference, pp. 217–224 (2021)
9. Cota, G., et al.: The landscape of ontology reuse approaches. Appl. Pract. Ontol. Des. Extract. Reason **49**, 21 (2020)

Track on Open Repositories, Research Information Systems & Data Infrastructures, and Metadata, Linked Data, Semantics and Ontologies - General Session

Materials Science Ontology Design with an Analytico-Synthetic Facet Analysis Framework

Jane Greenberg[1(✉)], Scott McClellan[1], Xintong Zhao[1], Elijah J Kellner[2], David Venator[3], Haoran Zhao[1], Jiacheng Shen[1], Xiaohua Hu[1], and Yuan An[1]

[1] Metadata Research Center, Drexel University, Philadelphia, USA
jg3243@drexel.edu
[2] College of Science and Engineering, Winona State University, Winona, USA
[3] McCormick School of Engineering, Northwestern University, Evanston, USA

Abstract. Researchers across nearly every discipline seek to leverage ontologies for knowledge discovery and computational tasks; yet, the number of machine readable materials science ontologies is limited. The work presented in this paper explores the Processing, Structure, Properties and Performance (PSPP) framework for accelerating the development of materials science ontologies. We pursue a case study framed by the creation of an Aerogel ontology and a Battery Cathode ontology and demonstrate the Helping Interdisciplinary Vocabulary Engineer for Materials Science (HIVE4MAT) as a proof of concept showing PSPP relationships. The paper includes background context covering materials science, the PSPP framework, and faceted analysis for ontologies. We report our research objectives, methods, research procedures, and results. The findings indicate that the PSPP framework offers a rubric that may help guide and potentially accelerate ontology development.

Keywords: Ontology · Facet Analysis · Facets · Automatic Indexing · Materials Science

1 Introduction

An ontology is an explicit language that includes a vocabulary. An ontology, and hence the underlying vocabulary, frequently represents a domain or area of knowledge. Machine readable ontologies are made explicit by adhering to grammatical rules and through the application of enabling technologies, such as the Resource Description Framework (RDF) and Web Ontology Language (OWL). These technologies have advanced the development of ontologies, including the transformation of analog disciplinary vocabularies into machine readable ontological structures. Furthermore, they enable ontologies to support information discovery, reasoning, data interoperability, linked data applications, and other

This work is supported by NSF-OAC 2118201, NSF-IIS 1815256.

E. Garoufallou and A. Vlachidis (Eds.): MTSR 2022, CCIS 1789, pp. 211–221, 2023.
https://doi.org/10.1007/978-3-031-39141-5_18

computational tasks. Today hundreds of ontologies in biomedicine, biology, and related disciplines are accessible via portals, such as the National Center for Biomedical Ontology's Bioportal [13] and the OBO Ontology register [12]–both of which have been operational since the early and mid-2000's. In comparison, the number of machine readable materials science ontologies is limited, with MatPortal [14] hosting approximately 25 ontologies. The limited number of materials-science ontologies challenges researchers to identify approaches for accelerating their development.

The research presented in this paper seeks to address this challenge by exploring analytico-synthetic faceted classification [24] as a framework for accelerating the development of materials science ontologies. In pursing this task, it is important to examine why there are a relatively small number of materials science ontologies. One likely factor is R&D (research and development) funding allocations with the life-sciences, which includes medicine and biology, has generally exceeded other disciplines [25]. A more obvious factor is the broad context that materials science encompasses, spanning engineering, physics, chemistry, and other interconnected disciplines. Finding a unifying approach to any knowledge-based task is difficult across any interdisciplinary and transdisciplinary field, and materials science is among one of the more extensive disciplines in its topical and disciplinary span. A final factor to note here is the absence of a clear underlying semantic framework. While materials scientists may examine biomedical ontologies for guidance and research support, ontological structures from these disciplines may not resonate or sufficiently to inform development of material science ontologies. This predicament motivates us to examine the Processing, Structure, Properties and Performance (PSPP) framework for ontology development. The work presented in this paper specifically investigates the application of the PSPP model for developing materials science ontologies. We present a case study framed by the creation of two exploratory ontologies, one focused on Aerogels and another on Cathode Batteries. Additionally, we demonstrate the use of these ontologies with the Helping Interdisciplinary Vocabulary Engineer for Materials Science (HIVE4MAT) indexing application to illustrate PSPP relationships extracted materials science literature. The following sections include background context, the guiding objectives, methods, research procedures, and results. The last two sections include a discussion and a conclusion, which underscores key takeaways and next steps.

2 Background and Motivation

2.1 Materials Science and PSPP

In exploring the PSPP framework, it is important to understand the expanse and context of materials science. Materials science is an interdisciplinary field that utilizes physics, chemistry, and engineering principles to identify new materials and improve existing ones. The field focuses on solids, which have a defined structure unlike liquids or gases. These defined structures give rise to specific properties, and understanding how and why certain structures correspond to useful properties is central to the field. There are four general classes of materials - metals, polymers, ceramics, and composites - each with a different type of structure that make the class more favorable for certain applications. In each field there are infinite potential materials, each with a unique set of properties.

At a very general level, materials science research follows two pathways. The historical and still significant path is method-driven. Research following this pathway focuses on the scientific relationships between materials processing and performance. This approach allows a researcher to gain a thorough understanding of how certain processes lead to certain structures, which give rise to unique properties, and allows a material to perform in specific ways. This has long been achieved through experimentation. As understanding of these relationships across processing, structure, properties, and performance has grown, an inverse research pathway has emerged, and has become crucial to material-related engineering. The goal of this other pathway is to find a material and materials processing method that achieves the desired material performance. This method has advanced as researchers pursue data-driven approaches, and allow researchers to more efficiently simulate processing in order to measure performance. This framework is illustrated in Fig. 1.

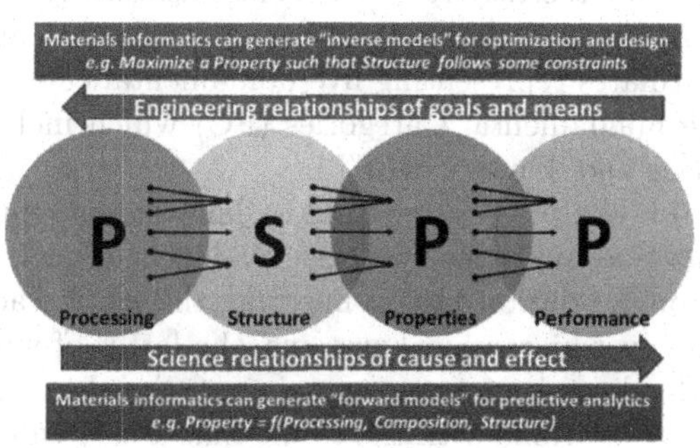

Fig. 1. Materials Paradigm showing the scientific and engineering approaches to the field [10]

This framework may inform the development of materials science ontologies, which are increasingly important for data-driven research including AI. The next section discusses facet analysis and how this approach connects with ontology development.

2.2 Facet Analysis and Ontologies

The fundamental approach to facet analysis and organization has been practiced since ancient times. Facets are defined as mutually exclusive categories. The Pinakes, the catalog Callimachus (310/305-240 BCE) created for the Library of Alexandria, provided disciplinary classes, which knowledge organization researchers have discussed as topical facets. Supporting this view is the Aristotelian notion of classification, where categories are determined by necessary and sufficient conditions of their existence [17]. As direct evidence is scarce, knowledge of these developments descended through the writings of Pliny the Elder and other classical writers who studied at the library.

Faceted knowledge organization systems gained popularity in the late 19th and early 20th century schemes, such as the Dewey Decimal System's use of tables for geographic regions, languages, and other areas [16,21]; Bliss's methodological organization of agents, operations, properties, materials, processes, parts, types, and thing [15]; and, Colon Classification System [22], perhaps the most recently referenced classification system, developed by the mathematician/librarian Shialy Rammarita Ranganathan. Colon classification is based on postulates representing five fundamental categories, each an isolated facet, with five Fundamental Categories (FC) which include: Personality, Matter, Energy, Space and Time (PMEST).

In all of these examples, knowledge representation follows an approach known as analytico-synthetic classification, where a class notation is constructed through relationships connecting the facts. Faceted approaches have an advantage over hierarchical systems, the latter of which tend to isolate related topics and sub-topics in a taxonomic way that can lead to overlapping and redundant representations with the result that a user can miss relevant information having to in initiate their search at a lower than intended level [2]. While faceted systems frequently have an element of hierarchy, the level plane for entry enables a more flexible, accommodating approach, and one that is worth exploring in materials science as viewed in the work of [6]. In sum, the guiding principles underlying faceted systems and the significance of the PSPP framework motivate further exploration of the analytico-synthetic approach for materials science ontologies, and shape the objectives that have guided our work.

3 Research Goals and Objectives

Our overall goal is to investigate the PSPP framework as a method for streamlining the development of materials science ontologies. The individual component of PSPP provides a top-level scaffold of facets and can support analytico-synthetic classification, leading to discovery of new knowledge. We pursued this work by developing two materials science ontologies, one focused Aerogels, which are low-density, open-pored nanostructured materials that support low thermal conductivity, and high adsorption capacity (Feng et al. 2020), and the other focused on Battery Cathode materials, as lithium-ion batteries have rapidly become the standard for many applications [19]. Specific objectives guiding our work include:

1. Exploring literature covering these two areas
2. Developing two baseline/preliminary ontologies, one for aerogels and one for lithium-ion battery cathode materials
3. Demonstrating the application of the ontologies for displaying relationships and knowledge discovery, using the HIVE4MAT ontology application [23].

4 Methods and Research Design Procedures

We pursued the above objectives using a mixed methods approach combining the case study approach, card sorting, and demonstration. The case method, drawing from classic work of Fidel [26], allows researchers to explore a topic at a more indepth level as we explicitly defined the ontology space covering Aerogels and Battery Cathode materials using the PSPP framework. The card-sorting method informed this process, as we grouped terms according to the PSPP framework, under the facets processing, structure, properties, and performance. Finally, we demonstrated the application of both ontologies for knowledge extraction, using the HIVE4MAT ontology application. This offered a proof of concept.

Our procedures involves following seven steps:

- **Step 1: Locate and confirm an area of study**. We started with broader materials science categories which were then narrowed to increase specificity of the vocabulary. The initial categories of gels and batteries were viewed as overly broad, which led to the selection of battery cathodes and aerogels which provide a balance of specificity and breadth. It was important to confirm that the area of study had a definable aspect of materials science and yielded a manageable, useful set of terms for the ontology.
- **Step 2: Term collection**. Term collection was pursued using both automatic and manual review of relevant literature. Terms were selected that related to the two defined topical areas, Aerogels and Battery Cathode materials.
- **Step 3: Term sorting**. Terms were sorted into relevant PSPP facets based upon common features. Following the initial faceted analysis, terms were arranged hierarchically, defined by "is-a"relationship between parent and child concepts.
- **Step 4: Establishing Relationships**: The process of defining relationships between terms as introduced as the sorting activity, and exclusively focused when the sorting was completed.
- **Step 5: Ontology Encoding**: We used WebProtege to visualize the hierarchy and code the terms and their relationships, resulting in the two example ontologies. During this process, some ontology refinement also took place, discarding extraneous terms from each ontology, and the terms that remained were further scoped. During this step, we were able to also examine several symmetrical relationship functions, including their domains and ranges. These qualifications of the relationships and concepts reinforced the interconnections among the categories.
- **Step 6: HIVE4MAT integration**: The baseline Aerogel Ontology and the Battery Cathode Ontology were both integrated into the HIVE4MAT ontology server, and general functionalities of search, browse and index were confirmed.
- **Step 7: Demonstration**: The final step in ontology development was deployment and testing in HIVE4MAT, which offered a proof of concept.

5 Results

Results reported here cover the ontology structures, their display in Protege, and HIVE4MAT outputs.

Aerogel Ontology. This aerogel ontology contains terms that are related to the processing, structure, properties, and performance of aerogels. It should be noted that this is only a baseline ontology and that many terms relating to aerogels, especially newly developed terms, are likely not contained within the ontology and that future updating and expansion of the ontology is recommended. This case study ontology contains 7 performance terms, 38 processing terms, 30 property terms, and 32 structure terms, for a total of 107 terms. These counts include both the preferred label and any synonyms for the listed concepts. The aerogel ontology also contains 4 relationships, which are *isSynthesizedBy*, *isDependentOn*, *isDerivedFrom*, and *isPrecededBy*. The *isSynthesizedBy* relationship connects structures with the process used to synthesize them; the *isDependentOn* relationship connects property terms to performance terms that are based on them; the *isDerivedFrom* relationship connects performance terms to the property terms that they are mathematically derived from; and the *isPrecededBy* relationship connects process terms in the order that they occur in a standard synthesis or procedure (Fig. 2).

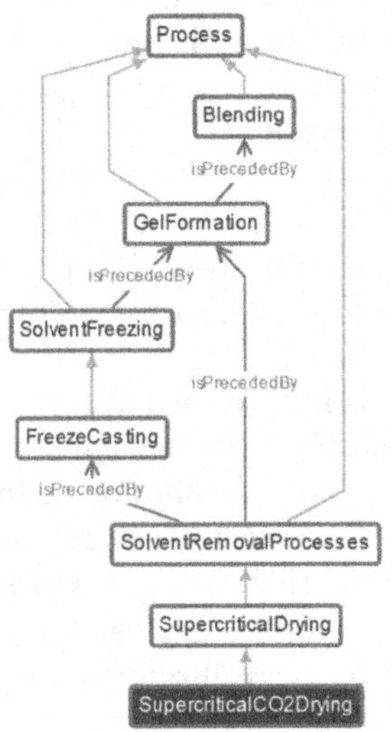

Fig. 2. Aerogel Ontology: Entity and Relationship Display

Battery Cathode Ontology. As an area of high research interest, there are a wealth of terms associated with the study of lithium-ion battery cathodes. This ontology serves as a baseline, capturing many of the foundational terms involved in the processing, structure, properties, and performance of cathode materials. This ontology is not comprehensive; with studies focusing on certain aspects of the cathode (introducing novel processing methods or using constituents of novel composition) likely to have relevant terms not captured in this ontology.

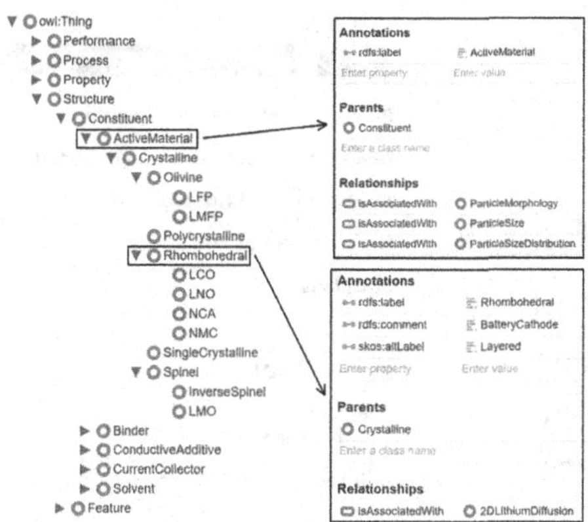

Fig. 3. Battery Cathode Ontology: Protege Faceted and Hierarchical Structure

In order to truly capture all terms in this space, the process would likely have to be automated.

This ontology contains 153 independent terms, exclusive of alternative labels, across each part of the materials science paradigm. There are 20 processing terms, 58 structure terms, 39 property terms, and 36 performance terms. These terms are organized hierarchically, as shown in the figure below. Relationships are also used to connect terms among separate branches. One example, as shown in the figure below, is relating certain structure terms (particle size/size distribution/morphology) to the part of the composite cathode that they relate to (the active material) through the relationship *isAssociatedWith*. Other relationships include *isPreceedεdby*, to connected processes in the general synthesis procedure, and *isDerivedFrom*, to connect performance metrics to the properties they are mathematically derived from (Fig. 3).

Finally, we tested the functionality of the ontologies in the HIVE4MAT ontology server. Figs. 4 and 5 show that the ontologies are browsable and support knowledge extraction when tested with unstructured scholarly big data. The work with HIVE4MAT offers a proof of concept. Figures 4–5 demonstrate the use of HIVE4MAT. Figure 4 presents knowledge extraction results (left-hand side) in using the Battery Cathode Ontology in HIVE4MAT. The right-hand side includes the term display for "CurrentCollector" and associated ontological relationships. Figure 5 presents the HIVE4MAT browse display for Aerogel Ontology which situates a term, "SolventFreezing," within the hierarchy of terms and relationships of the Aerogel ontology.

6 Discussion

The case study presents a proof of concept using the PSPP framework for the Aerogel and Battery Cathode ontologies. The case study also demonstrates the

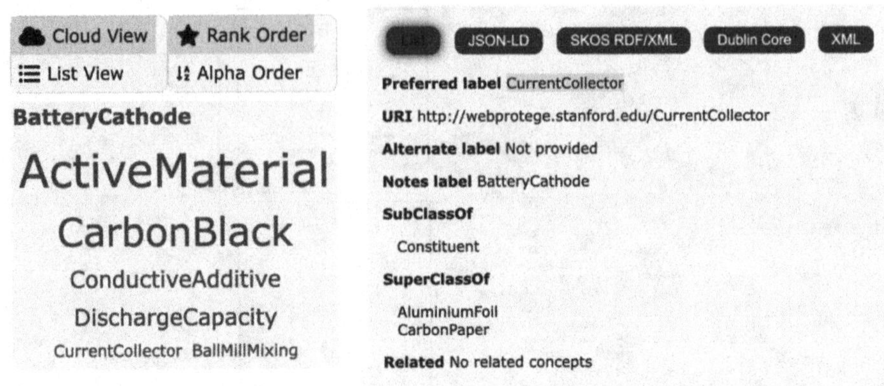

Fig. 4. HIVE4MAT: Knowledge Extraction Demonstration with Battery Cathode Ontology

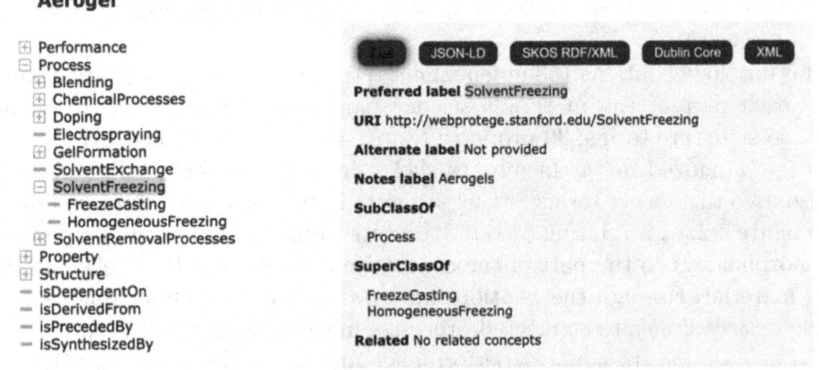

Fig. 5. HIVE4MAT: Browse display for Aerogel Ontology

HIVE4MAT application for knowledge extraction and the ontology browse feature. The narrowed scope of the two ontologies allowed them to extract specific topical aspects of documents. Moreover, the narrow scope underlying the exploratory ontology construction largely falls in line with contemporary methods which focus on area-specific topics and link to broader domain- or upper-level ontologies for general terms. However, the limited scope of the vocabularies similarly narrows the applications of the ontologies to smaller tranches of materials science and possibly the relationships between and among concepts. These limitations are partly the result of decreased time and human resources; most ontologies are the result of subject matter experts reaching consensus about terminology and relationships, sometimes over the course of several years, such as the Elemental Multiperspective Materials Ontology (EMMO), which is an ongoing initiative since 2016 (https://github.com/emmo-repo/EMMO/). It's also important to point out that the ontologies developed for exploring faceted classification have an extensive genealogy stemming primarily from [27] which describes a set of core ontologies for materials science based around the following aspects: substance, process, property, and environment. In addition, the ontologies postulated in this paper align closer with early efforts such as the Plinius ontology of ceramic materials [28] for using ontologies for automatic classification of materials science literature. The use of HIVE4MAT broadens the graph of possible ontology and vocabulary classification structures to show possible unknown connections between smaller test ontologies such as our Aerogel or Battery Cathode as well as those such as EMMO (to be tested at a future date).

The exploration of facet analysis for material science ontology construction proved a useful heuristic for the constructors and deciding how to categorize terms. The method sparked interesting discussions about how to classify terms which seemed to fall into several facets. The Performance facet proved the most complex to handle as it attempts to represent a more dynamic aspect of a material or process. Relationships between the facets proved somewhat complex to model given their more dynamic nature. The discussions regarding relationships offer insight into future HIVE4MAT improvements, including future support for OWL relationships beyond *isA* and *hasA*. Finally, this discussion and earlier efforts in the faceted ontology space demonstrate this topic warrants further exploration.

7 Conclusion

This paper reports on research investigating analytico-synthetic faceted analysis for building material science ontologies. The case study approach, along with the card sorting exercise, supported the construction of two base-level ontologies following the PSPP framework, and we demonstrated the application of both ontologies for knowledge extraction using the HIVE4MAT ontology application.

Ontology development in any area generally involves a team of multiple people and is an interactive process, with refinements over time. Reaching consensus among team members often proves problematic due to disparate theoretical or methodological stances of the participants. Additionally, terms are pruned and added as knowledge changes and new term relationships evolve. The work presented here provides a foundation for further exploration of PSPP facets for ontology development. The framework proved useful overall in guiding the term sorting and overall ontology construction; although, not all of the facets had equal representation. Future work will address issues surrounding the distribution of terms across the facets and how the relationships can be better deployed and displayed as part of an automatic indexing pipeline supporting knowledge extraction.

Acknowledgment. This work is supported by NSF-OAC 2118201, NSF-IIS 1815256.

References

1. Sciences, Medicine, others. frontiers of materials research A decadal survey. National Academies Press (2019)
2. Ghosh, S., Panigrahi, P.: Use of Ranganathan's analytico-synthetic approach in developing a domain ontology in library and information science (2015)
3. Zhao, X., Lopez, S., Saikin, S., Hu, X., Greenberg, J.: Text to insight accelerating organic materials knowledge extraction via deep learning. Proc. Assoc. Inf. Sc. Technol. **58**(1), 558–562 (2021)
4. Author, A.-B.: Contribution title. In: 9th International Proceedings on Proceedings, pp. 1–2 (2010)
5. Himanen, L., Geurts, A., Foster, A., Rinke, P.: Data-driven materials science: status, challenges, and perspectives. Adv. Sci. **6**(21), 1900808 (2019)
6. Kumaraguru, S., Rachuri, S., Lechevalier, D.: Faceted classification of manufacturing processes for sustainability performance evaluation. Int. J. Adv. Manuf. Technol. **75**, 1309–1320 (2014). https://doi.org/10.1007/s00170-014-6184-x
7. Zhao, X., Greenberg, J., Meschke, V., Toberer, E., Hu, X.: An exploratory analysis: extracting materials science knowledge from unstructured scholarly data. Electron. Libr. **39**, 469–485 (2021)
8. Simperler, A., Goldbeck, G.: OntoTrans benefits for industry (2021)
9. Materials Genome Initiative strategic plan: Executive Office of the President. National Science and Technology Council, Committee on Technology, Subcommittee on the Materials Genome Initiative (2021)
10. Agrawal, A., Choudhary, A.: Perspective: materials informatics and big data: realization of the "fourth paradigm" of science in materials science. Apl Materials **4**(5), 053208 (2016)
11. Hey, A., Tansley, S., Tolle, K., et al.: The fourth paradigm: data-intensive scientific discovery. (Vol. 1) Microsoft research Redmond, WA (2009)
12. Obo foundry. http://www.obofoundry.org/
13. Ncbo bioportal. http://bioportal.bioontology.org/
14. http://matportal.org/
15. Bliss, H., et al.: System of bibliographic classification (1935)
16. Dewey, M.: A classification and subject index, for cataloguing and arranging the books and pamphlets of a library. Brick row book shop, Incorporated (1876)
17. Falcon, A.: Aristotle on causality (2006)
18. Feng, J., et al.: Printed aerogels: chemistry, processing, and applications. Chem. Soc. Rev. **50**(6), 3842–3888 (2021)
19. Hawley, W., Li, J.: Electrode manufacturing for lithium-ion batteries-analysis of current and next generation processing. J. Energy Storage **25**, 100862 (2019)
20. Bayerlein, B., et al.: A perspective on digital knowledge representation in materials science and engineering. Adv. Eng. Mater. **24**, 2101176 (2022)
21. Guerrini, M.: Dewey Decimal Classification and Relative Index, devised by Melvil Dewey, Ed. 22. Bollettino AIB (1992–2011), 44(2), 199–201 (2004)
22. Ranganathan, S.R.: Colon classification. In: Madras Library Association, vol. 1933, p. 1v (1933)
23. Greenberg, J., Zhao, X., Adair, J., Boone, J., Hu, X.: HIVE-4-MAT: advancing the ontology infrastructure for materials science. In Research Conference on Metadata and Semantics Research, pp. 297–307 (2020)
24. La Barre, K.: The use of faceted analytico-synthetic theory as revealed in the practice of website construction and design. Indiana University (2006)

25. Federal Funds for Research and Development: Fiscal Years 2013–15
26. Fidel, R.: The case study method: a case study. Libr. Inf. Sci. Res. **6**(3), 273–288 (1984)
27. Ashino, T.: Materials ontology: an infrastructure for exchanging materials information and knowledge. Data Sci. J. **9**, 54–61 (2010)
28. Vet, P., Speel, P., Mars, N.: The Plinius ontology of ceramic materials. In: Eleventh European Conference On Artificial Intelligence (ECAI 1994) Workshop On Comparison Of Implemented Ontologies, pp. 8–12 (1994)

A Primer on Open Science-Driven Repository Platforms

Alessia Bardi, Paolo Manghi, Andrea Mannocci(✉), Enrico Ottonello, and Gina Pavone

Institute of Information Science and Technologies, National Research Council, Pisa, Italy
{alessia.bardi,paolo.manghi,andrea.mannocci,enrico.ottonello, gina.pavone}@isti.cnr.it

Abstract. Following Open Science mandates, institutions and communities increasingly demand repositories with native support for publishing scientific literature together with research data, software, and other research products. Such repositories may be thematic or general-purpose and are deeply integrated with the scholarly communication ecosystem to ensure versioning, persistent identifiers, data curation, usage stats, and so on. Identifying the most suitable off-the-shelf repository platform is often a non-trivial task as the choice depends on functional requirements, programming and technical skills, and infrastructure resources.

This work analyses four state-of-the-art Open Source repository platforms, namely Dryad, Dataverse, DSpace, and InvenioRDM, from both a functional and a software perspective. This work intends to provide an overview serving as a primer for choosing repository platform solutions in different application scenarios. Moreover, this paper highlights how these platforms reacted to some key Open Science demands, moving away from the original and old-fashioned concept of a repository serving as a static container of files and metadata.

Keywords: Repository · Repository platforms · Repository software · Dryad · Dataverse · DSpace · InvenioRDM · Open Science · FAIR · Research Data

1 Introduction

Following Open Science mandates, institutions and communities increasingly demand repositories with native support for publishing scientific literature together with research data, research software, and other scientific products. As envisioned by the COAR Next Generation Repositories Working Group [1] and other initiatives in the digital libraries' domain [2], repositories form "the foundation for a distributed, globally networked infrastructure for scholarly communication, on top of which layers of value-added services will be deployed, thereby transforming the system, making it more research-centric, open to and supportive of innovation, while also collectively managed by the scholarly community". The increasing adoption of Open Science and Open Access mandates further urges this process, with many institutions, infrastructures, and research communities setting the ambitious goal of providing an "Open Science-driven" repository for their

E. Garoufallou and A. Vlachidis (Eds.): MTSR 2022, CCIS 1789, pp. 222–234, 2023.
https://doi.org/10.1007/978-3-031-39141-5_19

community of users. Such repositories may focus on research datasets or become the holders of all kinds of research products, including publications, datasets, and software, and aim at supporting out-of-the-box features such as FAIRness, collaboration, access control, and data curation. Their instances should be able, to some extent, to adapt to community-specific requirements and ensure the degree of interoperability required to be part of scientific workflows (e.g., to fetch-analyse or generate-deposit products) and interact with third-party scholarly communication services, such as monitoring platforms (e.g., MakeDataCount), altmetrics, and PID registries (e.g., ORCID.org, ROR.org, Crossref.org, DataCite.org).

However, researchers' and policymakers' requirements often make choosing the suitable repository platform a non-trivial choice for organisations, as institutional and community demands may vary in terms of kinds of research products, metadata descriptions, and functionalities (e.g., data curation, collaboration). Typically, repository platforms may satisfy these requirements to some extent and then require adaptation to fit additional specific needs better [3, 4]. Some solutions are designed to maximise flexibility, e.g., enabling customisation of metadata descriptions and facilitating the modular integration of new functionalities, while others exhibit less flexibility in favour of a tailored, one-stop-shop product. Besides, local requirements, e.g., available skills and resources, may pose constraints and limitations to software choices and following customisation.

In the attempt to facilitate such a choice, this work analyses four state-of-the-art repository solutions, namely Dryad, Dataverse, DSpace, and InvenioRDM, from both a functional and a software perspective, addressing the selection needs of organisations willing to become repository providers (for an end-users-oriented survey, please refer to [13]). The investigation is intended as a "primer" for choosing repository platform solutions in different institutional and community application scenarios. Most importantly, the paper highlights how such known platforms reacted to Open Science demands [5], moving away from the old-fashioned concept of a repository as static containers of files and metadata.

2 Repository Platforms

The four Open Source repository platforms at the centre of this analysis were picked among others due to the following reasons. Firstly, because of their wide adoption by institutions and communities worldwide, a trend often followed by company uptake. Secondly, their design and functionalities evolved to address the demands of Open Science scientific workflows [6]. Finally, the authors have familiarity with the four platforms and could rely on feedback from adopters; this explains why software platforms such as ePrints[1] and Fedora/Islandora[2] have not been included. This paper aims to analyse the platforms to identify their specific reactions to such demands, moving away from old-fashioned repositories conceived as static containers of files and metadata.

For this analysis, we referred to the work of the COAR Next Generation Repositories Working Group[3], for which a "next generation repository" should:

[1] www.eprints.org.

[2] https://duraspace.org/fedora.

[3] http://ngr.coar-repositories.org.

- **Support a diversity of research products** and thus manage, preserve, version, curate, and provide access to a broad range of *research products*, including published articles, pre-prints, datasets, working papers, images, and software;
- **Support a diversity of research communities and institutions**, and thus be to some extent customisable to satisfy community/local requisites [7] in terms of products, metadata, and functionalities;
- **Be part of an ecosystem of repositories and scholarly communication services** by interlinking via persistent identifiers their resources to relevant entities, such as author identifiers (e.g., ORCID IDs), project identifiers (e.g., FundRef), organisation identifiers (e.g., ROR.org, ISNI), other resources (e.g., data, software, literature via DOIs, arXiv IDs);
- **Be machine-friendly and interoperable** by adopting standards [8] that enable a broader range of scientific services, such as scientific workflows, discovery, access, annotation, sharing, quality assessment, content transfer, analytics, provenance tracking, recommendations, and so on.

The following two sections point out the desiderata that can be derived from such a vision in terms of functionalities and software features. *Functional desiderata* capture the ability to address Open Science resources and workflows and the proactivity expected by modern repositories in the context of scholarly communication. *Software desiderata* instead frame a software project's maturity, flexibility, and modularity, pointing out the degree of customisation the platform can meet.

For the sake of space, we deliberately left out *operational desiderata*, which may depend on the individual installation policies and resources. The most prominent ones identified during the investigation are *long-term preservation* [12] (i.e., terms of commitment towards long-term storage of resources) and *free deposition strategies* (e.g., quota allowed per research product/user, which demands fees to be exceeded).

2.1 Functional Desiderata

After reviewing the selected repository platforms, the following relevant functional desiderata emerged (see Table 1 for a summary):

Research Product Types. Following the approach of resource modelling recommended by the European Open Science Cloud[4] (EOSC), research products can be classified into four meta-entities: *publications,* e.g., articles, theses, reports, presentations, *research data,* e.g., tables, images, archives, *research software,* e.g., code, *and others,* i.e., all products whose nature does not match one of the other entities. The metadata descriptions of such products may differ profoundly, ranging from bibliographic descriptions to provenance and community-specific tags. Moreover, metadata may include semantic links to other products to capture the entire research lifecycle for the sake of discoverability and reproducibility.

Data (Metadata & File) Curation Functionalities. The ability to engage scientists in data curation and validation processes is becoming prominent, as trust in research

[4] https://eosc-portal.eu.

data and software is undermined by a general lack of policies, practices, and tools for certification of quality [9–11]. Data curation functionalities (where "data" means everything that is metadata or files) regard two main aspects. The first is to offer collaboration and validation tools to a group of community curators to ensure the data matches the expectation of the community at hand in terms of quality, formats, and so on. The second is to ensure that end-users, i.e., the scientists, can establish virtuous interactions with the curators to make sure data is published with the expected quality.

Integration with Entity Registries. To adhere to Open Science demands and mandates, repositories use persistent identifiers (PIDs) for scholarly communication entities. On the one hand, they provide PIDs for the products uploaded by the users. On the other hand, they enable referencing to scholarly communication entities via PIDs by connecting to the related registries; examples are ORCID for authors and ROR.org for organisations. Integration with PID systems, i.e., registries, can be supported at two different degrees. The basic integration level is one where the repository metadata includes fields dedicated to interlinking with external entity registries, managing entity identities (via PIDs, cool URIs, handles, and so on), such as DataCite, Crossref, ORCID, ROR, Commons. The approach is subject to human mistakes in the format of PID, which may be "misspelt", or in the referencing, i.e., an existing, yet wrong, PID may be used. A deeper and optimal level of integration is one where the insertion of a PID is supported by direct interaction with the related registry APIs, ensuring both format and PIDs are correct.

Access Control. Access control provides users with different levels of restriction options and granularity regarding research product access. Users may deposit research products and fine-tune access rights (e.g., restricted, open access, embargo) for metadata and/or files and to all users or groups of users (e.g., a research community).

Table 1. Functional desiderata.

Desiderata	*Description*
Research product types	Type of research products that users can deposit (e.g., publications, datasets, and/or software)
Data curation functionalities	Validation, rejection, and curation of metadata and/or files of research products
Integration with entity registries	Integration with PID systems to support and contribute to a non-ambiguous scholarly record
Access control	Users can rule access to metadata and files they deposit

2.2 Software Desiderata

Open Source repository platforms may be deployed by organisations with ICT capacity, whose requirements may derive from local technological constraints, peculiar functionalities, or, conversely, due to lack of ICT resources, by organisations that require ready-to-go solutions. After reviewing the candidate repository platforms, the following relevant software desiderata were identified (see Table 2 for a summary):

Software Project Sustainability. The maturity, traction, and licencing of a software package are key requisites for an organisation to invest in a software product.

Functionality Customisation. Repository platforms are typically modular, meaning new functionalities can be easily plugged into the system, but to different degrees, with a trade-off between out-of-the-box and customisation.

Metadata Model Customisation. The repository can be more or less flexible concerning the metadata model, e.g., the attributes, the vocabularies, and references to external PID systems or registries in the scholarly communication infrastructure. Customisation of the metadata format measures the potential reuse across different communities and use cases. Still, as a counterpart, it impacts the out-of-the-box capabilities of a repository, which cannot be grounded on data model assumptions.

Custom Storage Infrastructure. Repository software must be configured and deployed to address potentially different scenarios, such as the cross-institutional, cross-country deployment setting, or community one. Different storage requirements may apply in terms of scalability, preservation, and availability of resources. Examples are Amazon S3 standard storage or simpler local storage solutions, typically provided by institutional data centres. The extent of customisation of the storage infrastructure is therefore relevant to making the right choice.

Integration with Scientific Services. Programmatic access enables third-party services to perform product depositions, metadata searches, exports, and downloads via APIs. The former allows for the implementation of scientific workflows capable of depositing into the repository on behalf and prior authorisation of the scientists. The latter ensures the repository can expose its content to other scholarly communication services, such as aggregators, ultimately enabling the realisation of customs UIs using the repository as a back-end (e.g., Zenodo.org).

Persistent Identifiers. Repositories must rely on persistent identifiers, typically issued at the record level, to uniquely refer to the pair metadata-files. Software platforms may be more or less flexible concerning the identifiers scheme to be used (e.g., handles, DOIs) by offering support to one or more specific PID Agencies (e.g., DataCite, EZID) and by enabling the integration with any PID agency.

Usage Statistics. Repository platforms are increasingly integrating with usage statistics infrastructures (e.g., IRUS-UK[5], MakeDataCount[6], OpenAIRE[7]) compliant with COUNTER Code of Practice[8]. Repositories, on their occurrence, centrally share views and downloads events of research products via the related PIDs, enabling aggregation of PID usage statistics across different repositories.

[5] https://www.jisc.ac.uk/irus.

[6] https://makedatacount.org.

[7] https://www.openaire.eu.

[8] https://support.datacite.org/docs/counter-code-of-practice.

Table 2. Software desiderata.

Desiderata	*Description*
Software project sustainability	Software project trust is measured by the engagement of developer communities
Functionality customisation	Modular design enabling the extension/customisation of functionalities
Metadata model customisation	Degree of research product types, metadata customisation, vocabularies, etc.
Custom storage infrastructure	Degree of customisation of storage infrastructure
Integration with scientific services	Ability to integrate with scientific services to publish products and/or provide access to products programmatically via APIs
Persistent Identifiers	Platform embeds functionality to mint PIDs for deposited research products
Usage statistics	Availability of modules to integrate with usage statistics infrastructures

3 Repository Platforms Analysis

3.1 Dryad

"Dryad is an open source, community-driven project that takes a unique approach to data publication and digital preservation. Dryad focuses on search, presentation, and discovery and delegates the responsibility for the data preservation function to the underlying repository with which it is integrated"[9]. Research data are uploaded with metadata representing the dataset landing pages. Still, they are formatted as an online version of a data paper that can be downloaded as an individual PDF file or as part of the complete dataset download package, incorporating all data files for all versions.

Functionality. Dryad supports research data deposition only, although software deposition is possible via integration with Zenodo.org. For the official Dryad installation, curation is performed at the instance level, ensuring metadata is complete and both metadata and files comply with the platform recommendations[10]. Automatic validation tools are available for tables. The platform is integrated with ORCID, as it requires an ORCID to log in and supports ROR.org and FundRef IDs to refer to organisations and projects/grants funding, respectively. Metadata and files in Dryad are by the policy under CC0 waiver, so no fine-grained access control is supported.

Software. Dryad's software is released on GitHub[11] under the MIT Licence and maintained by a community of 21 contributors (as of August 2022). The software is modular

[9] https://datadryad.org.

[10] https://datadryad.org/stash/faq#files.

[11] https://github.com/CDL-Dryad/dryad-app.

and based on the Stash software, organised into three modules: *Store* (deposition of metadata and files), *Harvest* (export of metadata to third-party services and a full-text Solr index), and *Share* (GeoBlacklight UIs). Its design enables the extension/customisation of metadata export protocols and the personalisation of metadata schemas. The Store module supports the DataCite format, but can be extended to include extra fields. It supports SWORD 2.0 to temporarily enable programmatic access from journal publishing platforms during article submission to deposit research data for peer review. The Harvest module supports OAI-PMH and ResourceSync and can be customised to support different export protocols.

3.2 Dataverse

"The Dataverse Project is an open-source web application to share, preserve, cite, explore, and analyse research data. It facilitates making data available to others and allows you to replicate others' work more easily"[12]. A Dataverse repository hosts multiple archives called Dataverses, each intended as a collection of datasets consisting of descriptive metadata and data files. As a design choice, Dataverse collections may also be nested. Dataverse has been conceived to automate archivists' and librarians' tasks and to provide services for and to distribute credit to the data creator.

Functionality. The Dataverse platform focuses on publishing research data and related supplementary material (e.g., code and docs supporting the data). Dataverses are created by super-users that can assign to users nine different roles, establishing rights for publishing (draft, public, to be validated), accessing (read-only, update, delete, access to the record, access to files), and curating (right to update and publish). By creating a Dataverse and assigning the proper user roles, Dataverse installations can support custom data curation workflows. The platforms support user interfaces for manually reviewing tabular data.

Dataverse repositories are integrated with ORCID and ROR.org via APIs to ensure up-to-date references to authors and institutions. Access to research data can be controlled at the level of the Dataverse collection, at the fine-grain level of metadata records and individual files. The restricted mode, i.e., download upon request to the owner, is optional.

Software. Dataverse's software is released on GitHub[13] under Apache Licence v2.0, maintained by a community of 144 contributors (as of August 2022). Designed as a ready-to-deploy package, which can be customised in some core capabilities such as the underlying storage system and the data model. Further customisation is possible via plugins, for example, to fetch vocabulary or entity data from external information systems such as registries.

---

[12] https://dataverse.org.

[13] https://github.com/iqss/dataverse.

Dataverse software supports three levels of metadata: metadata for citation (standard DDI), metadata for journal info (linking to external publications), and disciplinary metadata (provided with six default templates). The three come with a Dataverse schema, which can be further customised to include application-specific fields. It is possible to create new templates for the discipline metadata, to be shared with the community. The platform is also compliant with schema.org to support Google's data search crawlers.

Dataverse user interfaces can be extended via different tools developed by third parties[14], e.g., for data previewing and data curation. Dataverse is designed to be integrated with other systems via SWORD protocol for data deposition. Examples are OJS[15] and publisher platforms, supporting publication and data submission workflows, but also integration with existing scientific workflows, e.g., Lab notebooks in RSpace[16]. The platform also supports OAI-PMH protocol standards for metadata harvesting. Its storage layer supports object and file system preservation via S3 or Swift and is configurable at the collection and dataset level.

3.3 DSpace

"DSpace is a web application allowing researchers and scholars to publish documents and data. [...] It is free and easy to install "out of the box" and completely customisable to fit the needs of any organisation"[17]. DSpace repositories are organised into *communities* (e.g., departments or institutions) that include *collections*, which are groups of *items*, i.e., data files and metadata descriptions.

Functionality. DSpace items can be set to model any kind of research product. For data curation, DSpace enables the definition of "Tasks" as plugins via a customisable curation framework[18]. Tasks enable checks and controls over metadata and files upon their deposition. The platform is integrated with ORCID for login and reference to authors. DSpace allows controlling read/write permissions at the instance level or per community, collection, item, and file. Administrative permissions per community or per collection can be delegated to users.

Software. DSpace is a mature project released on GitHub[19] under a BSD 3-Clause Licence and is maintained by a community of 166 contributors (as of August 2022), including companies doing business out of its custom extensions and installations.

The component pair UI/index (metadata store) is decoupled from the file storage. Files in DSpace can be stored either using a local filesystem (default) or a cloud-based solution, such as Amazon S3.

---

14 https://guides.dataverse.org/en/latest/admin/external-tools.html#inventory-of-external-tools.

15 https://openjournalsystems.com.

16 https://www.researchspace.com.

17 https://dspace.lyrasis.org.

18 https://wiki.lyrasis.org/display/DSDOC6x/Curation+System#CurationSystem-Tasks.

19 https://github.com/dspace/dspace.

DSpace comes with a suite of tools (e.g., batch ingest, batch export, batch metadata editing) and plugins for translating content into DSpace objects. By default, DSpace uses a Qualified Dublin Core (QDC) based metadata schema. Institutions can extend that base schema or add custom QDC-like schemas. DSpace can import or export metadata from other major metadata schemas, such as MARC or MODS. DSpace supports the Handle system by default but also integrates with DOI DataCite and EZID identifiers (ARK, DOIs). The platform offers custom APIs for the deposition of files and metadata and OAI-PMH for harvesting metadata.

3.4 InvenioRDM

"InvenioRDM is a turn-key research data management repository platform based on Invenio Framework and Zenodo"[20]. Its instantiations offer deposition and access functionalities to a set of communities (i.e., collections) of research products, which in turn can be of any kind.

Functionality. InvenioRDM includes communities to model collections of research products. Deposited research products can be managed by multiple users (i.e., shared submissions). Communities support curation/management workflows, where different users with different roles (i.e., curator, manager, reader, owner) are involved to ensure smooth, tracked deposition workflows. The deposition of metadata and files is structured as a "pull request" in software repositories, in which the submitter and curators (who can modify the metadata) are engaged in a discussion via an internal ticketing system. Workflows can be customised to include specific steps of approval at the community level: assigning roles of submitters subject to validation and curators notified of new submissions and in charge of the evaluation. Multiple curators can interact with the same submitter for the same submission. Also, requests for extra storage may be sent and handled by community managers.

Users can specify ORCID and ROR IDs for creators and related affiliations via the UIs. The selection of PIDs is enabled by ORCID and ROR APIs for validation; otherwise, textual values can be typed in by users.

Access can be controlled at the level of the community (restrictions to community and non-community members) or at the level of the record, at the granularity of the metadata and the files. The embargo function ensures that a record is made public at the expiring date without users performing any manual action.

Software. InvenioRDM is a rather young project, active since June 2019, released on GitHub[21] under an MIT licence, and maintained by a community of 32 contributors (as of August 2022). The software is developed as a specialisation of the Invenio Framework v3.0, glueing known Open Source tools such as Elasticsearch, OpenSearch, and Postgres, and based on JSON and DataCite format. The software comes with a ready-to-deploy configuration to deliver a repository instance similar to Zenodo.org.

[20] https://inveniosoftware.org/products/rdm.

[21] https://github.com/inveniosoftware/invenio-app-rdm.

The metadata data model implements the DataCite guidelines, but can be customised with extra fields to match community requirements. Interaction with vocabularies can be implemented by integrating external APIs into vocabulary systems or PID registries (e.g., ORCID, ROR).

Due to the flexibility of the Invenio Framework, the software is highly modular: storage can be of any kind (e.g., S3, file systems), and using different indexing and database systems is possible via programming efforts. The software supports OAI-PMH protocols and offers custom APIs for file and metadata deposition. The index offers indexing synchronisation functions, which mirror a new deposition in the InvenioRDM full-text index on external indexes.

4 Discussion

The four platforms offer ready-to-go mature or experience-based software solutions and can also benefit from companies for the configuration and installation of custom solutions. However, differences exist; Table 3 and Table 4 offer a high-level comparison of the functionality and software desiderata we have identified for the four platforms. In summary:

Research products and metadata model customisation beyond research data are addressed by InvenioRDM and DSpace. Instead, Dryad and Dataverse specialise in research data, offering dedicated and rich data management functionalities. All platforms generally offer a degree of customisability of the metadata descriptions. Dataverse, however, is designed to be extremely flexible in this respect, supporting a set of community profiles and a fully flexible metadata framework.

Data Curation is addressed in InvenioRDM by enabling interaction via UIs between data curators and end-users, integrating validation modules, and going beyond the validate-reject workflows. Similarly, but disregarding end users-curators interactions, DSpace offers a "Task" framework that developers can use to implement research data validation checks. Dryad and Dataverse offer manual validation and rejection procedures at the repository instance and the Dataverse level, respectively.

Customisability of functionalities and storage is equally addressed. InvenioRDM and DSpace seem to be the solutions that meet, at best, a scenario where the customisability of functionalities is a strong requirement. InvenioRDM's software has been designed after the lesson learned in realising Zenodo.org using the Invenio Framework and meeting the requirements of Zenodo users and Invenio repository providers. Similarly, DSpace 7 has built on the core platform, and experience reached up to the release of DSpace 6 to bring a "single, modern user interface and REST API and integrates current technological standards and best practices". As such, the platforms offer a good balance of out-of-the-box functionalities and flexibility of customisation and software extension. Dataverse also shows a high degree of customisability and a rich set of functional modules shared by the community. The four platforms allow the integration of different kinds of storage layers by modularly decoupling them from the user interfaces.

Integration with entity registries is well covered by Dryad, followed by InvenioRDM, and then DSpace and Dataverse, which only support ORCID. All platforms enable the integration of entity registries of reference via custom plugins.

Persistent identifier minting is thoroughly addressed by DSpace, supporting the open Handle system and optionally DOIs from DataCite and EZID identifiers. Dataverse follows with DOIs and Handles, while Dryad and InvenioRDM support DOI from DataCite. Plugins to other PID services are, in general, allowed.

Integration with scientific services is supported by all platforms for both deposition and harvesting. SWORD is provided by Dryad, DSpace, and Dataverse, while InvenioRDM implements a proprietary API. All platforms implement OAI-PMH, while DSpace offers ResourceSynch out-of-the-box.

Usage statistics are supported by all platforms via Make Data Count and COUNTER Code of Practice implementation.

Table 3. Functional desiderata comparison.

Desiderata	*Dryad*	*Dataverse*	*DSpace*	*InvenioRDM*
Research product types	Research Data	Research Data	All research products	All research products
Data curation functionalities	Manual rejection or approval at repository instance level	Manual rejection or approval at “dataverse” level	Customisable data “curation tasks” as validation controls over metadata and files upon deposition	Customisable data curation workflows, the interaction between submitters and collection managers/curators
Integration with entity registries	ORCID, ROR, FundRef	ORCID	ORCID	ORCID, ROR.org
Access control	Records and files are under CC0 waiver by default	At the granularity of “dataverses”, record, and files in the record	At the granularity of “sites”, “community”, collection, item and files per item	At the granularity of “communities”, record, metadata and files of the record; embargo functionality

Table 4. Software desiderata comparison.

Desiderata	*Dryad*	*Dataverse*	*DSpace*	*InvenioRDM*
Software project sustainability	21 contributors, MIT Licence	144 contributors, Apache Licence v2.0	166 contributors, BSD-3-Clause Licence	32 contributors, MIT Licence
Functionality customisation	Customisation of metadata export protocols	Integration with entity registries, customisation metadata exports and UI functions	Extendible software, a large pool of extensions is available	Extendible software. Building on the Invenio integration framework
Metadata model customisation	Metadata is DataCite but can be customised	Sets community metadata schemas which can be customised; supports schema.org	Metadata is Qualified Dublin Core and can be customised	Metadata is DataCite but can be customised
Custom storage infrastructure	Decouples storage from indexing and web portals	Decouples web portals from storage	Decouples web portals from storage	Decouples web portals from storage and indexing
Integration with scientific services	SWORD and OAI-PMH	SWORD and OAI-PMH	Deposition API, OAI-PMH, ResourceSynch	Deposition API, OAI-PMH, index synchronisation
Persistent identifiers	DOIs via DataCite	DOIs and Handles	Handle system, optional DOI from DataCite and EZID identifiers (ARK, DOIs)	DOIs via DataCite
Usage statistics	Make Data Count	Make Data Count	COUNTER Code of Practice	COUNTER Code of Practice

References

1. Rodrigues, E., et al.: Next generation repositories: behaviours and technical recommendations of the COAR next generation repositories working group. Zenodo (2017). https://doi.org/10.5281/zenodo.1215014
2. Dempsey, L.: Library collections in the life of the user: two directions. LIBER Q.: J. Assoc. Eur. Res. Librar. **26**(4), 338–359 (2016). https://doi.org/10.18352/lq.10170
3. Austin, C., Brown, S., Fong, N., Humphrey, C., Leahey, A., Webster, P.: Research data repositories: review of current features, gap analysis, and recommendations for minimum requirements (Version 0) (2015). https://doi.org/10.29173/iq904
4. Assante, M., Candela, L., Castelli, D., Tani, A.: Are scientific data repositories coping with research data publishing? Data Sci. J. **15**, 6 (2016). https://doi.org/10.5334/dsj-2016-006

5. Jean-Claude, B., et al.: Open science, open data, and open scholarship: European policies to make science fit for the twenty-first century. Front. Big Data (2) (2019). https://doi.org/10.3389/fdata.2019.00043
6. RepOSGate: Open Science Gateways for Institutional Repositories, Michele Artini, Leonardo Candela, Paolo Manghi & Silvia Giannini
7. Jwa, A.S., Poldrack, R.A.: The spectrum of data sharing policies in neuroimaging data repositories. Hum. Brain Mapp. **43**(8), 2707–2721 (2022). https://doi.org/10.1002/hbm.25803
8. Forero, D.A., Curioso, W.H., Patrinos, G.P.: The importance of adherence to international standards for depositing open data in public repositories. BMC Res. Notes **14**, 405 (2021). https://doi.org/10.1186/s13104-021-05817-z
9. Liaw, S.-T., et al.: Quality assessment of real-world data repositories across the data life cycle: a literature review. J. Am. Med. Inform. Assoc. **28**(7), 1591–1599 (2021). https://doi.org/10.1093/jamia/ocaa340
10. Löffler, F., Wesp, V., König-Ries, B., Klan, F.: Dataset search in biodiversity research: do metadata in data repositories reflect scholarly information needs? PLoS ONE **16**(3), e0246099 (2021). https://doi.org/10.1371/journal.pone.0246099
11. Bashir, S., Gul, S., Bashir, S., Nisa, N.T., Ganaie, S.A.: Evolution of institutional repositories: managing institutional research output to remove the gap of academic elitism. J. Librarianship Inf. Sci. **54**(3), 518–531 (2022). https://doi.org/10.1177/09610006211009592
12. Barrueco, J.M., Termens, M.: Digital preservation in institutional repositories: a systematic literature review. Digit. Libr. Perspect. **38**(2), 161–174 (2022). https://doi.org/10.1108/DLP-02-2021-0011
13. Boch, M., et al.: A systematic review of data management platforms. In: Rocha, A., Adeli, H., Dzemyda, G., Moreira, F. (eds.) WorldCIST 2022. LNNS, vol. 469, pp. 15–24. Springer, Cham (2022). https://doi.org/10.1007/978-3-031-04819-7_2

Integrated Access to Multidisciplinary Data Through Semantically Interoperable Services in a Metadata-Driven Platform for Solid Earth Science

Daniele Bailo[1,2(✉)], Rossana Paciello[1,2], Valerio Vinciarelli[2], Andrea Orfino[1], Keith G. Jeffery[3], Jan Michalek[4], and Claudio Goffi[2]

[1] Istituto Nazionale di Geofisica e Vulcanologia, Rome, Italy
daniele.bailo@ingv.it
[2] European Plate Observing System, EPOS ERIC, Rome, Italy
[3] Keith Jeffery Consultants, Faringdon, UK
[4] Universitetet i Bergen (UiB), 5020 Bergen, Norway

Abstract. The ability to use data produced by different sources (social networks, governments, weather sensors etc.) is widely recognized as a key to capitalize the value of data. In the scientific field, such usage may incredibly boost the innovation and foster new discoveries. However, one of the main hurdles is currently represented by the difficulties in achieving the required interoperability to provide integrated access to multi-disciplinary data. The current work presents a metadata-driven approach that uses in a combined way metadata, semantics, and services as key components for providing integrated access to heterogeneous data sources. The integration occurs within a central data integration system, which is driven by a rich metadata catalogue and that can present the data provided by the different data sources in a harmonised way to the end user, by means of RESTful APIs. A real application demonstrating metadata-driven semantic and service interoperability for achieving homogeneous access to multi-disciplinary heterogeneous data sources is illustrated in the case of EPOS, a Research Infrastructure for Solid Earth Science. The advantages in terms of ease of maintenance, of flexibility in plugging different standard without perturbating communities' long-lasting technical practices, and of ability to track provenance are discussed. Future work for providing open-source implementation of a system built following the proposed approach is also envisaged.

Keywords: Metadata · Interoperability · Semantics · Multidisciplinary Data · Heterogeneous datasets · Services integration · EPOS

1 Motivation

In the era of the "data deluge" [1] where data is considered as a strategic assets and its economic value is more and more recognized [2, 3], the access to datasets is hindered by the proliferation of different (meta)data formats, (meta)data standards and protocols to

E. Garoufallou and A. Vlachidis (Eds.): MTSR 2022, CCIS 1789, pp. 235–247, 2023.
https://doi.org/10.1007/978-3-031-39141-5_20

access data. Getting advantage of the data value and potential is therefore a real challenge as also recognized by the EU, which foster the re-use of Open Government Data in Member States [4] and – at the same time – tried to lay the foundation of a common framework for data exploitation by releasing the European interoperability framework [5] and the FAIR principles [6]. The challenge of data access is particularly relevant for the Research Infrastructures (RIs), huge facilities – often at European level – that put together institutions, researchers, data centres from different European countries with the goal of improving open science and open innovation by providing an harmonized access to data and services from specific science domains [7]. In particular, this is true for the RI in the ESFRI (European Strategic Forum on Research Infrastructures) Roadmap [8]. Leveraging on the work carried out in an ESFRI RIs, namely the European Plate Observing System EPOS [9] – the current work describes an approach to face the challenge of providing homogeneous access to heterogeneous federated resources in a true interoperable way. It uses in a synergic way techniques, concepts, and standards concerning *metadata*, *semantics*, and *services*, and is currently used to integrate in a single portal datasets from more than 220 data sources that adopt different standards in terms of data formats (more than 30) and of (meta)data standards (more than 20) [10].

2 Background

2.1 Integration Through FAIR Principles

With the relatively recent advent of the European Open Science Cloud, established by the European Commission since 2016 [11], making research data publicly available for its exploitation by public or private institutions is a mandatory commitment for all RIs in the European galaxy.

The FAIR principles have been adopted as criteria to harmonize access to data. Officially established in 2016 [6], they provide a set of non-prescriptive principles to guarantee and enhance Findability, Accessibility, Interoperability and Reusability of datasets. Since their release, several scientific contributions have been provided on this topic, spanning from metrics to assess the "FAIRness" of datasets [12–14], to guidelines and best practices for FAIR implementation [15, 16], but also providing comments and thoughts about the cost of FAIR data [17], or even by extending the FAIR concept to other digital assets (e.g., Software, Services) [18–20].

However, beyond metrics and academic contributions, in the real world the adoption of FAIR principles is still a huge challenge, especially for the Research Infrastructures, and the final proof of their "FAIRness" is demonstrated by the true availability of datasets that can be consumed either by humans or machines. Such data integration challenge is already tackled by different initiatives, as shown in the next section.

2.2 Portals for Data Integration

Without claiming to be exhaustive, a few examples of platforms for data integration are presented (either multi-disciplinary or domain specific) with the goal of having a grasp on the real status of implementation of FAIR by huge Research Infrastructures.

The first example is from AuScope, Australia's provider of research infrastructure to the national geoscience community working on fundamental geoscience questions and grand challenges[1]. AuScope displays geospatial data obtained from several organizations around Australia, providing a way to find geospatial data and display that data on the map. It relies on the adoption of Open Geospatial Consortium (OGC)[2] standards by all integrated data providers. Such an approach is very effective but hard to replicate in contexts where data sources cannot adopt a common standard.

The Global Earth Observation System of Systems (GEOSS)[3], one of the key products of the Group on Earth Observation (GEO)[4], is based on the brokering approach for achieving multi-disciplinary interoperability. The advantage of this approach [21] is that it does not impose any standard to the data providers. However, its application presumes the implementation of a set of brokers to convert all formats to all formats, with a consequent combinatory explosion ($O(n)^2$) and potential issues in software maintenance.

Finally, other initiatives like Maracoos[5] in the Ocean domain, consist of a set of portals[6] for accessing several assets. Data is integrated by using different approaches, according to the specific use cases, spanning from techniques requiring the adoption common standards, to using proprietary tools, and to approaches based on metadata ingestion.

All the examples above use of course metadata for storing information about data sources, but – according to the available documentation – they do not consider metadata for driving semantic interoperability of data and services.

2.3 Use of Web Services for Integration

Although web services are recognized since at least a decade as a key element for interoperability (see for instance [22]), they do not seem to find explicit mentions in the FAIR principles, as also discussed elsewhere [23]. Therefore, many scientists and data practitioners seek for (and find) out of the box solutions for data integration available on the market like GeoNetwork[7], Esri, CKAN[8], which actually do what they promise. In the FAIR galaxy, a more flexible approach that explicitly relies on metadata, semantics, and web services to homogenise the access to heterogenous data sources from one single system is not yet present in literature. The current work aims at filling this gap by describing a metadata-driven approach using semantic and web services to integrate data from a single integration system, as described in the reminder of the paper.

---

1 https://www.auscope.org.au/ (accessed on 24th of August 2022).

2 https://www.ogc.org/ (accessed on 24th of August 2022).

3 https://www.geoportal.org/?m:activeLayerTileId=osm&f:dataSource=dab (accessed on 24th of August 2022).

4 https://www.earthobservations.org/index.php (accessed on 24th of August 2022).

5 https://maracoos.org/ (accessed on 24th of August 2022).

6 https://maracoos.org/index.php/tools/ (accessed on 24th of August 2022).

7 https://geonetwork-opensource.org/ (accessed on 25th of August 2022).

8 https://ckan.org/ (accessed on 25th of August 2022).

3 A Metadata-Driven Approach for Interoperability

Beyond the usual search and discovery of digital resources, metadata can be used to drive an entire system, as already introduced in [24]. The method described in this paper elaborates on such an approach where a rich metadata catalogue is used by a data management system to manage semantics attached to metadata and to manage the interoperability with data sources through web-services as depicted in Fig. 1.

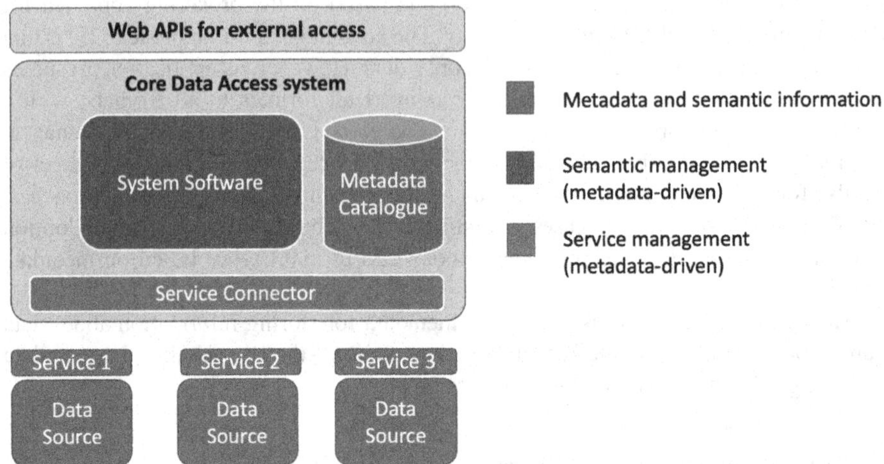

Fig. 1. A simplified diagram of the proposed approach. Web APIs for external access are used for autonomic access to the central data integration system by external clients or software agents. The metadata catalogue includes entities for describing domains specific core concepts (e.g., dataset, web service, person, organizations). It also supports sematic descriptions of classes, properties, and relationships to enable mappings from/to metadata schema of different data sources. Semantics are also needed to support different requests and responses syntaxes (e.g., RESTful URLs) from/to heterogeneous data sources. This action is technically performed by the service connector module, that interacts with the data sources by means of (web) services.

In the proposed metadata-driven interoperability approach, semantic plays a key role at a *data discovery level*, i.e., at query level. Indeed, the queries received by the main data integration system are – by means of the semantic information associated to the data source - mapped to queries expressed in the appropriate semantic used by the web services protocol of a specific data source, as shown in Fig. 2a.

At *data visualization level* (response) the semantic information in the metadata catalogue is used to drive appropriate conversions from the data sources payloads to canonical payloads used internally by the system as output of the Web APIs for external access (Fig. 2b). Payload responses harmonization enables client applications to visualize heterogeneous data sources in a unique format in a User Interface as exemplified in Sect. 4.3

The implementation of both levels guarantees integrated access, but also – through mapping and conversions – an integrated and homogeneous visualization of assets that are potentially very different in terms of data formats, metadata standards, data access standards.

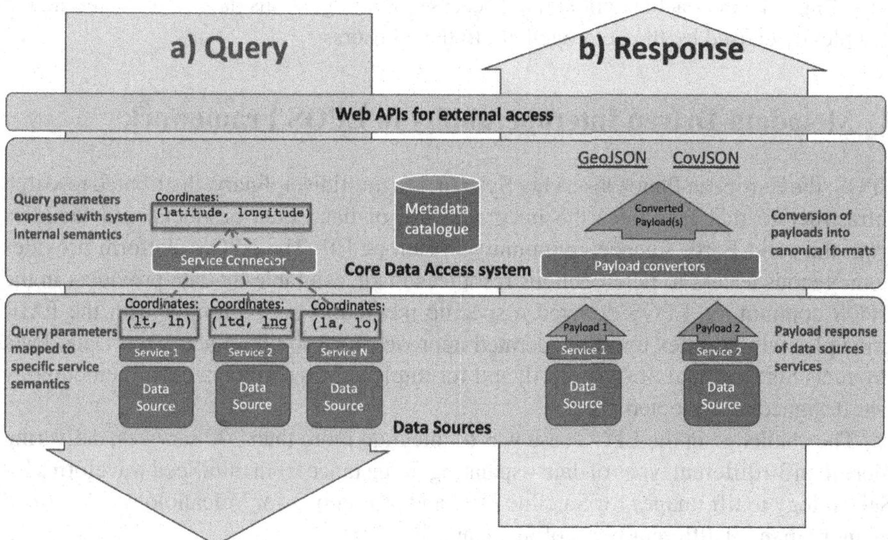

Fig. 2. An example case of semantic interoperability driven by metadata, using web services. In the **query** case **(2a)**, a query performed by a user requires the usage of spatial coordinates. This occurs for instance when a bounding box is selected. The coordinates are provided by the user (ar machine) in the query done at through the *Web APIs for external access.* They are then expressed with an internal semantics, where latitude and longitude concepts are defined by the terms (respectively) *latitude* and *longitude.* Then, on the basis of the semantic information contained in the metadata catalogue, the system can map the term *latitude* to the corresponding terms in the different data sources. In the example, three mappings are done for three different services on the data sources: 1) in service 1: *latitude* → *lt, 2) in* service 2: *latitude* → *ltd, 3)* in service 3*: latitude* → *la.* Same occurs for the longitude term. In the **response** case **(2b)**, the data sources respond to the query with different payload formats. On the basis of the information from the metadata catalogue, appropriate convertors can be selected, and the responses can be converted into one or more canonical formats (e.g., GeoJSON[9], CovJSON[10]). In both cases, the behaviour of the system is driven by the semantic information embedded in the metadata.

Another key role is played by web services, which in this framework are considered as a dynamic element that changes according to the data source to be integrated. In other words, the integration system interoperates with data sources implementing different web services. Details about services, including semantic information, are stored in the metadata catalogue, and the selection of the service protocol to be used for accessing a specific data source (e.g., query case in Fig. 2) is therefore managed by the system software based on the information stored in the metadata catalogue.

[9] https://geojson.io/#map=2/20.0/0.0 (accessed on 25th of August 2022).
[10] https://covjson.org/ (accessed on 25th of August 2022).

This allows covering a broad spectrum of services that includes both global well-established and community specific standards for web services [26].

Access to datasets by means of services is therefore completely metadata-driven, thus providing a mean to achieve integrated access to heterogeneous data sources, hiding the complexity caused by the heterogeneity to the ed users.

4 Metadata-Driven Interoperability in EPOS Framework

EPOS, the European Plate Observing System, is a multidisciplinary, distributed research infrastructure that facilitates the integrated use of data, data products, and facilities from the solid Earth science community in Europe [9]. The EPOS platform provides homogenous access to heterogenous resources made available by data providers in the EPOS community. EPOS adopted a specific methodology to comply with the FAIR principles which relies upon a federated approach for providing access to Data, Data Products Services and Software [10] and for implementing which a clear methodology was designed and adopted [16].

The challenge in the EPOS case was to integrate more than 200 services, delivering more than 30 different types of data – spanning for instance from miniSeed waveforms for Seismology to tiff images for Satellite Data and pdf reports for Volcanology - described by more than 20 different types of metadata.

For tackling such a challenge EPOS relies on the core elements of metadata-driven approach: a) *metadata*, for driving the entire system Interoperability, b) *semantic*, to improve interoperability of the different (meta)data description and c) *web-services*, to enable accessing and integrating heterogeneous data sources i.e., to data providers adopting different standards, not natively interoperable (e.g., OGC WMS and FDSN services). In the following subsections we describe how these are implemented in EPOS.

4.1 Metadata

To properly represent the EPOS ecosystem, a first conceptual model was done and discussed in the community. This is known as the EPOS data model, and it ensures that all necessary metadata is captured and that it is sufficient to inform the central data integration system. The model includes a wide range of concepts including those for capturing the needed information from the Data, examples of which are user, equipment, organization, dataset, web service, person, publication, and others.

The metadata catalogue that demonstrated to best address the requirements of the EPOS data model was CERIF, the Common European Research Information Format (CERIF[11]) [27–29]. CERIF is a conceptual model with formal syntax and declared semantics for representing research information and is structured natively into entity types, also providing the support for multilinguality and semantics. The intensive use of relationships with attributes enables the model to record timestamps (for provenance) and links to the so-called semantic layer, a set of entities and relationships that can represent any classification scheme or even mapping between schemes.

[11] https://eurocris.org/services/main-features-cerif (accessed on 25th of August 2022).

To better adapt the CERIF basic scheme, which is standard and somehow generalist, and tailor it to the specific EPOS needs, a refactoring operation was undertaken. It focused mainly on the creation of new base entities or on updating the existing ones, while maintaining the strengths of references to the timestamps and to the semantic layer.

The semantic layer was also reviewed to better describe EPOS Data Model domain: the potential of CERIF's classification classes was expanded to better represent ontologies, classes, and attributes, and support for mapping between different ontologies was added.

Although metadata can be created, updated, deleted (CRUD operations) by means of APIs and through dedicated User interface interacting with the metadata catalogue (i.e., the so called Backoffice Client), it became apparent that providing a way to bulk ingest such information described with a well-known and widespread metadata standard, including serializations that metadata practitioners are used to, would represent an added value. For this reason, an extension of DCAT-AP was created (EPOS-DCAT-AP[12]) which can be used for describing the data sources details. The EPOS-DCAT-AP extension is also discussed in another work in the current volume [30]. A dedicated software component then maps the information, expressed as RDF Turtle-serialised content, into the internal metadata catalogue relational representation and then persist it to a relational database. This step is called "ingestion process" An excerpt of an EPOS-DCAT-AP RDF/turtle description is shown in Fig. 3.

```
hydra:mapping[ a hydra:IriTemplateMapping;
        hydra:variable "starttime"^^xsd:string;
        hydra:property "schema:startDate";
        schema:valuePattern "YYYY-MM-DDThh:mm:ss";
        rdfs:range "xsd:dateTime";
        rdfs:label "Start time"@en;
        schema:minValue "1000-01-01T00:00:00";
        schema:maxValue "1899-12-31T23:59:59";
        schema:defaultValue "1000-01-01T00:00:00";
        hydra:required "true"^^xsd:boolean;
];
hydra:mapping[ a hydra:IriTemplateMapping;
        hydra:variable "endtime"^^xsd:string;
        hydra:property "schema:endDate";
        schema:valuePattern "YYYY-MM-DDThh:mm:ss";
        rdfs:range "xsd:dateTime";
        rdfs:label "End time"@en;
        schema:minValue "1000-01-01T00:00:00";
        schema:maxValue "1899-12-31T23:59:59";
        schema:defaultValue "1899-12-31T23:59:59";
        hydra:required "true"^^xsd:boolean;
];
hydra:mapping[ a hydra:IriTemplateMapping;
        hydra:variable "minlongitude"^^xsd:string;
        hydra:property "epos:westernmostLongitude";
        rdfs:range "xsd:float";
        rdfs:label "Minimum longitude"@en;
        schema:minValue "-34.0000";
        schema:maxValue "34.0000";
        schema:defaultValue "-34.0000";
        hydra:required "false"^^xsd:boolean;
];
hydra:mapping[ a hydra:IriTemplateMapping;
        hydra:variable "maxlongitude"^^xsd:string;
        hydra:property "epos:easternmostLongitude";
        rdfs:range "xsd:float";
        rdfs:label "Maximum longitude"@en;
        schema:minValue "-34.0000";
        schema:maxValue "34.0000";
        schema:defaultValue "34.0000";
        hydra:required "false"^^xsd:boolean;
];
```

Fig. 3. Excerpt of an EPOS-DCAT-AP RDF/turtle description where semantic information about services query parameters are detailed by using the *schema.org* vocabulary (e.g., "schema:startDate", "schema:endDate"). These are used by the system to drive the connection to the services of the data sources and to semantically harmonize queries meaning across heterogeneous services, as also detailed described in Fig. 2. Such information can be expressed by metadata editors in rdf/turtle, and are then mapped and ingested into the main CERIF based metadata catalogue.

[12] https://epos-eu.github.io/EPOS-DCAT-AP/#data-service (accessed on 25th of August 2022).

The ability of providing descriptive information regarding each service - such as the geographical area and the time range of data coverage, service provider and maintainers details, the thematic area, licenses, and other generic information, used for discovery and contextualization – in one single EPOS-DCAT-AP turtle file, rather than interfacing with a complex relational database, was highly appreciated by the metadata practitioners of the data sources, thus contributing to the engagement dimension and also ensuring that the metadata shall be frequently and easily updated.

4.2 Usage of Semantics for Services Interoperability

The metadata and semantic descriptions ingested into the metadata catalogue are used by the system to enable harmonized programmatic access to different data services. By means of the semantics associated to services information, the system can connect with the data sources using appropriate protocols and querying syntax. Semantics indeed describe HTTP methods (e.g., POST or GET), specify the endpoint to be accessed and provide detailed descriptions of each query parameter, as shown in Fig. 3 and Fig. 4.

In the example in Fig. 4, in the EPOS APIs (called Web APIs for external access in Fig. 1 and Fig. 2) the *latitude* parameter in the URL in the upper light-gray box is mapped to the corresponding data source parameter term (*bbox*, in the bottom dark gray box). This is done through the semantic descriptions of services and parameters (table views in the mid-gray block in the center) in two steps. Firstly, with a semantic mapping (with *Service Parameter* table view) that associates terms from the EPOS APIs to terms used in the data source web service request template. Secondly, by rearranging mapped terms according to the syntax of the data source web services request (*template* attribute in the *Service* table view). In the example, parameters defining geographical coordinates in the EPOS APIs (*lat*, *lon)* are mapped and rearranged to compose the request of an OGC WMS web service, which uses the *bbox* parameter with all coordinates rather than a parameter for each of the coordinates as in the EPOS APIs.

In other words, the semantics allow to match parameters that, in different services, have the same meaning but are named differently: these can be identified through specific properties that describe their meaning (the two table views in Fig. 4).

Metadata and semantics are also used, in the EPOS case, for the conversion of data sources payload responses from their original format to two canonical formats, the first based on GeoJSON[13] (for maps, and geo-refenced objects visualisation) and the second on CovJSON[14] (for time-series visualisation). Such formats were selected because of their versatility and widespread use, that enable developers to easily set-up Graphic User Interface clients for consuming and visualizing the response of the EPOS APIs. Examples of this visualization in the EPOS case can be found in the work from Bailo et al. [10].

The two levels of interoperability (harmonized data discovery and harmonized visualization) are therefore entirely driven by metadata and semantics. In addition, these can be controlled by external agents by means of a set of RESTful APIs for external access (EPOS APIs in Fig. 4) and may enable any third-party stakeholder to build custom

---

[13] https://geojson.io/#map=2/20.0/0.0 (accessed on 25th of August 2022).

[14] https://covjson.org/ (accessed on 25th of August 2022).

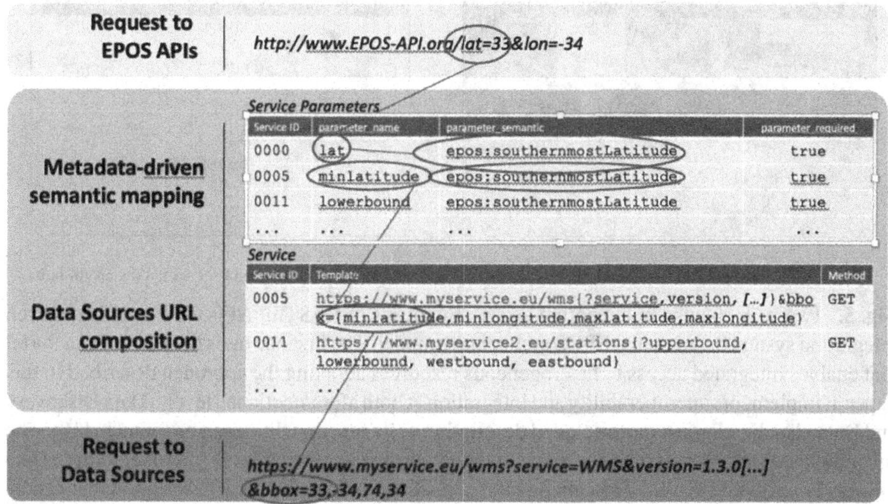

Fig. 4. Services interoperation driven by metadata and semantics. Web services are described in detail in the EPOS metadata catalogue (mid gray block in the center) here simplified with two table views: the first one (*Service Parameters* view), associates services (with *Service ID* attribute) to semantic descriptions of each parameter of the service. The *parameter_semantic* attribute defines the semantic meaning of each of the *parameter_name* attribute. It enables a semantic crosswalk that links parameters (*parameter_name*) of different services with the same meaning. In this example, the crosswalk is done for mapping the EPOS APIs (top, light gray block) request to the Data Source request (bottom, dark gray box). The second table contains, for each service (*Service ID*) the *template* describing the syntax to be used for web service request. Such template is used, together with the *http* method (*method* attribute in *Services* table) to compose the URL of the service request.

user interfaces or software agents to access programmatically to the integrated data, as exemplified in the next section.

4.3 Metadata and Semantic Driven Data Integration Portals for End Users

The implementation, in the EPOS system, of a set of RESTful APIs for external access to the integrated assets, allows the exposure of the metadata stored within the catalogue. The APIs also implement a set of additional methods allowing the development of clients that integrate the heterogeneous resources described above.

Just for the sake of example, we show in Fig. 5 two clients that take advantage of this set of RESTful APIs: the EPOS Data Portal[15] and the ENVRI-Hub[16]. The former is already available in its test version, while the latter is being developed in the context of the ENVRI-FAIR initiative [31].

---

15 https://www.ics-c.epos-eu.org/ (accessed on 26th of August 2022).

16 https://envri.eu/envri-hub/ (accessed on 26th of August 2022).

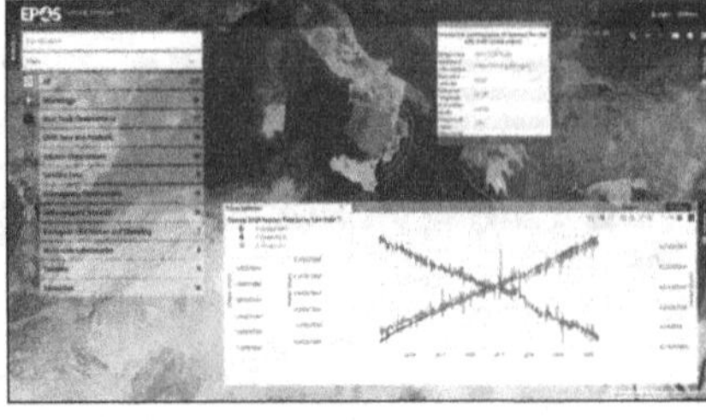

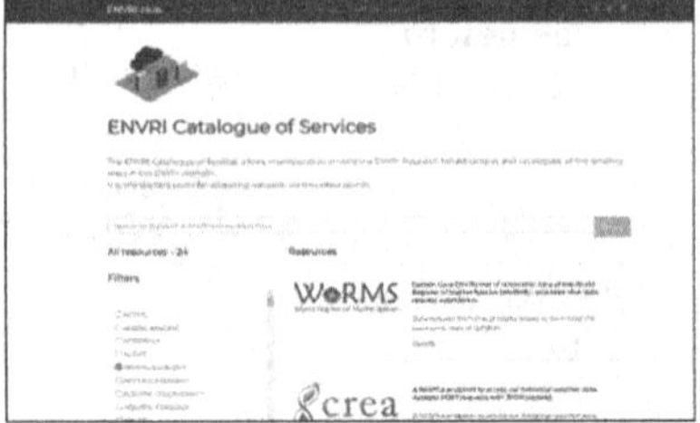

a) EPOS Data portal b) The ENVRI catalogue of services in the ENVIR-hub

Fig. 5. Two web clients implementing access, by means of RESTful APIs, to a metadata-driven integration system based on the EPOS architecture model. The first one (a) is the EPOS Data Portal that enables integrated access to heterogeneous resources adopting the approach described in this paper. It implements interoperability and integration at both aforementioned levels (Data Discovery and Data visualization). A more detailed description of its functionalities can be found in [10]. The second one, although based on the same approach, implements first-level interoperability (Data Discovery only) and is used as a catalogue of services, providing detailed description that can be used by external agents to directly access the data sources. This is one of the components of the ENVRI-hub, an open access hub for interdisciplinary environmental research data in the European Research Area interoperable with the EOSC, and was done in the framework of ENVRI-FAIR Task Force 1.

5 Discussion and Conclusions

In the proposed approach the combined usage of three elements, sometimes considered in an isolated way for interoperability, namely *metadata*, *semantic*s and *web-ervices*, is presented as a powerful combination that fully exploits the possibilities of the existing technologies for tackling the challenge of data integration. Metadata alone is indeed not enough for data interoperation, as it can – in the best case – provide a rich description of a data resource that needs then to be integrated by an external agent (human or machine). The usage of metadata to drive interoperability enables integration at system level and presents some interesting advantages.

An integration system following the proposed approach can be considered as a sort of metadata-driven middleware that stands between the data sources and the data consumers, providing advantages for both: data sources are indeed not forced to adopt one common standard but only to implement basic recommendations based on the FAIR principles and providing metadata descriptions of the data sources; data consumers can, by means of the APIs on top of the integration system (e.g., "Web APIs for external access" mentioned in Fig. 2), consume heterogeneous resources as if they were homogeneous in terms of communication protocols, metadata description and data formats.

In the Research Infrastructures domain, as exemplified by the EPOS case, the low perturbation level of Data Source providers is quite a remarkable advantage considering that changing the data sources data provision systems is often an impossible task for organizational, financial and – last but not least – historical reasons. Community practitioners are reluctant to change well established IT practices and approaches they are used to.

In addition, by means of the metadata-driven approach, the system can be updated and maintained easily as its configuration entirely depends on the metadata and not on hardcoded information or procedures that would require to update and re-deploy the entire system software. Plugging in new data sources is therefore relatively easy, given that they respect some basic FAIR constraints.

The presented approach also enables to manage provenance and lineage in a relatively easy way, which is useful for tracking changes in the metadata and for keeping metadata records also when metadata is not available, in compliance with the FAIR principles. Also, creating provenance relationship between datasets is the key to reproducibility of scientific results and a requirement that paves the way to scientific workflows management, that was the subject of previous exploration also in the EPOS context [32].

Furthermore, such an approach allows the integration of non-standard services. In most of the examples reported in the Background section, the assumption is that there is a standard technology to rely upon, which means forcing the adoption of services (e.g., OGC) that may not fully respond to the requirements of the data providers and for which an ad hoc protocol or implementation is required.

Finally, and perhaps most importantly, by means of the semantic descriptions embedded in the metadata catalogue, the system can adapt itself to consume different APIs at the data source level and to manage the different payload responses, thus hiding to the end user (human or machine) the underlying complexity.

Further work is still required to take full advantage of the semantic descriptions, for instance for providing metadata-and-semantic-driven data conversions and visualization (or processing) functionalities.

The presented approach, in conclusion, allows true integration as it enables the access to multidisciplinary data resources from one single portal which is not simply a catalogue of resources, but a one stop shop where user can discover, download, and previsualize resources from a single User Interface.

Of course, the cost of setting up such a system, as demonstrated in the case of EPOS, can be considerable in terms of sustainability, governance, and technical efforts. In order to ease other RIs facing the same challenge of accessing heterogeneous multidisciplinary data, EPOS is making further efforts in producing an open-source version of the system that will be openly available and surely described in a future work.

Acknowledgements. The authors would like to acknowledge the following projects and initiatives for financing part of the activities: EPOS-IP, European Commission H2020 program, Grant agreement ID 676564; ENVRI-FAIR, European Commission H2020 program, Grant agreement ID 824068; EPOS-ERIC (https://www.epos-eu.org/epos-eric) for sustainability and management.

References

1. Hey, T., Tansley, S., Tolle, K.: The fourth paradigm. Data-Intensive Scientific Discovery Microsoft Research (2009). http://scholar.google.com/scholar?hl=en&btnG=Search&q=intitle:the+fourth+paradigm#3. Accessed 07 Apr 2014

2. Humby, C., Bugowski, A.: Data is the new oil. In: Proceedings of the ANA Sr. Mark. Summit. Evanston, IL, USA (2006). https://see.techdata.com/CatAdminHtmlContentEditor/uploads/Country/SL/UMAGpresentations/Dataisthenewoil_Andrzej_Bugowski_TechData.pdf. Accessed 24 Aug 2022
3. T.E.G. Limited. The world's most valuable resource is no longer oil, but data. Economist 1–4 (2017)
4. European Commission. Directive 2003/98/EC of the European Parliament and of the Council of 17 November 2003 on the re-use of public sector information. Off. J. Eur. Communities, vol. L 269, no. November 2003, pp. 1–15 (2003). http://eur-lex.europa.eu/legal-content/EN/TXT/PDF/?uri=CELEX:32003L0098&from=en. Accessed 08 Feb 2018
5. European Commission. European Interoperability Framework - Implementation Strategy, p. 40 (2017). https://ec.europa.eu/isa2/publications/communication-european-commission-european-interoperability-framework-implementation_en
6. Wilkinson, M.D., et al.: The FAIR guiding principles for scientific data management and stewardship. Sci. Data **3**, 160018 (2016). https://doi.org/10.1038/sdata.2016.18
7. European Commission. European Charter for Access to Research Infrastructures: Principles and Guidelines for Access and Related Services (2015). https://ec.europa.eu/research/infrastructures/pdf/2016_charterforaccessto-ris.pdf
8. ESFRI-European Strategy Forum on research Infrastructures. Roadmap & Strategy Report on Research Infrastructures (2018). https://doi.org/10.2777/23127
9. Cocco, M., et al.: The EPOS research infrastructure: a federated approach to integrate solid Earth science data and services. Ann. Geophys. **65**(2), 1–15 (2022). https://doi.org/10.4401/ag-8756
10. Bailo, D., et al.: Data integration and FAIR data management in Solid Earth Science. Ann. Geophys. **65**(2), DM210 (2022). https://doi.org/10.4401/ag-8742
11. EC - European Commission, "European Cloud Initiative - Building a competitive data and knowledge economy in Europe (2016)
12. Wilkinson, M.D., Sansone, S.A., Schultes, E., Doorn, P., Da Silva Santos, L.O.B., Dumontier, M.: Comment: a design framework and exemplar metrics for FAIRness. Sci. Data **5**, 7–10 (2018). https://doi.org/10.1038/sdata.2018.118
13. RDA FAIR Data Maturity Model Working Group. FAIR Data Maturity Model: specification and guidelines. Res. Data Alliance, no. June, pp. 2019–2020 (2020). https://doi.org/10.15497/rda00050
14. Sustkova, H.P., et al.: Fair convergence matrix: optimizing the reuse of existing fair-related resources. Data Intell. **2**(1–2), 158–170 (2020). https://doi.org/10.1162/dint_a_00038
15. Collins, S., et al.: Turning FAIR data into reality: interim report from the European Commission Expert Group on FAIR data. Interim Rep. from Eur. Comm. Expert Gr. FAIR data, no. June (2018). https://doi.org/10.5281/zenodo.1285272
16. Marti, M., Haslinger, F., Peppoloni, S., Di Capua, G., Glaves, H., Dallo, I.: Addressing the challenges of making data, products, and services accessible: an EPOS perspective. Ann. Geophys. **65**(2), DM212 (2022). https://doi.org/10.4401/ag-8746
17. European Commission. Cost of not having FAIR research data (2018)
18. Lamprecht, A.-L., et al.: Towards FAIR principles for research software. Data Sci. **3**(1), 37–59 (2019). https://doi.org/10.3233/ds-190026
19. Hasselbring, W., Carr, L., Hettrick, S., Packer, H., Tiropanis, T.: From FAIR research data toward FAIR and open research software. IT - Inf. Technol. **62**(1), 39–47 (2020). https://doi.org/10.1515/itit-2019-0040
20. Koers, H., Bangert, D., Hermans, E., van Horik, R., de Jong, M., Mokrane, M.: Recommendations for services in a FAIR data ecosystem. Patterns **1**(5), 100058 (2020). https://doi.org/10.1016/j.patter.2020.100058

21. Nativi, S., Craglia, M., Pearlman, J.: The brokering approach for multidisciplinary interoperability: a position paper. Int. J. Spat. Data Infrastruct. **7**, 1–15 (2012). https://doi.org/10.2902/1725-0463.2012.07.art1
22. Nagarajan, M., Verma, K., Sheth, A.P., Miller, J., Lathem, J.: Semantic interoperability of Web services - challenges and experiences. In: IEEE International Conference on Web Services, ICWS 2006, pp. 373–380 (2006). https://doi.org/10.1109/ICWS.2006.116
23. Bailo, D., Paciello, R., Sbarra, M., Rabissoni, R., Vinciarelli, V., Cocco, M.: Perspectives on the implementation of FAIR principles in solid earth research infrastructures. Front. Earth Sci. **8** (2020). https://doi.org/10.3389/feart.2020.00003
24. Nativi, S., Jeffery, K.G., Koskela, R.: RDA: brokering with metadata. ERCIM News, no. 100, pp. 26–27 (2015)
25. Minadakis, N., et al.: X3ML framework: an effective suite for supporting data mappings. In: CEUR Workshop Proceedings, vol. 1656, pp. 1–12 (2015). https://pdfs.semanticscholar.org/0eb9/eaa92f051b629691426f70200dec98262b27.pdf. Accessed 06 April 2018
26. Trani, L., Atkinson, M., Bailo, D., Paciello, R., Filgueira, R.: Establishing core concepts for information-powered collaborations. Futur. Gener. Comput. Syst. **89**, 421–436 (2018). https://doi.org/10.1016/j.future.2018.07.005
27. Jeffery, K., Houssos, N., Jörg, B., Asserson, A.: Research information management: the CERIF approach. Int. J. Metadata Semant. Ontol. **9**(1) (2014). http://inderscience.metapress.com/index/VL5422N2U7112669.pdf. Accessed 16 Apr (2014)
28. Bailo, D., Jeffery, K.G.: EPOS: a novel use of CERIF for data-intensive science. Procedia Comput. Sci. **33**, 3–10 (2014). https://doi.org/10.1016/j.procs.2014.06.002
29. Jeffery, K.G., Bailo, D.: EPOS: using metadata in geoscience. In: Closs, S., Studer, R., Garoufallou, E., Sicilia, M.-A. (eds.) MTSR 2014. CCIS, vol. 478, pp. 170–184. Springer, Cham (2014). https://doi.org/10.1007/978-3-319-13674-5_17. Accessed 19 Nov 2014
30. Paciello, R., Trani, L., Bailo, D., Sbarra, M.: EPOS-DCAT-AP 2.0 – State of play on the Application Profile for metadata exchange in the EPOS RI (2022)
31. Petzold, A., et al.: ENVRI-fair-interoperable environmental fair data and services for society, innovation and research. In: Proceedings - IEEE 15th International Conference on eScience, eScience 2019, no. 824068, pp. 277–280 (2019). https://doi.org/10.1109/eScience.2019.00038
32. Spinuso, A., Veldhuizen, M., Bailo, D., Vinciarelli, V., Langeland, T.: SWIRRL. Managing provenance-aware and reproducible workspaces. Data Intell. **4**(2), 243–258 (2022). https://doi.org/10.1162/dint_a_00129

EPOS-DCAT-AP 2.0 – State of Play on the Application Profile for Metadata Exchange in the EPOS RI

Rossana Paciello[1,2](✉), Luca Trani[3], Daniele Bailo[1,2], and Manuela Sbarra[1]

[1] Istituto Nazionale di Geofisica e Vulcanologia (INGV), Rome, Italy
rossana.paciello@ingv.it

[2] European Plate Observing System, EPOS ERIC, Rome, Italy

[3] Department of R&D Seismology and Acoustics, Royal Netherlands Meteorological Institute (KNMI), Utrechtseweg 297, 3731 GA De Bilt, The Netherlands

Abstract. Metadata application profiles are widely employed to enable the exchange of metadata between different systems or platforms.

DCAT-AP is an application profile of the W3C Data Catalog Vocabulary (DCAT) used as a cross-domain and cross-platform metadata interchange format for data catalogues operated in the European Union. Several extensions of DCAT-AP have been created to address domain-specific requirements. Due to the inherent evolving nature of Research Infrastructures, maintenance and regular updates of such profiles are necessary activities in order to assess the matching with existing and new community requirements.

In this paper, we give an overview of the new release of the EPOS-DCAT Application Profile based on DCAT-AP v2.1.0. EPOS-DCAT-AP has been developed, maintained, and adopted by the European Plate Observing System (EPOS) Research Infrastructure to capture the heterogeneity of the assets provided by diverse scientific communities and to increase findability, accessibility, and usability of multidisciplinary data.

EPOS-DCAT-AP is the result of a collaborative ongoing effort of various expertise. This application profile addresses several requirements, and it is suitable for a wide range of applications therefore it can be adopted by other Research Infrastructures.

Keywords: EPOS-DCAT-AP · DCAT-AP · Metadata · RDF · Application Profile · Interoperability · Research Infrastructure

1 Introduction

Metadata application profiles represent a key element in interoperability of metadata instances. They can be seen as "*schemas which consist of data elements drawn from one or more namespaces, combined by implementors, and optimized for a particular application*" [1]. Application profiles define what types of entities are described and how they are related to each other, what controlled vocabularies are used, the cardinality

E. Garoufallou and A. Vlachidis (Eds.): MTSR 2022, CCIS 1789, pp. 248–258, 2023.
https://doi.org/10.1007/978-3-031-39141-5_21

of fields/properties, data types, and guiding notes for a consistent use of fields/properties. Application profiles usually mix only those relevant properties from different standard metadata schemas, combined for the purpose of describing resources in a particular context [2].

The DCAT Application Profile (DCAT-AP[1]) is a specification based on the Data Catalogue Vocabulary (DCAT[2]) and developed by W3C to meet the specific application needs of data portals in Europe. DCAT-AP aims at facilitating data findability, cross-reference, as well as improving the interoperability between data catalogues in the public sector data.

Applications within a national domain, or applications in a particular domain, that have different requirements and want to create extensions of the basic profile of DCAT-AP need to follow the guidelines published by the ISA[3] Programme.

Currently, two extensions of the DCAT-AP have been defined at the European level. GeoDCAT-AP [3] for describing geospatial datasets, dataset series and services, and StatDCAT-AP [4] for describing statistical datasets.

Several states of the European Union (Belgium, Germany, Ireland, Italy, the Netherlands, Norway, Sweden, Switzerland, and Spain) have extended DCAT-AP to meet their own needs [5].

Other DCAT-AP extensions like DCAT-AP-JRC[4] for multi-disciplinary research data, CiteDCAT-AP[5] for citation, EPOS-DCAT-AP[6] for European Plate Observing System[7], and TransportDCAT-AP[8] for the transport domain, are emerging in order to address domain specific requirements. As the context evolve new requirements might arise thus triggering revisions and adjustments of such application profiles. To ensure long-term adoption and facilitate uptake it is important to define clear policies, identify responsibilities and embed the maintenance process within established organizations. For instance, DCAT-AP has a well-defined change and release management policy[9].

In this work we present an update on EPOS-DCAT-AP, an extension of DCAT-AP, developed, adopted, and maintained by the European Plate Observing System Research Infrastructure in order to describe the diversity and heterogeneity of assets in solid-Earth domain.

1 https://joinup.ec.europa.eu/collection/semantic-interoperability-community-semic/solution/dcat-application-profile-data-portals-europe.

2 https://www.w3.org/TR/vocab-dcat-2.

3 https://ec.europa.eu/isa2/home_en/.

4 https://ec-jrc.github.io/dcat-ap-jrc/.

5 https://ec-jrc.github.io/datacite-to-dcat-ap/.

6 https://epos-eu.github.io/EPOS-DCAT-AP/.

7 https://www.epos-eu.org.

8 https://github.com/dachafra/TransportDCAT-AP.

9 https://joinup.ec.europa.eu/collection/semantic-interoperability-community-semic/solution/dcat-application-profile-data-portals-europe/document/change-and-release-management-policy-dcat-ap.

2 Motivation

The European Plate Observing System (EPOS) is a Research Infrastructure "*committed to enable excellent science through the integration, accessibility, use and re-use of solid Earth science data, research products and services; and to promote physical access to research facilities*" [6].

The architecture of the EPOS Delivery Framework consists of four high level components (Fig. 1).

1. Thematic Core Services (TCS), that provide access to data and metadata generated, quality-controlled and standardized by scientific communities.
2. Integrated Core Services Central HUB (ICS-C), that is responsible for collecting, aggregating, and integrating data and metadata from different sources.
3. Integrated Core Services Distributed (ICS-D), which provide access to distributed resources (e.g., HPC, HTC, data storage and data transport).
4. Users, who have access to multidisciplinary Solid Earth data, products, software, and services provided by the TCS, integrated within the ICS-C, and made available and accessible through the EPOS Data Portal[10].

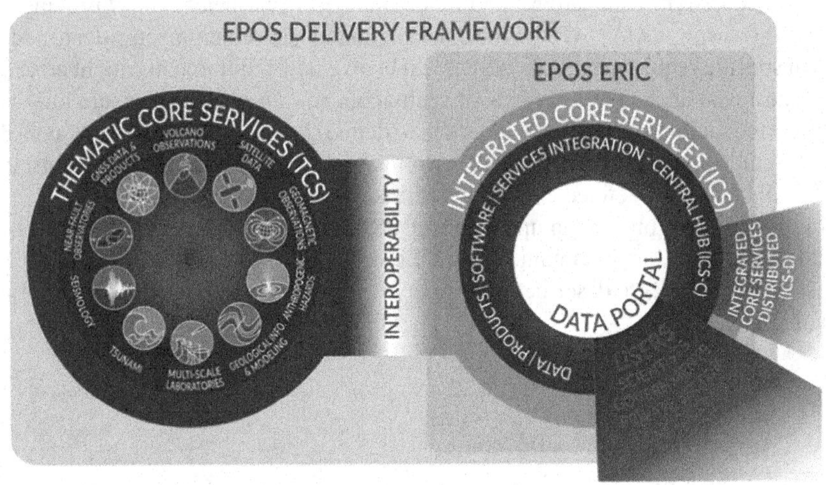

Fig. 1. The architecture of the EPOS Delivery Framework.

[10] https://www.ics-c.epos-eu.org/.

Providing users with a single homogeneous access to heterogeneous resources means implementing an interoperability layer which enables the interaction between TCS and ICS. TCS have various degrees of maturity and are highly heterogeneous. Indeed, some of them adopt ad-hoc service architectures based on years of experience in that specific domain. Others are based on common and standard services, architectures, and protocols. Some rely on a federated architecture, others on a single sited data center. The data and products accessed via the TCS are heterogeneous in terms of encoding formats, vocabularies, and metadata standards [7]. To implement the interaction between the TCS and ICS and to achieve the integration of heterogeneous data sources, a common knowledge representation has been defined in the form of a metadata application profile.

Due to the scale and complexity of EPOS, the definition of such a profile followed an incremental approach and a well-defined methodology [8, 9].

In the next section details about the EPOS-DCAT-AP profile are presented.

3 The EPOS-DCAT-AP Extension

3.1 Overview

EPOSDCAT-AP is a metadata profile designed to achieve a powerful, flexible, and extensible representation of the EPOS Canonical Core which contains Core Concepts (CC) agreed among the EPOS communities [8]. The current Canonical Core includes concepts such as: *Dataset, Equipment, Facility, Organization, Person, Publication, Service, Software, Webservice.*

The profile has been developed and evolved by applying incremental refinements. To facilitate the implementation of the profile and its adoption by the EPOS communities the process has been organized in stages by focusing on chosen aspects. At each stage features of the model were refined depending on their priority thus leading to new releases. Figure 2 shows a timeline with a description of the main milestones.

The first release, based on DCAT-AP v1.1[11], was in February 2018. The model contained all the relevant entities and correspondent relationships. However, major attention and focus was given to the entities and attributes considered of high priority for the EPOS context at that time, i.e., *Dataset, Organization, Person, Webservice.* The profile included controlled vocabularies and an initial set of metadata descriptions to be exchanged between TCS and ICS. In February 2019 a second release was made to improve the quality of the metadata descriptions and refine property constraints i.e., recommended or mandatory properties. In June 2019, the profile was updated to better support entities such as *Software, Service, Equipment* and *Facility*. The September 2020 release addressed bugs detected in the previous releases and requests coming from the communities.

---

[11] https://joinup.ec.europa.eu/collection/semantic-interoperability-community-semic/solution/dcat-application-profile-data-portals-europe/release/11.

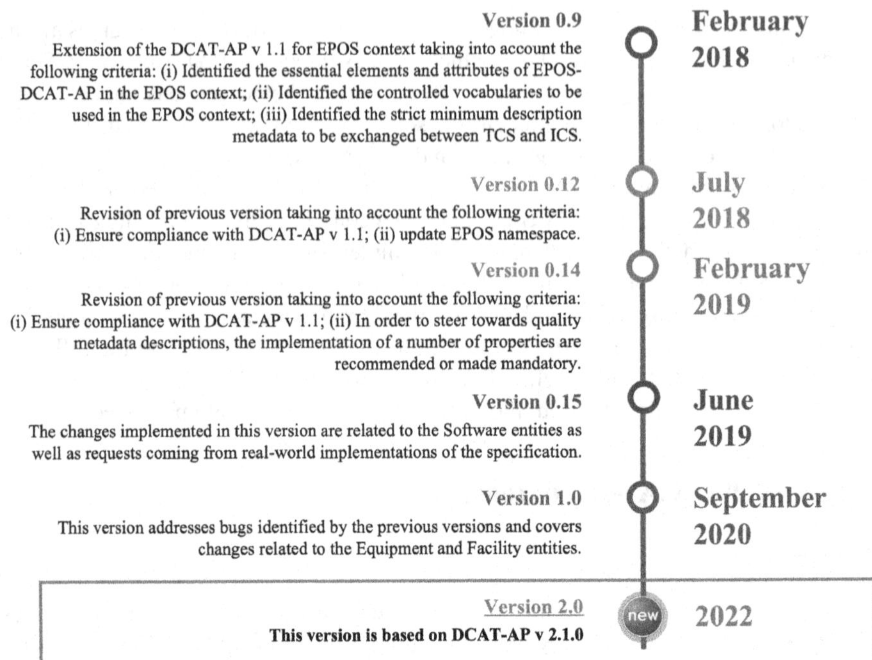

Fig. 2. EPOS-DCAT-AP development timeline.

In the meantime, DCAT-AP v2.1.0[12] became available, that version solved most of the previous shortcomings which were addressed by EPOS-DCAT-AP. Therefore, a new version of EPOSDCAT-AP has been made based on DCAT-AP v2.1.0. In the next section we give an overview of the changes and features introduced. The new version of EPOS-DCAT-AP (v 2.0) is currently under testing to assess the metadata consistency with previous versions.

All EPOS-DCAT-AP releases followed the DCAT-AP recommendations[13] for the extensions. Those recommendations are listed below:

- *Extensions must not widen but may only narrow down the usage notes as specified in DCAT-AP, so that all information provided according to the extension remains valid for DCAT-AP.*
- *Extensions may add classes that are not specified for DCAT-AP; however, an extension should not add classes that are similar to DCAT-AP classes.*
- *Extensions may add properties that are not specified for DCAT-AP; however, an extension should not add properties that are similar to DCAT-AP properties.*
- *Extensions may change the cardinalities for properties defined for DCAT-AP respecting the following rules:*

[12] https://joinup.ec.europa.eu/collection/semantic-interoperability-community-semic/solution/dcat-application-profile-data-portals-europe/release/210.

[13] https://joinup.ec.europa.eu/release/dcat-ap-how-extend-dcat-ap.

- *Mandatory properties in DCAT-AP must be mandatory in the extension.*
- *Recommended properties in DCAT-AP may be declared optional or mandatory in the extension.*
- *Optional properties in DCAT-AP may be declared recommended or mandatory in the extension.*
- *Recommended and optional properties in DCAT-AP may be removed from the extension.*

• *Extensions may add mandatory controlled vocabularies.*

3.2 EPOS-DCAT-AP Main Features and Use Cases

The EPOS-DCAT-AP extension consists of the DCAT-AP core classes and additional classes, relationships, and roles from other standard vocabularies introduced to represent the EPOS Canonical Core.

The core classes of DCAT-AP are: i) *Catalog*, that represents a dataset catalog; ii) *Dataset*, that represents a dataset in the catalog; iii) *Distribution*, that represents an accessible form of a dataset, i.e., a downloadable file or a Web service; iv) *DataService*, that provides access to one or more datasets. Access-specific properties for Application Programming Interface (API) descriptions are partially supported by DCAT-AP version 2 and 3[14]. Therefore, exploiting the principle of reuse, the EPOS-DCAT-AP extension makes an extended use of the *Schema.org*[15] and *Hydra Core*[16] vocabularies for describing a programmatic access to datasets via API. More specifically, the extension uses classes of Hydra vocabulary such as: *Operation, IriTemplate and IriTemplateMapping*, to describe: i) IRI template; ii) list of parameters that enable data access; iii) each parameter of the IRI template. Moreover, additional properties coming from the *Schema.org* vocabulary are also introduced to better describe the features of the web service parameters (e.g., defaultValue, maxValue, minValue).

Adopting this approach, the *Distribution* can point to a resource described with the *Hydra* vocabulary, thus allowing to have flexible and fine-grained representations covering the broad EPOS spectrum that includes both global, well-established and community specific standards for web services.

DCAT-AP uses *vcard:Kind* as range of *dcat:contactPoint*, and uses *foaf:Agent (Person or Organization)* as range for describing other roles like *creator*, *publisher and contributor.* Both *vcard:Kind* and *foaf:Agent* do not specify a minimum set of properties thus not ensuring a robust interoperability between applications. EPOS- DCAT-AP defines a set of alignments and range extensions by using the *Schema.org* vocabulary in order to enable a more detailed representation of Person and Organization. The use of *schema:ContactPoint* class enables a flexible definition of roles and responsibilities.

[14] https://www.w3.org/TR/vocab-dcat-3/.

[15] https://schema.org.

[16] www.hydra-cg.com.

Table 1 describes the EPOS Core Concepts which underpin the profile (first and second columns); how they are covered by DCAT-AP classes (third column); how they are reported in the EPOS-DCAT-AP extension (fourth column). Table 2 presents an alignment of the properties in DCAT-AP 2.1.0 and EPOS-DCAT-AP 2.0.

Figure 3 illustrates the UML class diagram of the latest version of EPOS-DCAT-AP[17] where the gray boxes denote the DCAT-AP core classes, the orange boxes represent the EPOS-DCAT-AP additional classes, that together with relationships and roles, address the EPOS requirements.

Table 1. Showing the alignments of the EPOS Core Concepts with the classes of DCAT-AP v 2.1.0 and EPOS-DCAT-AP v 2.0.

EPOS Core Concept	Description	DCAT-AP v 2.1.0 Classes	EPOS-DCAT-AP v 2.0 Classes
Data Product	Data and Data Product.	dcat:Dataset	dcat:Dataset
Distribution	A specific representation of a data or data product available in multiple serializations and provided in different ways.	dcat:Distribution	dcat:Distribution
Web Service	API which enables to programmatically access the given resource.	dcat:DataService	dcat:DataService
Web Service Operation	A description of a web service operation which consists of a ULR template literal and a set of parameters used in the template.	dcat:endpointDescription (property of dcat:DataService)	Extended the range rdfs:Resource in order to include hydra:Operation, hydra:IriTemplate, hydra:IriTemplateMapping
API Documentation	API documentation of a Webservice.	dct:conformsTo (property of dcat:DataService)	dct:conformsTo (property of dcat:DataService)
Service	A generic service.	-	schema:Service
Person	A person which represents a contact point of a resource.	foaf:Person or vcard:Individual (i.e., it depends on the relationship type)	schema:Person (as equal to foaf:Person)
Organization	Institution or organization which represents the Data provider or Service provider.	foaf:Organization or vcard:Organization (i.e., it depends on the relationship type)	schema:Organization (as equal to foaf:Organization)
ContactPoint	A contact point of a resource.	vcard:Kind	schema:ContactPoint (as equal to vcard:Kind)
SoftwareApplication	Software packages, applications and programs.	-	schema:SoftwareApplication
SoftwareSourceCode	A computer programming source code.	-	schema:SoftwareSourceCode
Category	A subject of a resource.	skos:Concept	skos:Concept
CategoryScheme	A concept collection in which categories are defined.	skos:ConceptScheme	skos:ConceptScheme
Equipment	A device (e.g., Seismic Station).	-	epos:Equipment (as subclass of schema:Product)
Facility	A facility used by a scientific community to conduct top-level research (e.g., Seismic Network).	-	epos:Facility
Publication	A publication related to a dataset, data product or other.	-	epos:Publication (as subclass of schema:CreativeWork)

[17] https://epos-eu.github.io/EPOS-DCAT-AP/.

Table 2. Overview of the properties characterizing EPOS-DCAT-AP 2.0 with respect to DCAT-AP 2.1.0

URI	Type	Description	DCAT-AP 2 Action	EPOS-DCAT-AP 2 Action
dct:isReferencedBy	Optional **(Dataset)**	Range : rdfs:Resource This property is about a related resource, such as a publication, that references, cites, or otherwise points to the dataset.	New	Added
dcat:qualifiedRelation	Optional **(Dataset)**	Range : dcat:Relationship This property provides a link to a description of a relationship with another resource	New	Added
dct:creator	Optional **(Dataset)**	Range : foaf:Agent This property refers to the entity primarily responsible for producing the dataset	New	Added and extended the range to include schema:Organization
prov:qualifiedAttribution	Optional **(Dataset)**	Range : prov:Attribution This property refers to a link to an Agent having some form of responsibility for the resource	New	Added
prov:wasGeneratedBy	Optional **(Dataset)**	Range : prov:Activity This property refers to an activity that generated, or provides the business context for, the creation of the dataset.	New	Added
dcat:spatialResolutionInMeters	Optional **(Dataset)**	Range : xsd:decimal This property refers to the minimum spatial seperation resolvable in a dataset, measured in meters.	New	Added
dcat:temporalResolution	Optional **(Dataset)**	Range : xsd:duration This property refers to the minimum time period resolvable in the dataset.	New	Added
dct:spatial	Recommended **(Dataset)**	Optional property → Recommended property	Updated	Updated
dct:temporal	Recommended **(Dataset)**	Optional property → Recommended property	Updated	Updated
dcat:mediaType	Optional **(Distribution)**	Range: dct:MediaTypeOrExtent →dct:MediaType	Updated	Updated
odrl:hasPolicy	Optional **(Distribution)**	Range: odrl:Policy This property refers to the policy expressing the rights associated with the distribution if using the ODRL vocabulary	New	Added
dcat:accessService	Optional **(Distribution)**	Range: dcat:DataService This property refers to a data service that gives access to the distribution of the dataset	New	Added
dcat:spatialResolutionInMeters	Optional **(Distribution)**	Range : xsd:decimal This property refers to the minimum spatial separation resolvable in a dataset distribution, measured in meters.	New	Added
dcat:temporalResolution	Optional **(Distribution)**	Range: xsd:duration This property refers to the minimum time period resolvable in the dataset distribution.	New	Added
dcat:compressFormat	(Optional **(Distribution)**	Range: dct:MediaType This property refers to the format of the file in which the data is contained in a compressed form, e.g. to reduce the size of the downloadable file.	New	Added
dcat:packageFormat	Optional **(Distribution)**	Range: dct:MediaType This property refers to the format of the file in which one or more data files are grouped together, e.g. to enable a set of related files to be downloaded together.	New	Added
dcatap:availability	Recommended **(Distribution)**	Range : skos:Concept This property indicates how long it is planned to keep the Distribution of the Dataset available. It MUST take one of the values: temporary, experimental, available, stable.	New	Added
dcat:endPointURL	Mandatory **(Data Service)**	Range : rdfs:Resource The root location or primary endpoint of the service (an IRI).	New	Added
dct:title	Mandatory **(Data Service)**	Range : rdfs:Literal This property contains a name given to the Data Service. This property can be repeated for parallel language versions of the name.	New	Added
dct:identifier	Mandatory **(Data Service)**	Range: rdfs:Literal This property contains the main identifier for the Data Service.	-	Added
dcat:servesDataset	Recommended **(Data Service)**	Range : dcat:Dataset This property refers to a collection of data that this data service can distribute.	New	Added
dcat:endpointDescription	Recommended **(Data Service)**	Range: rdfs:Resource This property contains a description of the services available via the end-points, including their operations, parameters etc. The property gives specific details of the actual endpoint instances.	New	Added and extended the range to include hydra:Operation
dcat:contactPoint	Recommended **(Data Service)**	This property contains contact information that can be used for sending comments about the Data Service.	-	Inherited from superclass dcat:Resource
dct:description	Recommended **(Data Service)**	This property contains a free-text account of the Data Service. This property can be repeated for parallel language versions of the description.	New	Added Optional property → Recommended property
dct:issued	Recommended **(Data Service)**	This property contains the date of publication of the Data Service.	-	Inherited from superclass dcat:Resource
dct:modified	Recommended **(Data Service)**	This property contains the most recent date on which the Data Service was modified.	-	Inherited from superclass dcat:Resource
dct:publisher	Recommended **(Data Service)**	This property refers to an Organization responsible for making the Data Service available.	-	Inherited from superclass dcat:Resource
dcat:theme	Recommended **(Data Service)**	This property refers to a category of the Data Service. A Data Service may be associated with multiple themes.	-	Inherited from superclass dcat:Resource
dct:accessRights	Optional **(Data Service)**	Range: dct:RightsStatement This property MAY include information regarding access or restrictions based on privacy, security, or other policies.	New	Added
dct:license	Optional **(Data Service)**	Range: dct:LicenseDocument This property contains the licence under which the service is made available.	New	Added
dct:conformsTo	Optional **(Data Service)**	This property refers to the Data Service API Definition URL.	-	Inherited from superclass dcat:Resource
dcat:keyword	Optional **(Data Service)**	This property contains a keyword or tag describing the Data Service.	-	Inherited from superclass dcat:Resource
dct:spatial	Optional **(Data Service)**	This property refers to a geographic region that is covered by the Data Service.	-	New property
dct:temporal	Optional **(Data Service)**	This property refers to a temporal period that the Data Service covers.	-	New property

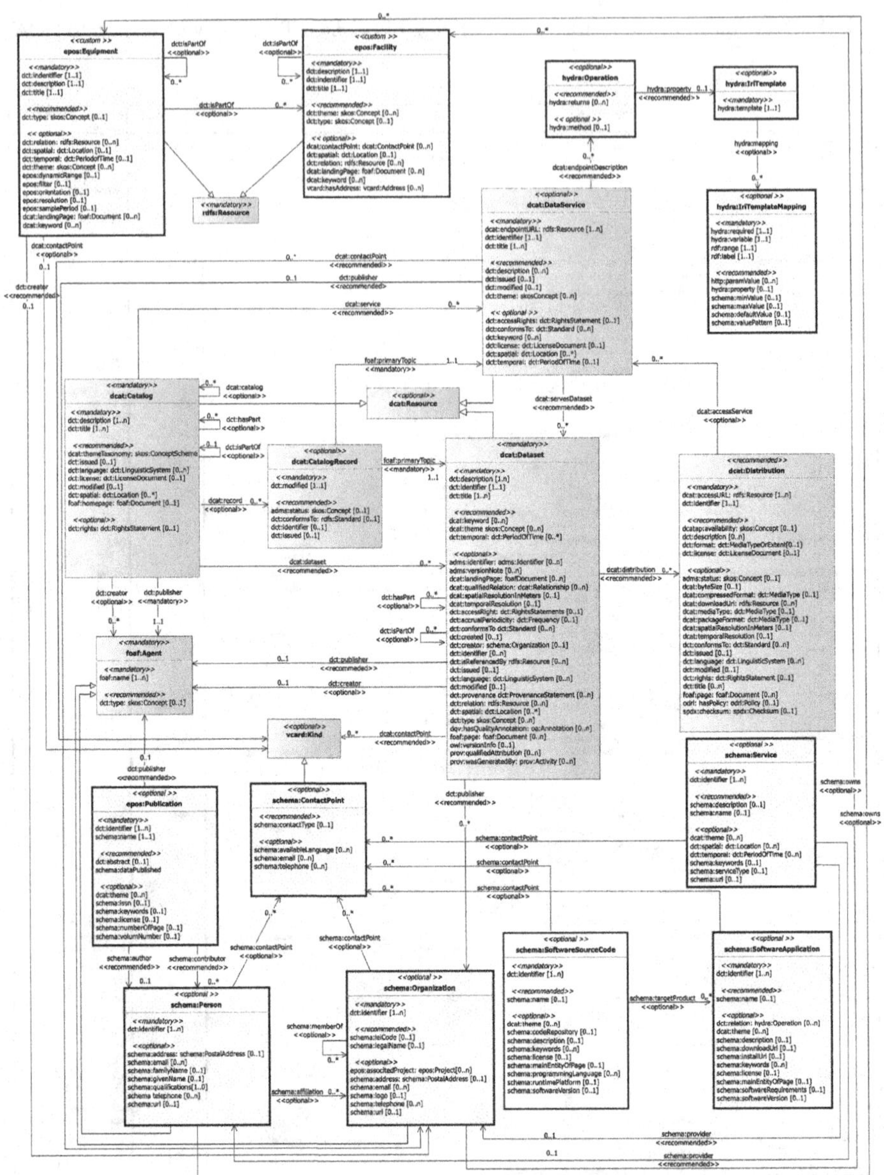

Fig. 3. The EPOS-DCAT-AP UML class diagram that highlights the additional classes (in bold), relationships and roles introduced to address the EPOS requirements.

EPOS-DCAT-AP is successfully adopted to enable integrated use of data, data products, software and services from distributed research infrastructures in EPOS. The EPOS platform implements a metadata-driven-approach [10] that provides users with homogenous access to heterogenous assets made available by ten Thematic Core Services:

Seismology, Near Fault Observatories, GNSS Data and Products, Volcano Observations, Satellite Data, Geomagnetic Observations, Anthropogenic Hazards, Geological Information and Modelling, Multi-scale laboratories and Tsunami.

Information about communities' assets e.g., how they are distributed and how to access them, are described by EPOS-DCAT-AP metadata instances in RDF/Turtle format. Metadata are stored in a centralized catalogue, exposed via RESTful APIs and consumed by the EPOS Data Portal to drive its features and support primary use cases. For instance, assets (*dcat:Dataset* and *dcat:Distribution*) can be searched by exploiting keywords (*dct:keyword*), spatial coverage (*dct:spatial*), temporal coverage (*dct:temporal*) and data/service providers (*schema:Organization* and *schema:Person*); query results can be browsed by thematic areas (*dcat:theme* and *skos:Concept*); queries can be performed by exploiting services URL and query parameters (*dcat:DataService, hydra:Operation, hydra:IriTemplate* and *hydra:IriTemplateMapping*). To enable the data visualization in different formats (e.g., GeoJSON, CovJSON), several software converters are described by using *schema:SoftwareApplication* and *schema:SoftwareSourceCode.*

The description of transnational access to various research facilities (e.g., analogue modelling laboratories, high-pressure, high-temperature melt, rock physics and mineralogical experiments) is implemented by exploiting *epos:Facility*, *epos:Equipment* and *schema:Service* [11].

EPOS-DCAT-AP is also used within the ENVRI-FAIR [12] project to create the ENVRI Hub[18] – an open access hub for interdisciplinary environmental research data in the European Research Area. In this context, the metadata catalogue underpinning the hub is populated with EPOS-DCAT-AP metadata instances which enable the description of the services provided by the ENVRI Research Infrastructures [13].

4 Conclusion

In this paper we have presented the current status of the EPOS-DCAT Application Profile that extends the DCAT Application profile to enable metadata exchange, and thus implementing the interoperability, within the European Plate Observing System (EPOS[19]) Research Infrastructure (RI).

The complexity and scale of EPOS require an incremental and agile approach to maintain the interoperability layer by accommodating evolving requirements. For instance, new communities should be able to join the RI and it should be possible to integrate new assets without disrupting the EPOS delivery framework. EPOS-DCAT-AP has demonstrated the ability to fulfill those requirements. The management of the profile is guaranteed by a strong commitment and a continued engagement with users and stakeholders of the EPOS RI. These organizational characteristics together with the technical aspect can foster the adoption by other communities.

Acknowledgements. The authors would like to acknowledge the following projects and initiatives for financing part of the activities: EPOS-IP, European Commission H2020 program, Grant agreement ID 676564; ENVRI-FAIR, European Commission H2020 program, Grant agreement ID

[18] https://envri.eu/envri-hub/.

[19] https://www.epos-eu.org/.

824068; EPOS-ERIC for sustainability and management. The authors would also like to acknowledge the EPOS TCS-ICS team for providing feedback on the development of the EPOS-DCAT-AP specification.

References

1. Heery, R., Patel, M.: Application profiles: mixing and matching metadata schemas. Ariadne **25**, 27–31 (2000). http://www.ariadne.ac.uk/issue25/app-profiles/
2. Tennis, J.T.: Metadata Application Profiles. Encyclopedia of Archival Concepts, Principles, and Practices. Rowman & Littlefield (2015). https://ssrn.com/abstract=3225431
3. Perego, A., Cetl, V., Friis-Christensen, A., Lutz, M.: GeoDCAT-AP: representing geographic metadata by using the "DCAT application profile for data portals in Europe". In: Joint UNECE/UNGGIM Europe Workshop on Integrating Geospatial and Statistical Standards, 06–08 September 2017, Stockholm, Sweden, UNECE Workshop on Integrating Geospatial and Statistical Standards, JRC107410 (2017)
4. Dekkers, M., Kotoglou, S., Nelson, C., Pellegrino, M., Hohn, N., Peristeras, V.: StatDCAT-AP, a common layer for the exchange of statistical metadata in open data portals. SemStats@ISWC (2016)
5. PwC EU Services, Analysis of the DCAT-AP extensions, European Commission (2017). https://joinup.ec.europa.eu/sites/default/files/document/2017-10/DCAT-AP%20extensions%20analysis_v1.00.pdf
6. Cocco, M., et al.: The EPOS Research Infrastructure: a federated approach to integrate solid Earth science data and services. Ann. Geophys. (2022). https://doi.org/10.4401/ag-8756
7. Bailo, D., et al.: Data integration and FAIR data management in Solid Earth Science. Ann. Geophys. (2022). https://doi.org/10.4401/ag-8742
8. Trani, L.: A methodology to sustain common information spaces for research collaborations. University of Edinburgh (2019)
9. Trani, L., Atkinson, M., Bailo, D., Paciello, R., Filgueira, R.: Establishing core concepts for information-powered collaborations. Futur. Gener. Comput. Syst. **89**, 421–437 (2018). https://doi.org/10.1016/j.future.2018.07.005
10. Bailo, D., et al.: Integrated access to multidisciplinary data through semantically interoperable services in a metadata-driven platform for solid earth science. In: MTSR 2022, 16th International Conference on Metadata and Semantics Research, London, 7th–11th November 2022 (2022)
11. Wessels, R., et al.: Transnational access to research facilities: an EPOS service to promote multi-domain Solid Earth Sciences in Europe. Ann. Geophys. (2022). https://www.annalsofgeophysics.eu/index.php/annals/article/view/8768
12. Jeffery, K.G., Bailo, D., Paciello, R., Vinciarelli, V.: European environmental metadata. In: MTSR 2022, 16th International Conference on Metadata and Semantics Research, London, 7th–11th November 2022 (2022)
13. Petzold, A., et al.: ENVRI-fair-interoperable environmental fair data and services for society, innovation and research. In: Proceedings - IEEE 15th International Conference on eScience, eScience 2019, no. 824068, pp. 277–280 (2019). https://doi.org/10.1109/eScience.2019.00038

Metadata, Linked Data, Semantics and Ontologies - General Session, and Track on European and National Projects

Metadata for Clinical Narrative

Udaya Varadarajan[1,2(✉)] and Biswanath Dutta[1(✉)]

[1] Documentation Research and Training Centre, Indian Statistical Institute, Bangalore, Bangalore, India
{udayav,bisu}@drtc.isibang.ac.in

[2] Department of Library and Information Science, University of Calcutta, Kolkata, India

Abstract. The purpose of the current work is to develop metadata for clinical narrative information. For the metadata development, studies were conducted to identify the resources for patient stories. The resource consulted for the current work is the medical journals and case records. With the patient stories, medical narratives were developed. To identify the elements of narration, narrative theories and electronic health records were studied. These elements were identified in the medical narratives developed. By conducting this study, it was found that the medical narratives lack metadata for describing the clinical narration. Thus, metadata elements were composed for the patient-doctor narration. The work stands out by developing a metadata framework for medical narrative information. This framework addresses the lack of metadata for narrative information in a clinical setting. As a result, this research aids in the recording of patient-doctor dialogue.

Keywords: Narrative Information Metadata · Narrative Ontology · Clinical Narration · Medical Narrative Metadata

1 Introduction

Narrative has acquired its place in the current century. The area has found a place in various domains such as cognitive sciences, political science, digital library, archaeology and so on. Narrative is used from business to software development (Schwabe, Richter, and Wende, 2019). The medical field has also adopted the narrative into their folds. Those narratives describe events, experiences and illnesses in a medical setting. Clinical narratives are 'story', detailed description of any specific situation or event including the details such as where, when, patient details, special conditions and so on by clinicians. The narratives in medical situations are considered as a mix of fact and creativity (Wood, 2005). They generally are part of pharmacovigilance and patient safety. These narratives back the epistemological basis for medical cognition, analysis of patient illness and research on medical models for efficient healthcare delivery (Goyal, 2013). The concept of narrative medicine is a product of this (Charon et al., 2017).

Other than this branch of medicine, there are other narratives that occur in the medical domain. These narratives are important as they capture relevant information of the

E. Garoufallou and A. Vlachidis (Eds.): MTSR 2022, CCIS 1789, pp. 261–273, 2023.
https://doi.org/10.1007/978-3-031-39141-5_22

people and roles associated in the healthcare domain. According to Le et al (2017) other narratives that occur in the medical domain are:

- Patient narration describes the details of the patient such as age, gender, clinical condition, occurrence and duration of illness
- Narrative medical writing, describing the adverse events experienced by the patient
- Health and illness narrative are the details of the illness and its effect on the patient in a personal way

On one hand, the patient narration is recorded using the electronic health records (EHRs). Few components of this narratives such as age, gender, condition and occurrence are captured by the EHRs in a structured manner. EHRs are the electronic counterpart to the paper patient records. Evolving from paper, the records become electronic (Shortliffe, 1999). Generally, EHRs contain daily charting, medication administration, physical evaluation, admission nursing note, nursing care plan, referral, current complaint (such as symptoms), prior medical history, way of life, physical examination, diagnoses, tests, procedures, treatment, medication, discharge, history, diaries, problems, findings, and immunisation. The common fields in an EHR are Patient details/profile, Hospital details, Doctor/Physician details, Measurements details and Drugs details (Alabbasi et al., 2014). There are standards for the EHRs. Some of these are discussed in detail the literature review section.

On the other hand, narrative medical writing and health and illness narratives mostly existing in the form of videotaping, audio recording or in the form of note taking, captured as unstructured data types, often, for subject interviews, observations (Harris, P. (n.d.)). As identified by Varadarajan and Dutta (2021a) these data are not exploited beyond the immediate use of treatment. Data collected through videotaping, audio recording, or note taking can be used to infer improved outcome. These narratives consist of information important for better healthcare delivery. These unstructured data need to be structured for discoverability and reuse. In order to better understand the data, there is a need for describing them. With this motivation, the current work attempts to structure these narratives by defining the metadata. As detailed in the literature section, designated electronic health records (EHRs) fields nor any data standards exist for it. Despite the significance and importance of this type of clinical narratives, there is a lack of metadata for narrative information in medicine.

The paper is divided as follows. The literature study follows the introduction. The methodology is Sect. 3. The Narrative framework is detailed in Sect. 4. The findings and discussion are detailed in Sect. 5. The paper concludes by mentioning future works.

2 Literature Study

In order to understand about the metadata for clinical narratives, a study of the relevant literature was performed. There have been multiple works undertaken for the study of metadata in general. Metadata can be generic or domain specific. Metadata schemas are present for resources on the web, for archaeological and cultural artefacts, biodiversity and natural history, for data, for describing ontologies. Some of the standards are Dublin core, a domain independent standard for describing resources, VRA Core for visual culture, images and the document that describes them, CIDOC-CRM for museum and cultural heritage documentation, Darwin Core for biological diversity information exchange, ABCD for data exchange in the domain of biological specimen data, DDI for data in the domain of social and behavioural sciences, DCAT for datasets in data catalogues, MOD for describing the ontologies Dutta et al., (2017) and so on. There are projects undertaken to identify the best possible metadata set for describing the resources in libraries. Some of the literature are a guideline for the current work is detailed here. For digital archiving and preserving, through a collaborative approach, the University of Houston Libraries developed a set of 23 metadata elements. This is in addition to the already existing element set for their digital assets (Washington and Weidner, 2017). In another collaborative work, libraries at the University of Nebraska-Lincoln (UNL) worked together to create a metadata application profile (MAP). This was done in order to record and disseminate information about the metadata standards and content procedures used by each of the four digital repositories. Platform-specific restrictions, content limitations, approaches to metadata and description, and contrasting ideologies were the main roadblocks. Through cooperative work, the group discovered similarities and decided on a minimal set of necessary metadata components for all of their repositories. After deciding on the bare minimum of metadata components, the team created and made available a LibGuide for the UNL MAP. (Mering & Wintermute, 2020). Works on metadata mapping or extension are also significant in this study. These works help in understanding the kind of metadata creation, modification and extension that happens in the same domain or among domains. A crosswalk of the standards (either of the same domain or of the same purpose) will also enable interoperability among the standards. Works such as Marketakis et al (2017), Habermann (2019), Martin et al (2019) and Jung et al. (2022) discuss metadata unification and information integration with respect to cultural heritage, geographical data, digital humanities or computational engineering. This study has given a glimpse into the ways metadata is developed and enriched across libraries, museums and archives.

Particular to narrative, there are frameworks that play the role of descriptors or metadata. Certain works were studied to develop ideas on the metadata for narratives. The Archetype Ontology (Damiano and Lieto, 2013) was built to navigate the digital archive using the narrative relations among the resources. The founding idea of the model has been the narrative situation (Klarer, 2013). Narrative situations demand characters and objects which are part of a larger story once connected. The major classes of this framework are Artifact, Archetype, Entity, Dynamics, Story. These entities are connected to each other via the relations such as evokes (connecting Artifact and Archetype) and displays (connecting Artifact and Entity). Fisseni et al. (2013) conducted a preliminary study to compare the stories. In order to perform the study, they studied the aspects of narratives. The findings of the work identify elements such as characters, entities and the relationship between them. Since the case is to compare stories, the other elements identified were the pattern of the stories, any metaphorical or allegorical interpretation, and the recipient's perspective. Ciotti (2016) initiates a formal ontology towards developing narratives. The ontology has classes, namely - Action, Object, Event, Actor, Place, Quality and Actant. The classes are major components of any narrative. Bartalesi et al., (2016) is a formal model for narratives based on the classical theory of narratology.

The elements of the models are Fabula- sequence of events in a chronological order, Narration- text that narrates the fabula, Narrative fragments- a portion of the narration, Event- something that happens at a time and place and Action- a subdivision of event, is doing something. The elements of narratives identified by Bartalesi et al (2016) are the Generalised event (where action and objects exist in a particular time and space), Process (events with a beginning, middle and end), Time (temporal factor including the start, end and interval), Physical objects (physical object present in particular time and space), Mental events (events occurring in the mind of the agent) and Mental objects (objects present in the mind of the agent). Lombardo et al (2018) developed an ontology for encoding the drama and its elements. Four major classes of the model are DramaEntity (the dramatic entities), DataStructure (class that organises the elements of the ontology into common structures), DescriptionTemplate (contains the patterns for the representation of drama) and ExternalReference (class that bridges the description of drama to common sense and linguistic concepts situated in external resources). Meghini et al (2021) developed Nont ontology. The work is an attempt to describe the resources in museums or archives using narratives. The ontology provides provision for extending NOnt with other existing narrative models.

With regard to clinical narratives, the closest works are the modelling of EHR or of clinical case reports. Ogbuji (2011) developed Computer Based Patient Record (CPR). The ontology contains the elements of clinical finding, procedure, bodily feature, organism, pharmacological substance, recorded clinical situation and clinical artifact. In another work, the co-occurrence matrices of the pair of terms that occur in the EHRs were mapped to the medical concepts. This matrix helps establish relationships between the disease, drugs and devices (Finlayson et al., 2014). The unstructured data in the clinical case report make it difficult for it to be machine readable. In order to efficiently do this a Metadata Acquired from Clinical Case Reports (MACCR) was developed containing the terms for the demographics, disease presentation, treatments, and outcomes. The work also curates' diseases into 15 groups and maps them to the ICD-10 diagnostics codes (Caufield et al., 2018). Developed as an annotation tool for clinical records, the ACROBAT categories, events, properties and entities in the clinical document. For example, the events are classified as clinical event, diagnostic procedure, medication, therapeutic procedures etc. The entity types contain the demographic information like age, sex, occupation and so on (Caufield et al., 2019). Studying the existing theories for narration and the ontology models, a partial knowledge graph was constructed to capture the patient-doctor narration. This identifies the narrative elements in general that can be reused for the medical narrative domain. The elements identified were Story, Actor, Event, Action, Theme, Time and Space (Varadarajan & Dutta, 2021b).

As is evident, there are still research arena in the metadata standard for the clinical narratives. With this work, we hope to contribute to the elements that aid in the description of clinical narration and help in the efficient healthcare delivery.

3 Methodology

Once the literature study was conducted, a methodology was adopted to achieve the objective of the current work. The methodology consists of four steps. The detailed step by step is given below. The figure illustrates the workflow of the process (Fig. 1).

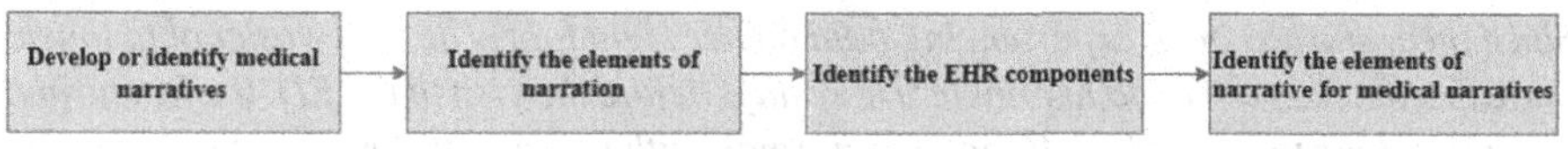

Fig. 1. The workflow for developing elements for medical narratives

Step 1: Develop or identify a medical narrative

As a first step, we need to identify the patient stories. There are various sources that will assist in providing the patient stories. Sources include interview the patient for their experience of the disease, refer the first hand reports in medical journals, newsletters and openly available case records and secondary sources such as newspapers that reports the patient stories. The source of patient stories will contain many stories and cases. From the multiple sources identify the medical narrative that suits the purpose. If the stories were collected from the patient through interviews, there is a need for developing the transcript into stories.

Step 2: Identify the elements of narration

Once the stories are developed and at hand, we need to identify the elements of narration. For this, we need to have an overview of the theories of narrative. The theories were identified by searching across the academic databases such as SCOPUS, ScienceDirect, JSTOR and so on. In addition to the theories from narrative domain, the narrative frameworks can also be used to identify the possible elements that can aid in describing the medical narrative.

Step 3: Identify the EHR components

The work proceeds to identify the elements present in the EHRs that can aid in the description of medical narratives. To achieve this, a study of the EHRs element and their standards can be performed.

Step 4: Identify the elements of narrative for medical narratives

The theories studied help in identifying the elements of narration. Once the elements are identified, these elements are mapped to the medical narrative that was identified in step 2. The elements of narration in medical narratives are described in the following section.

4 Descriptors for Medical Narratives

The first step is to identify the various resources available for patient stories. For the purpose of the current work, medical data openly available in medical journals, newsletters, openly available case records and newspapers were referred to. The details of the patient are still protected even in these platforms. Few resources that contain the clinical stories are The New England Journal of Medicine, Journal of American Medical Association and the New York Times Magazine Column 'Diagnosis'. Stories in a free-text manner are available from these resources. Following the identification of the resources for patient story collection, these stories were gathered. The stories were downloaded as text files in.pdf format. Following is an example of the kind of stories that were identified for the work.

One such patient story is that of a 41 year old woman. She visits the emergency department (ED) with cold feet on New Year's eve. On Christmas she received new boots.

Since then, she has been experiencing pain on her right foot. The foot was cool to touch. She experienced pain up to her ankle. Three days before the visit to the ED, the feet turned into the colour purple. The left foot was normal, with no pain or discoloration. She also had chills 2 days before arrival to the ED. She had received treatment for endocarditis 2 years before this presentation and sought evaluation because she was worried, she had another infection. The patient undergoes examination for numbness, tingling or weakness in the legs. Followed by this, the patient was asked about the cramping of the legs. The family history on the clotting disorder was checked. The patient did feel numbness in the legs, but was able to move the toes, but did not experience any cramping of the legs nor has any history of clotting disorder. The physical examination of the patient did not reveal any abnormality with the lung, heart, abdomen, hair loss, ulcerations or any region of atrophy. But the physical sensation was missing in the right foot.

After the story was selected, in order to identify the elements of narrative, a study was performed of the existing narrative theories. Aristotle's theory identified the elements as exposition (initial situation in a narrative), crisis (disturbances in the initial situation), and denouement (resolution of the crisis leading to new exposition) (Klarer, 2013). Todorov and Weinstein (1969) discuss the elements of narration in terms of the balance in the story. They structure the narrative as beginning with 'equilibrium'. A 'problem' in the balance causes 'disequilibrium'. When the problem is resolved, they attain a new 'equilibrium'. This is similar to Aristotle's classification. Freytag's Pyramid or Freytag's analysis (Abbott, 2003; Freytag, 1900) is narrative theory that explains the plot structure of the story. The elements of the Pyramid are:

a) Exposition
b) Rising action
c) Climax
d) Falling action
e) Catastrophe

Propp proposed 31 functions and 8 roles for a fairy tale. The 31 functions include introduction of the hero, manipulation of the hero, action by the central character, resulting in victory for the hero and defeat for the villain. The eight roles in the fairy tales are the villain, the hero (character with grey shades, the central character), the donor and helper (who aids with object with some special property), the princess (a character of the fairy tale and object of the villain's schemes), her father, the dispatcher (who sends the hero on the quest) and the false hero (Propp, 2009). Greimas's contribution to the narrative has been to propose six actants (the actantial model). They are paired as binary units. The six actants are-subject/object, sender/receiver, helper/opponent. Some tasks are performed by the actants. They are search, aim, desire (by subject/object), communication (by sender/receiver), and support or hindrance (by helper/opponent) (Hébert, 2020). Similar to this theory is the philosophy of Levi-Strauss (Puckett, 2016). "Stories have shapes which can be drawn on graph paper, and that the shape of a given society's stories is at least as interesting as the shape of its pots or spearheads" (Case Western Reserve University, 2016). This theory comes from Kurt Vonnegut. He plots a line on the mathematical x and y axis. The 'Beginning-End' (BE axis) or the x-axis traces the time of the story. The 'Ill Fortune-Great Fortune' (GI axis), or the y-axis, follows the fortune of the protagonist.

Once the narrative theories are studied, the next step is to study the EHRs and their standards. Some majorly referred and cited standards developed to bring about a standardisation in the EHR data entry and exchange are mostly for varying purposes such as (a) transmission of patient data (ASC X12 (EDI)), image or radiology data (DICOM); (b) communication standards for EHR system (CEN's TC/251, EN 13606, and HISA (EN 12967) and for text messages (HL7 (HL7v2, C-CDA)) (c) standardise the continuity of care (CONTSYS (EN 13940), Continuity of Care Record) and (d) technical protocol (ISO – ISO TC 215, ISO 18308). The Government of India and Germany have set up recommendations for the country. The Government of India recommends a minimum dataset (MDS) that the EHR vendors have to confirm. While the German standard of xDT is developed for data exchange among physicians and healthcare administrators. For clinical narratives, there is a data standard for nursing information developed in the 1990s.

Table 1. Elements for describing narratives

Elements	Definition
Storyline	Whole story
Plot	What happens
Agent	Person present in the story
Behaviour	Way an agent behaves towards another agent(s)
Day-to-day	Change in the way an agent behaves towards another agent(s) day-to-day
Healthcare professional	Change in the way an agent behaves towards another agent(s) who is a health professional
Physical behaviour	Change in the way an agent behaves physically
Emotional state	The state of a person's emotions
Event	Something that happens at a given place and time
Event type	The type of the event
Action	Series of events that form a plot
Action type	The type of action
Spatial factor	Space or location where an event occurs
Temporal factor	Time in which event occurs
Object	Object present during the event
Role	Function of the agent in the event
Direct participant	Function of the direct involvement of agent in the event
Indirect participant	Function of the indirect involvement of agent in the event
Cause	Phenomenon that provides the generative force for other event
Effect	Phenomenon that follows and is caused by some previous phenomenon
Theme of a story	Subject matter

The aim of the project was to develop a standard for clinical nursing data and incorporate the standard into the EHRs. The total of 16 elements are in three categories of Nursing care elements, patient or client demographics and service elements (Werley et al., 1991). EHR systems are constantly involving, adding, modifying and deleting components. But the components are from the administrative, technical and medical point of view. Narrative components such as the details of the events, actions and persons, though captured, are recorded as unstructured data information. They are generally recorded in the Notes field of EHRs. Apart from the history of the EHR system, there are studies on the components and standards of the EHR.

In 2008, Hayrinen et al., (2008) performed a study to understand the EHRs. The study took note of the structured and unstructured data types in the EHRs. They indicate the need to develop a standard or vocabulary so as to use these EHRs efficiently. Daily charting, medication administration, physical evaluation, admission nursing note, nursing care plan, referral, current complaint (such as symptoms), prior medical history, way of life, physical examination, diagnoses, tests, procedures, treatment, medication, discharge, history, diaries, problems, findings, and immunisation were among the data elements that were documented in EHRs. Alabbasi et al. (2014) performed a study of the components of the EHR. The authors identified 5 common components across EHRs. They are Patient details/profile, Hospital details, Doctor/Physician details, Measurements details and Drugs details. They were further classified as static (patient details), semi-static (hospital details), static but growing (drug details) and dynamic and new data (measurement details). The study by (Graña and Jackwoski, 2015) presents the then state

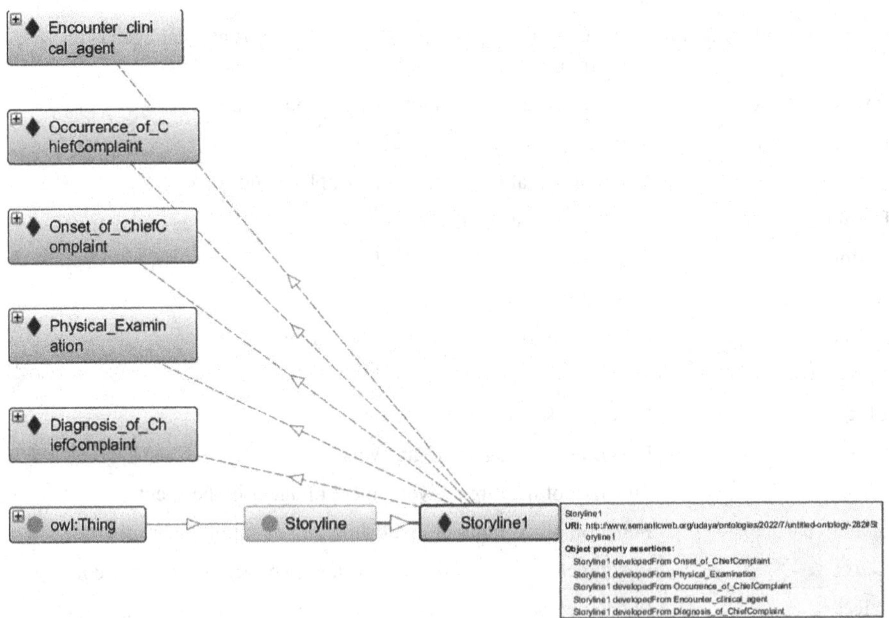

Fig. 2. An example storyline. The popup dialogue box details the Plots that form one single storyline.

of numerous facets of EHR, including security, privacy, decision support system design, and system deployment. Another study by Evans (2016) identifies the components of EHR present in the years 1992 and 2015. The components were mostly in hierarchical or relational databases. The components developed were for scheduling or for billing. Later as technology advanced many components such as statistical packages, physician notes, orders, laboratory results, patient measurement, nursing assessment, patient care procedures, radiology and respiratory therapies were incorporated into the EHR systems. Work by Wasylewicz and Scheepers-Hoeks (2019) indicate a move towards developing a clinical decision support system (CDS). Such CDS included components such as drug-allergy, drug-drug interactions and specific laboratory results. These systems were targeted at the physician who can make sense of the data and help diagnose. From the previous steps of studying the narrative theories EHRs and their standard, we can list the elements that can be used to describe the medical narratives. This is listed in Table 1 and illustrated in Figs. 2, 3 and 4.

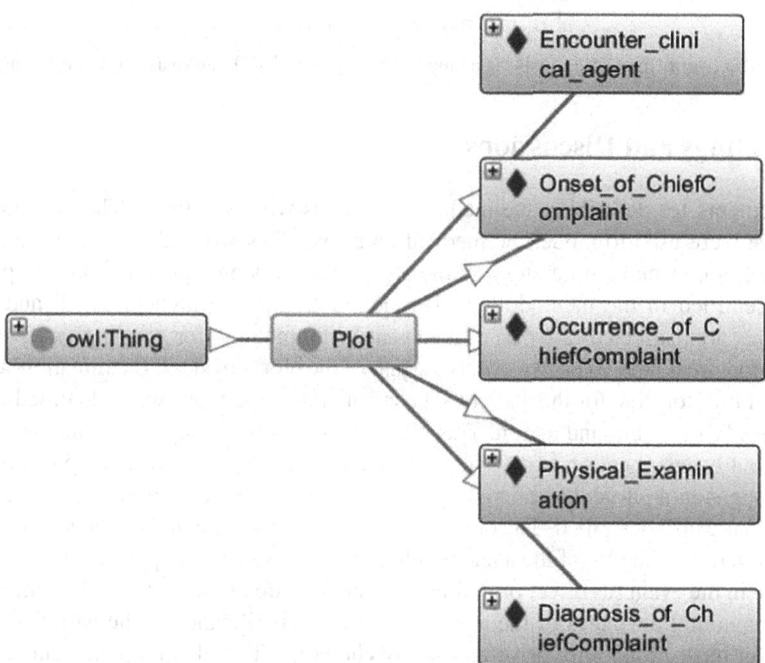

Fig. 3. Plots that form the example storyline

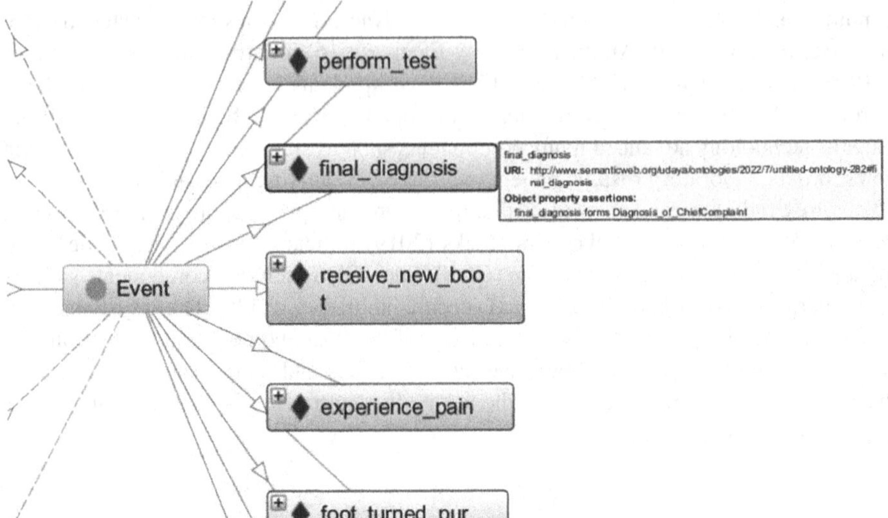

Fig. 4. The event 'final_diagnosis' is a single event in the plot 'Diagnosis_of_ChiefComplaint'

5 Findings and Discussions

The elements for describing the medical narratives were identified. The metadata for narrative were used to model the medical narrative. This work identified events, plots and actions that make up a story or the storyline of a single person from the patient story identified in the methodology. The action 'touch_the_area_affected' and 'pin-prick_the_area_affected' are part of the event 'examination _for_tingling' and 'examination_for_weakness'. The two events are part of the plot 'Physical_Examination' which is part of the storyline for this patient. The event and action types were identified to further classify the event and action. This classification helps in organising the medically significant event or action from others. By the definition of event, it is a phenomenon that happens in a particular time and place. The spatial and temporal metadata for the narration are also described. The objects and agents participate in the plot development, event or action. The role of the agents such as a professional role (physician, nurse etc.) or a role in the event (as direct or indirect participant) are also described. The emotional and behavioural attributes of the agents are also of significance to the narrative. Such factors in most probability drive the plot of the story. The identified elements can be seen as an initial work towards the goal of metadata for medical narratives. The values for the identified metadata are the medical data derived from the medical use cases.

6 Conclusion

The aim of the work was to describe the metadata for medical narration. This was achieved by identifying a patient story and the narrative elements in the story. A study on the existing models and theories of narrative were conducted to understand the components of a narrative. EHRs and the standards were also studied. The existing studies on modelling the clinical narratives are all an attempt made towards improving healthcare delivery. The realisation that the narratives hold the significance in opening up to information never captured before makes these types of works significant. Works such as (Varadarajan and Dutta, 2021a) and (Varadarajan and Dutta, 2021b) have attempted to develop a machine processable artefact for narratives in the medical domain. In the future, work will include expressing the metadata using the OWL language and to expand it by further studying EHRs and consult experts such as doctors and nurses. In addition, future work will include identifying more aspects particular to the medical domain to form the medical narration metadata. Though the use case at hand does not have a variety of roles, in the future with more use cases, it will be modelled efficiently.

References

Abbott, P.H.: The Cambridge Introduction to Narrative. Cambridge University Press, Cambridge (2003)

Alabbasi, S., Ahmed, A., Rebeiro-Hargrave, A., Kaneko, K., Fukuda, A.: Design of a personal health book for ensuring healthcare data portability. In: International Conference on Applied and Theoretical Information Systems Research 2014 (2014)

Bartalesi, V., Meghini, C., Metilli, D.: Steps towards a formal ontology of narratives based on narratology. In: Miller, B., Lieto, A. Ronfard, R., Ware, S.G., Finlayson, M.A. (eds.) Workshop on Computational Models of Narrative 2016, Dagstuhl, Germany, pp. 4:1–4:10 (2016)

Case Western Reserve University. Kurt Vonnegut Lecturel Shape of Story [Video]. YouTube. (2016)

Caufield, J. H., et al.: A comprehensive typing system for information extraction from clinical narratives. MedRxiv, 19009118 (2019). https://doi.org/10.1101/19009118

Caufield, J.H., et al.: A reference set of curated biomedical data and metadata from clinical case reports. Sci. Data **5**(1), 1–18 (2018). https://doi.org/10.1038/sdata.2018.258

Charon, R., et al.: The Principles and Practice of Narrative Medicine. Oxford University Press, New York (2017)

Ciotti, F.: Toward a formal ontology for narrative. MATLIT: Materialidades Lit. **4**(1), 29–44 (2016)

Damiano, R., Lieto, A.: Ontological representations of narratives: a case study on stories and actions. In: CMN'13 Computational Models of Narratives 2013. Dagstuhl Publishing, Germany (2013)

Dutta, B., Toulet, A., Emonet, V., Jonquet, C.: New generation metadata vocabulary for ontology description and publication. In: Garoufallou, E., Virkus, S., Siatri, R., Koutsomiha, D. (eds.) MTSR 2017. CCIS, vol. 755, pp. 173–185. Springer, Cham (2017). https://doi.org/10.1007/978-3-319-70863-8_17

Evans, R.S.: Electronic health records: then, now, and in the future. In: Yearbook of Medical Informatics, vol. 25.S 01, pp. S48–S61 (2016)

Finlayson, S.G., LePendu, P., Shah, N.H.: Building the graph of medicine from millions of clinical narratives. Sci. Data **1**(1), 1–9 (2014)

Fisseni, B., Kurji, A., Sarikaya, D., Viehstädt, M.: Story comparisons: evidence from film reviews. In 2013 Workshop on Computational Models of Narrative. Dagstuhl Publishing, Germany (2013)

Freytag, G.: Freytag's Technique of the Drama, an Exposition of Dramatic Composition and Art. Dr. Gustav Freytag: An Authorized Translation from the Sixth German Edition by Elias J. MacEwan, M.A., 3rd edn., pp. 13–283 Foresman and Company, LCCN, Chicago (1900)

Goyal, R.: Narration in Medicine. In: Hühn, P., et al. (eds.) The Living Handbook of Narratology. Hamburg University, Hamburg (2013). http://www.lhn.uni-hamburg.de/article/narration-medicine

Grana, M.: Jackwoski, K.: Electronic health record: a review. In: 2015 IEEE International Conference on Bioinformatics and Biomedicine (BIBM). IEEE (2015)

Habermann, T.: Mapping ISO 19115–1 geographic metadata standards to CodeMeta. PeerJ Computer Science **5**, e174 (2019)

Harris, P.: Research data planning 1. Coursera (n.d). https://www.coursera.org/learn/clinical-data-management/lecture/8gU2k/researchdata-planning-1126

Häyrinen, K., Saranto, K., Nykänen, P.: Definition, structure, content, use and impacts of electronic health records: a review of the research literature. Int. J. Med. Inform. **77**(5), 291–304 (2008). https://doi.org/10.1016/J.IJMEDINF.2007.09.001

Hébert, L., Tabler, J.:An Introduction to Applied Semiotics: Tools for Text and Image Analysis. Routledge, London (2019). https://doi.org/10.4324/9780429329807/INTRODUCTION-APPLIED-SEMIOTICS-LOUIS-H

Jung, K., Schembera, B., Gärtner, M.: Best of both worlds? Mapping process metadata in digital humanities and computational engineering. In: Garoufallou, E., Ovalle-Perandones, MA., Vlachidis, A. (eds.) MTSR 2021. Communications in Computer and Information Science, vol. 1537, pp. 199–205. Springer, Cham (2022). https://doi.org/10.1007/978-3-030-98876-0_17

Klarer, M.: An Introduction to Literary Studies. Routledge, Devon (2013)

Le, A., Miller, K., McMullin, J.: From particularities to context: refining our thinking on illness narratives. AMA J. Ethics **19**(3), 304–311 (2017)

Lenzi, V.B., Marcelloni, F., Meghini, D.C., Niccolucci, F., Doerr, D.M., Luise, M.: An ontology for narratives. Doctoral thesis (2017)

Lombardo, V., Damiano, R., Pizzo, A.: Drammar: a comprehensive ontological resource on drama. In: Vrandečić, D., et al. (eds.) ISWC 2018. LNCS, vol. 11137, pp. 103–118. Springer, Cham (2018). https://doi.org/10.1007/978-3-030-00668-6_7

Marketakis, Y., et al.: X3ML mapping framework for information integration in cultural heritage and beyond. Int. J. Digit. Libr. **18**(4), 301–319 (2016). https://doi.org/10.1007/s00799-016-0179-1

Martin, P., Remy, L., Theodoridou, M., Jeffery, K., Zhao, Z.: Mapping heterogeneous research infrastructure metadata into a unified catalogue for use in a generic virtual research environment. Future Gener. Comput. Syst. **101**, 1–13 (2019)

Meghini, C., Bartalesi, V., Metilli, D.: Representing narratives in digital libraries: the narrative ontology. Semant. Web **12**(2), 241–264 (2021)

Mering, M.: Wintermute, H.E.: Mapping metadata: ingenta connect. J. Digit. Media Manage. **9**(1), 71–85 (2020). https://www.ingentaconnect.com/content/hsp/jdmm/2020/00000009/00000001/art00008

Ogbuji, C.A.: Framework ontology for computer-based patient record systems. In ICBO (2011)

Propp, V.: Morphology of the Folktale. University of Texas Press, Texas (2009)

Puckett, K.: Narrative theory. Cambridge University Press, Cambridge (2016)

Schwabe, G., Richter, A., Wende, E.: Special issue on storytelling and information systems. Information Systems Journal **29**, 1122–1125 (2019)

Shortliffe, H.: The evolution of electronic medical records. Acad. Med. Philadelphia **74**, 414–419 (1999)

Todorov, T., Weinstein, A.: Structural Analysis of Narrative. NOVEL: A Forum on Fiction, vol. 3, no. 1. Duke University Press (1969)

Varadarajan, U., Dutta, B.: Towards development of knowledge graph for narrative information in medicine. In: Villazón-Terrazas, B., Ortiz-Rodríguez, F., Tiwari, S., Goyal, A., Jabbar, M. (eds.) KGSWC 2021. CCIS, vol. 1459, pp. 290–307. Springer, Cham (2021a). https://doi.org/10.1007/978-3-030-91305-2_22

Varadarajan, U., Dutta, B.:Models for narrative information: a study. arXiv preprint. arXiv:2110.02084 (2021b)

Washington, A., Weidner, A.: Collaborative metadata application profile development for DAMS migration (2017)

Wasylewicz, A.T.M., Scheepers-Hoeks, A.M.J.W.: Clinical decision support systems. Fundam. Clin. Data Sci. 153–169 (2019)

Weibel, S., Kunze, J., Lagoze, C., Wolf, M.: Dublin core metadata for resource discovery (No. rfc2413) (1998)

Werley, H.H., Devine, E.C., Zorn, C.R., Ryan, P., Westra, B.L.: The Nursing Minimum Data Set: abstraction tool for standardized, comparable, essential data. Am. J. Public Health **81**(4), 421–426 (1991). https://doi.org/10.2105/ajph.81.4.421

Wood, J.H.: Interventional : form and function of the narrative medical write-up. Lit. Med. **24**, 283–96 (2005)

SHAPEness: A SHACL-Driven Metadata Editor

Rossana Paciello[1,2(✉)], Luca Trani[3], Daniele Bailo[1,2], Valerio Vinciarelli[2], and Manuela Sbarra[1]

[1] Istituto Nazionale di Geofisica e Vulcanologia (INGV), Rome, Italy
rossana.paciello@ingv.it

[2] European Plate Observing System, EPOS ERIC, Rome, Italy

[3] Department of R&D Seismology and Acoustics, Royal Netherlands Meteorological Institute (KNMI), Utrechtseweg 297, 3731 GA De Bilt, The Netherlands

Abstract. The Shapes Constraint Language (SHACL) has been recently introduced as a W3C recommendation to define constraints for validating RDF graphs. In this paper a novel SHACL-driven multi-view editor is presented: SHAPE*ness*. It empowers users by offering them a rich interface for assessing and improving the quality of metadata represented as RDF graphs. SHAPE*ness* has been developed and tested in the framework of the European Plate Observing System (EPOS). In this context, the SHAPE*ness* features have proven to be a valuable solution to easily create and maintain valid graphs according to the EPOS data model. The SHACL-driven approach underpinning SHAPE*ness*, makes this tool suitable for a broad range of domains, or use cases, which structure their knowledge by means of SHACL constraints.

Keywords: SHACL shapes · RDF validation · knowledge graph quality · graphs visualization · metadata editor

1 Introduction

Over the past decade, the use of standard semantic technologies and linked data principles have become general practice in structuring metadata and related data. For instance, semantic representations such as ontologies are applied to address FAIR data principles [10, 25], that require rich metadata descriptions for scientific datasets. These principles have gained consensus within scientific communities, fostered by pan-European initiatives such as the European Open Science Cloud (EOSC) [18], where they are used as driving concepts to support data interoperability among standardized repositories compliant to a shared set of requirements [7]. According to the FAIR principles, metadata can facilitate data usage and exchange, data findability [16] and access [5].

Resource Description Framework[1] (RDF) is a popular format for exchanging semantic (meta)data, structured as dynamic and schema-less graphs. However, the RDF flexibility turns out to be the source of many data quality and knowledge representation issues.

[1] https://www.w3.org/RDF/.

E. Garoufallou and A. Vlachidis (Eds.): MTSR 2022, CCIS 1789, pp. 274–288, 2023.
https://doi.org/10.1007/978-3-031-39141-5_23

The lack of constraints or of a schema often generates ambiguities in the structure of the data [17].

The validation of the RDF graphs structure against a set of constraints is a requirement shared by many users with different expertise levels, and it represents an actual and relevant research topic [4, 13].

Constraint languages, such as SHACL[2] or ShE[3], meet this need by providing models and vocabularies for expressing structural and semantic relationships [12]—they typically support different data types and multiple severity levels.

The Shapes Constraint Language (SHACL) is a recent W3C recommendation and a powerful formalism to define a set of constraints (called *shapes*) on the content of RDF data graphs thereby improving their quality. SHACL addresses various use cases and application scenarios, for instance, it can be adopted to validate RDF data structures, as a template to model RDF and as an RDF structure query mechanism.

The modelling of such constraints is usually performed by experts with a deep understanding of the concepts of a target domain (e.g., environmental sciences, humanities, biology) and who are also knowledgeable in the language's syntax. In this way they can describe the desired data structure by adhering to the domain requirements.

Due to the potential size of the data structure and the complexity of the restrictions needed to model a knowledge domain, several approaches and tools have been proposed for supporting experts in the above-mentioned modelling task [3, 6, 8, 9].

Nevertheless, defining SHACL constraints is just the first step towards assessment and improvement of knowledge graphs quality [21]. It is equally important to provide visual tools to create, edit and maintain graphs compliant with such constraints, even when users have a limited knowledge of the domain's concepts and data structures.

In this paper we present SHAPE*ness*, a SHACL-driven application that provides users with a rich interactive and user-friendly environment where they can generate, visualize and work with RDF data and structures complying to defined SHACL constraints (*shapes*). RDF data graphs can be easily created by loading a set of *shapes* into the SHAPE*ness* application; graph properties (e.g., nodes and relationships' properties) can be edited and visualized using simple forms; and the resulting graphs can be inspected and serialized to RDF/Turtle[4] format. SHAPE*ness'* features are enabled by combining three types of views in a single user interface: *graph-based*; *form-based*; and *tree-based*. This approach enables users to easily perform their tasks by hiding data structure complexity, thus overcoming possible lack of technical expertise. The SHACL-driven mechanism, implemented by SHAPE*ness*, aims at providing an innovative visual tool for creating and validating metadata as RDF graphs, suitable for any knowledge domain described by means of SHACL constraints. In this paper we prove its added value in the context of solid-Earth sciences.

The remainder of this paper is organized as follows: Sect. 2 provides an overview of the existing tools for creating and validating RDF data against a set of constraints. Section 3 describes the main features of SHAPE*ness*. Section 4 gives an overview of the SHAPE*ness* architecture. Section 5 describes the application of SHAPE*ness* in a

2 https://www.w3.org/TR/shacl/.

3 https://github.com/shexSpec/shex/wiki/ShEx.

4 https://www.w3.org/TR/turtle/.

real case scenario. Section 6 discusses approach and results of a user testing. Finally, Sect. 7 summarizes the outcomes of this research and provides directions for future developments.

2 Related Tools

At present a limited set of visual tools is available for supporting users in the creation and validation of RDF data by means of user-friendly user interfaces. This might be due to the recent standardization of constraint languages for Linked Data such as SHACL. This section introduces some of those tools and provides considerations about their supported features.

Schímatos [26] is a form-based Web application that helps users to create and edit RDF data, validated against SHACL constraints. The web forms are automatically generated by using the SHACL content and the acquired data are stored in a triple store. It also offers a client-side validation which allows users to minimize the input of erroneous data. Schímatos serializes the created data to Turtle format in order to store data in a triple store. The software is available for download as a React.js application.

ActiveRaUL [11] is a web forms generator that helps users, who have limited knowledge about semantic technologies, create and maintain RDF data. ActiveRaUL creates input forms using an arbitrary RDF ontology or a RaUL RDF model in order to acquire data from users and store them in a triple store. XHTML + RDFa is the format used to consume and export data. However, the tool does not support validation of the edited metadata.

Zazuko SHACL Playground[5] is a client-side application built on top of a JavaScript library that can be easily installed via docker[6]. The tool consists of web forms used to validate RDF data against a given set of SHACL constraints, and supporting a wide variety of RDF serializations. The validation report is provided both in a human-readable format for a quick analysis of the issues within a web form, and in a downloadable format for offline reading (e.g., RDF/XML, JSON-LD).

The VitroLib Metadata Editor[7] is one of the outputs of the LD4L project (Liked Data 4 Libraries[8]) a collaboration of Cornell, Harvard, Iowa, and Stanford Universities to promote the use and value of linked data in libraries. VitroLib extends Vitro [15] which is an open-source community driven web application development platform, known as the software underlying the VIVO[9] research networking tool. VitroLib assists users in data editing and, as the data storage is managed by a triple store, VitroLib provides a serialization of data by querying the database and retrieving the result also in JSON format.

To summarize, the presented tools allow users to edit RDF data by means of input forms. However, none of these tools combines the form-based editing functionality with a graph-based visualization of edited data. This feature is beneficial as it offers

5 https://github.com/zazuko/shacl-playground.

6 https://www.docker.com/.

7 https://wiki.lyrasis.org/display/ld4lLABS/The+VitroLib+Metadata+Editor.

8 https://www.ld4l.org/.

9 http://vivoweb.org/.

users a complete overview of the data structure. Most of the reported tools support the serialization of RDF data as a database storage mechanism. Finally, some of these tools support a template-driven approach, which allows users to customize the features offered, including the data validation, on the basis of a configured template (like SHACL) at installation stage.

SHAPE*ness* supports a SHACL-driven approach at the execution stage and this key feature, along with the others, will be described in Sect. 3.

3 SHAPE*ness* Features

The main goal in developing SHAPE*ness* was to create a rich application suitable for any context, domain, and use case that needs to browse, edit and validate RDF graphs, according to a set of input SHACL constraints (schema).

SHAPE*ness* provides a rich user interface which combines: i) a graph-based visualization, for helping users analyze and better understand graphs' structures and semantic relationships; ii) a form-based visualization for easily editing graphs; iii) a tree-based visualization for exploring the graph. The user interface is depicted in Fig. 1 and described in Sect. 3.1.

SHAPE*ness'* features are completely driven by a given SHACL schema (see Sect. 3.2), thus enabling users to easily structure RDF graphs according to the provided SHACL constraints (see Sect. 3.3). The application assists users in editing property values: a) by focusing only on relevant parts of the schema, thus hiding its complexity; b) by helping avoid typos while entering property values (see Sect. 3.4); and c) by validating property types and mandatory properties (see Sect. 3.5). Section 3.6 describes how users can export the created RDF graphs.

3.1 User Interface

The SHAPE*ness* user interface consists of five views: *Graph View (*Fig. 1a), *Palette View* (Fig. 1b), *Outline View* (Fig. 1c), *Properties View* (Fig. 1d), *RDF/Turtle View* (Fig. 1e).

Users can customize the appearance of the application by resizing views and rearranging them using drag and drop within the main window.

The *Graph View* is a visual representation of an RDF graph. The nodes represent resources and the edges represent relationships. Each node-edge-node connection represents a subject-predicate-object statement. A node is represented by an oval shape. An edge is represented by a labeled arrow which indicates the direction of the relation: from subject to object.

The view also includes: i) a toolbar (upper right-hand corner, Fig. 1f) which provides access to the common commands on the graph (e.g., zoom in, zoom out, change graph layout, add and remove nodes or relationships, etc.); ii) a filter panel which allows users to visualize or hide specific node classes on the graph (Fig. 1g); iii) a context menu on nodes and edges which gives users a shortcut to common commands (Fig. 1h).

The *Palette View* shows the shapes' target classes defined by the uploaded SHACL schema, through a list of colored circles. The purpose of this view is to allow users to create nodes of an RDF graph by simply dragging the shapes from this view to the Graph View, or alternatively by right-clicking on the shapes.

The *Outline View* represents the RDF graph as a tree-like structure where the nodes are grouped according to the shape types and the edges are represented by arrows showing the relationship to objects. This view is automatically updated according to the changes made in the Graph View.

The *Properties View* implements a form-based inspection and editing of node properties by providing several form fields (e.g., text fields, tables, dropdown lists, etc.). Each property is labeled by using its compact IRI expressed as `prefix:localPart` (e.g., `foaf:name`). The view can group the properties into mandatory, recommended and optional categories based on their cardinality (as defined by the uploaded SHACL schema).

The *RDF/Turtle View* provides the RDF/Turtle serialization of the graph. By default, this view is hidden. When activated the application goes into a split-view mode and shows the Turtle serialization automatically generated according to the changes made in the Graph View or Properties View.

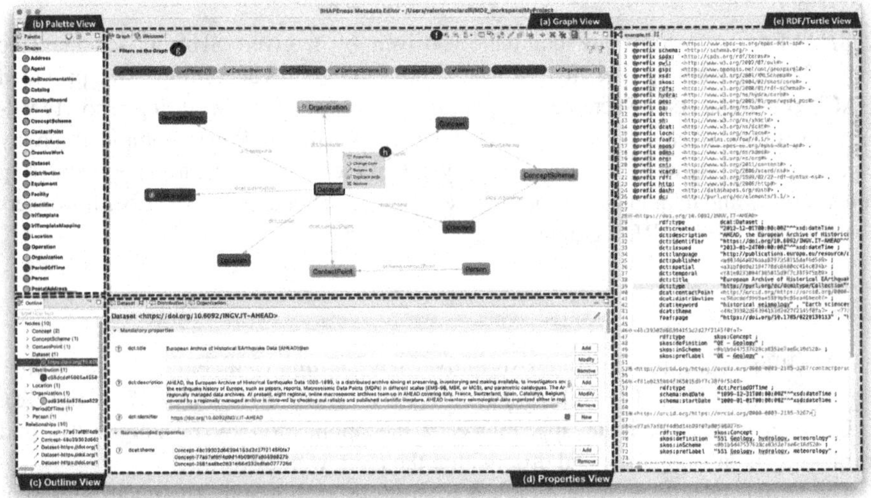

Fig. 1. Showing the SHAPE*ness* user interface which consists of: *Graph View* including (a) a toolbar (f), a filter panel (g), a context menu on nodes and edges (h); *Palette View* (b); *Out-line View* (c); *Properties View* (d); *RDF/Turtle View* (e).

3.2 Using a SHACL Schema to Set up a SHAPE*ness* Project

SHAPE*ness* implements a SHACL-driven approach for creating, editing and validating RDF graphs. A typical user interaction workflow includes a) selection of a SHACL schema (from URL or local file); b) creation of a new RDF graph compliant with the selected SHACL schema; or c) import of an existing RDF data graph serialized in

RDF/Turtle format (from URL or local file). Finally, the application dynamically generates the user interface and its underlying data model based on the SHACL shapes and enables users to work with graphs. After these steps a SHAPE*ness* project is created and saved by default in a dedicated folder inside the user workspace. SHAPE*ness* creates two subfolders for each project folder. The first is used for saving the SHACL schema (which drives the project) and all standard ontologies needed for the graph validation (e.g., `foaf`, `vcard`, `skos`, `dcat`). The second is used for saving the graph serialized in Turtle format. In this way users can work on a project in successive stages and also share it with colleagues.

3.3 Browsing and Authoring RDF Graphs

The Palette View, Graph View and Outline View provide a suite of operations for exploring and structuring RDF data graphs.

The Graph View presents an overall picture of the entities and relationships via an intuitive graph-based interface and enables customizations of the visual elements. SHAPE*ness* assigns different colors to the shapes type listed in the Palette View. Nodes on the graph are labeled and color-coded according to their shape type. Users can customize these colors by means of the palette toolbar or the context menu on the nodes.

The graph is interactive, nodes and edges can be moved around for a better inspection and selection. Nodes and edges of the graph can be highlighted by clicking on them.

To manage readability of large graphs SHAPE*ness* provides zoom functionalities and a filter panel which allows users to hide specific nodes on the graph. The Outline View provides a free-text search which allows users to quickly look up nodes and edges on the graph.

3.4 Supporting Property Editing

SHAPE*ness* empowers metadata authors and data curators to meet SHACL compliance requirements faster and more accurately by supporting property values editing.

The Properties View enables users to view and edit the properties of a selected node on the graph. In order to facilitate the population of property values, SHAPE*ness* gathers dynamically information about types, allowed values and cardinality of the properties from the SHACL schema, and it provides users with suitable form fields (e.g., text fields, dropdown lists, tables, etc.) with syntax checks and dedicated widgets. For example, an interactive Map, shown in Fig. 2a, is available to enter geospatial information (points or polygons) -- users can draw a rectangle on a map or insert geographic coordinates. Another example of widget enables users to select a date/time from a graphical calendar (Fig. 2b).

SHAPE*ness* gathers information about the meaning of the properties from the SHACL schema or related ontologies and presents it via a help button. For instance, in the case of `dct:isVersionOf` property for a `dcat:Dataset` entity users can get the term definition, i.e., *"A related resource of which the described resource is a version, edition, or adaptation."*, as defined by the *Dublin Core*[10] ontology (Fig. 2c).

[10] https://udfr.org/docs/onto/dct_isVersionOf.html.

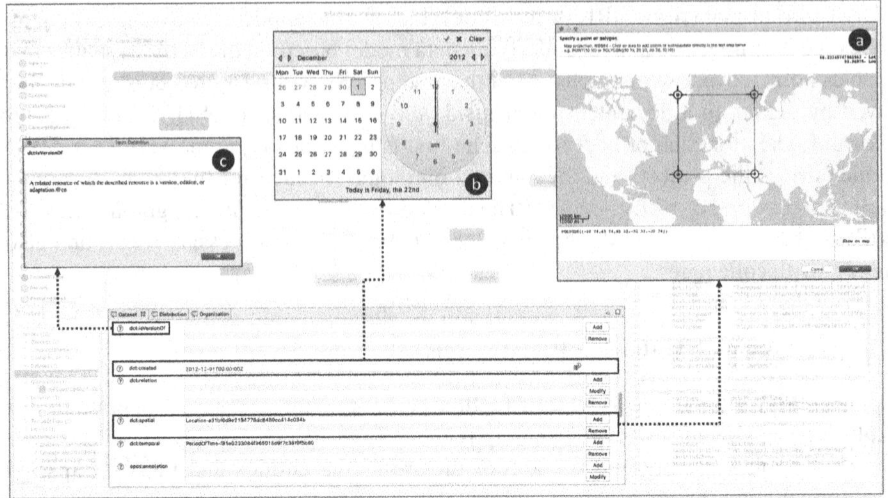

Fig. 2. The SHAPE*ness* user interface helps users populate valid node properties by providing suitable form fields and dedicated widgets such as: an interactive Map for geospatial information (a), a graphical calendar for date/time (b); and semantic information about properties(c).

3.5 Validating RDF Graphs

SHAPE*ness* implements on-the-fly quality and consistency check of the graph, validating its content according to the SHACL constraints. Users are notified about possible constraint violations with errors and warnings. An error represents a critical problem, related to mandatory properties which invalidates the graph. A warning refers to recommended properties and provides advice for improving the quality of the graph.

Constraints violations are shown in two views of the user interface (Fig. 3). In the Graph View, an alert icon is visualized inside the oval shapes of those nodes that contain faulty properties. In the Properties View, an alert icon appears close to the property fields that fail the validation. In the upper side of the view, an error message dialog reports the total number of detected violations and a brief description.

3.6 Exporting RDF Graphs

SHAPE*ness* automatically serializes the RDF graph into Turtle format and saves the file to a dedicated folder. Users may export the Turtle file to another local folder or push it to a Git repository. In this case, users can perform the push by supplying the Git repository URL, the branch name and the authentication credentials. This feature is useful for sharing RDF graphs within collaborative frameworks, or even for triggering a data ingestion pipeline within automated processes.

Furthermore, SHAPE*ness* offers the possibility to export the RDF graph as a PNG image, this is particularly convenient for documentation purposes.

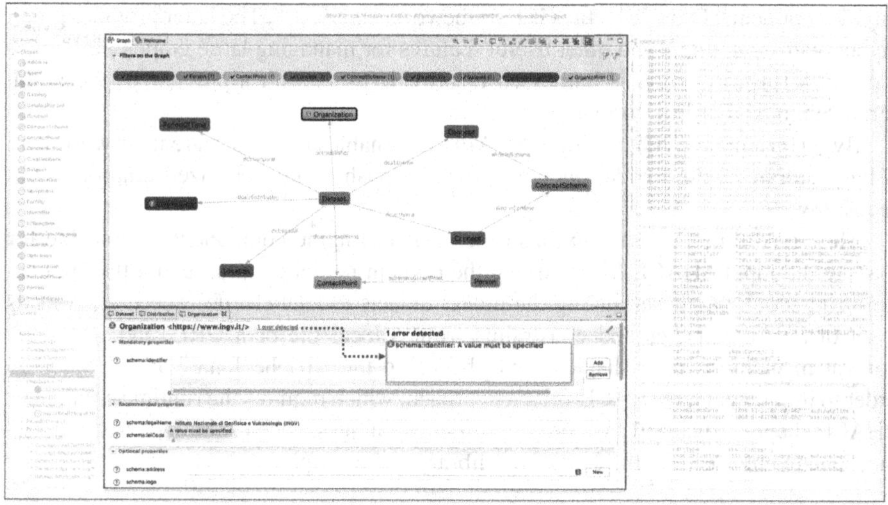

Fig. 3. The SHAPE*ness* user interface notifies users about the detected SHACL violations on the graph.

4 The SHAPE*ness* Architecture

The current version of SHAPE*ness* is based on Eclipse Rich Client Platform[11](RCP) which provides a minimum set of plugins to build a rich desktop application. SHAPE*ness* uses the dynamic plugin model, and the user interface is built with a set of toolkits and extension points. Eclipse's extension points mechanism enables the creation of applications with loosely coupled components which can be easily added, removed and replaced. Third-party tools can be easily integrated in the application by registering them as extensions. Such a plugin-based approach overcomes the maintainability and lack of modularity issues that may arise with monolithic applications. In addition, it provides great development flexibility, as new functionalities can be implemented by adding new components without having to rewire the entire application.

The SHAPE*ness* user interface is based on the Workbench plugin which offers the overall structure of Eclipse and common extension points used to customize the application. Several views are designed to present the underlying SHAPE*ness* data model and enable users to perform data ingestion. The views and other visual parts are developed by using the SWT[12] and JFace[13] frameworks, those are adopted to build a form-based interface which includes widgets (such as text fields, dropdown lists, tables, trees, wizards, dialogs) and simplifies data editing.

By default, Eclipse does not include any toolkit to create and manipulate graphs. Therefore, SHAPE*ness* uses the Graphical Editing Framework[14] (GEF) which bundles

[11] https://wiki.eclipse.org/Rich_Client_Platform.
[12] https://www.eclipse.org/swt/.
[13] https://wiki.eclipse.org/JFace.
[14] https://www.eclipse.org/gef/.

three components: Draw2d[15], the GEF framework, and Zest[16]. The latter provides graph layout managers, filters and other useful features for managing large graphs.

The XTurtle[17] plugin is harnessed to provide users with a preview of the graph serialized in RDF/Turtle format.

By integrating the JGit[18] plugin SHAPE*ness* enables users to share their work with collaborators or with a wider audience, e.g., by pushing the serialized graph to a Git repository.

The SHAPE*ness* architecture also includes an Engine component responsible for loading the input SHACL file, building the domain model classes behind the application, and serializing/deserializing the model objects to RDF/Turtle. The Engine loads a set of SHACL shapes and constraints from a local file or a URL, and stores the content in memory, as a shapes graph, by using the Apache Jena[19] Java library. In order to implement the SHACL-driven approach, which requires the runtime creation of SHACL shapes, advanced Java programming techniques, such as the Java Reflection[20] mechanism enhanced by the Javassist[21] library, were adopted.

5 Application of SHAPE*ness* in EPOS

The motivation for developing SHAPE*ness* was triggered by the concrete requirements of a challenging Research Infrastructure (RI) for solid Earth sciences: the European Plate Observing System (EPOS) [7]. EPOS is a prominent example of Information-Powered Collaborations (IPC)—the approach devised and adopted to enable cross-disciplinary knowledge pooling in such complex environments is extensively described in previous work [22, 23]. A major challenge in EPOS is the integration of multi-disciplinary, multi-organizational, distributed resources into a single overarching RI—the EPOS Integrated Core Services (ICS). ICS provide users with a harmonized view of diverse community assets, i.e., Thematic Core Services (TCS), that contribute domain-specific resources such as data and metadata products, software and services. Interoperability is achieved via canonical representations of such resources. Since EPOS is committed to provide the integrated resources according to the FAIR principles, the metadata challenge is of primary importance and the provision, management and production of metadata descriptions plays a fundamental role in the EPOS Software Development Life Cycle [1].

To tackle the inherent socio-technical challenges in EPOS, a methodology was applied to separate concerns and build a common information space that underpins the IPC. The CRP methodology encompasses three dimensions to be addressed independently: "*Conceptual definition (C), Representation (R), Population (P). C develops the ways of thinking, introducing terminology and meaning into the knowledge space, R*

15 https://www.eclipse.org/gef/draw2d/index.php.

16 https://www.eclipse.org/gef/zest/.

17 https://aksw.org/Projects/Xturtle.html.

18 https://www.eclipse.org/jgit/.

19 https://jena.apache.org/.

20 https://www.oracle.com/technical-resources/articles/java/javareflection.html.

21 https://www.javassist.org/.

develops detail and how to organise concepts, P deals with the gathering of instances of concepts in order to meet a community's requirements" [22].

A rich and flexible data model was designed for the representation of such concepts and their relationships, namely EPOS-DCAT-AP[22], which is a DCAT[23] application profile available in RDF format and structured as a SHACL *Shapes* graph, thus supporting validation and consistency checks [24]. To populate such a representation an ingestion process (*pipeline*) was devised. SHAPE*ness* elaborates on those results and offers a generic and scalable solution for the implementation of knowledge graph population pipelines.

In EPOS, major requirements focused on usability by non-technical domain experts and applicability to the diverse and heterogeneous communities composing the RI. Although each domain might have different policies for data and metadata management, they eventually exchange the information required by the EPOS RI by populating the EPOS-DCAT-AP model. In the first phases of the project, the population and curation were mostly human-based processes, e.g., by manually editing and validating RDF/Turtle files according to the EPOS-DCAT-AP model.

The SHAPE*ness* editor provides a significant added value and its features, described in Sect. 3, fulfil EPOS' requirements. It enables automation and enhancements in the creation and population of quality checked EPOS-DCAT-AP graphs by distributed and heterogeneous communities.

Figure 4 illustrates the processes that compose the EPOS Metadata Ingestion Pipeline. *Community Metadata Authors* have the responsibility to provide ICS with the metadata from their TCS according to ICS' requirements i.e., by populating EPOS-DCAT-AP RDF graphs. The creation of an EPOS-DCAT-AP RDF graph is followed by a validation of its SHACL constraints (e.g., structural and syntactical) and a visual inspection and curation of its content. In the next phase, the RDF graph is serialized in a file and deposited onto a dedicated TCS shared space (e.g., GitLab). This action triggers the automated ingestion of the file to the ICS. ICS receives inputs from multiple TCS pipelines, which represent the ten EPOS communities, and integrates the corresponding EPOS-DCAT-AP RDF representation in a consistent, consolidated knowledge graph. Once the integrated metadata is validated, it requires the final approval of an *EPOS Metadata Curator* in order to be applied in the production environment.

As illustrated in Fig. 4, SHAPE*ness* plays a crucial role in several steps of the ingestion pipeline: a) it provides TCS Metadata Authors with a powerful environment where they can create new EPOS-DCAT-AP RDF files and validate them; b) it offers an interactive tool for browsing and assessing the quality of the RDF graph content; c) it integrates with shared repositories such as GitLab; and d) it can be adopted to support content validation and approval by the EPOS Metadata Curators in the ICS.

In the next section, the approach adopted to assess the usability of SHAPE*ness* in the EPOS community is described and the evaluation results are presented.

[22] https://github.com/epos-eu/EPOS-DCAT-AP.

[23] https://joinup.ec.europa.eu/collection/semantic-interoperability-community-semic/solution/dcat-application-profile-data-portals-europe.

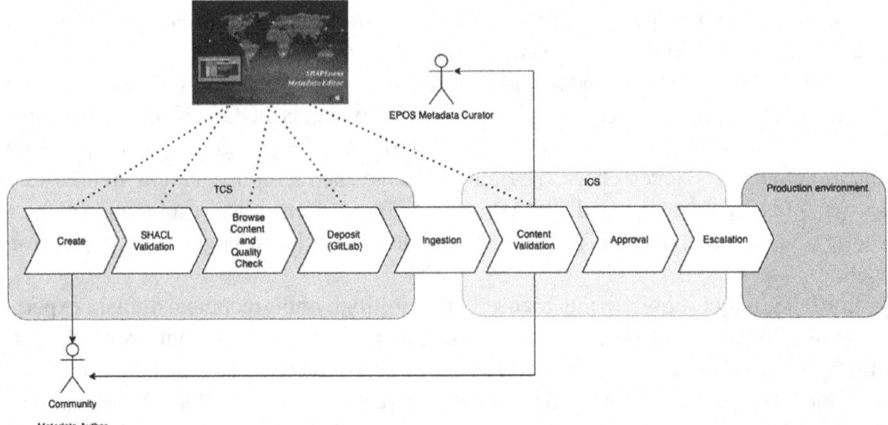

Fig. 4. Application of SHAPE*ness* to enable automation in the EPOS Metadata Ingestion Pipeline.

6 User Testing

A testing plan was performed for the first release of the application in the framework of the EPOS community. The testing included four main steps: a) definition of the objectives; b) definition of the methodology; c) submission of a testing questionnaire; d) collection of results. The testing provided inputs for further software developments and engaged a wider user base by advertising the application in the EPOS community.

We decided to focus on user testing because technical testing, such as the structural or behavioral testing [2], which aims at validating the quality or structure of the architecture and code, was embedded as routinely procedure in the software development practice (Continuous Integration through GitLab[24]). Therefore, our aim was to:

- validate the tool in terms of a) functionalities, to verify that the software meets user's expectations, and b) usability, to check that the software usage is effective and efficient.
- collect user feedback to improve the quality and utility of the software; this includes collection of new requirements, bugs notification, improvement of existing functionalities.
- collect user profile related requirements: different types of users may have different or even divergent expectations with respect to the SHAPEness application; knowing the requirements raised by specific user profiles allows us to prioritize implementation of new features on the basis of available resources, time constraints and target user groups.

Inspired by existing approaches [14], a testing methodology was designed and included four main activities: a) definition of user groups; b) definition of a questionnaire; c) questionnaire submission; d) collection and analysis of results.

[24] https://about.gitlab.com/stages-devops-lifecycle/continuous-integration/.

The testing program was advertised during EPOS meetings. Six out of fifteen beta testers who had been selected accepted to respond to the Google web forms questionnaire. They all belong to research institutions. 2 out of 6 users have a technical background (computer science), 1 has a hybrid technical/scientific background and 3 come from the scientific community (i.e., seismology and remote sensing).

Users were required to test the software being guided by two use cases: 1) *Creation of an RDF/Turtle file from scratch*; 2) *Creation of a project from an existing RDF/Turtle file*; each of which composed by several tasks.

The execution of the first use case was considered easy. Comments by users also provided additional information, in particular: a) small bugs were reported; b) no criticalities where emphasized with respect to the current functionalities, no new functionalities were required, some improvements of current functionalities were suggested, e.g., licenses metadata field; c) usability of a few layout parts or actionable elements within the GUI needed to be improved—for instance, the spatial coverage has been ameliorated thanks to users' feedback.

The execution of the second use case was considered moderately easy. Comments in each task were valuable and provided the following information: a) small bugs were reported, for instance deletion not saved upon closing the application; b) a few criticalities were emphasized with respect to the current functionalities mostly related to the graph visualization; c) as a consequence, the application needs to improve the usability of the graph, and suggestions provided by users are very useful in this perspective.

Questions were included to have a general evaluation of the satisfaction about software. 50% of the testers never used a similar application before. The overall evaluation is positive, emphasizing that the application needs to be improved to fully match users' expectations. Final questions focused on features, unexpected behavior or bugs, and additional comments/suggestions. Interestingly, the most appreciated features are those that the authors consider as the innovative added value of the software, i.e., a) graph automatic validation, b) easy to use by unexperienced person, c) configurable on the basis of runtime loadable SHACL files, d) easy creation of nodes and relationships. The least interesting features are those related to the coloring of nodes (4 out of 6 consider these not important). Few bugs were also reported, related to lag in the GUI response, and to different behavior on OSX operating systems. New features were required, but a few features for improving the graph navigation were suggested (e.g., additional dynamic layout for the bubble graph).

Based on the questionnaire' s results, the SHAPE*ness* application demonstrated to be easy to use in the proposed use cases, to have a good overall usability, and to satisfy the expectations of expert users. Improvements are needed e.g., to fix bugs and add new features for the graph navigation.

In addition, SHAPE*ness* was presented in the training activities of the ENVRI-FAIR European cluster project [20] and encountered positive feedback.

7 Conclusions and Future Work

In this paper we presented SHAPE*ness* -- an application that helps metadata authors, curators, and non-expert users fulfil SHACL compliance requirements in RDF data.

Based on a given SHACL content, SHAPE*ness* creates:

- a graph-based user interface which allows users to easily explore and structure RDF data as graphs according to the SHACL shapes;
- a form-based user interface which assists users in populating nodes properties by providing suitable widgets and useful suggestions;
- a tree-based user interface which allows users to browse nodes and edges by means of a common structure;
- a validation process on RDF graphs which includes visual alerts about detected SHACL violations and suggestions on how to fix them.

SHAPE*ness* has been developed within the European Plate Observing System (EPOS) framework, where in order to exchange knowledge between the diverse EPOS Thematic Core Services (TCS) and the Integrated Core Services (ICS), an extension of DCAT Application Profile, called EPOS-DCAT-AP, has been conceived.

SHAPE*ness* was tested by different users of the EPOS community who have evaluated its features, provided feedback about few bugs, partially fixed in the latest version, and who generally appreciated its added value as a tool for supporting the creation and validation of RDF graphs within the EPOS ingestion pipeline. An informal feedback provided by the ENVRI-FAIR community confirmed that the tool is fit for purpose and innovative.

Future plans include: a broader user testing in order to cover the remaining identified user groups and to target additional communities; tackling open issues reported on the GitHub repository[25] (e.g., drawing an arrow between two nodes in order to create relationships); addressing the inputs provided by current users; and updating the tool accordingly.

The following additional features are planned and considered for future releases:

- serialization and deserialization of RDF graphs to other standard formats (e.g., RDF/XML, Notation-3);
- import and export of graphs from/to a persistence layer such as triple stores in order to enable collaborative knowledge management;
- development of a web version of the tool.

Thanks to its self-adaptability, i.e., its capability to dynamically modify its behavior, based on a set of SHACL shapes given as input, SHAPE*ness* proves to be suitable for any context, domain, and use case which uses SHACL language for describing and constraining the contents of RDF data.

Because of its ease of use, SHAPE*ness* is a promising metadata management tool for metadata curators and practitioners, but specifically targeted to scientific experts who manage metadata with a limited semantic technology background. This happens for instance when non-experts are required to take the responsibility for the creation, maintenance and update of quality and rich metadata produced in the framework of initiatives that aim at addressing the FAIR guiding principles for data stewardship.

Acknowledgments. The authors would like to acknowledge the following projects and initiatives for financing part of the activities: EPOS-ERIC for sustainability and management; ENVRI-FAIR, European Commission H2020 program, Grant agreement ID 824068.

[25] https://github.com/epos-eu/SHAPEness-Metadata-Editor/issues.

Software Availability. SHAPE*ness* source code and binaries [19] are freely distributed under the GNU General Public License GPL-3. Download, setup instructions, user manual and video tutorials are available on GitHub[26].

References

1. Bailo, D. Paciello, R., Sbarra, M., Rabissoni, R., Vinciarelli, V., Cocco, M.: Perspectives on the implementation of FAIR principles in solid earth research infrastructures. Front. Earth Sci. **8** (2020). https://doi.org/10.3389/feart.2020.00003
2. Black, R.: Managing the Testing Process: Practical Tools and Techniques for Managing Hardware and Software Testing (1999)
3. Boneva, I., Dusart, J., Alvarez, D.F., Labra Gayo, J.E.: Shape designer for ShEx and SHACL constraints. In: ISWC 2019–18th International Semantic Web Conference (2019)
4. Bosch, T., Acar, E., Nolle, A., Eckert, K.: The role of reasoning for RDF validation. In: ACM International Conference Proceeding Series, pp. 33–40, 16–17-September 2015. https://doi.org/10.1145/2814864.2814867
5. Brewster, C., Nouwt, B., Raaijmakers, S., Verhoosel, J.: Ontology-based access control for FAIR data. Data Intell. **2**, 66–77 (2020). https://doi.org/10.1162/dint_a_00029
6. Cimmino, A., Fernández-Izquierdo, A., García-Castro, R.: Astrea: automatic generation of SHACL shapes from ontologies. In: Harth, A., et al. (eds.) ESWC 2020. LNCS, vol. 12123, pp. 497–513. Springer, Cham (2020). https://doi.org/10.1007/978-3-030-49461-2_29
7. Cocco, M., Freda, C.: Scientific and technical description of the European Plate Observing System (EPOS) Research Infrastructure, pp. 1–22 (2017). https://doi.org/10.5281/zenodo.4475633
8. De Meester, B., Heyvaert, P., Dimou, A., Verborgh, R.: Towards a uniform user interface for editing data shapes. In: CEUR Workshop Proceedings, vol. 2187, pp. 25–36 (2018)
9. Ekaputra, F.J., Lin, X.: SHACL4P: SHACL constraints validation within Protégé ontology editor. In: Proceedings of the 2016 International Conference on Data and Software Engineering ICoDSE 2016, pp. 1–6. IEEE (2017). https://doi.org/10.1109/ICODSE.2016.7936162
10. Garijo, D., Poveda-Villalón, M.: Best Practices for Implementing FAIR Vocabularies and Ontologies on the Web, ArXiv. (2020). https://doi.org/10.3233/ssw200034
11. Haller, A., Rosenberg, F.: A semantic web enabled form model and restful service implementation [replaces: ActiveRaUL: A model-view-controller approach for semantic web applications]. In: 2010 IEEE International Conference on Service-Oriented Computing and Applications (SOCA), 2010, pp. 1–8 (2010). https://doi.org/10.1109/SOCA.2010.5707158
12. Labra Gayo, J.E., Prud'hommeaux, E., Boneva, I., Kontokostas, D.: Validating RDF Data, Synthesis Lectures on the Semantic Web: Theory and Technology, vol. 7, no. 1, pp. 1–328 (2018). https://doi.org/10.2200/S00786ED1V01Y201707WBE016
13. Labra-Gayo, J.E., García-González, H., Fernández-Alvarez, D., Prud'hommeaux, E.: Challenges in RDF validation. In: Alor-Hernández, G., Sánchez-Cervantes, J., Rodríguez-González, A., Valencia-García, R. (eds.) Current Trends in Semantic Web Technologies: Theory and Practice. SCI, vol. 815, pp. 121–151. Springer, Cham (2019). https://doi.org/10.1007/978-3-030-06149-4_6
14. Lewis, J.R.: The system usability scale: past, present, and future. Int. J. Hum.-Comput. Interact. **34**(7), 577–590 (2018). https://doi.org/10.1080/10447318.2018.1455307
15. Lowe, B., Caruso, B., Cappadona, N., Worthington, M., Mitchell, S., Corson-Rikert, J.: The vitro integrated ontology editor and semantic web application. In: CEUR Workshop Proceedings, vol. 833, pp. 296–297 (2011)

[26] https://epos-eu.github.io/SHAPEness-Metadata-Editor/.

16. Mons, B., Neylon, C., Velterop, J., Dumontier, M., da Silva Santos, L.O.B., Wilkinson, M.D.: Cloudy, increasingly FAIR; revisiting the FAIR data guiding principles for the European open science cloud. Inf. Serv. Use. **37**, 49–56 (2017). https://doi.org/10.3233/ISU-170824
17. Muñoz, E.: On learnability of constraints from RDF data. In: Sack, H., Blomqvist, E., d'Aquin, M., Ghidini, C., Ponzetto, S.P., Lange, C. (eds.) ESWC 2016. LNCS, vol. 9678, pp. 834–844. Springer, Cham (2016). https://doi.org/10.1007/978-3-319-34129-3_52
18. Muscella, S., et al.: PROMPTING AN EOSC IN PRACTICE - Final report and recommendations of the Commission 2nd High Level Expert Group on the European Open Science Cloud (EOSC) (2018). https://doi.org/10.2777/620195
19. Paciello, R., Vinciarelli, V.: SHAPEness Metadata Editor (2021). https://doi.org/10.5281/zenodo.5702869
20. Petzold, A., et al.: ENVRI-fair-interoperable environmental fair data and services for society, innovation and research. In: Proceedings of the - IEEE 15th International Conference EScience, EScience 2019, pp. 277–280. IEEE (2019). https://doi.org/10.1109/eScience.2019.00038
21. Spahiu, B., Maurino, A., Palmonari, M.: Towards improving the quality of knowledge graphs with data-driven ontology patterns and SHACL. In: CEUR Workshop Proceedings, vol. 2195, pp. 52–66 (2018). https://doi.org/10.3233/978-1-61499-894-5-103
22. Trani, L.: A Methodology to Sustain Common Information Spaces for Research Collaborations, University of Edinburgh (2019). http://hdl.handle.net/1842/36139
23. Trani, L., Atkinson, M., Bailo, D., Paciello, R., Filgueira, R.: Establishing core concepts for information-powered collaborations. Futur. Gener. Comput. Syst. **89**, 421–437 (2018). https://doi.org/10.1016/j.future.2018.07.005
24. Trani, L., Paciello, R., Sbarra, M., Ulbricht, D.: Representing Core Concepts for solid-Earth sciences with DCAT – the EPOS-DCAT Application Profile, In Geophysical Research Abstracts, vol. 20. and the EPOS IT Team. https://meetingorganizer.copernicus.org/EGU2018/EGU2018-9797.pdf
25. Wilkinson, M., Dumontier, M., Aalbersberg, I., et al.: The FAIR guiding principles for scientific data management and stewardship. Sci. Data **3**, 160018 (2016). https://doi.org/10.1038/sdata.2016.18
26. Wright, J., Rodríguez Méndez, S., Haller, A., Taylor, K., Omran, P.: Schímatos: a SHACL-based web-form generator for knowledge graph editing. In: Proceedings of the International Semantic Web Conference, ISWC2020 (2020)

European Environmental Metadata

Keith G. Jeffery[1], Daniele Bailo[2,3(✉)], Rossana Paciello[2,3], and Valerio Vinciarelli[3]

[1] British Geological Survey, Keyworth, UK
[2] Istituto Nazionale di Geofisica e Vulcanologia, Rome, Italy
daniele.bailo@ingv.it
[3] European Plate Observing System, EPOS-ERIC, Rome, Italy

Abstract. Research Infrastructures (RI) of the Environment Domain as defined by ESFRI cover the main four subdomains of the complex Earth system (Atmosphere, Marine, Solid Earth, and Biodiversity/Terrestrial Ecosystems), thus forming the cluster of European Environmental and Earth System Research Infrastructures (ENVRIs). The overarching goal is that at the end of the proposed project, all participating RIs have built a set of FAIR (Findable, Accessible, Interoperable, Reusable) data services which enhances the efficiency and productivity of researchers, supports innovation, enables data- and knowledge-based decisions and connects the ENVRI Cluster to the European Open Science Cloud. The focus of the proposed work is on the provision of an environmental metadata catalogue describing in detail the FAIR services produced (or enhanced) in each subdomain; the complete set of thematic data services and tools provided by the ENVRI cluster can then be exposed to the EOSC catalogue of services.

1 Background

1.1 ENVRI Community

ENVRIs are crucial pillars for environmental scientists in their quest to understand and interpret the complex Earth System. They are the most comprehensive producers and providers of environmental research data in Europe collected from the in-situ and space-based observing systems. ENVRIs often contribute to global observation systems and they generate relevant information for Europe and worldwide.

1.2 ENVRI Projects

The ENVRI community has evolved over more than a decade through a series of projects: ENVRI[1], ENVRI-Plus[2] and now ENVRI-FAIR[3]. In each step FAIRness and interoperability were the key aspects and in ENVRI-FAIR[1] interoperation with European Open

[1] https://envri.eu/ (accessed on 13.10.2022).
[2] https://www.envriplus.eu/ (accessed on 13.10.2022).
[3] https://envri.eu/home-envri-fair/ (accessed on 13.10.2022).

E. Garoufallou and A. Vlachidis (Eds.): MTSR 2022, CCIS 1789, pp. 289–294, 2023.
https://doi.org/10.1007/978-3-031-39141-5_24

Science Cloud (EOSC[4]) [2] is an objective. ENVRI is the science cluster representing the environment in the European Commission view of research.

ENVRI-FAIR is the connection of ENVRI to the European Open Science Cloud (EOSC). Participating research infrastructures (RI) of the environmental domain cover the subdomains Atmosphere, Marine, Solid Earth and Biodiversity/Ecosystems and thus the Earth system in its full complexity.

The overarching goal is that at the end of the proposed project, all participating RIs have built a set of FAIR data services which enhances the efficiency and productivity of researchers, supports innovation, enables data- and knowledge-based decisions and connects the ENVRI Cluster to the EOSC.

This goal is reached by: (1) well defined community policies and standards on all steps of the data life cycle, aligned with the wider European policies, as well as with international developments; (2) each participating RI will have sustainable, transparent and auditable data services, for each step of data life cycle, compliant to the FAIR principles[5] [3]. (3) the focus of the proposed work is on the implementation of prototypes for testing pre-production services at each RI; the catalogue of prepared services is defined for each RI independently, depending on the maturity of the involved RIs; (4) the complete set of thematic data services and tools provided by the ENVRI cluster is exposed under the EOSC catalogue of services.

2 Interoperability Through Metadata

The various approaches to interoperability were re-examined and evaluated. The classical programmatic brokering method [4] was rejected because of (a) the many different metadata standards; (b) the evolutionary changes of those standards which would involve constant re-programming and (c) the number of brokers required at each asset supplier node of the architecture implying much programming effort repeated when any changes occurred at either of the asset suppliers being brokered. Manual interoperability by constructing mappings as required for each interoperation was also rejected, although mapping is a necessary step for any approach used. A further problem with brokering is that it does not provide a homogeneous view over all the assets, but only pairwise mediated views so that research challenges requiring assets from multiple suppliers with heterogeneous metadata standards become unworkable.

Interoperability has evolved from the idea of any two asset suppliers being able to intercommunicate, to the provision for an end-user of a homogeneous view across multiple heterogeneous asset suppliers such that relevant assets can be brought together to address a research challenge.

2.1 Overall Architecture

The overall architecture is based on the concept that asset suppliers which contribute to each of the RIs define – through metadata – a description of the assets made available

[4] https://eosc-portal.eu/ (accessed on 13.10.2022).

[5] https://www.go-fair.org/fair-principles/ (accessed on 13.10.2022).

to the wider community and any conditions of asset usage. Thus, the asset suppliers control the 'view' that users have of their assets. However, the many thousands of asset suppliers each have their own metadata standard for asset description. As an example, in the European Plate Observing System (EPOS[6]) RI with > 250 asset suppliers, 17 different metadata standards are used [5, 6].

Clearly, to provide homogeneous user access to these heterogeneous assets a canonical common rich metadata description is required so that an end-user can discover and contextualize assets from all four sub-domains of ENVRI to achieve cross-disciplinary science. The choice of such a canonical rich metadata model also implies conversion to it from all the other local standards. However, converting *n* local standards to *1* canonical standard is feasible, whereas converting each standard to every other standard *(n*(n-1))* is not.

2.2 Catalog Metadata CERIF

Within the community, and specifically in the Task Force 1 (TF1) of ENVRI-FAIR, it was decided (a) to use CERIF (Common European Research Information Format, Fig. 1)[7] [7] for the catalog of ENVRI-Hub and (b) to convert from local standards to EPOS-DCAT-AP[8] and thence to CERIF to provide an easier pathway for ingestion and one that could be validated using SHAPES/SHACL[9]. CERIF provides a fully connected graph data model whereas EPOS-DCAT-AP provides the model for serialization through e.g., JSON.

2.3 Ingestion Metadata EPOS-DCAT-AP

The mechanism used in EPOS is used more widely within ENVRI. EPOS-DCAT-AP is a much richer representation than DCAT-AP[10] and includes many more entities used in the research domain (Fig. 2).

---

[6] https://www.epos-eu.org/ (accessed on 13.10.2022).

[7] https://eurocris.org/eurocris_archive/cerifsupport.org/cerif-in-brief/ (accessed on 13.10.2022).

[8] https://github.com/epos-eu/EPOS-DCAT-AP (accessed on 13.10.2022).

[9] https://www.w3.org/TR/shacl/ (accessed on 13.10.2022).

[10] https://joinup.ec.europa.eu/collection/semantic-interoperability-community-semic/solution/dcat-application-profile-data-portals-europe/release/210 (accessed on 13.10.2022).

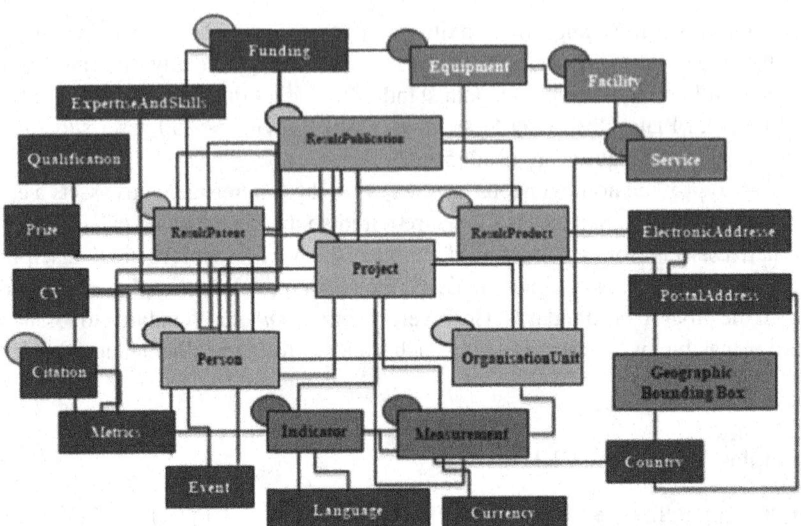

Fig. 1. CERIF 1.3 Entities and their relationships categorized as base entities, result entities, 2nd level entities and infrastructure entities. The model also includes measurement and geographic entities. Full description of entities with color codes is available in the CERIF 1.3 Full Data Model (FDM)[11]

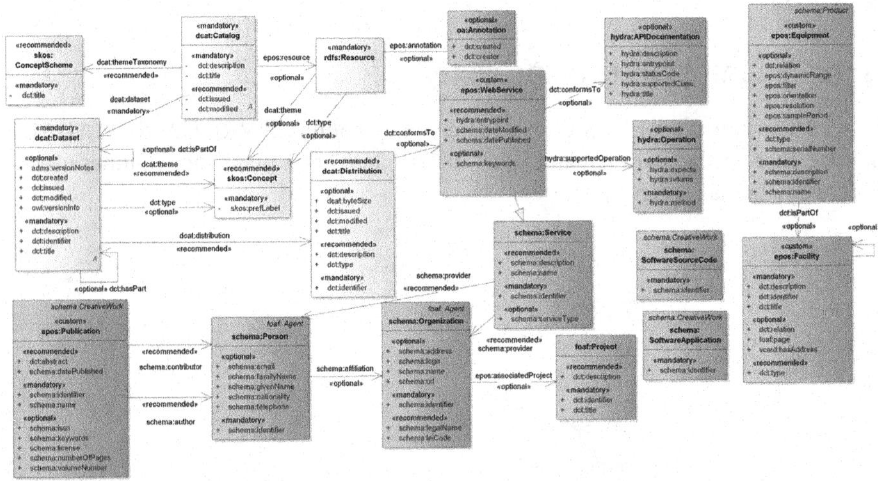

Fig. 2. The EPOS-DCAT-AP UML diagram that highlight the DCAT core entities in silver and the EPOS-DCAT-AP extensions in gold.

11 https://eurocris.org/Uploads/Web%20pages/CERIF-1.3/Specifications/CERIF1.3_FDM.pdf (accessed on 13.10.2022).

3 Current State

3.1 The Catalog

The ENVRI-Hub catalog is implemented as CERIF and is currently loaded with some representative metadata logical records. Each logical record is a complex record of base entities with groups of attributes and linking entities with their own attributes such as role and temporal duration between the base entities. The current state of the catalog is as a proof of concept with representative metadata records from various asset suppliers. The use of a rich metadata catalog (CERIF) ensures FAIRness – even for difficult principles like I3 (qualified references).

3.2 The Ingestion Pipeline

The ingestion pipeline for ENVRI asset suppliers to provision the central ENVRI-Hub catalog is taken directly from that of EPOS. It has been demonstrated to work although it required a tutorial and documentation to assist asset suppliers in utilizing the EPOS-DCAT-AP format.

4 Challenges

The current work on the catalog addresses the problem of the syntax – i.e., the representation of the information – in a canonical, homogeneous way. However, not only each sub-domain but - in many cases – individual asset suppliers within the sub-domain, have their own vocabulary of terms which may or may not be stored formally (to validate values in attributes) in a vocabulary, lexicon, thesaurus, or domain ontology. CERIF allows for a semantic layer – with the same concept of base entities (in this case sets of terms) and link entities (in this case relationships between terms). The structural congruence in CERIF between the syntactic layer (the structure of the metadata of entities and attributes) and the semantic layer (the meaning of the terms used as values in attributes) is very powerful in ensuring consistency.

Current work is ongoing in each sub-domain to harmonize the vocabularies where possible and to provide crosswalks between them where not. This is slow work and has to take account of standard or widely used vocabularies in each domain internationally.

In parallel, over several years, mappings have been done between CERIF and the evolving EOSC profiles (metadata schemas) for suppliers and assets. There is no problem with the mapping (and hence conversion) but there is real concern that the profiles are insufficiently rich for EOSC users to be able to discover and contextualise the assets for their purposes because of the poor metadata. In parallel, the science clusters (such as ENVRI) have been discussing with OpenAIRE[12] (which is based on CERIF) whether a route to onboarding scientific asset metadata through OpenAIRE exists – with the advantage of linking the assets to already existing information on publications, organisations, projects etc. all in the rich CERIF model.

[12] https://www.openaire.eu/ (accessed on 13.10.2022).

5 Way Forward

The current state indicates that ENVRI can provide a canonical homogeneous catalog describing the assets with rich data ensuring FAIRness. As indicated above, the current activity is concerned mainly with harmonizing the vocabularies and populating the catalog with the semantic layer.

Concerning interoperation with EOSC the way forward is less clear and discussions continue. However, the current EOSC profiles are agreed to be insufficient for scientific discovery and contextualization so a way forward with richer metadata must be found.

Acknowledgements. The authors would like to acknowledge the following projects and initiatives for financing part of the activities: ENVRI-FAIR, European Commission H2020 program, Grant agreement ID 824068; EPOS-ERIC (https://www.epos-eu.org/epos-eric) for sustainability and management.

References

1. Petzold, A., Glaves, H.: ENVRI-FAIR - the next step towards FAIRer environmental research. In: American Geophysical Union, Fall Meeting 2018, vol. 21, p. 15684 (2019)
2. European Commission, "Implementation Roadmap for the European Open Science Cloud" (2018). https://ec.europa.eu/research/openscience/pdf/swd_2018_83_f1_staff_working_paper_en.pdf#view=fit&pagemode=none
3. Wilkinson, M.D., et al.: The FAIR guiding principles for scientific data management and stewardship. Sci. Data **3**, 160018 (2016). https://doi.org/10.1038/sdata.2016.18
4. Nativi, S., Craglia, M., Pearlman, J.: Earth science infrastructures interoperability: the brokering approach. Top. Appl. Earth **6**(3), 1118–1129 (2013). http://ieeexplore.ieee.org/xpls/abs_all.jsp?arnumber=6506981. Accessed 08 Apr 2014
5. Cocco, M., et al.: The EPOS research infrastructure: a federated approach to integrate solid earth science data and services. Ann. Geophys. **65**, (2), DM208 (2022). https://doi.org/10.4401/ag-8756
6. Bailo, D., et al.: Data integration and FAIR data management in solid earth science. Ann. Geophys. **65**(2), DM210 (2022). https://doi.org/10.4401/ag-8742
7. Jörg, B.: CERIF: the common European research information format model. Data Sci. J. **9**, CRIS24–CRIS31 (2010). https://doi.org/10.2481/DSJ.CRIS4

Designing PIDs for Reproducible Science Using Time-Series Data

Wen Ting Maria Tu and Stephen Makonin(✉)

Simon Fraser University, Burnaby, Canada
{maria_tu,smakonin}@sfu.ca

Abstract. The use of persistent identifiers (PIDs) is seen as a part of the solution to the problem of reproducible research and science. This short paper proposes a preliminary method using PIDs to reproduce research results using time-series data. Furthermore, we feel it is possible to use the methodology and design for other types of datasets.

Keywords: PID · ARKs · time-series · datasets · reproducibility

1 Introduction

Reproducible research and science has become an urgent problem as machine learning, and Ai algorithms become more complex (e.g., deep learning). Part of this reproducibility problem is the lack of specificity as to the exact data used for training and testing these learning systems. Part of the investigative work done by IEEE Standards Association P2957 Data Governance and Metadata Management Working Group (BDGMMWG) is to look at how to create a persistent identifier (PID) system that point to specific data from a given data repository.

2 Methodology

A federated metadata registry (as in Fig. 1) is an extensive database that stores and manages datasets in a given repository. Within the registry, a federated data catalog system provides a single point of access across all data regardless of the location data is stored. The use of Archival Resource Keys (ARKs) as persistent identifiers (PIDs) means that specific data can be queried and accessed from a request originating outside the system. Using Nice Opaque Identifier (NOID) software tool to implement ARKs provides a way to mint unique ARK strings, bind location URLs to those strings, and serve as a name resolver to redirect requests to the proper location of each dataset. We explain the method details in this section.

2.1 Federated Data Types Registry

Automated processing of large volumes of data requires implicit details about the data types. Data federation combines all the autonomous data stored to

E. Garoufallou and A. Vlachidis (Eds.): MTSR 2022, CCIS 1789, pp. 295–301, 2023.
https://doi.org/10.1007/978-3-031-39141-5_25

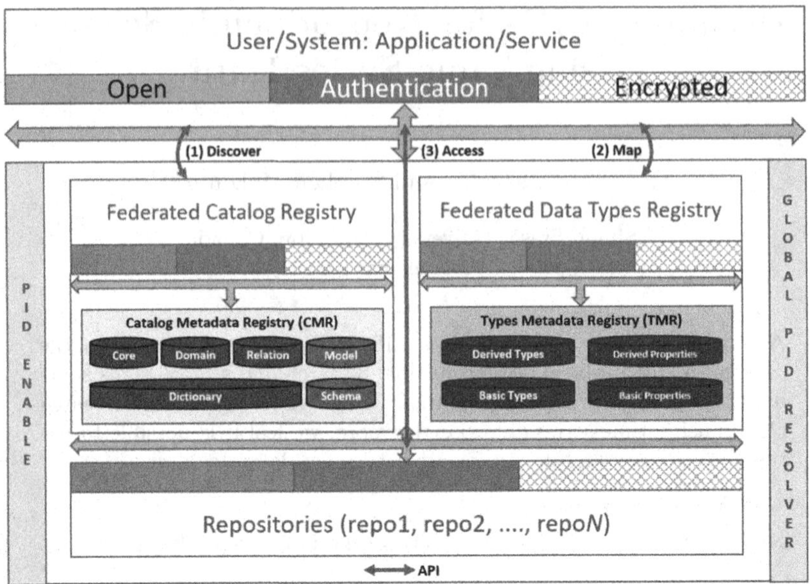

Fig. 1. Block diagram of a federated metadata registry (BDGMMWG Draft Fig. 1 [4]).

form one extensive database. Data federation stores data into a heterogeneous set. The data is accessible to users as one integrated database using on-demand data integration [10]. A data user using data federation should be able to access different types of database servers and files with various formats from all data sources and be accessible through multiple APIs.

Types Metadata Registry (TMR). A metadata registry is a database used to store, organize, manage, and share metadata [2]. An issue often encountered in building an extensive metadata registry is that the participants may have used diverse schemas and description methods to create their metadata records [3]. Building one integrated metadata registry enables one search from the user's end to retrieve the information needed rather than searching through all the different existing individual databases. Therefore, interoperability will be a critical component in such development. Most of the time, different types of resources are already classified under a variety of specialized schemas [3].

Data Types are characterizations of data at any level of granularity. Data types identified, defined and registered data. When encountering unknown data, the registry can explicate those types and output the type definitions, relationships and properties. *Basic Types* are used for interpreting and later processing data. A Data Type Registry provides a detailed and structured description of inputted data. Some of the basic types are listed below in Table 1 (left column). *Derived Types* are more specific cases/instances of the basic types. For example, the derived types are listed in Table 1 (right column).

Table 1. Derived Types

Basic Types	Corresponding Derived Types
text	character, varchar
number	integer, long, real, float, double, percentage, scientific
currency	USD, RMB, $, Euro, Yen
boolean	check box, yes/no, true/false, on/off
date/time	timestamp, short date, medium date, long date, time am/pm, medium time, time 24 h
blob	rich text, attachment, memo, attachment
calculated	lambda unction, imaginary number
pointer	hyperlink, lookup

Basic Properties describe the nature of the data. These descriptions are essential to understanding and performing any statistical analysis on the data. Different Exploratory Data Analysis (EDA techniques) can be used to identify the properties of data so that the appropriate statistical methods can be applied to the data. Here is a list of different basic properties of a set of data as shown in Table 2 *Derived Properties* are properties that do not exist on the Entity Type associated with the Entity Set; rather, it exists on a type that is derived from the base type of the entity set.

Table 2. Basic Properties

Basic Properties
Centre of data
Skewness of data
Spread among the data members
Presence of outliers
Correlation among the data
Type of probability distribution that the data follows

2.2 Federated Catalog Registry

A data catalog system provides a single place where all available data can be catalogued, enriched, searched, tracked and prioritized. Federation provides a single view across all data of interest to a user, regardless of where the data is stored or sourced. When there are changes to the external data, the system can quickly crawl external data sources, track changes, make automatic enhancements and push notifications when changes occur. A federated registry is used when user and group information is spread across multiple registries. If the information is stored in various systems, a federated registry can provide a unified view without changing the platform providing a single point of access to reliable data.

Catalog Metadata Registry (CMR). A metadata Catalog System provides a single place where all data can be catalogued, enriched, searched, tracked and prioritized. Data catalog is a collection of metadata, combined with data management and search tools. The combination serves as an inventory for data and provides tools for data analysis. The analyst can search and find data quickly, see all of the available datasets, evaluate and make informed choices for which data to use, and perform data preparation and analysis efficiently.

Core is the main classifications and groups among the Catalog Metadata Registry. *Domain* has three types: environmental domain, object class domain and object format domain. Environmental domain is the discipline and the community that the scheme services. Object class domain is the assembly and grouping of similar objects by type and offer multiple ways to define type. Object format domain is the object's composition and what it is made of [6]. *Relation* defines a related resource. The recommended practice is to identify the related resource by means of a URI. If this is not possible or feasible, a string conforming to a formal identification system may be provided [1]. *Model* describes the physical raw data files such as: binary, images, or text containing numeric values [11]. *Dictionary* is a set of well defined terminology. The goal for a dictionary is to eliminate ambiguity, control the use of synonyms, establish formal relationship among terms and validate terms [7]. *Schema* is also called Formats or Element Sets. It is a set of semantic properties used to describe resources; examples include: MARC 21, Dublin Core, MODS, and ONIX [7].

2.3 ARKs as Persistent Identifiers (PIDs)

A Persistent identifier (PID) is a long-lasting reference/resolve to a digital resource. There are many online organizations that provide PID resolving services; for exmaple, DOIs, ORCIDs, and ARKs. Digital object identifiers (DOI, https://www.doi.org) are paid-for persistent identifiers used for scholarly communication, such as in journal articles, books and datasets. DOIs as a paid for service. Open Researcher and Contributor Identifiers (ORCID, https://orcid.org) is financially sustained by membership fees from organizational members; however, participants in research, scholarship or innovation can register an ORCID ID for free. Archival Resource Keys (ARKs, https://arks.org) are persistent identifiers (PIDs) that are open, decentralized and can be applied to any type of object (digital, physical or abstract). Like any modern PID system, ARKs rely heavily on URL redirection. To use ARKs, the following items are needed: a Name Assigning Authority Number (NAAN), a minter, a resolver, an assignment plan, and an access persistence policy.

The NAAN indicates the organization that creates the persistent identifier. To eliminates duplicates, the minter only generates unique string. Once a string is assigned to a resource and its location, the resolver can redirect the persistent ARK identifier to the current access URL where the resource resides. Preplanning of ARK features such as suffix pass-through (which allows one ARK to be a single point of management for millions of other ARKs) or ARK shoulders (a way of subdividing and managing your own namespace) should be considered during the implementation. If the resource is kept with persistent access, it needs to be securely preserved to prevent accidental loss and deletion [9].

The Nice Opaque Identifier (NOID) tool lets one establish any number of minters, Each NOID minter comes with a template specifying the length and combinations of numbers and letters in the strings that it will generate. These strings become ARKs when they are assigned to the objects they identify. In order to prevent duplication, a database will check that no identifier is minted more than once. The published URL is kept persistent while NOID can also be used to run as a name resolver to redirect to the new location of where the object resides. You can publish your ARKs with your own hostname (decentralized ARKs) or with the N2T.net hostname (centralized mode, in case your own hostname is subject to some instability).

3 Designing PIDs for Time-Series Data

Time-series data is a collection of observations made chronologically. For example, where sensor measurements are recorded over a period of time. Given the length of time and the frequency of reading, these datasets can become large in size, and have high dimensionality if reading more than one value, observation, or measurement [5]. Each value from each sensor can be marked with a timestamp — the date and time of reading — a unique identifier. As the timestamp is unique we can use it to reference a specific reading. Row number cannot be used as a unique identifier because it can change based on data manipulation and information processing functions such as row sorting.

For our demonstration we use the AMPds: Almanac of Minutely Power dataset [8] which contains electricity, water, and natural gas metering data. Sensors measure different consumption characteristics. In each CSV file (one per sensor) the timestamp (per minute) is the a unique identifier or primary key.

An example of a PID might be:

Ex.1: https://n2t.net/ark:/57460/AMPds/DWE/V@13332~13400

where https is a secure HTTP RESTful request, n2t.net is the global resolver, ark means the URL is an ARK, 57460 is the NAAN for our lab, AMPds is the name of the dataset, DWE is the meter or sensor, V is the measurement (column), and @13332˜13400 is the timestamp range of the readings (rows). To select all the readings for a given sensor (e.g., DWE or dishwasher meter) for a give measurement (V or voltage), the following URL would be used:

Ex.2: https://n2t.net/ark:/57460/AMPds/DWE/V@*

or multiple timestamp (i.e., ID) ranges we would use @13332˜13400+24300˜25500. To return multiple values (e.g., V for voltage and I for current) we use:

Ex.3: https://n2t.net/ark:/57460/AMPds/DWE/V+I@*

And, for multiple sensors (e.g., HPE, DWE, and WOE; heatpump, dishwasher, and wall oven) we would use:

Ex.4: https://n2t.net/ark:/57460/AMPds/HPE+DWE+WOE/V+I@*

Lastly, using cross-fold validation is important for training and testing learning algorithms. Here is an example when we want to exclude a range of timestamps:

Ex.5: https://n2t.net/ark:/57460/AMPds/DWE/V@@24300~25500

In this case, we are requesting all data except for the data in the inclusive timestamp range of @@24300˜25500. The double-at @@ is used as *exclusion* rather than the minus sign as this avoids potential URL corruption with text formatting software where hyphens as used for line breaks.

4 Conclusions

We show how PIDs can be used for persistent access to specific data from a dataset. ARKs provides a flexible, inexpensive way to make data more accessible and provide an easy way to describe the data for easy reproducibility of research and scientific results. Next steps include releasing a prototype that can used as part of the IEEE Standards Association P2957 Data Governance and Metadata Management Working Group (BDGMMWG) standard. Further, we plan to demonstrate using PIDs for other types of non-time-series data.

Acknowledgements. We would like to thank the IEEE Standards Association for allowing us to particulate in the creation of P2957 and for the members of BDGMMWG for there discussions and views. Special thanks to John Kunze of ARKs and the Ronin Institute for his valuable feedback and suggestions.

References

1. Baker, T., Coyle, K.: Guidelines for Dublin core application profiles. DCMI (2009)
2. Bargmeyer, B.E., Gillman, D.W.: Metadata standards and metadata registries: an overview. In: International Conference on Establishment Surveys II, Buffalo, NY (2000)
3. Chan, L.M., Zeng, M.L.: Metadata interoperability and standardization-a study of methodology part I. D-Lib Mag. **12**(6), 1082–9873 (2006)
4. Chang, W., et al.: IEEE IC big data governance and metadata management: standards roadmap. In: IEEE SA Industry Connections, p. 62 (2020)

5. Fu, T.C.: A review on time series data mining. Eng. Appl. Artif. Intell. **24**(1), 164–181 (2011)
6. Greenberg, J.: Understanding metadata and metadata schemes. Catalog. Classif. Quart. **40**(3–4), 17–36 (2005)
7. Hillmann, D.I., Marker, R., Brady, C.: Metadata standards and applications. Ser. Libr. **54**(1-2), 7–21 (2008)
8. Makonin, S., Popowich, F., Bartram, L., Gill, B., Bajić, I.V.: AMPDS: a public dataset for load disaggregation and eco-feedback research. In: 2013 IEEE Electrical Power & Energy Conference, pp. 1–6 (2013)
9. The ARK Alliance: Getting started: What to plan for as you implement arks (2022). https://arks.org/about/getting-started-implementing-arks/
10. Van Der Lans, R.: Data Virtualization for business intelligence systems: revolutionizing data integration for data warehouses. Elsevier (2012)
11. Yang, E., Matthews, B., Wilson, M.: Enhancing the core scientific metadata model to incorporate derived data. Future Gener. Comput. Syst. **29**(2), 612–623 (2013)

Author Index

E. Garoufallou and A. Vlachidis (Eds.): MTSR 2022, CCIS 1789, pp. 303–304, 2023.
https://doi.org/10.1007/978-3-031-39141-5

Printed in the United States
by Baker & Taylor Publisher Services